The Wages of Conquest

The Wages of Conquest

The Mexican Aristocracy in the Context of Western Aristocracies

Hugo G. Nutini

THE UNIVERSITY OF MICHIGAN PRESS

Ann Arbor

1998   1997   1996   1995   4   3   2   1

A CIP catalogue record for this book is available from the British Library.

Library of Congress Cataloging-in-Publication Data

Nutini, Hugo G.
   The wages of conquest : the Mexican aristocracy in the context of
Western aristocracies / Hugo G. Nutini.
      p.   cm.
   Includes bibliographical references and index.
   ISBN 0-472-10484-5 (alk. paper)
      1. Aristocracy (Social class)—Mexico—History.   I. Title.
HT653.M6N88   1995
305.5'2'0972—dc20   94-24553
                                                               CIP

A la Memoria de Carlos de Ovando:
Entrañable Amigo, Eximio Colaborador, y Profundo
Concedor de la Historia y Configuración de su Clase

Contents

Preface

This study departs radically from my seven-volume series on the ethnography and ethnology of rural Tlaxcala and other regions of the Central Mexican Highlands. The present book describes and analyzes the inception, development, and decline of a social class that has played an inordinately important role in the life of the Mexican nation for more than four hundred years. Like most of my work, this book examines culture loss and decay. My proclivity for these themes does not necessarily reflect a pessimistic personality—simply the conviction that in Mexico, perhaps more than in most modern countries, the present cannot be entirely understood without reference to the past. The Mexican aristocracy is now on the verge of disappearing as a distinct social class, and a limited ethnographic, synchronic study of its situation today would provide only a hint of the great power and wealth that it wielded until the 1910 Revolution. It has played a leading role in the history of the country; at every turn the aristocracy was determinantly instrumental in forging the course of the nation. In the egalitarian, democratic ambiance of modern countries it is easy to forget, and easier still to denigrate and distort, the role of the aristocracy in two and a half millennia of Western Civilization. Throughout this monograph, I have done my best to steer away from panegyric and blanket criticism. Though objectivity is a difficult stance, I have tried to present a balanced account of the evolution of the Mexican aristocracy from its inception to the present. I hope this account will offend neither aristocratic sensibilities nor political and intellectual proclivities of colleagues and general readers.

The paucity of studies of upper-class stratification originally led me to investigate the aristocracy and how it had changed since the onset of the Mexican Revolution, when, by all accounts, it was at the pinnacle of its power. It seemed as if social scientists had ignored this social class almost by design. Though few works on Mexico and Latin America proved useful, historical studies of the nobility and several European aristocracies from the tenth to the twentieth centuries were quite valuable for comparative purposes, since the Mexican aristocracy is a variant of the Spanish aristocracy and was forged when Spain dominated most of the New World. Historians, unencumbered by sociological constraints, have been able to ascertain empirically that, say, within the predominantly capitalistic mode of production characteristic of European society during the last 250 years, distinct and often significant elements of the seigneurial period have survived as distinct categories. Thus historians and an occasional gifted social critic analyze the contemporary nobility, aristocracy, or socially exalted in England, Spain, or France as significant groups, whereas most social scientists dismiss them as irrelevant, spurious survivals or include them indiscriminately in a contemporary bourgeois ruling class. Politically powerless and economically relatively insignificant as these social elites may be, they nonetheless retain a distinct existence.

Shortly after beginning the systematic collection of data in 1978, I realized two things. First, a traditional structural study of an upper class would result either in another description of a classical aristocracy in the process of being replaced by a new plutocracy (a process that has occurred and has been documented by historians several times since the close of the Middle Ages), or in just another urban ethnography in the usual anthropological manner. Second, neither alternative entailed explanatory elements, and, at best, both represented descriptive exemplifications of processes that are already well known after more than one hundred years of historical and sociological investigation. I turned in my predicament to the expressive approach. As a complementary analytical tool, it could generate answers to fundamental questions of social mobility and persistence, as well as amplifying the concept of social class, particularly at the higher echelons of the stratification system. Class position, mobility, and consciousness are admittedly caused by economic forces in action, concomitantly discharged in a number of cultural domains, of which the most prominent are the social, the political, and the religious, and supported by an ideological superstructure designed to perpetuate the status quo. But this general economic explanation by no means exhausts the conceptualization of class and related phenomena; indeed, evidence has been accumulating for the past twenty years that these concepts are replete with expressive components.

To say, then, that this study is an expressive description and analysis of the Mexican aristocracy means that, based on a solid structural base, the expressive focus is the main analytical tool. It generates explanations in domains that the traditional approach to social stratification is never likely to explain. In my approach, structural (economic, political, and other) variables constitute the necessary conditions for the conceptualization of social stratification, and expressive variables constitute the sufficient conditions, which in specified settings and in several domains account for social mobility and the persistence of class ideology. The complementary relationship of these two approaches is necessary to generate a theory of social class and mobility that is neither circular, incomplete, nor ideologically self-serving. After placing the aristocracy in historical and structural perspective within the context of Mexican culture and society, I offer an expressive ethnography and comparative assessment of this social class in the twentieth century. Thus will the stage be set for an explanation of class persistence, mobility, and emulation of manners and behavior that characterize social stratification.

The historical development of the Mexican aristocracy presented in this book is based mostly on published sources, the quality of which is uneven. I have benefited, however, from access to the private archives and collections of nine aristocratic informants. I was able, therefore, to peruse the following documents: genealogies, some of them extending to the sixteenth century; an extensive array of documentation pertaining to *haciendas* (landed estates), extending to the middle of the eighteenth century; accounts of seigneurial houses in Mexico City and important provincial cities from the late seventeenth century onward; and an extensive body of legal documents pertaining to wills, marriage contracts, sales contracts, entails, property settlements, and so on. I also relied heavily on many private publications of family histories, memoirs, accounts of houses and *haciendas,* anecdotes, and genealogical and heraldic materials (what the French call *petite histoire*) written by members of the aristocracy up until the beginning of the nineteenth century. Most of these publications were written by amateurs and may be biased and self-serving, but they are useful for reconstructing the milieu of several periods.

This eclectic material provides both raw data and some insightful piecemeal analyses of the Mexican aristocracy from the Spanish Conquest to the present. Though my historical account could have benefited by original research in the standard archives of Mexico and Spain, such monumental research would have required a separate three-year project. Inasmuch as my primary aim is to present a synchronic expressive analysis of the Mexican aristocracy (Volumes 2 and 3), with an immediate short-range historical perspective, I opted for mostly published sources, sufficient to place this social class in proper historical perspective.

As in the past, I have extended the ethnographic present to the Porfirio Díaz regime (Nutini 1988; Nutini and Bell 1980; Nutini and Roberts 1990). Data for this part of the work (1880–1985) consist of in-depth, open-ended, sporadic interviews (collective and individual) with several dozen informants, at least ten of whom were more than eighty years old in 1978–1980, and who were able to give accurate accounts of the social, economic, religious, and political milieu before Mexico's great transformation radically changed their lives. When systematic data collection began in 1978, I had so honed the techniques of short-range historical reconstruction that, with the assistance of approximately thirty-five male and female informants ranging from seventy-five to ninety years of age, the critical period between 1910 and 1950 was well accounted for. The aristocratic milieu of Mexico City, where the majority of the aristocracy had by then congregated, became intelligible ethnographically. The past forty years is, of course, a standard ethnographic period.

Although the Mexican aristocracy no longer has residential unity, nor does it constitute a community in the conventional sociological or anthropological sense, the great majority of its members reside in circumscribed areas of Mexico City. It is not a rigidly bounded group, but by standard criteria of self-identification the great majority of its married members know each other personally or by reference, and individuals can always be placed genealogically by ancestral place of origin and other characteristic attributes. The Mexican aristocracy today has an approximate membership of six thousand, including roughly seven hundred households (nuclear family households with a sprinkling of extended family households) constituting some fifty identifiable networks. The adult population constitutes roughly 45 percent of the group. From this pool, informants were chosen on a voluntary and opportunity basis. A total of 157 male and female informants, ranging in age from the late teens to the late eighties, were interviewed at least once, and 35 of them as many as ten times. The bulk of the ethnography was gathered from 12 key informants who were interviewed at least ten hours each, 3 for more than one hundred hours. Most informants were interviewed individually, but on many occasions collective interviewing of 3 to 5 people was appropriate and usually highly profitable.

Quantitative data were gathered by the administration of questionnaires and several other fairly formal techniques. Questionnaires were administered to men and women, ranging in age from twenty-five to eighty, who were asked anywhere from a dozen to as many as a hundred questions, some of which required short essays to answer. Depending on the task at hand, questionnaires were administered to samples of as few as twenty-five to as many as a hundred respondents. The subjects of investigation varied considerably, but the most common were expressive domains and the expressive array; expressive participation and withdrawal; expressive differentiation and clustering; voluntary association and membership rosters; dyadic and relational data on social, political, and economic interaction; career development and differentiation; status differentiation within the group; hierarchization of families and subgroup differentiation; strategies of relative upward and downward mobility; patterns of interaction and intermarriage; and genealogy. Male and/or female respondents ranging from twenty-five to fifty years old were asked to complete short (fifteen to thirty minutes' duration) psychological tests, self-awareness tests, expressive participation tests, triad tests, attitudinal tests, card-sorting tasks, clustering tasks, and identification and correlation tasks.

I wish to emphasize three points. First, the samples of respondents for the administration of questionnaires and tests and for the application of other data-gathering techniques were not random. Randomness would have been an impossible goal, given the aristocratics' commitments, schedules, and general constraints. Rather, response was dictated by the availability, willingness, and knowledge of informants. Second, in addition to the wide-ranging roster of data-gathering methods described above, I also culled significant information on the social, religious, and "cultural" life of the aristocracy from newspapers and magazines for the past seventy-five years. Third, although this study deals exclusively with the aristocracy, it was not pursued in isolation. The new plutocracy of Mexico complements the study, and a significant amount of data was collected and analyzed on this social class. Most of the categories of data detailed above were also gathered for the plutocracy, and while the sample of plutocratic informants and respondents was not nearly as large and diversified as that of the aristocracy, I generated a corpus of data sufficient to describe and analyze the relationship between these two critical components of the Mexican haute bourgeoisie today.

This three-volume study is primarily an exercise in expression; I have termed the accompanying conceptual approach "expressive focus and strategy." The book also clarifies and refines several of the most salient aspects of expression as a tool for understanding social class and stratification. Two other conceptual approaches, network analysis and the renewal of elites, complement the primary expressive thrust. Network analysis has been successfully employed in studies of ritual kinship (*compadrazgo*). The network approach has proven most useful in the analysis of plutocratic upward mobility and the accommodations made by aristocrats in order to survive. The renewal or circulation of elites, as originally postulated by Pareto (1935) and around which the diachronic description is organized, best explains the evolution of the Mexican aristocracy over 450 years.

The book is divided into three volumes that share the same central goal: an evolutionary, expressive, and network description and analysis of the Mexican aristocracy in a changing structural setting. The three volumes are concerned respectively with the historical-evolutionary, structural-expressive, and formal-expressive components of the Mexican aristocracy. You have Volume 1 in hand. Volumes 2 and 3 will be published as separate monographs and should be ready within four years.

Volume 1 presents an extended description and analysis of superordinate stratification in Western Civilization from classical times to the present. Part 1 discusses the concepts of aristocracy and nobility, the relationship between class and estate, upward and downward mobility, the demise of the estate system, and the rise of class stratification. It places all Western aristocracies within a single framework of stratification, and it discusses the rise of the bourgeoisie in modern times. Part 2 chronicles the evolution of the Mexican aristocracy from the Spanish

Conquest to the present and analyzes the structural milieu, the changes in personnel, and the various stages. Conquistadors and early settlers constituted the original nucleus of the Mexican aristocracy; by the end of the sixteenth century it had become the dominant social class in New Spain. Early in the seventeenth century, the first titles of nobility were granted to members of the Creole aristocracy by the Spanish Crown, which throughout the century dominated the social and economic life of the colony. As early as the second half of the sixteenth century, the ranks of the aristocracy began to swell with newly rich members, both of Creole and *peninsular* (Spaniard born in Spain) origin. The process continued throughout the Colonial period. Beginning around 1725, the great mining boom of New Spain created an important group of plutocratic magnates, most of whom acquired titles of nobility and came to dominate the Creole aristocracy. For the first thirty years after Independence, the Mexican aristocracy continued to dominate the life of Mexico, but not until after the Reform Laws and the French intervention did it reach its zenith of power as a ruling class, throughout the Díaz regime until 1910. The Mexican Revolution radically transformed the aristocracy: it lost all political power, and, as a result of the land reform of President Cárdenas in the 1930s, it also lost almost all of its once great wealth. Since the Second World War, particularly after the early 1950s, the aristocracy has had to share social prominence with a new class of plutocrats, the last massive renewal of elites in 450 years of Colonial and Republican evolution.

Volume 2 constitutes the synchronic part of the study and includes standard and expressive ethnographies of the Mexican aristocracy in its period of rapid decline as a social class (1950–90, the ethnographic present of Part 2). The standard ethnography of this social class is in principle no different from the ethnography of a tribal society or folk community, particularly given the fact that the aristocracy exhibits a high degree of cultural uniformity. A standard ethnography of the Mexican aristocracy offers a new twist, however, for it is located in an urban setting, firmly grounded in the culture of Mexico City. Accordingly, the description and analysis touch significantly on the life and configuration of several segments of Mexican society: the plutocracy, the political sector of the country, the upper-middle class, and the network of services and facilities that support the aristocratic-plutocratic milieu. The expressive ethnography, on the other hand, is altogether novel. It explores the domains that are mainly expressive or have an expressive coloration—including most standard ethnographic domains—but that are concentrated in the social, familial, and recreational life of aristocrats. This description and analysis allow me to generalize a standardized approach for the comparative study of expression in various sociocultural settings. Last, the standard and the expressive ethnographies of Volume 2 link the aristocracy and plutocracy in several contexts and domains, reflecting their rapid coalescence into an undifferentiated haut bourgeois class.

Volume 3 is the most formal part of the study. It consists of several short, independent studies of expressive domains or problems that would have proved intractable within the more traditional ambiance of the expressive ethnography. These short studies illustrate specific aspects of the expressive culture of the Mexican aristocracy while pointing toward the comparative implementation of the expressive focus and strategy. The configuration of data for these studies is more exacting and controlled than the expressive ethnography, and it has a significantly higher psychological component. Employing some of the methods of behavioral analysis (multidimensional scaling, clustering analysis, constant-sum ratio scaling, semantic differential analysis), these studies clarify segments, patterns, and contexts of the expressive behavior of the aristocracy that are best approached individually in more controlled substantive environments.

For the generous financial support that enabled me to gather the historical, ethnohistorical, and ethnographical data on which this book is based, I thank the National Endowment for the Humanities, the American Philosophical Society, the Wenner-Gren Foundation for Anthropological Research, the Pittsburgh Foundation, the University of Pittsburgh Center for Latin American Studies, and the University of Pittsburgh Faculty of Arts and Sciences Research Fund. Without their assistance, I could not have completed the eleven years of research this study demanded.

It would be impossible to single out every individual or institution who, in one way or another, helped in the fieldwork and archival research on which it is based, but I would like to express my appreciation to those who made the most significant contributions: To the Academia Mexicana de Genealogía y Heráldica (Mexican Academy of Genealogy and Heraldry) I am grateful for electing me to its membership. To its president, Don Teodoro Amerlinck y Zirión, in particular, and to academy members in general, I am grateful for discussions that bear directly on the present volume. To the countless informants who provided specific facts or led me to information contained in books and private archives, I am grateful for their openness and willingness to help and for the time and effort they devoted to answering questions and guiding me through the intricacies of family histories.

I am intellectually and professionally indebted to L. Keith Brown, María Teresa Cervantes, Rosa María Cervantes, Douglas R. White, Lilyan Brudner-White, Thomas S. Schorr, Doren L. Slade, Lisa Moskowitz, Vinigi L. Grottanelli, Italo Signorini, Alessandro Lupo, James S. Boster, Lola R. Ross, Ronald C. Carlisle, William Smole, and Desiderio H. Xochitiotzin, who either read parts of the text, made constructive criticisms, and suggested changes in style, presentation, and organization, or discussed theoretical or methodological matters with me. The last two sections of chapters 7 and 8, which cover the time period from the onset of the Porfirio Díaz regime until the present, contain ethnographic information elicited or reconstructed from informants. Of the dozens of respondents, I wish to thank particularly José Luis Pérez de Salazar, Fernando Cervantes Palomino, José Ignacio Conde Díaz Rubín, Juan Cervantes Palomino, Carlos Cervantes Escandón, Marita Martínez del Río de Redo, Cucú Cabrera Ypiña de Corsi, the late Landolfo Colonna di Stigliano, and Carlotta Mapelli-Mozzi. I am very grateful for their detailed information, comments, and suggestions, which were extremely valuable for the analysis of the aristocracy's decline.

I am especially grateful to Solange Alberro for her insightful notions on the socialization of conquistadors during the sixteenth century, and how they were transformed by contact with several levels of Indian society. For more than twenty years, Solange has read the manuscripts of my most important publications, improving my works with her creative criticisms and offering an inexhaustible source of information and ideas on the history of mentalities. Her intellectual generosity and her willingness to exchange ideas have been two of the pleasures of working in Mexico for more than three decades. I am indebted to Daniel Rábago for allowing me to consult his family papers, which shed considerable light on several aspects of downward aristocratic mobility, the landed estates during the Porfirio Díaz regime, and early land reform.

To the late John M. Roberts, I owe most of the ideas concerning the expressive components of the aristocracy in particular and of social stratification in general. He was for many years an invaluable source of inspiration concerning the quantitative analysis of data and the expressive configuration of sociocultural systems. Indeed, the structural and expressive study of the aristocracy was a collaborative enterprise; he was instrumental in designing several domains of its implementation, and his untimely death leaves a vacuum that will be very difficult to fill. More than any other anthropologist, he influenced my mature analytical development; for this I shall always be grateful. He was a dear friend, and his memory will never wane.

This book is dedicated to the late Carlos de Ovando Gutierrez. I owe Carlos my greatest debt of gratitude, for his friendship, intellectual collaboration, and profound knowledge of the history and configuration of his class have been of inestimable importance to the realization of the study. He was a peerless informant, collaborator, and friend. The rich texture of his data—elicited in several hundred hours of conversation—will illuminate subsequent volumes. He directed me to important sources of historical information and provided me with unpublished documents that enhanced this monograph. His precise, penetrating descriptions of the behavior and expression of his class contribute immeasurably to the study. He opened his house to my wife, Jean F. Nutini, and I. I was allowed unrestricted use of Carlos's family papers as well as those of his father-in-law, Don Francisco Pérez de Salazar. My wife and I are equally grateful to Carmelita Pérez de Salazar de Ovando, Carlos's wife: not only the most generous and hospitable of hostesses, but an accurate and insightful informant as well. We shall always treasure the engrossing days that we spent in Carlos and Carmelita's homes in Mexico City and the country, eliciting information, analyzing data, and enjoying each other's company. Carlos and Carmelita not only enriched this study, but our lives, as did many of their kinsmen and friends who also became our informants and friends. This kind of human interaction is one of the glories of the anthropologist's craft, and I thank Fortuna for having blessed me with such rewarding and unforgettable experiences.

Introduction

This book is concerned with the Mexican aristocracy: its formation in the sixteenth century, its development throughout Colonial times, its florescence in the nineteenth century, and its persistence and decline in the twentieth century. More than any other social class in Mexico, with the exception of the Indian population until the Mexican Revolution of 1910, it exhibits unparalleled continuity of structure, form, and content. Indeed, one could make the case that these two classes (or ethnic groups) at the opposite extremes of the social system have always been, and to some extent still are, the most conscious of their social strata, the most ideologically self-contained, and the most structurally identifiable. Even in its terminal stage, the Mexican aristocracy retains an integrity and uniformity of behavior and a self-awareness unmatched by any other segment of Mexican society. Like most Western aristocracies, it has been from the beginning intimately tied to the land, and its possession was always the main source of its social, economic, and political strength. At its inception (during the fifty years after the Spanish Conquest) and at the pinnacle of its power (in the second half of the nineteenth century), it thoroughly dominated the social, economic, and religious life of the nation. Though always a small group, the Mexican aristocracy has played an inordinately significant role in Mexican history, thus sometimes resembling the European seigneurial aristocracy out of which it arose.

No social scientist or historian has ever presented an exhaustive description and analysis of the Mexican aristocracy. Though some good studies describe the aristocracy for circumscribed historical periods, no comprehensive account exists of the formation, development, and decline of this social class. Historians have been particularly good in describing, and to some extent analyzing, segments of the Mexican aristocracy and its economic and political roles in the seventeenth, eighteenth, and nineteenth centuries. Social scientists, on the other hand, primarily sociologists and political scientists, have not done as well, and anthropologists have displayed a conspicuous lack of interest in any aspect of upper-class stratification in Mexico. Under the rubrics of "elites," "political elites," "oligarchies," "bourgeoisies," and other categories to identify the rich and politically powerful, several publications have appeared during the past twenty-five years (see Mendizábal 1972; Urías 1978). Most of these studies by American, Mexican, and European scholars conflate a number of disparate stratification categories either in ideologically committed, often Marxist, accounts of local (provincial) and national elites or in quantitative, empirical accounts modeled on the conceptions of class, power, and political participation (mostly variants of the functional paradigm) prevalent among sociologists and political scientists in the United States but not always applicable to the Mexican situation without significant modifications or calibrations. The paucity of comprehensive, empirically sound, and analytically unbiased studies of class and mobility in Mexico is striking, given the great changes that the stratification system has been undergoing since the Mexican Revolution of 1910.

For the foregoing reasons alone the present study is fully justified, for we know almost nothing about how the old landed aristocracy of Mexico has evolved during the past three generations to occupy a marginal, almost invisible niche in the stratification system. Stripped of wealth and political power, its social status and prestige on the verge of disappearing as a desirable commodity, the Mexican aristocracy is nonetheless still a viable social entity, recognized by Mexico's plutocracy and the most upwardly mobile sectors of the upper-middle class. The term *aristocracy* itself, as applied to the once very wealthy landed class of Mexico, would not be accepted by most social scientists, for whom this upper-class sector is an anachronism or a rather insignificant part of the contemporary oligarchy or *alta burguesía*, as most Mexican Marxists call the ruling class. Yet more than any other discernible social class or ethnic group in Mexico, the aristocracy is self-conscious—one of the significant attributes of Marx's definition of class. Here we reach the crux of the matter, which exemplifies the expressive components and underpinnings of social stratification that are the main thrust of the study. Admittedly, the aristocracy today is not a significant economic and political category in the Mexican stratification system; its significance rests solely on expressive considerations. But after three generations of having lost all political power and most of its wealth, it is still a social class to reckon with.[1]

Some Methodological and Theoretical Considerations on Western Stratification

Except for studies of caste, class differentiation in tribal societies, and the position of folk societies in national states, anthropologists have been traditionally concerned with societies that are essentially egalitarian. Only rarely have they ventured into the realm of complex societies and made significant contributions to the conceptualization of class and mobility. Sociological scholarship, on the other hand, offers rich theories and descriptions of stratification and its complexities, but still avoids the upper reaches of the class system and eschews the historical study of the estate system and its implications. Since this book is concerned with upper-class stratification and how it arose out of an estate system, I include the following remarks to place the discussion in methodological and theoretical perspective.

THE HISTORICAL AND CONTEMPORARY SETTING OF STRATIFICATION STUDIES

Since sociology has become an academic discipline, society's groups, and particularly the stratification thereof, have received as much attention as kinship has received in anthropological studies. The golden age of sociological studies of class, mobility, and other aspects of stratification occurred between 1920 and 1960, when, stimulated by what are now considered classical theories and positions, sociologists postulated new approaches, debated old issues, and occasionally formulated new theories. Since the reprint of Bendix and Lipset's (1966) volume on class, status, and power (an excellent compendium on stratification until that time), stratification studies have received little attention and no theoretical innovations, let alone theories, have arisen. I do not know the reason for this decline in stratification studies, but it is probably related to the overall decline of the Marxist and functional paradigms and the inordinate concern of sociology for the past twenty-five years with practical problems and quantifying methodologies. Nothing written during the past generation can contribute to the theoretical focus of the present study. I shall therefore briefly discuss the most significant theoretical positions on stratification insofar as they are, or are not, relevant to the present study.

In an unfinished chapter of *Capital: A Critique of Political Economy,* Marx says, "The first question to be answered is this: What constitutes a class?—and the reply to this follows naturally from the reply to another question, namely: What makes wage-laborers, capitalists, and landlords constitute the three great social classes?" (Bendix and Lipset 1966:5). This telling passage points, as critics have often noted, to Marx's a priori reasoning concerning social relations and his general conception of society. Specifically, he answers a question with a question; before setting up an empirical inquiry he already knows the analytical outcome of what he is about to investigate—in this case, the nature and number of classes that his a priori reasoning tells him exist in the real world. Upon close examination, Marxism, despite the much vaunted claims of Marx and his followers that it offers the only truly objective analysis of society, is little more than a marshaling of evidence for ideological constructs that have been nonscientifically established. Everything in Marx that is scientifically (structurally) useful and profitable (for example, the determinant effect of material and economic factors in structuring much of social life) has been internalized by the majority of social scientists and is now part of the canon of social science. The contemporary importance of Marx and Marxism is ideological and practical. Everything he conceptualized along these lines, such as the class struggle and the dictatorship of the proletariat, has certainly helped to change the modern world. Marxism may still nourish revolutions—although there are many who doubt even this aspect of Marxism—but it contributes little to the scientific explanation of sociocultural phenomena, in the light of the advances made in the second half of the twentieth century on methodology, data gathering, and scaling down problems for more exacting solutions.

Post-Marxian conceptions of class vary considerably. From the turn of the century until the 1950s, several approaches led to a good deal of work in sociology and history. Shortly before the turn of the century, Ferdinand Toennies (1931) addressed the question of distinguishing the three main manifestations of stratification: caste, estate, and class.

He suggests that although classes and estates are determined by economic constraints and access to the rewards of production, that their encompassing domains differ, particularly because they are sanctioned by legal mechanisms: estates and classes are not equal before the law, and in the overall organization of society estates approach the constitution of castes. Similarly, Max Weber's (1946) discussion of class, status, and parties posits class membership as an economic concomitant and status as a social concomitant (tradition, expression), while characterizing political parties as an extension of class into the political domain. Weber maintains that classes are not communities but amorphous groups linked by the position they occupy in the structure of production, whereas status groups are communities with a higher degree of cohesion. For example, classes, as defined by most sociologists, exist in the United States, but so do proper Bostonians, mainline Philadelphians, and Virginia gentry. What Weber evidently has in mind is the difference within the upper echelons of the stratification system, between elite and social class.

Among U.S. sociologists, a number of scholars have directly or indirectly addressed problems of upper-class stratification in ways relevant to the present study. Thorstein Veblen's (1931) theory of the leisure class has significant implications for the structural and expressive conceptualization of the upper classes. His notions on honor, manners, the value of leisure, and other characteristic attributes of the haute bourgeoisie relate directly to the expressive analysis of the aristocracy and its relationship, in turn, to the plutocracy in the modern context. The work of Joseph Schumpeter (1951) specifies the variable empirical and conceptual nature to which the term *class* applies, as used by Aristotle, the philosophers of the Enlightenment, and contemporary sociologists. This clarification is particularly important in the analysis of classes, defined as significant groups within larger divisions of society (for example, estates) that are customarily or legally constituted.

Much work of U.S. sociologists on stratification has been in the functionalist mold (see Davis and Moore 1945; Gordon 1958; Riesman 1959; Ossowski 1963), although when the functional theory of class stratification was first formulated by Davis and Moore (1945), it elicited mostly an unfavorable reception. Starting from the implicit empirical premise of social inequality (that there has never been a complex classless society), Davis and Moore maintain that class stratification is inevitable. Davis and Moore's theory should be rejected on structural grounds (it is tautologous, as most functional generalizations are). I need not detail the functional theory of class and its variations, for they are not relevant to the present study. There are, however, several scholars whose work has influenced the historical and ethnographic description and analysis of the Mexican aristocracy.

ESTATE AND CLASS IN STRUCTURAL AND EVOLUTIONARY PERSPECTIVE

After more than a hundred years of academic social science, class has become a byword in sociology and anthropology. Not so with the word *estate,* which remains vague, sometimes used and defined as a variety of class and almost always as denoting something arcane that need not concern those engaged in the study of sociocultural phenomena. The current sociological concept of class is rooted in the eighteenth century, and its properties and configuration were elaborated as a concomitant aspect of the rise of representative democracy, although Aristotle was the first to use the term *class* to refer to the basic divisions of civic society (in Sir Henry Maine's sense). The term *estate,* on the other hand, conceptually and in common parlance, is much older, going back to the thirteenth century, at least in constitutional law, but it has never received the sociological treatment and elaboration that have been applied to the concept of class in recent generations.

The term *estate* or *order* appears as early as the late seventeenth century in the work of Vico (1965), and the term was common in the work of the French philosophers of the Enlightenment. Though the founders of the social sciences were primarily concerned with the legal framework and formal political divisions of France and other European nations, they indirectly addressed the sociological concept of estate and its social and economic implications. Not until the beginning of the twentieth century, however, did the concept of estate receive systematic treatment and configuration with respect to class.

In the prevailing tradition of assigning primacy to material and economic considerations, Toennies (1931) asserts that estates, like classes, result from economic conditions. Classes and estates, however, are not simply entailed by economic conditions; they have political and social components and consequences as well. He points out that though classes and estates are different, up to his time they were

regarded as nearly synonymous—indeed, the terms were used inter-
changeably—and he proceeds to differentiate them. Under the rubric
of "collectives," he categorizes estates and classes and places them in an
evolutionary relationship to one another: estates are transformed into
classes by a process of class or estate struggle. He then systematically
distinguishes estate and class.

> But scientifically we want to distinguish these terms in the
> sense that estates are conceived as *communal* and classes as *societal*
> collectives. Another distinction between them consist in the
> greater rigidity of estates as against the often extreme fluidity of
> classes. Classes are more frequently determined by environmen-
> tal conditions, which as a rule remain the same for generations,
> but which become more changeable in the course of social devel-
> opment and which cause individuals and families to rise or fall
> to a higher or lower class. It follows, on the other hand, that an
> estate becomes more identical with a class, the more it disinte-
> grates, i.e., the more the mobility of its members increases.
> (Toennies 1966:12–13)

Confused as the foregoing quotation is, it details the main attributes and relationship of estate and class: their different constitution in
terms of personnel and the political structure of the state; the rigid,
self-contained nature of estates contrasted with the fluidity of class; and
the evolutionary nature, at least of Western stratification, in which
estates evolve into classes. Toennies (1966:13–14) further identifies
the social and honorific components of estates as an intrinsic aspect of
societies for most of the duration of Western Civilization, meaning, of
course, those of the superordinate estate until its demise. The fundamental property of estates and classes, however, is encapsulated in his
characterization of the former as *communal* and the latter as *societal*. The
source of his differentiation evidently comes from Maine's distinction
between *societas* and *civitas* in their evolutionary context. Like societies
organized largely on the basis of kinship, estates are subdivisions of
society in which kinship, heredity, and lineage play an important role
in the organic structure of the grouping; meanwhile, the loose constraints of territory and state organization account for the basic structure of classes.

Toennies' key terms—communal and societal—and their elaboration offer a slight shading of Maine's characterization. Estates are major subdivisions of society, based largely on occupation, ruling (political) attributes, and/or lineage and heredity. Estates are unequal before the law or customarily entail differential access to whatever economic, political, and social rewards the society offers; they are largely endogamous, without approaching the structure of castes; and they are characterized, particularly superordinate estates, by a high degree of consciousness of membership and status. Classes, on the other hand, are what Toennies calls "collectives" exhibiting "significant societal tendencies" (read, rather disparate groups of people exhibiting significant mobility), characterized by a modicum of consciousness, largely agamous, and in a constant state of flux. Although Toennies does not say so explicitly, classes, as defined, can only exist when all members of a society are equal before the law. Toennies' definition of class is inadequate, particularly in its relationship to estate, as it will be discussed below (Toennies 1966:12–20).

Classes—defined as the loose, fluid, agamous, and mobile global (societal) subdivisions of the body politic—have existed in Western Civilization for barely two hundred years, preceded by two hundred years of gestation. Before the French Revolution, extending back to Homeric times, for which we can dimly reconstruct the basic configuration of society, the universal form of European stratification was the estate system. The Indo-European peoples at the dawn of Western Civilization, the classical Greeks and Romans, the peoples of the Roman Empire, the Germanic monarchies founded on the ruins of the empire, the feudal monarchies, the monarchies of the late Middle Ages, and the monarchies of early modern times were fundamentally stratified into a superordinate and a subordinate estate. The superordinate estate—most commonly known as the aristocracy, the nobility, or the ruling class—possessed social, economic, and political privileges that sharply distinguished it from the subordinate estate—usually known as the common people or the commonality—to whom these privileges were denied by law and/or custom. Each discernible historical period had specific terms to designate the superordinate and subordinate estates: eupatridae and thetes among the Greeks; patricians and plebeians among the Romans; lords and serfs in feudal times; nobles and commoners from the onset of the late Middle Ages onward. Of course, the sharp distinction between the estates shaded at times into gray zones of class differentiation, but until the end of the ancien régime the estate system constituted the determinant factor of stratification.

The fundamental principle of Western stratification for two and a half millennia was thus inequality before the law and the social, economic, and political privileges that buttressed it. Properly speaking, then, until the rise of modern democracy, defined as equality before the law for all members of the body politic, Western Civilization had no classes that could be defined as the primary building blocks of stratification. It is easy to misinterpret developments in ancient and medieval policies as political tendencies toward the democratization of society and hence the establishment of social classes. In fact, the so-called Greek democracies, the struggle of the plebeians for economic and political recognition in Republican Rome, and the existence of the city in the early Middle Ages as a semi-independent entity of Feudalism did not entail the rise of primary classes, for these developments took place under the umbrella of a firmly established estate system. It should be noted, however, that the estate system was never a caste system, since comparatively early in the development of stratification in the West an intermediary order arose, alternately called by historians an estate and a class. This development is first documented in the rise of a knightly estate or class (order is perhaps a better term) during Republican Rome that persisted until the end of the empire. This order completed the basic stratification system that characterized Western Civilization for two millennia, until the end of the eighteenth century: a superordinate and a subordinate estate somewhat mediated by an intermediate order. Straddling the nobility and the commonality, the knightly order bridged the two estates throughout the Dark and Middle Ages and well into modern times, until the rise of modern class stratification.

Defined as distinct groups of people, classes have existed at least since Roman times. During the early Republic, the entire population was categorized into classes based on wealth, mostly for political purposes. Though Roman classes were not quite equivalent to the modern concept of class, they are the earliest example in Western Civilization of categorizing part of the population according to principles akin to those we employ today. More pertinent to the present discussion is the medieval subdivision of the estate into classes. During feudal times, the nobility was divided into a number of ranks with many characteristics of classes, while the commonality was divided into freeholders, villeins, and serfs. In early modern times, the aristocracy was further categorized as upper and lower nobility, while the commonality was divided into the bourgeoisie, the peasantry, and possibly other identifiable groups that can be construed into classes. Status before the law was largely defined by estate, but within each estate social, economic, and political access was in principle egalitarian, mobility was possible, and endogenous interaction permissible. Thus, the differences between the higher or titled nobility and the lower nobility or gentry were those of class, in the sociological definition of the term operating largely in an endogenous context; the same can be said of the component classes of the commonality.

Dating from the formation of the Germanic monarchies, and particularly from the onset of modern times, the passage from commoner to noble status was most characteristically embodied in the knightly class. In this ambiance of relative mobility and upward aspirations commoners became knights, and the upper segments of the commonality were structured into a bourgeoisie and ultimately into a plutocratic class that begat the gentry of late modern times. Two additional points are in order. First, historians and jurists have traditionally distinguished between hereditary and occupational estates, but from the viewpoint of stratification only the former are estates, strictly speaking. Thus, the statuses of noble and commoner until the end of the ancien régime were inherited, whereas status in the clerical or priestly estate was acquired upon formal admission. Since the early Middle Ages, the priestly estate (including bishops, priests, nuns, and other church officials above the laity) had legal recognition and entailed specific rights and privileges that set them apart from both superordinate and subordinate estates, but its members came from both the nobility and commonality. Such legally recognized estates are not stratificational and are best regarded as occupational groups or classes. The primary and secondary divisions of the body politic must be precisely established, and when we discuss the period when the estate system was in place, the only sociologically sensible approach is to speak of classes as subdivisions of the superordinate and subordinate estates.

Second, classes in the strict sociological sense of primary divisions of the body politic are of recent occurrence in the long life of Western Civilization. The condition sine qua non for the inception of classes is equality before the law: lineage and heredity do not play a determinant role in configuring the primary groupings of society. Thus, classes are a concomitant aspect of the rise of political democracy, which by definition does not tolerate the presence of hereditary estates as constitutive parts of the body politic. The much vaunted democracies of classical Greek city-states were not democracies in this sense, for they were founded on slavery and had an estate system entailing inequality before the law. That certain hereditary attributes, perhaps proclivities is a better term, have survived in the contemporary class system is a fact, but in principle and in most of its attributes class membership is acquired.

Classes came into existence in Western society when the last important privileges of the aristocracy (higher and lower nobility) were abolished, that is, when European monarchies became republics or constitutional monarchies. This occurred between the French Revolution and the social upheavals of the mid-nineteenth century, when the legal and constitutional framework of European nations changed radically and irreversibly. But the change from estate to class stratification was not swift; several aspects of the former survived until the twentieth century, and some vestigially until the present. More important to the present study and for the overall conceptualization of Western stratification is the realization that the class system had a long period of gestation extending to the second half of the fifteenth century. Class stratification gathered momentum by the middle of the seventeenth century, and by the end of the eighteenth century it had become a fact of social life in most European nations.

The key factor in the development of class stratification was the rise of the bourgeoisie, which originated among segments of European society that were not directly subject to Feudalism or seigneuralism in the thriving urban centers of the early to the late Middle Ages. From the middle of the fifteenth century, this class of the commonality began to usurp some of the privileges of the aristocracy, and by the end of the seventeenth century the bourgeoisie had become an established powerful segment of the commonality: a rich and bureaucratically important class competing directly with the lesser nobility. By the end of the eighteenth century a powerful, plutocratic haute bourgeoisie was in existence, which in self-awareness and configuration must be regarded as the first real class in the modern sociological sense. With the establishment of republics and constitutional monarchies by the middle of the nineteenth century, the haute bourgeoisie came into its own, striving with the aristocracy, primarily by virtue of the great wealth that it had created as the main architect of the Industrial Revolution. The landed wealth of the aristocracy, which in the main survived the loss of privilege, could not compete with the industrial, banking, and manufacturing wealth of the haute bourgeoisie, and from the middle of the nineteenth century a process of class acculturation began. The haute bourgeoisie emulated the aristocracy, and the aristocracy acquired significant bourgeoislike elements as its once-great wealth dwindled. This process of accommodation has characterized the upper reaches of the class system for the past hundred years or so, until, after the middle of the twentieth century, the aristocracy had become little more than a social elite.

From Homeric times to the sixth century B.C., custom or kinship, not law, most likely sanctioned the division of society into superordinate and subordinate estates. Similarly, during the early Middle Ages, certain privileges were sanctioned by custom rather than law, a good example being the *jus prima noctis* or *droit de seigneur,* insofar as we can determine that it was actually exercised. In other words, in the history of Western stratification, the estate system is the product of legislation, usually as the result of conquest—witness the Germanic conquest of the western Roman Empire, political and economic domination, and customary practice usually based on kinship and religion. Thus, the foundations of the aristocracy's privileges from the late Middle Ages until the French Revolution were legal and customary, and not infrequently custom was as strong as law. This dual basis of privilege is important to keep in mind, for it may explain why customary privileges of the nobility survived the legal abolition of the noble estate by more than a century.

A century and a half after the establishment of the first well-configured class system, the last vestiges of the estate system have mostly disappeared from Western society, and in a few instances, particularly in Great Britain, some linger even still. The survival of the aristocracy is an interesting phenomenon inseparable from the rise and predominance of the haute bourgeoisie from the early nineteenth century to the present. Aristocratic manners, mores, and institutions have survived the expressive and structural process of acculturation as part of a class system that values an expressive life that the haute bourgeoisie was not able to reproduce.

SOCIAL CLASS, POLITICAL CLASS, AND RULING CLASS DEFINED AND CONFIGURED

The concept of class is not only complex but involves several levels of analysis. With a few notable exceptions, anthropologists have contributed practically nothing to the conceptualization of class, while sociologists, who have done most of the work, have tended to view the concept one-dimensionally. A polarization in the study of stratification has emphasized on the one hand the so-called objective criteria of class (wealth, power, occupation, education, residence, and so on) and on the other so-called subjective criteria of class (most of what is included under the rubrics of social life and expressive components) (Baltzell 1966:267). I find this a spurious dichotomy. One approach without the other at best offers incomplete accounts of stratification and at worst leads to a distorted perception of stratification in structuring society. Epistemologically, objective criteria constitute the necessary attributes of class, whereas expressive criteria constitute its sufficient attributes.

Another effect of the rigidity that has characterized the sociological treatment of stratification has been a lack of discrimination concerning the types of classes that constitute a given polity. Classes are not just social entities—that is, major subdivisions of society entailing an endogenous tendency of mutual recognition and consciousness of kind; they have varied compositions determined by their function in society. This point is necessary to a proper appreciation of the evolution of class and estate, as well as crucial to an understanding of the relationship of wealth, power, and position at the top of modern national states. Most historical polities for which there is sufficient information seem to have developed a division of labor in public life. In fact, monolithic stratification structures rarely come into being. Perhaps the two most notable exceptions are the early Roman patriciate from the fifth to the third century B.C. and the last centuries of effective Feudalism. The most common form of stratification in Western history, at least in the superordinate or ruling sector of society, has been embodied in classes that perform some but not all of the functions of social, economic, political, and public life. Moreover, the evidence suggests that superordinate estates are made up of classes with diverse interests and attributes that shade and overlap but do not necessarily present a monolithic confrontational stance with respect to the subordinate estate.

United States sociologists have dealt with the differentiation of classes in terms of the social, economic, and political functions they perform (see Kornhauser 1966; Baltzell 1966; Gordon 1949; Mills 1966), but none has presented this aspect of stratification with the clear focus of the French sociologist Raymond Aron. In a concise but densely written article, Aron (1966:201—10) presents a very useful and somewhat novel way of looking at class, particularly the relationship between classes in general and the superordinate or dominant class in contemporary society. He sketches and configures a model of the leading strata of modern industrial societies that has wide-ranging implications for the study of stratification from an evolutionary perspective. The model he proposes applies not only to contemporary European societies but to their past and future evolution.

Aron sketches the transformation of stratification from the estate system of the ancien régime to the establishment of classes in the nineteenth century. He delineates the transformation of the aristocracy to a social class and, concentrating on the upper strata (ruling classes, oligarchies), demonstrates, on the basis of what follows the demise of the estate system, that although there has been a definitive change in the legal and juridicial foundations of the stratification system, there remains in place a superordinate group vis-à-vis a subordinate group. As there was a differentiation of functions in the superordinate estate of the ancien régime, Aron demonstrates that the same differentiation survived transformation to a class system. Aron conceptualizes this class oligarchy as a threefold division or grouping with distinctive functions. Following Pareto's designation of this class oligarchy, Aron defines elite, political class, and ruling class:

> I use the term *elite* in the broadest sense: all those who in diverse activities are high in the hierarchy, who occupy any important privileged position, whether in terms of wealth or of prestige. The term *political class* should be reserved for the much more narrow minority who actually exercise the political functions of government. The *ruling class* would be situated between the *elite* and the *political class:* it includes those privileged people who, without exercising actual political functions, influence those who govern and those who obey, either because of the moral authority which they hold, or because of the economic or financial power they possess. (Aron 1966:204)

Aron expresses concern over the use of the term *elite* because of its ambiguous implications and particularly because of the very broad categories of people it designates. I share Aron's qualms, which is why I use *social upper class*, or social class for short, to denote this category.

In this respect, I adopt Digby Baltzell's (1966) distinction between elites and upper classes. He defines elites as those, and the families of those, who have achieved great prominence in whatever endeavor they are engaged in (from politics and religion to artistic and intellectual pursuits). Elites are on the whole transitory, and they lack the continuity to constitute a discernible "class." Upper classes, on the other hand, do constitute genuine classes, for they exhibit a significant permanence through generations, and their membership is determined by sufficiently maintained ancestral influence. Baltzell implies that what lends significant unitary meaning to an upper class is a behavioral component, particularly an expressive behavioral component, that identifies members of the class as having good lineage, good breeding, and proper manners. Thus, of Aron's threefold categorization, social class is the main concern of this monograph, defined as embodying social exaltedness, as possessing the highest honors and dignities that society can confer above and beyond economic or political considerations but in direct relationship to the other classes of the oligarchy.

Though less central to this book, Aron's quite straightforward definitions of political class and ruling class do need some clarification for our purposes. Of the two, political class is the most visible, but not necessarily the easiest to conceptualize, for it is more transitory and less permanently configured than the ruling class. Nonetheless, political class is not simply an elite in the restricted sense. The ruling class, on the other hand, is undoubtedly more permanent but even more difficult to visualize, as it is composed of all the powerful segments not directly engaged in administering or making immediate political decisions. The most powerful of these segments are those with economic power who are allied directly or indirectly with the holders of political power. The ruling class includes ancillary elements, but all are centered on the exercise of power, whether intellectual, scientific, administrative, or artistic. Although in the context of estate-organized societies, the ruling class is easy to differentiate from the political class, class-organized societies offer no such tractable interpretation.

In the context of contemporary stratification, the three superordinate classes are more differentiated from one another than they were in the past. How much, then, do these classes still overlap, and to what extent are they more or less self-contained groups? As a rule, social class stands somewhat apart, whereas political and ruling classes generally function in unison by virtue of their greater overlapping.

Perhaps not in the United States, but certainly in Europe and many Latin American countries, this overlapping is a natural result of the survival of the aristocracy and certain aspects of the estate system. As the aristocracy loses political power and wealth, political classes and ruling classes emerge concomitantly with the haute bourgeoisie. Differentiation of the political and ruling classes is not easily discerned by scholars in the contemporary setting. This fuzziness of outline is nothing new, however: before the demise of the ancien régime the superordinate estate was by no means always a monolithic composite of these three classes. Indeed, a significant degree of variation characterized the evolution of Western Civilization from classical to modern times.

Only twice during major periods of Western stratification was the superordinate estate constituted by an undifferentiated social, political, and ruling class: during the Roman Republic until the first Punic War (roughly from 500 to 250 B.C.) and during most of the early Middle Ages under Feudalism (roughly from 900 to 1100). Throughout these two periods, the Roman patriciate and the feudal aristocracy, respectively, constituted the undisputed political leadership, owned most of the wealth, and epitomized social exaltedness. Whether similar situations existed before the end of the eighteenth century I do not know, though it is likely that they did for short periods of time in marginal societies of the West. An opposite situation obtained during the Roman principate (roughly from the time of Christ until the reign of Diocletian), which exhibited the greatest differentiation of functions of the three social classes until late modern times: the old patriciate and a newly created imperial aristocracy constituted the socially exalted; the army and imperial bureaucrats formed the political class; and the ruling class consisted of imperial favorites, a knightly plutocracy, and assorted regional magnates. In all other periods, and particularly from the late Middle Ages until early modern times (roughly from 1250 until 1800), the superordinate estate was variously differentiated, offering as the most common combinations the following: (1) the aristocracy constituted the social and ruling classes, and the monarchy constituted the political class but overlapped the aristocracy as the ruling class; (2) the aristocracy was the social class but shared some political and ruling functions with the monarchy; and (3) the aristocracy as a social class shared honors with a rising bourgeoisie, while the monarchy shared ruling and political functions with the aristocracy and rising bourgeoisie, respectively.

How, then, does the Mexican case fit into the puzzle? The Mexican aristocracy has had an unbroken existence since its inception right after the Spanish Conquest until the present. From the middle of the sixteenth century to the Mexican Revolution of 1910, the aristocracy was an example of combination (1): it was the undisputed pinnacle of social exaltedness, and its great landed and, at times, mining wealth made it the undisputed ruling class of the Colonial and Republican periods. They were never an effective political class, for Crown officials monopolized Colonial government, and after Independence political leadership was primarily in the hands of a professional middle class. With the 1910 Revolution and the attendant loss of all its landed estates, the aristocracy became a mere social class essentially of type (3), sharing, in Aron's terms, oligarchical functions with a new plutocracy and "revolutionary" political class.

This conceptualization of the dominant strata has two advantages over any other analysis of class that has been formulated by contemporary sociologists. First, in combination with Pareto's theory on the renewal of elites, it uses good evolutionary sense to explain the various forms of the superordinate estate and, with the rise of class systems, of the leading strata of society over millennia. In particular, the distinction between social class and ruling class is of paramount importance to this monograph, for the Mexican aristocracy has survived exclusively as an expression of the former while interacting intimately with a new plutocracy with political components. Second, the threefold classification of the dominant stratum allows for the expressive component of stratification in a manner not facilitated by most other conceptions. Social class thus embodies primarily expressive components, whereas the ruling and political classes embody primarily the structural components of stratification.

RENEWAL OF ELITES, LINEAGE, AND HEREDITY

To endow my account of the evolution of social stratification with a dynamic element, I turn to the work of Vilfredo Pareto (1935, 1980). Pareto's work offers rich insights on upper-class stratification and the conditions under which it takes place: empirically sound, methodologically feasible, and surprisingly free of ideological obstruction. Pareto is not interested in changing society but in understanding it: once it is established that men are as unequal in intellect as in power and wealth (a tradition that goes back to the French philosophers of the Enlightenment and shared by Mosca and Michels), the problem for the social scientist or social philosopher is not to eliminate these natural and social inequalities but to ensure that the best possible form of government mediates between the rulers and the ruled (Pareto 1980:371). Without categorically dichotomizing the dominant and dominated strata, Pareto agrees with Marx that class (or estate) struggle occurs periodically, changing the structure of historical societies as new dominant classes emerge and subordinate classes regroup. Pareto and Marx agree about the oligarchical interpretations of revolutions, that is, that significant restructuring of society is brought about by a succession of ruling classes. But Pareto does not maintain that every revolution establishes a new oligarchy that is more progressive than the one it replaced; changes in the organization of society result from particular, at times serendipitous, economic, political, and religious forces that may or may not represent an improvement on previous conditions. For Pareto, important societal changes, especially those reflected in the stratification system, are as much the product of violent confrontation as of slow accommodation and agreement, and both take place in a more fluid organization of classes and estates than Marx was willing to recognize.

Pareto's analysis of the circulation of elites leads to empirical generalizations worth testing. In outlining the replacement of ruling classes or elites, Pareto attributes to them certain psychological characteristics. He describes leadership of the new ruling class as adaptive-innovative; it achieves power by manipulating the social, economic, political, and religious conditions of the time—by force, if necessary, but also by compromise and concession. Once a new ruling class is established, and generally after a long period of time, it becomes complacent and ultimately conservative and regressive, thereby sowing the seeds of its own demise (Parsons 1965:411–16). The renewal of elites (dominant strata in Aron's terminology, superordinate class or estate in my terminology) is not intrinsically progressive in the Marxist sense, as it is primarily determined by the ability of a new group, with a foothold in the established oligarchy, to take advantage of the sociocultural conditions of the time and transform the social system. Pareto's conception of stratification, as Aron (1966:208) puts it, "is better adapted to the interpretation of revolutions which claim to follow Marx than is Marxism."

At the end of the eighth chapter of his treatise on general sociology, Pareto discusses the form and nature of elites and their circulation. He divides society into two strata, the elite and the nonelite, and further subdivides the former into a governing elite and a nongoverning elite, which correspond, respectively, to my superordinate and subordinate estates (or classes) and Aron's distinction between political and ruling classes. He then discusses social mobility, or, as he puts it, "the mixing of the elite and the non-elite," and the circumstances that lead to the incorporation of nonelite personnel into the elite (Homans and Curtis 1934:250–51). In the context of mobility, Pareto considers the rapidity of circulation (that is, the time and means that it takes for individuals to become part of the elite) and the mechanisms of acceptance and rejection at play in the formation of elites. Despite mobility and fluidity in periods of transition and in the decaying stages of a ruling elite, the composition of the superordinate strata is sharp and well defined, in harmony with the prevalent military, religious, and political tenor of the times. These aristocracies and plutocracies, as Pareto sometimes calls them, are the heart of the ruling elites; they are ultimately transformed either by force (revolution) or, when upwardly mobile members of the subordinate strata gain control of the principal assets of the superordinate stratum, by the slower workings of evolution.

Pareto's overall conception of aristocracies is essentially correct and, modified, has been instrumental in structuring my account of the evolution and development of upper-class stratification in the Mexican aristocracy. In particular, I have expanded and modified three points. First, Pareto overemphasizes the contribution of upwardly mobile personnel to the dominant strata of society, thereby downplaying the contributions of those in social, economic, and political control. The entrenched superordinate class or estate unquestionably decays, and as complacency sets in, it loses initiative and the ability to innovate in order to stay in power. But the power and effect of residues (the common denominator of ascending or decaying stratification systems) cannot be underestimated, and in the transformation, replacement, or circulation of classes and estates, that which is decaying determines to a variably significant extent (depending on the pace of change) the form and content of that which is ascending. In other words, the circulation of elites resembles an ongoing process of stratification acculturation. Emerging dominant classes or estates embody attributes, elements, and behavior of both ascending and decaying structures. The result favors the former in cases of revolutionary situations and the latter in cases of evolutionary situations. Thus, the barbarian monarchies of Europe and the estate system they established by conquest on the ruins of the empire (a revolutionary change) preserved most of the Germanic kinship and structure of the ruling class, but in forms significantly modified by equivalent Roman institutions. Conversely, in the transformation of the estate system into a class system in late modern times (an evolutionary change) the haute bourgeoisie preserved most of the expressive underpinnings and much of the general configuration of the aristocracy as a ruling class.

Second, though there is no reason to doubt that elites transform slowly but constantly, Pareto exaggerates change at the expense of permanence. The history of Western stratification demonstrates that the circulation of elites has been ceaseless, but also that certain fundamental structures have remained fairly static for very long periods. Another way of putting it is that individuals move up and down but the basic institutional framework of the stratification system often persists unchanged for an extended time. From the long-range historical perspective, since Homeric times until the establishment of the Roman Empire, there was an aristocratic estate that changed very little in structure and ideology, and yet, throughout this millennium, no lineage of eupatridae or patricians was indisputably part of the ruling class for more than two or three centuries. By the same token, very few, if any, noble houses in Europe can trace uninterrupted descent from the demise of the ancien régime back to the foundation of Feudalism early in the ninth century, and yet there was a nobiliary system that, in form and orientation, experienced few changes for more than nine centuries. From a more short-range perspective, we might observe of the Mexican aristocracy from the Spanish Conquest to the Revolution of 1910 that very few families today can trace descent to original conquistadors. There were many changes in memberships in nearly four hundred years, but with the same orientation and very few changes in configuration, the aristocracy persisted unbroken.

Third, Pareto's overemphasis on the circulation and impermanence of elites probably derives from his almost exclusive concern with the ruling and political classes and his only tangential reference to social class. Had he dealt extensively with the latter, he would have realized that superordinate classes and estates have much more institutional and configurational permanence than he was willing to acknowledge. That a social class can persist for considerably long periods of time independently, without sharing in political and ruling functions, has been amply demonstrated by the survival of European aristocracies past the end of the estate system. Pareto underestimates the force of kinship, lineage, and heredity, omnipresent and powerful elements in Western Civilization that shape and perpetuate social institutions. Everything we know about the psychology and sociology of upper-class (or estate) stratification indicates that once individuals achieve such status, they want to make it hereditary—and generally invoke an array of ideological rationalization in order to do so. Within this framework upper-class stratification must be conceptualized; power and wealth alone do not exhaust its overall configuration, for of the various forms of stratification social elites survive the longest, either as separate entities or as residual structures, once they have lost their ruling and political associations. The classic estate system, an integral part of Western stratification for millennia, may be regarded as an institution forged by legally sanctioning hereditary membership while allowing for sufficient mobility from the subordinate estate. In the modern class system, though hereditary membership is abolished, elite class status persists for generations, and the subterfuges and strategies employed in this endeavor become a sort of customary heredity.

I have refined the foregoing three points within the context of the evolution of the Mexican aristocracy since the Spanish Conquest and its contemporary development since the Revolution of 1910. The aristocracy has had a continuous existence of 450 years, and though it has undergone four major episodes of reorganization, throughout its tenure it has preserved a relatively constant ideological and structural integrity, despite several revolutions and the political and economic vicissitudes of its members. Mobility has been high, followed by periods of endogenous retrenchment, only to return again to periods of relative mobility. Circulation has been high; many plutocrats achieved aristocratic status, and many more aristocrats sank to the obscurity of middle-class existence.

The Expressive Components and Configuration of Upper-Class Stratification

The expressive focus and strategy are the most recent approaches to the study of the Mexican aristocracy, and in this case constitute almost

terra incognita. Expression constitutes a determinant aspect of stratification, and the following remarks are designed to put the present study
in perspective with respect to the standard analyses of class and related
phenomena. Inasmuch as in subsequent monographs I will demonstrate what the expressive analysis of stratification entails and advance a
number of propositions on the approach, what follows is an outline of
what is now known about the general parameters of expressive culture
in complex societies. (For a more complete account of the expressive
focus and strategy, see Nutini [1988:377–97].) Though I am concerned here with the structural components of stratification in diachronic perspective, underlying expressive themes impinge directly on
the evolutionary form and social content of estate and class.

SOME GENERAL CONSIDERATIONS ON THE EXPRESSIVE FOCUS AND STRATEGY

Most people—particularly anthropological researchers—are not aware
of expression. Otherwise, expression, as a concept, would occupy almost as much space as structure in the anthropological literature. The
reason for this neglect is probably twofold. The distinction between
structure and expression is not easy to visualize or to conceptualize. In
the intellectual climate of the past three generations, dominated by the
various forms of functionalism and historical materialism, the general
practice has been to regard expression (and, by extension, values,
beliefs, and ideology) as a residual aspect of the social structure or as
altogether outside the conceptual domain of individuals and groups in
interaction. Furthermore, expression, insofar as anthropologists have
dealt with it, has been regarded as essentially idiosyncratic, individually discharged, and as not only inadequate for but not applicable to a
large proportion of human activity.

Probably the most characteristic and universal attribute of expressive behavior is that it is essentially noninstrumental, that is, individually it represents an end in itself. John M. Roberts expresses this
property of expression by saying that "it is linked to antecedent psychological states," that is, enactment or representation of culturally conditioned individual experience. Put another way, the motivation and
discharge of expressive behavior are conditioned by the individual's
reaction or adaptation to changing aspects of the social structure. It
should be emphasized, however, that although expressive behavior is

psychologically motivated (at least most kinds of it) and individually manifested, it nonetheless has a collective, structured manifestation closely related to the social structure. Thus, expressive behavior may be nominally defined as the individual and collective choices that the members of a group or of an entire social system can make. By themselves they do not necessarily alter the group or system, but they express whatever changing conditions the group or system is experiencing. The motivation of expressive behavior makes it nonutilitarian or noninstrumental. In functional terms, expressive behavior is an integral part of the social structure as it manifests or exhibits certain diagnostic processes of the social system.

Though this conception of expressive behavior is the most useful sociologically, it is only one of several ways to approach the study of these concepts and what they mean for social structural studies. Expressive behavior is a universal of culture that either is associated with manifestly noninstrumental domains (art, music, play, games, manners, etiquette, dress) or colors certain aspects of structurally utilitarian domains (religion, warfare, stratification, subsistence and diet, even strictly economic pursuits). Indeed, any significant domain of culture or circumscribed aspect of the social structure may have an expressive component, which, temporarily or permanently, continuously or intermittently, configures behavior. Essentially, I have defined the basic forms of expression that may be called "structurally motivated" and "inherent." The former are directly linked to an antecedent psychological state, while the latter are inherent components of human behavior; both are discharged in structured ways within generally well delineated sociocultural domains.

Just as the organization and constituent elements of social structure vary in time and space, so also do the configuration and form of social expression. To pursue the analogy, if social expression is to become a field of scientific inquiry, it requires a technical vocabulary like the one anthropologists have devised to analyze social structure. Thus have Roberts and his collaborators (Roberts 1976; Roberts, Chiao, and Pandey 1975; Roberts and Chick 1979; Roberts and Golder 1970; Roberts, Koening, and Stark 1969; Roberts, Meeker, and Aller 1972; Roberts and Natrass 1980; Roberts and Sutton-Smith 1962; Roberts, Williams, and Poole 1982) formulated the concepts of expressive "array" and "domain" as the basic units in the analysis of expressive culture and behavior. Aware of the significant core of expressive forms in cultures throughout the world, Roberts has aimed to systematize the study of expressive behavior by delineating basic categories and units.

First, the expressive array is defined as the total of all patterns and contexts in a given culture that entirely or partially realize expression. Every culture has an expressive array that is peculiar to itself, both in terms of intensity and the contexts in which expression is realized. In the absence of a working theory of expression, and without systematic, cross-cultural data on expression, we can assert little about the intensity and extent of expressive behavior or about the most common contexts where expression is realized. We may, however, generalize: First, the contexts of play, what Westerners call the arts, the various kinds of crafts, several aspects of religion, and some features of kinship and interpersonal relations are the most likely to have significant expressive components; whereas the more intrinsically utilitarian components of culture such as subsistence patterns, economics, and politics are the least likely to realize expression.

Second, although every expressive array offers a unique organization of contexts, and no two arrays are exactly alike, total content and form show more overlap. One of the most characteristic attributes of the expressive array is that its global content and form, as well as those of specific contexts, are shared by several social systems, many spatially and temporally adjacent cultures, and perhaps by all subcultures of a cultural tradition. Thus, the expressive arrays of Italians, Frenchmen, Spaniards, Englishmen, Germans, perhaps even Americans and Australians, manifest a degree of content and form that is exclusively their own while sharing the bulk of the array with Western society as a whole. Can one say anything meaningful about the proportion of exclusive and inclusive content and form of expressive arrays in this macrocontext? The answer is a tentative yes. Observations among Araucanian Indians, rural Tlaxcalans, and Mexican aristocrats suggest that the expressive array of any subculture is about 20 percent exclusive in content and form, while 80 percent of it is shared by all sister subcultures. In other words, roughly 20 percent of the expressive array of the English is exclusively their own, while 80 percent of it is shared with the French, Italians, Spaniards, Americans, and the other nationalities of Western Civilization.

Third, let us consider the complicating factors of class, by itself and as it crosscuts the boundaries of cultures and subcultures. In terms of expressive culture and behavior, class (and certainly caste, and estates in the past) is probably the most salient and effective social assorter. Class appears always to have been the compound variable most efficacious in generating differential expressive arrays, both within a single cultural tradition and across several, sometimes quite different, cultural traditions. That is, the expressive arrays of equivalent social classes generally reflect more similarities across subcultures, and not infrequently even across different cultural traditions, than they do across classes within the same subculture. Given certain social, economic, industrial, and commercial constraints and the efficient networks of communication and diffusion in the world today, one could speak of the expressive array of the rich and powerful, of international business and political bureaucracies, of diplomats, and even of so-called jet-setters. Likewise, the expressive arrays of the middle and lower classes cut across all of Western society, perhaps even of the world, again due to the homogenizing effects of industrialization and the diffusion of other Western cultural complexes. The Mexican aristocracy displays an expressive array, for example, that resembles more closely the expressive array of the Spanish or Italian aristocracy than that of, say, Mexican plutocrats or upper-middle classes, despite the fact that inclusively the aristocracy shares most of its expressive contexts in varying proportions with the entire Mexican stratification system, from its rural Indian sector to its upper sector in Mexico City. The inclusive bulk of content and form of expressive arrays, then, is much more culturally or subculturally bound. If one takes the expressive array of Mexican aristocrats, the exclusive core is most of the content and form of that 20 percent identified previously; while the remaining 80 percent is shared in varying proportions with all other classes in the Mexican stratification system, for they have the same religion, are bound by many social customs, and are constrained by the same political, environmental, and ecological variables. But that 20 percent is what distinguishes Mexican aristocrats as an expressive class from all other classes in Mexican society and secures their membership in the larger class of Western aristocrats.

Fourth, though the main contexts of expression are the nonutilitarian aspects of culture, any aspect of culture may realize expressive behavior, regardless of manifestly utilitarian attributes and functions. No significant aspects of culture lack potential expressive coloration. Just as cultures organize around contexts and themes that exceed the exigencies of subsistence and shelter, so does the expressive array organize around characteristic contexts and themes. In addition to the universal contexts of art and play, an expressive array derives its characteristic configuration and flavor from the contextual loci of its realization. Sports, dress, and etiquette, for example, are important loci of expressive behavior in Western culture, whereas in many tribal societies, ritual, certain aspects of religion, and oral tradition seem to be the main loci of the expressive array.

Fifth, one of the most characteristic attributes of expressive culture—and one of the most difficult to handle conceptually and methodologically—is that expressive behavior is contextual in the sense that the same content of social practice may sometimes be discharged structurally, other times expressively. Therefore, expression must be regarded as an individual's epistemological options within the social structure: expressive behavior represents the psychological and social alternatives, the available leeway between structural requirements and individual choices. Expression is realized in three basic contexts: those in which realized behavior is primarily expressive, those in which behavior is at times expressive and at times instrumental, and those in which behavior is primarily instrumental.

Most forms of art and play are good examples of the first kind of expressive environment. The games people play and the paintings, music, and sculpture produced by artists are essentially forms of expressive behavior, that is, their realized intent is noninstrumental. Admittedly, there are professional athletes and game players, as there are artists whose main goal is monetary gain rather than artistic production for its own sake. Nonetheless, the most permanent, and hence the most universal, expressive contexts are those with an intrinsic expressive component. Perhaps all cultures have particular contexts and practices (often class-bound or structured by the division of labor or social segmentation) that are overwhelmingly expressive for most actors in the system. The tea ceremony in traditional Japan, the horse complex of Western aristocrats, and the cult of the dead among Mesoamerican Indians are good examples of this type of permanent expression.

Most expression in societies occurs in the second kind of environment. The elucidation and decomposition of this type of expressive behavior are the most difficult, for the contextual situations are multiple and involve sociopsychological options about which we can now make only tentative comments. Two examples suffice to illustrate the difficulties: Shopping for clothes can be alternately expressive and instrumental. For many women, especially in the upper sectors of the stratification system, buying items of attire is an expressive context. It can be decomposed into smaller parts that may variously include patronizing certain stores, selecting brand names, window-shopping, trying on garments, searching for patterns and styles, and so on. For most men, on the other hand, buying clothes is an instrumental activity that may or may not have an expressive coloration. Furthermore, the general activity of buying clothes may involve both expressive and instrumental components (simultaneously or sequentially), depending on social class, ethnic background, age, and other variables.

Some kinds of contextual expression are highly specialized, often confined to members of certain classes and interest groups. Belonging to clubs, doing charity work, organizing benefit balls, and participating in volunteer work are expressive activities usually associated with the socially prominent upper classes, whereas more specifically, philanthropy, patronizing the arts, and exhibiting art are expressive activities generally associated with the rich and powerful sectors of these classes. Storytelling, religious devotions, ritual and ceremonial involvement (in both sacred and secular events), and even many eccentricities may be regarded as expressive activities of individuals sharing certain psychological proclivities or belonging to certain special-interest groups.

The third context occurs least frequently but is quite important within the entire expressive array, in terms of both antecedents and consequences for the social structure. This type of expression is the most difficult to detect, for it is intertwined with instrumental contexts and goals. Indeed, the contexts and practices of this usually appear on the surface to be entirely instrumental; their expressive components must be sought beneath the instrumental goals and motivations. Politicians, religious seers, or captains of industry, while seeking manifestly utilitarian aims, may be powerfully motivated by such expressive goals as the desire to assert their individuality or to gain attention for their effect (positive or negative) on the society. Becoming an activist for a cause, running for a local office, or joining a street gang offer more mundane examples of this phenomenon. These seemingly instrumental but expressively laden contexts are crucial to understanding how psychological input affects socially determined outcomes.

The expressive domain is the basic component of the expressive array. It may be defined as any cultural context in which expressive behavior is realized with some degree of semantic unity. The domain is not a fixed unit or entity of expressive realization; it can aggregate to higher levels (broader domains) or decompose to lower levels (narrower domains) according to the needs of the analysis. For example, in all subcultures of Western society sports constitute a major expressive domain. This domain may be broken down into the domains (or subdomains) of individual sports and team sports; within these, into the sub-subdomains of track and field, golf, tennis, bowling, and so on, football, basketball, hockey, soccer, and so on. Some of these sports can be further decomposed into still narrower domains—track and field into sprints, middle-distance running, and field events, and even further into particular events such as the hundred-yard dash, the mile run, the marathon, the shot put, and the high jump. Each event has its own expressive configuration, but it also shares some aspect of expression with the sport of track and field as a whole. This notion of a shared semantic field of expression probably cannot be extended beyond the major domains of a given global array. That is, the expressive array of a well-defined culture, subculture, or permanently organized social segment such as a class.

The expressive array of the Mexican aristocracy includes more than 230 domains, many of which can be decomposed into subdomains. The array includes domains in all the usual ethnographic categories (kinship, religion, the life cycle, political life, economy and material culture, games and play) with different degrees of intensity and saliency. It contains many domains shared with plutocrats in what might be called the international set in Mexico City and with the upper-middle class. Aristocrats also share many expressive domains with all classes in the Mexican stratification system.

In summary, the expressive array of social class, subculture, culture, or perhaps an entire culture area is the totality of expressive domains and their subdivisions configured in terms of inclusive and exclusive categories with reference to the three basic environments I have enumerated. The breakdown of inclusive and exclusive domains generally identifies the environments of greatest expressive realization and of most universal incidence in the social unit under consideration, for it is the 20 percent or so of exclusive domains of the global array that distinguishes the expressive behavior of the group.

No doubt many different kinds of expressive behavior exist, but so far it has been possible to distinguish only three: the "natural" (or "inherent"), the "conflict," and the "terminal" types. The first two are of immediate relevance.

Natural expression is a universal attribute of sociocultural systems, a manifestation of the psychic unity of mankind. The concept is a reflection of the fact that, for whatever psychological reasons, the social life of humans inevitably contains nonutilitarian elements that shape the social structure. Although expression obeys psychological motivation above all, it is realized within concrete sociocultural settings, and its explanation therefore involves the confluence of psychological and sociological variables.

Although any sociocultural domain may be the locus of expression, each culture tends to concentrate expression in some environments over others, and these "dense" loci must be central to an expressive analysis. If the differential density of loci is the distinctive sociocultural manifestation of expressive behavior, idiosyncratic expression is the clearest manifestation of the psychological underpinnings thereof. Idiosyncratic expression here means expression by atypical (and therefore few) members of the group, whether in common or uncommon domains. The description of an expressive array must specify not only the most intensive and extensive domains and subdomains, but also idiosyncratic domains and subdomains. The realization of expression has a significant diachronic component. Although the psychological nature of expression does not change, the domains of its realization most certainly do: What is today central to the expressive array of a social group may have been peripheral a generation or two ago, and vice versa.

One of the most difficult problems in investigating expression is how to determine what is expressive and what is instrumental in the causation of behavior. There is no operational definition of expression, but given even the nominal definition of expression presented here, the expressive components of behavior are not at an epistemological disadvantage with respect to its instrumental components. Assuming the ontological reality of expression, it should be possible to determine the expressive and instrumental composition of input in any behavioral outcome.

Conflict expression entails special kinds of behavior that are tied to changes in the social structure of such groups as are often associated collectively with revolutions and individually with changes of socioeconomic standing. This type of expression is a good example of the importance of determining why some members of a social group are involved in certain patterns of expressive behavior while others are not, since those domains that claim no one's involvement generally disappear from the expressive array (Roberts 1976). In order to address this type of expression, Roberts and Sutton-Smith (1962) developed a "conflict-enculturation theory of model involvement." This theory postulates that conflict among individuals and groups is likely to lead to involvement in a model (an expressive style) that represents the area of conflict to a greater or lesser degree and that the greater the conflict, the less representative or realistic the model must be to assuage the conflict-induced involvement. The theory also maintains that actions by actors within the "model-world" provide training (that is, enculturation), which in turn may or may not affect performance or activity in the "real world."

Another application of conflict expression can be seen in the history of traditional Western European aristocrats. For more than a century, these groups have been disintegrating. As the result first of the loss of political power, then of wealth and economic power, and more recently of social prestige and a position as role models for the rising plutocracies, they have seen their expressive arrays undergo considerable change. Expressive involvements that were once modest and peripheral have become central. As in the case of Mexican aristocrats, these changes appear to be the expressive outcome of the loss of status.

A theory of expression must address how the individual psychological realization of expression reflects collective social implications. In the present formulation, individual expression is a necessary condition for understanding decision making and motivation, whereas collective expression is intimately connected to the wider context of social explanation. An appreciation of the various forms of expression and the contexts in which they take place is necessary to the conceptualization of the Mexican aristocracy.

EXPRESSION IN EARLY STUDIES OF SOCIAL CLASS

It is difficult to conceive of a social class that does not include either an explicit or implicit reference to the expressive component of stratification. Awareness of this component can be traced to the earliest systematic statements on class by the Scottish moral philosophers at the beginning of the nineteenth century but to pinpoint the first use of expression as a complementary or defining characteristic of stratification is impossible. For more than a century and a half, class has been defined and configured primarily in structural terms; whatever else characterizes class as a social institution has remained unspecified. The behavior of class membership has not been analyzed as constituting a primary variable but as a subsidiary aspect of the effect of economic, political, and other variables. Although the expressive component has perhaps always been latent in studies of class and other forms of stratification, it was never in any fashion verbalized or formulated. The first studies from an expressive perspective, implicit and unspecified as the premises of the approach were at the time, were accounts of the U.S. upper class in cities of the eastern United States. Thus, the expressive (class) life of proper Bostonians, Main line Philadelphians, New York plutocrats, Virginia gentry, and other circles of the eastern social establishment is well described, and the expressive array of these upper classes can be partially reconstructed from these accounts (see Adams 1896; Allen 1935; Amory 1947, 1952; Ashburn 1944; Martin 1911; Wecter 1937). To be sure, these accounts contain no analytical statements on expressive culture and its relationship to stratification, but they are unquestionably the first studies of urban and regional upper classes that emphasize some of the most salient expressive aspects of stratification. Of these studies, none is as significant as the work of W. Lloyd Warner.

Baltzell (1966:266–75) maintains that by midcentury a polarization had occurred in studies of social stratification between objective and subjective definitions of class (corresponding closely to my structural and expressive foci), as exemplified by the works of Warner (1942) and the Lynds (1937), respectively. At that stage of development of U.S. sociology, says Baltzell, Warner's approach represented the dominant trend in stratification studies; Baltzell reiterates the fact that the objective approach to stratification is in no sense more "real" than the subjective approach.

Warner contributed both to the expressive conceptualization of stratification and to the broad parameters of expressive culture. Let us take the latter contribution first. As an anthropologist trained in the functional and U.S. historical traditions, Warner emphasized culture more than the social system, and within this ambiance he identified and described several domains of expression in U.S. culture. Most of this work on expression stems from the *Yankee City* series. With an eye on the ideational, symbolic, and ritual aspects of culture, Warner describes and interprets several domains of expression: kinship (interpersonal relations, patterns of etiquette, entertainment), religion (ceremonialism, religious beliefs), sacred ceremonies (Memorial Day, death and burial, weddings), secular ceremonies, and other more restricted domains (Warner 1957, 1959, 1961; Warner and Hunt 1941; Warner 1963).

Warner's main contribution to social stratification studies was his rejection of a strictly economic interpretation of class as the predominant form of analysis, at least among U.S. sociologists. Warner's reaction offered a needed corrective to a strictly objective conceptualization of class, though one can go too far toward the subjective (expressive) position. In contrast to the then prevailing position, Warner emphasizes the social, hereditary, and behavioral aspects of stratification and correctly maintains that all classes of society display attributes that transcend the more easily measurable criteria of wealth and economic position. Thus, he defines class as "two or more orders of people who are believed to be, and are accordingly ranked by members of the community, in socially superior and inferior positions" (Warner 1942:81), clearly suggesting that economic position cannot be the sole, nor even the predominant, indicator and differentiator of class.

Warner successfully approached the form and content of class from the social and behavioral standpoints, most markedly with reference to upper-class stratification in Newburyport, Massachusetts, one of the oldest cities of New England, the site of his *Yankee City* series. His complex study touches upon the entire spectrum of stratification, but most important is his description of the behavioral and expressive life of the local upper class, the old Yankee families, some of whom could trace their ancestry to the seventeenth century. Warner's basic idea was to view modern communities as a global cultural ensemble—much as an anthropologist views a tribe—to extend the analogy, social stratification as an institution is as pervasive in a community as kinship is in a tribe. This view of stratification apparently led Warner to emphasize the social style and expressive behavior of the various classes of the traditional upper class of Newburyport. At his best, he insightfully describes several expressive domains of the old Yankee upper class as characteristically diagnostic: houses and households, family and class, patterns of entertainment and display, etiquettes and interpersonal relationships, voluntary association groups and class membership, ritual and ceremonialism, and symbolism and class consciousness.

One of the most pertinent aspects of Warner's conception of class is his realization that lineage and heredity are important determinant aspects of stratification, particularly in its upper sectors. Although Warner did not develop them, two sides of this position stem directly from his conception of class. First, in the quest for upward mobility entailed by estate and class systems, whatever social, economic, political, or any other attributes required to achieve superordinate status are ultimately attributed to inherent, hereditary causes. Second, lineage and heredity are powerful rationalizing elements, so much so that they may be regarded as self-fulfilling mechanisms operating superordinately as well as subordinately, guiding the behavior and expectations of those who are above and below in the social scale. The expectation of upward mobility and the actual development of superordinate status therefore create a situation in which the determinant attributes of the lifestyle or the exclusive array acquires an exaltedness above and beyond what wealth and power can confer. On the debit side, Warner's conception of class, useful as it is when trained on the upper classes, has limited application to the entire stratification system. Though the expressive array of the lower classes may be as rich and complex as that of the upper classes, the former is never as determinant as the latter in configuring class consciousness and upward mobility, and other unknown factors are undoubtedly at work. Furthermore, in addition to overemphasizing expressive variables at the expense of structural variables, Warner does not specify the relationship between these two aspects of stratification.

The work of Digby Baltzell (1966) is a conceptual improvement on Warner's approach to class. Realizing the basic shortcoming of Warner's position, Baltzell not only presents stratification in the United States as a complement of the objective and subjective criteria that determine and define class, but he implies that these criteria vary in duration and origin. Concentrating on upper-class stratification, he identifies qualitative differences that separate this sector of the stratification system from the rest, noting that the difference contains an expressive component. Although he does not state it explicitly, he considers lineage and heredity a significant component of upper-class stratification and feels that social exaltedness maintained over several generations leads people to believe in inherent psychosocial properties of class membership.

In his study of elite and class indexes in the metropolitan United States, Baltzell (1966:266–75) draws a distinction between elites and upper classes that corresponds quite closely to my own distinction between Mexican aristocrats and plutocrats and between European aristocrats and the haute bourgeoisie. Baltzell defines elites as those who have achieved great economic, religious, and political power; they are individuals who have achieved high position and great prestige in their chosen professions (law, medicine, the arts, the sciences). Elites, however, do not constitute classes, for they lack secure continuity. Political and religious elites, for example, are constantly being renewed every one or two generations. By contrast, an upper class is a more structured social group exhibiting a much higher degree of permanence and institutional cohesion. Membership in an upper class, as we have seen, is determined by an ancestor having achieved a position of influence that his or her descendants have managed to maintain. In the ambiance of sustained prominence, expressive behavior identifies an upper class and endows it with a significant measure of unitary meaning as the possessor of good lineage, good breeding, and the group to emulate in upward mobility.

CLASS STRUCTURE AND THE VISIBILITY AND PERSISTENCE OF EXPRESSION

In the foregoing sections the necessity of conceptualizing upper-class stratification with the benefit of an expressive component has been amply documented, particularly with reference to the relationship obtaining between so-called objective variables and conditions and so-called subjective components. Concentrating on surviving European aristocracies, and particularly on the Mexican aristocracy, the following remarks elucidate the most substantive aspects of expression vis-à-vis stratification.

Granting that power and wealth, or lack thereof, structure, configure, and set the parameters of the expressive culture of all social classes (and estates), it is nonetheless the case that though class consciousness, class recognition, and class position are determined by the possession of wealth and power, the perception of class, its visibility, and its place in the social system are provided by its social and expressive behavior.

What is observed, internalized, and made into the ostensible definition of a class by the members of all other classes in the stratification system are the product of objective conditions, but modified, in feedback fashion, by historical circumstances and the nonutilitarian choices allowed by the expressive array. This visibility—pervasive gestalt, one might say—of class perception is the most distinctive and universal characteristic of class. It defines its entire range of social relations with the other classes of the stratification system. Visibility here denotes not only that the exclusive expressive array of a class is its most immediately and globally perceived attribute, but that its perception entails the most desirable quality for upward mobility.

The exclusive expressive arrays of all Western aristocracies result from complex historical circumstances, not only from the fact that until a century and a half ago they were still the wealthiest and most powerful sectors of European society. Some of the most characteristic domains of their expressive arrays hearken back to classical Greece and Rome, and others can be traced to Feudalism and the Middle Ages. Though every discernible aristocracy in Europe (national, regional) has developed its own expressive array, they all share a core of domains that define them as the most distinct segment of European society. This core, centered on several domains of social interaction, patterns of ritual and display, and an inordinate concern with lineage and heredity, has powerfully influenced the configuration of upper-class stratification since the middle of the nineteenth century when the estate system de facto ceased to exist. The aristocratic expressive core contains a fundamental property of upper-class stratification: the notion that the most successful people are the best born.

Most concepts of class maintain that stratification is a social phenomenon that arises in complex societies either from certain specific cultural ensembles that require a social division of labor or from the unequal distribution of and access to resources. To explain a class system from this standpoint, one makes a historical assessment of economic, political, religious, and other variables and places them in synchronic interaction. This approach leaves unexplained, however, motivation and certain inherent aspects of stratification; here the expressive analysis of class is most useful. In the long evolution of Western stratification, from classical times to the present, every new stage in the rearrangement of estates and classes has been characterized by a fairly distinct expressive array, most notably exemplified by the super-

ordinate stratification discussed in this monograph. But the core of the
aristocratic exclusive array has remained virtually constant, and not
even the rationalistic, naturalistic worldview that fostered the transition from estate to class was able to obliterate it completely.

The expressive component of stratification has two main aspects.
On the one hand, the diachronic analysis of the expressive array reveals
the constant of stratification that structures so much of the life of
classes and estates, which in turn (as a feedback effect) influences the
economic, political, and other domains that ultimately change the
configuration of stratification. Granted the primacy of objective variables in the evolution of stratification, the expressive component occasionally acquires enough efficacy to change the general configuration of
a class or estate. Thus, the great emphasis of the Spanish aristocracy
(and the Mexican aristocracy by extension) on the entail (*mayorazgo*)
from the fifteenth to the seventeenth century significantly affected the
general organization of the noble estate; similarly, the penchant of the
British peerage in the eighteenth century for exhibition and display
forced many of its members into business activities that departed significantly from the traditional aristocratic *imago mundi*. These are clear
cases of expressive commitments influencing the structural discharge of
estates.

On the other hand, the strictly structural definition and determina-
tion of stratification are basically static and do not explain upward and
downward mobility. To explain: Western aristocracies have been declining since the French Revolution, and by the turn of the twentieth
century they had lost all political power and most of their wealth. Yet as
viable social classes they have survived until the present. This survival
is explained by the empirical claim that upwardly mobile individuals
and entire segments of society emulate the lifestyle and expressive
behavior of those in superordinate positions. Furthermore, upwardly
mobile individuals change and to some extent transform the expressive
array of the superordinate group. As long as the estate system was a
reality, changes in expressive behavior, even throughout such drastic
periods as conquests, were never major, and at least the core of the
expressive array remained constant. The aristocratic expressive array,
however, has survived for a century and a half within the context of a
class system. This survival differs qualitatively from survival within the
estate system: the upwardly mobile class (haute bourgeoisie), insofar as
it has not been aristocraticized, has caused notable changes in the

expressive array of the aristocracy by virtue of its great power and wealth. Despite their embourgeoisement, aristocracies remain viable, recognized segments of the European social system, and this staying power can only be explained by aspects of their expressive arrays that the rich and powerful have not been able to provide.

This book establishes empirically that it takes four generations for an individual and his family to be universally recognized and accepted as aristocratic. In the case of Mexico, plutocratic nouveaux riches at the turn of the century had finally been recognized as bona fide aristocracy by 1970. Baltzell (1966:271) reaches similar conclusions about upward mobility in the social establishment of the eastern seaboard. Antiquity of lineage is undoubtedly one of the important elements of aristocratic status, resulting in social exaltedness and eliciting awe in upwardly mobile individuals and groups.

Wealth and achievement in political, religious, and other endeavors are other sets of considerations in assessing aristocratic (and upper-upper class) position. Wealth, for example, is a crucial consideration that has two main components. First, more than eroded political power or the lack of excellence in any field of endeavor, poverty erodes and finally destroys individual aristocratic standing and the class as a whole. This new context of upward plutocratic mobility has characterized the decline of the aristocracy since the end of the ancien régime. The greater the loss of wealth, the more the haute bourgeoisie has contributed to the evolving expressive array of the still socially important aristocracy. Perhaps more relevant, it is in the general ambiance of aristocratic economic decline that the haute bourgeoisie asserts itself and the allure of the aristocratic expressive array as a beacon of upward aspirations diminishes and ultimately flickers out, to be replaced by a new dominant upper-upper class. The plutocracy finally creates its own expressive array independent of aristocratic constraints, no longer awed by lineage and heredity, but most certainly asserting their own: plutocrats who have been rich and powerful for two or three generations are already engaged in the time-honored subterfuge of mythologizing their descent and creating pedigrees that transform humble or modest ancestors into outstanding figures. We arrive here at the heart of the aristocratic tradition: mythologizing and glorifying of the past and justifying exalted status by the right of blood.

Second, the role of wealth has a determinant historical dimension. Though it is difficult to separate wealth from political power and control, the former is superordinately more determinant, confirmed by the fact that for several centuries after the demise of Feudalism, the European aristocracy, still firmly in control of the land, thrived with little political power. This control of the main sources of production has two subsidiary aspects. First and most important, wealth has always been the primary determinant of the aristocratic expressive array. Had the aristocracy adapted more readily to the Industrial Revolution and managed to retain much of its wealth by changing from a landed base to an industrial and manufacturing base, we could speak today of a plutocratic aristocracy. What I have termed the *haute bourgeoisie* denotes a transitory group of upwardly mobile plutocrats, of nonaristocratic extraction, on the way to acquiring aristocratic status, and not the social sector that is presently coalescing as the predominant, superordinate class. It is virtually certain that the failure of the European aristocracy to have played a leading role in the Industrial Revolution was due to a conscious or unconscious adherence to patterns of aristocratic behavior concerning work and making money in pursuits other than exploitation of the land.

The second aspect concerns the relationship between wealth and antiquity of lineage. It bears directly on the internal ranking of the aristocracy and indirectly on its relationship to the plutocracy, particularly in periods of rapid decline. Until early modern times, perhaps until the French Revolution, antiquity of lineage was the main factor in the internal ranking of the European aristocracy. Among titled nobilities, for instance, a mere baron of most ancient lineage could outrank a duke of recent creation, and many gentry of feudal origin outranked most of the recently created titles beginning at the onset of the seventeenth century. Other factors were involved, of course, but generally speaking, given a modicum of wealth, the older an individual's proven genealogy, the more aristocratic he was. This situation began to change with the rise of the bourgeoisie and wealth and achievement became increasingly important in assessing relative aristocratic rank. By itself, this fact indicates that the aristocratic ideology has changed in important ways; it acquires sociological relevance in relation to aristocratic-plutocratic interaction. Briefly, in the process of acculturation that characterizes the relationship between aristocrats and plutocrats, the most receptive interaction has occurred among entrepreneurial aristocrats, the least conservative and younger sector of the aristocracy, and those plutocrats most willing to learn and internalize the ways of aristocrats; the oldest and most distinguished families and, quixotically, the least affluent members of the aristocracy have been least receptive to plutocratic interaction. An understanding of these differences in ideology and the attendant consequences is crucial to a proper conception of upward and downward mobility in the superordinate sector of the stratification system.

In the historical and ethnographic environments of a surviving aristocracy of the Western mold, I demonstrate not only the viability but the necessity of the expressive approach to stratification studies, without which many aspects of class and mobility would remain unanswered. Without minimizing the relevance of the traditional structural approach to stratification, I show in detailed examples the benefits of the expressive approach.

The Mexican Aristocracy in Cultural and Structural Perspective

In the social sciences, "aristocracy" has no technical definition, and in common discourse it has several meanings not always consonant with each other. In Europe, the term is almost synonymous with nobility but it is also frequently used to denote, in a more encompassing fashion, the higher or titled nobility and the lower nobility or gentry. In the United States and, particularly, in many Latin American countries, the word *aristocracy* most often refers to the upper-upper sector of the class stratification system.

ARISTOCRACY IN ITS VARIOUS MEANINGS AND USAGES

Sociologically, aristocracy is an archaic term: its precise meaning and range of application in a bygone sociocultural milieu are known, but in the contemporary stratification system, it elicits mixed meanings and feelings or a sense of malapropism. Since language almost invariably outlives sociocultural contexts and milieux, it tends to perpetuate old meanings when new conditions arise, thereby paradoxically leading to misunderstanding and, often, denial of the original denotation. Thus the connotations of aristocracy, nobility, and other key terms of the European estate stratification system elicit a visceral reaction from many social scientists that clouds their objectivity. A clear definition, therefore, is in order here.

Historically and sociologically, aristocracy stood for the superordinate estate from Homeric times to the demise of the ancien régime at the end of the eighteenth century. The Greek eupatridae, the Roman patricians, the feudal nobility of Spain or France, and the titled nobility and gentry of England or Germany in early modern times are defined as aristocrats. They were members of the superordinate estate, beneficiaries of rights and privileges denied to the great majority of the population, and possessors of most of the political power, wealth, and social prestige. Aristocracy denotes and encompasses the political, ruling, and social estate that dominated all societies of Western Civilization until roughly two hundred years ago. From Homer to Napoleon all nations or polities of the West were stratified into a superordinate and a subordinate estate. Though the names changed and the interaction and configuration varied, the basic structure of the estate system remained remarkably constant. Thus, the most common and encompassing usage of aristocracy has been for the superordinate estate.

Aristocracy has played a preponderant role in Western Civilization: it has shaped society; it has been the subject of much literature; and it has always been the beacon of upward mobility and the model of expressive behavior. Its fundamental attributes have been political and economic privileges and social exaltedness, maintained by lineage and heredity. In this context, Aristotle's (1923:114–22) definition of aristocracy as "the rule of the best" may be regarded simply as the rationalization of "the rule of the best born." The rise of democracy during the past two centuries, and the concomitant development of class stratification, abolished the privileges of the aristocracy (a process that started at the beginning of modern times), and it ceased to exist as an estate, becoming a social class in the evolving system.

The baseline consideration in the analysis of Western stratification is that, as long as the estate system was in place, the aristocracy, however configured, constituted a political, economic, and social class by virtue of its privileges. Despite the French Revolution and its aftermath, the aristocracy as an estate did not die suddenly. The European aristocracy declined steadily—but slowly—until it lost the last of its privileges and became a mere social class. The aristocracy's privileges declined steadily beginning in the late Middle Ages. Likewise, its integrity as an estate faltered as the bourgeoisie emerged, prospered, and ultimately displaced the aristocracy as the undisputed or predominant holder of political power and wealth. By 1900, the change from estate to class was complete, and a diversified upper-upper class stepped forth, composed of a ruling or plutocratic sector, a political sector, and a social or aristocratic sector (Perrot 1968). By the mid-twentieth century, the aristocracy was strictly a social elite. Still, as long as the superordinate sector of the European stratification system retained some meaningful economic and political privileges, it warranted the name of aristocracy in the traditional, original sense, namely, as applied to the titled or higher nobility and the lower nobility or gentry.

Aristocracy as a form of government, defined by Aristotle, is as old as the fifth century B.C., but the term was not employed to denote the superordinate estate until well into modern times. The sociological concept of aristocracy, as configured above, did not exist until the late seventeenth century, and by the end of the eighteenth century it had become a common designation for the higher and lower nobility. The substantive referent of aristocracy, however, is as old as Western Civilization, though roughly between the French Revolution and the revolutionary upheavals of mid-nineteenth century, this referent changed, and aristocracy began to denote new circumstances. Its survival as a component of a class system was increasingly dominated by a new, politically powerful plutocracy, a haute bourgeoisie that had been forming for at least a century and a half. As its political power was lost and its wealth paled against that of the plutocracy, the aristocracy focused on its exaltedness as a social class (Powis 1984).

In this new mold, the aristocracy survives, still a significant aspect of class stratification, but embodying solely social and behavioral attributes. The survival of the aristocracy, in other words, rests almost exclusively on expressive attributes and the momentum that such a long-lived and fundamental institution of Western stratification is bound to generate. Structurally, the aristocracy is no longer a distinct unit of the stratification system, but expressively, socially, and behaviorally, its presence continues to be felt. To the average citizen, the aristocracy is an invisible entity, a phantom that elicits ambivalent feeling; to the upwardly mobile in the upper reaches of the stratification system, however, it is a reality still recognized. The European aristocracy has survived because it represents a symbol of social exaltedness; it embodies a model of expression and behavior for the rich and powerful (Moncrieffe 1970), even in the United States—until the

Second World War, at any rate, when the U.S. haute bourgeoisie began to look to Europe for manners and marriage alliances.

Until 1900 one could argue that the aristocratic model of manners and expressive behavior persisted in its pristine, traditional form as the beacon of upward mobility for the rich and powerful (haute bourgeoisie). It should be noted, however, that the loss of political power and wealth suffered by the aristocracy in the nineteenth century greatly reduced its expressive style. Unable to compete with the industrially generated wealth of the plutocracy, the aristocracy underwent a process of embourgeoisement, or acculturation to bourgeois values. Nonetheless, the aristocracy is dying hard. The higher nobility, particularly, because of the ostensible symbolism of titles, has been able to maintain a distinct social profile in the upper reaches of the stratification system. The lesser nobility has not fared as well: in fact, in the second half of the century it is no longer distinguishable from the lower-upper class and the less affluent members of the haute bourgeoisie. The aristocracy is still effective as a symbol of social exaltedness, for all the power and wealth of the haute bourgeoisie has not produced a viable alternative. Sociologically, this is a rather precarious situation. The basic conception of what constitutes proper behavior and the accompanying expressive array are still aristocratic, but they are increasingly influenced by plutocratic inputs. If we liken aristocratic-plutocratic interaction to a situation of acculturation, the balance in the overall configuration of this new upper-upper class is already leaning toward the latter (Montagu of Beaulieu 1970).

In sum, aristocracy, as a category of stratification within this study, has three main definitions: (1) Aristocracy is an estate, defined as the political, economic, and social superordinate sector of the Western stratification system. This traditional conception of aristocracy began to change in modern times, declining rapidly after the French Revolution, and disappearing de jure by the middle of the nineteenth century from the European scene with the establishment of republics and constitutional monarchies. De facto, however, it lingered in some European countries and indeed in countries around the world as an extension of Western Civilization. (2) Aristocracy is a class, defined as a social (elite) class at the top of the contemporary stratification system of many European nations. Aristocracy in this structural niche is not an independent entity but part of a haute bourgeoisie that functions both as a ruling and political class. So defined, aristocracy has been a sector of the stratification system roughly since the turn of the century, with the preceding fifty years regarded as a period of transition. (3) Aristocracy is a model, defined as the manners and expressive behavior to be emulated by the upwardly mobile at the top of the stratification system. Since the Second World War, the definition has been greatly strained by the inputs of the contemporary haute bourgeoisie.

All three definitions of aristocracy will be employed in the present study, sometimes exclusively and sometimes complementarily, depending on period and context. From the Spanish Conquest until Independence, the Mexican aristocracy was defined by (1) and (3). From Independence to the Revolution of 1910, the aristocracy was still defined by (1) and (3)—but only customarily so. From 1910, the aristocracy rapidly declined. By 1940 it had lost all residual elements of (1), and during the past decade or so it has been on the verge of losing all elements of (2) and (3). Significantly, in the case of Mexico and other Latin American countries, custom has proved as effective as law in perpetuating an aristocratic tradition despite the republican institutions that were established immediately after Independence.

THE MEXICAN ARISTOCRACY: A VARIANT OF THE SPANISH ARISTOCRACY

More than any of the European nations that have conquered and colonized so much of the world since the early age of exploration, Spain fashioned its vast possessions in its own image. By the end of the sixteenth century the various territorial subdivisions of the Spanish Colonial Empire in the New World were fairly faithful copies of Spain, modified, to be sure, by local constraints of culture, demography, and geography. Inevitably, the search for gold and silver and the subsequent exploitation of the land and its people propelled the Spanish conquistadors and configured the towns and cities they founded and permanently settled, but religion played nearly as important a role in the establishment of Hispanic society in the New World. Supported by the Crown, the Spanish church (mostly mendicant friars during the first hundred years, and secular priests from then on) engaged in a massive and thorough task of converting the Indians to Catholicism and organizing them into permanent congregations. Religion was a fundamental catalyzing and homogenizing force in Colonial society, and its effect is nowhere better exemplified than in the viceroyalty of

New Spain, that vast territory centered in Mexico and including all of Central America, the jewel of the Spanish Crown in the New World. In Mexico, under Catholicism, the institutional processes of syncretism and acculturation took place. By the end of Colonial times a nation had emerged that was basically Spanish but shot through with specific influences of pre-Hispanic, Indian origin. Thus, when Mexico became a federal republic shortly after Independence, it was firmly in the orbit of Western Civilization in government, law, politics, religion, and the general organization of society. The Indians, to be sure, constituted by far the largest segment of the population, but the formal framework of the nation and the general ambiance and configuration of the cities were basically Western and European.

Mexico was never a homogeneous society, and from its inception in the sixteenth century until well into the twentieth, the population has been stratified by ethnic divisions and classes and, during most of Colonial times, divided into estates in the traditional European pattern. The social system was essentially hierarchized along ethnic and racial lines. Changes occurred from the sixteenth to the eighteenth century, but the basic configuration remained constant: at the top ranked the Spaniards born in Spain (*peninsulares*) and those born in Mexico, called Creoles (*criollos*); in the middle were positioned the *Mestizos* (people of mixed Spanish and Indian ancestry); and at the bottom were the Indians. The situation is more complicated than it appears. First, though *peninsulares* and *criollos* constituted an undifferentiated social class, the former generally monopolized political power. Another complicating factor was that probably most *peninsulares,* who came to Mexico as Crown officials or in the military, did not return to Spain, and their children thereby became *criollos.* Second, not all full-blooded Spaniards in Mexico belonged to the superordinate group; many Spaniards engaged primarily in retail business and craft production, constituting a rather indeterminate segment of the Spanish population that shared the middle ground with Mestizos. Third, Mestizo itself is an ambiguous designation. Originally the term *Mestizo* was a strictly racial category: the issue of a Spaniard (usually a male) and an Indian (usually a female). But within three generations the term *Mestizo* had acquired cultural attributes. It was applied to an individual of mixed Spanish-Indian parentage (by now in varying proportions) who practiced the hybrid (acculturated) Spanish-Indian culture that in less than a century after the Conquest had emerged in the cities and non-Indian environments.

From then on, the definition of Mestizo, and that of Indian for that matter, became essentially cultural and only tangentially somatic. Despite attempts in the eighteenth century to categorize and regulate the interaction of the basic racial strains (Spanish, Indian, and Black) and their multiple mixtures (*castas*), the Mexican social and stratification systems in Colonial times were never rigid: there was a good deal of passing, and racial (somatic) categories often entailed cultural characteristics. One was defined as a Spaniard, Mestizo, or Indian not entirely, perhaps not even predominantly, in terms of somatic traits, but significantly in cultural terms—the way one lived and behaved. This relative fluidity has characterized the Mexican social system since the sixteenth century. Fourth, the Indian population, segregated and to some extent isolated in their communities (congregations), also developed a syncretic and acculturated culture, which was periodically reinvigorated by contact with the wider Colonial world. Mobility was also relative, but the Indians never constituted a caste: away from their communities, Indians had no difficulty in passing as Mestizos once they had learned the ways of the wider world (Nutini 1963).

To generalize, the stratification system of Colonial times follows the foregoing characterization of the overall social system but is not coterminous with it. Certain significant differences transcend the basic division of the population into three groups. Starting at the bottom, the Indians in congregations and those who temporarily chose to live in the cities (many cities had Indian wards) were undoubtedly at the bottom of the stratification system. They constituted the lower class (or estate), paying tribute to the Crown or individual Spaniards and subservient to them in a variety of ways. Although never legally slaves, the Indian population may be regarded as a villein class somewhat similar to that existing during the seigneurial period of European society. Although the entire spectrum of the Indian population has occasionally been described as a caste, the definition never applied, and at no time was there an apartheid system that thoroughly segregated the Indians from the rest of the Colonial population. Vis-à-vis the ruling class of New Spain, the Indian population may rather be conceived as an estate (Mendizábal 1972).

As in any stratification system, the middle stratum of Colonial society is the most difficult to conceptualize. Furthermore, the information on this domain is the poorest. The middle stratum of Colonial society in Mexico, and undoubtedly in other Spanish possessions in the

New World, was composed of two tiers. The lower tier contained the bulk of the Mestizo population and those Indians in the process of passing to Mestizo status, a phenomenon that persisted well after Colonial times. By the beginning of the seventeenth century a proportionally large lower-middle class of manual workers, small shopkeepers, craftsmen, and domestics had emerged. Its members inhabited the towns and cities of New Spain or found employment with the rural upper classes. The upper tier was a kind of middle class of specialized craftsmen, professionals, owners of medium-sized businesses, and lower and regional bureaucrats. With the exception of the latter, this middle class was urban and composed of both Mestizos and Creoles and perhaps a sprinkling of Spaniards born in Spain. In the sixteenth and seventeenth centuries, Mestizos undoubtedly predominated in this middle stratum, but from the early eighteenth century until Independence the Creole element tended to predominate, as most *peninsulares* stayed in New Spain and their descendants became Creoles. By the end of Colonial times, more than a million people comprised the upper tier of the middle stratum. They constituted the most visible element in the towns and cities of New Spain (Nutini 1963). Notice that in discussing the lower and middle strata of Colonial society, I did not account for the rather numerous Black slave population that was brought to New Spain beginning in the latter half of the sixteenth century. These people, numbering some three hundred thousand (brought to replace the rapidly decreasing Indian population of the colony), had until Independence the status of slaves, but by the late seventeenth century they were being absorbed into the much larger Indian and lower-Mestizo population. Also under the category of Mestizo are included the various racial mixtures or castes that never played a significant social or economic role in the life of New Spain (Aguirre Beltrán 1946:243).

The top stratum of Colonial stratification was composed of Creoles, *peninsulares*, and many somatic Mestizos who were culturally classified as Creoles. Again we observe the interplay of physical and cultural attributes that determined the social classification of individuals in Colonial New Spain. The higher one rose in the social and stratification scales (from Indian to *peninsular*), the higher the somatic attributes (vis-à-vis cultural considerations) in passing for a member of a superordinate category. Thus, at the lowest level, the general configuration of attributes of an Indian to pass and be accepted as a Mestizo was overwhelmingly cultural, whereas for a Mestizo, invariably a light-skinned one, to be categorized as a Creole entailed primarily somatic characteristics. Another complicating factor at the top of the stratification system was that a significant number of conquistadors and early Spanish settlers married noble Indian women, land being the main reason for these mixed marriages, but very few Spanish women married noble Indian men. For the most part, this intermarriage occurred within one or two generations of the Conquest. By the beginning of the seventeenth century, the Creole upper class had somatically "erased" these original Indian inputs. That there were further Indian inputs into the genetic pool of the Creole sector, particularly the aristocracy, there is no doubt, but until the present day, the top stratum of the stratification system has remained overwhelmingly Spanish.

The uppermost stratum of Colonial society in Mexico was always very small. Shortly after the Conquest it became configured as an aristocratic and a plutocratic class. By the last quarter of the sixteenth century, these two classes, though clearly distinguishable, interacted closely in the economic and social realms. Whereas class distinctions between the middle and upper strata were high, and passage from the former to the latter difficult, particularly for Mestizos, aristocrats and plutocrats constituted distinct groups in a constantly fluid relationship. Most successful plutocrats eventually became aristocrats, that is, those who sustained their wealth for two or three generations and made appropriate alliances with the aristocracy. This book examines the permanently successful and upwardly mobile elements of these changing classes, whose descendants, enriched by more successful plutocrats of nineteenth-century extraction, ruled Mexico until the Revolution of 1910 (Durand 1953).

The most important element in the formation of the Mexican aristocracy was the usufruct of original conquistadors to the conquered land. First, Cortés's host extracted gold from Moctezuma's treasury. But it quickly became clear to those who had come to stay that the real wealth of the colony lay in the land and in the Indians who could work it. Before any other Spaniards, participants in the original conquest were entitled to the vast fund of land and Indian labor that had become available. Thus the institutions of *encomienda* (original grants of Indians to an individual Spaniard) and the *repartimiento* (periodic allotment of Indians to a landholder or mine owner) came to structure the original ruling class of the colony. By the end of the sixteenth century, this class had already become an aristocracy.

Not all conquistadors were granted Indians and land. Indeed, the majority were not—but those who were granted *encomiendas* became ipso facto members of the budding aristocracy. Early settlers (*pobladores*), through Crown patronage, influence in the Council of the Indies, and membership in the entourages of the early viceroys and other high officials in the viceregal government, were also able to secure *encomiendas*. They thus became the equals of the conquistador *encomenderos*, but not without eliciting resentment. The conquistadors considered themselves alone deserving of benefices, for they had won the vast territories for the Spanish Crown. By the early seventeenth century, the *encomenderos* and early *pobladores* of Mexico were a true landowning aristocracy with various business and mining interests. A local ruling and social class was established, composed of Creoles and increasingly augmented by *peninsulares*, fashioned in the Spanish model, and retaining considerable expressive and political ties to the mother country (Nutini 1972).

The social composition of these *encomenderos* was mixed: a sprinkling of members was related to the titled nobility; perhaps as many as 30 percent were *hidalgos* (gentry, members of the lesser, nontitled nobility); but the majority were commoners (*pecheros, villanos*, members of the *estado llano*). Regardless of social extraction, the *encomenderos* considered themselves noble; they had, after all, conquered the land and founded the first cities and towns of the colony. They supported their claim with the reasons that had justified ennoblement during the Reconquest in the late Middle Ages (1200–1492): military conquest and the foundation of new Christian settlements. Having recently broken the power of the seigneurial nobility and transformed Spain into the first truly centralized monarchy in Europe, the Crown was not about to accede to the blanket ennoblement of New Spain's *encomenderos*, particularly in view of the large number of Indians that for military and political reasons it had deemed necessary to place under their control. But far away from the social and political constraints and conventions of the mother country and under the immediate control of bribable viceregal authorities, de facto if not de jure the *encomendero* class became an aristocracy fashioned in the peninsular image (Durand 1953). Parvenu as this aristocracy was, it was nonetheless variant of the European aristocracy of the time, divided, like the Spanish nobility, into an upper and lower sector. Titles were awarded to original conquistadors shortly after the Conquest. Not, however, until the first titles were awarded to Creoles at the beginning of the seventeenth century and a good number of them were granted access to the military orders did the Mexican aristocracy come to maturity: a division between a higher, titled nobility (marquises and counts) and a lower nobility or gentry (*hidalgos,* with genuine or spurious coats of arms, and many members in military orders); a social milieu and expressive life mirroring the metropolitan nobility; and a large tributary Indian population that made the local aristocracy look seigneurial.

Legally considered by the viceregal government an integral part of the Spanish nobility, the Mexican nobility was an estate enjoying the same social and economic privileges as their peninsular prototypes. Again, however, far away from the mother country, in a more fluid social and economic milieu, the Mexican aristocracy was most likely not an estate vis-à-vis the rest of the Creole and *peninsular* population in the exercise of privileges and in the exaltedness of social prestige. Nevertheless, in their vast landed domains, and with respect to the non-European population, the aristocracy of New Spain was certainly an estate in every sense of the term (Lira Montt 1976). As this uppermost stratum of Colonial society grew in the seventeenth century and many titles were awarded to upwardly mobile gentry and plutocrats in the eighteenth century, the Mexican aristocracy conformed to the classic patterns of structure and expression of the Spanish aristocracy. Thus, although the Creole aristocracy was never a political class during Colonial times, since all high positions in the viceregal government were in the hands of *peninsulares,* it undoubtedly was a ruling and social class at the very top of the stratification system.

Who were the Creoles and *peninsulares* that have been generically referred to as plutocrats, and what defines the Colonial plutocracy? Immediately after the Conquest significant but never large numbers of Spaniards settled in New Spain. Continuing the predominantly urban pattern of living that had characterized Spain during the late Middle Ages, they settled in dozens of towns and cities that had been organized for effective exploitation of the colony. By the second half of the sixteenth century, every urban settlement in Mexico contained many Spaniards who soon became Creoles. Though many cities were controlled by *encomenderos,* just as many were dominated by Spaniards who had not been granted land or Indians in the generation or so following the Conquest. Thus, in many cities, including the capital of the viceroyalty, merchants, traders, and manufacturers developed into a class that eventually coalesced into a rich plutocracy, particularly after the rich gold and silver mines of Mexico began to be systematically exploited in

the second half of the sixteenth century. As early as 1580, this new
plutocracy came into conflict with the Creole aristocracy. Creole aristocrats complained bitterly that these nouveaux riches were favored economically and in matrimonial alliances by officers of the viceregal
bureaucracy. But as the landed aristocracy engaged increasingly in
commerce, and merchants and businessmen acquired social standing
through the acquisition of wealth, the plutocracy came into its own, for
no clear socioeconomic distinction separated gentlemen from rich merchants or businessmen (Gómez de Cervantes 1944). They became interrelated by economic and social alliances, thereby establishing the basic
model of upper-class mobility that characterized the Mexican stratification system until the second half of the twentieth century.

By the end of the seventeenth century, the situation had become
relatively fluid, and considerable numbers of individuals of non-
encomenderos origin had been incorporated into the ruling aristocracy. By
the middle of the eighteenth century, the Colonial ruling class was
composed of three distinct ranks: the titled nobility, the *hacendados*
(owners of great landed estates) of original *encomendero* extraction, and
the businessmen-*hacendados* of merchant and trading extraction. *Peninsulares,* the political class, did not enter this equation, for throughout the
entire Colonial period they were directly responsible to the Crown,
which encouraged these military and administrative personnel to remain as aloof as possible from the social and economic affairs of the
colony. A few Crown officials remained in the colony after their tour of
duty, but, despite matrimonial alliances with the Creole aristocracy,
their social and economic influence was never great. Indeed, *peninsulares* who remained in New Spain were quickly assimilated into the
cultural life of the colony (Nutini, Roberts, and Cervantes 1982).

In the eighteenth century New Spain produced more millionaires
and bigger holdings than any other Spanish possessions in the New
World. The second half of the century reflected this boom particularly:
personal fortunes reached more than three million gold pesos, an astro-
nomical sum for the times. Although these fortunes included entailed
and nonentailed mining and trade, probably the bulk of the wealth
still derived from agriculture and the raising of cattle and other stock
(Ladd 1976:25). It is clear, however, that the wealth of Mexico had
been diversified to include manifold business activities under the rubrics of mining, manufacturing, trading, and banking.

The years from 1750 to 1810, when the wars of Independence

began, were a period of social and economic affluence. The powerful plutocracy that had been forming throughout the eighteenth century crystallized into an undifferentiated aristocracy, and the thirteen years of the wars of Independence changed very little the composition of the ruling aristocracy of Mexico, which by then included not only Creoles but *peninsulares,* many of whom stayed in Mexico after Independence. From the viewpoint of social class formation, the last sixty years of Colonial times represent the last period of Mexican history in which social and economic factors coalesced to structure a well-defined ruling class.

With Independence, the approximately one hundred titles of nobility that the Spanish Crown had granted to distinguished administrators and landed aristocrats from about 1600 to 1810 and to plutocrats and mine owners from about 1730 to 1810 were abolished, thus erasing the most visible symbol of aristocratic achievement. Although the ruling class had always been embodied in the aristocracy, the aristocracy had never been a political class, and the vacuum left by the Spaniards was occupied by new aspiring plutocrats and the few educated professionals, who were not about to perpetuate a system that had always limited their upwardly mobile aspirations.

The main change brought by Independence was the formation of a new political class composed primarily of aspiring plutocrats and members of a small, rising middle class. At times throughout the nineteenth century, aristocrats engaged in politics, but the political arena remained essentially a plutocratic, middle-class preserve. The power of the Mexican aristocracy, periodically reinvigorated by new plutocratic blood, was great, which explains its persistence as a ruling class while it allowed another sector of the stratification system to function as a de facto political class. Mexican *hacendados* were near-absolute powers in their domains, and the central government could do little to bring about change. Under Porfirio Díaz, the government acquired more control but never enough to permit access to significant political participation by the rising middle class. By the eve of the Mexican Revolution, the landed aristocracy and the magnate plutocratic sector constituted a socially differentiated but politically united force. It is against these rather monolithic social, economic, and political systems that, for different reasons, the middle and lower classes of Mexico took up arms.

The Mexican Revolution of 1910 brought cataclysmic changes to the aristocracy-plutocracy. Almost overnight they lost all political power as a ruling class. Although denied political participation, they did manage to retain a good deal of prestige as a social upper class until the Second World War. The traditional, behavioral, and expressive differences that had distinguished the aristocracy from the plutocracy until the end of the Porfirian era had disappeared by 1960, and the dying aristocracy was a mélange of surviving descendants of original conquistadors and *encomenderos* of the sixteenth century, *hacendados* and miners of the seventeenth and eighteenth centuries, plutocratic magnates of the nineteenth century, and more recent Porfirian plutocrats. Most catastrophic for the aristocracy-plutocracy was the loss of great wealth. By 1940, all their land had been confiscated, their businesses lay in ruins, and most of them were reduced, in American sociological parlance, to upper-middle-class economic status. In fact, the most serious consequence of the Mexican Revolution and its aftermath for the realignment of the upper sectors of the stratification system was the economic obliteration not only of the landed aristocracy but of the Porfirian plutocracy as well, which led to the formation of a totally new plutocracy (Cosío Villegas 1975).

PART I

An Outline of Western European Estate and Class Stratification from Classical Times to the Present

CHAPTER 1

The Formation of Western Stratification:
From Greco-Roman Times to the Dark Ages

In the following chapters, I analyze the evolution of Western stratification from its earliest recording to the present by focusing on the superordinate sectors. This extended discussion places the Mexican aristocracy thoroughly within the context of the European aristocracy as an extension of the Spanish aristocracy. This task is necessary in order to understand the rise, florescence, and decline of one of the last variants of this fundamental institution of the West. No other single, exclusive study traces the evolution of superordinate stratifications in Western Civilization; the present book seems an appropriate place to undertake this project, if only in outline form.

From the beginning, Western Civilization has been a conglomerate of stratified societies. As early as the Trojan War, Indo-European peoples were organized into stratified societies (Murray 1951). Indeed, the reconstruction of the Indo-European language clearly indicates that its speakers (the ethnic ancestors of most variants of Western Civilization) were organized into rather rigid class or estate systems (Terrence Kaufman, pers. comm.). As Western cultural traditions crystallized in the Greco-Roman civilization, most member societies became stratified along rigid estate lines. The stratification of these peoples developed a rich vocabulary to designate its various segments, particularly in the higher echelons of the system. The Greeks first, then the Romans, coined many terms to refer to the upper sectors of the stratification system, terms that persist as part of everyday language and as technical terms in the social sciences. The most common of these are aristocracy, nobility, oligarchy, plutocracy, patrician, knight, and *novus homus*. The first four terms are of particular relevance to the present study and they require careful definition.

Terminological Considerations and Social Perception

Classical terms such as *aristocracy* and *knight* (*eques*), which, at least in the writings of Greek and Roman scholars of antiquity, had specific meanings, are today employed mostly as reference terms to suit theoretical preferences or ideological biases. The following discussion purports not to present new definitions, but to determine how these terms reflect actual sociological situations. This study is primarily concerned with those sectors of Western stratification that have been conventionally, but not universally, denoted by the terms *aristocracy* and *plutocracy*. Directly related to them are the concepts of nobility and *novus homus* (new rich) and, indirectly, the notions of oligarchy and knight.

One may assume that when Aristotle (1923:114) defines "aristocracy" as "the rule of the best" he is not simply projecting an ideological judgment, but that the societies in the Greek and barbarian worlds that he describes as aristocracies were in fact ruled by a class of individuals consensually regarded as the best by the majority of citizens or subjects. But it is difficult, perhaps impossible, to ascertain how Greek and barbarian aristocracies conceived and rationalized their rule and how they were viewed by society at large. The same holds true to a significant extent for the other main forms of government described by Aristotle, namely, democracy, monarchy, oligarchy (plutocracy), and tyranny. Aristotle's conception of man as *homo politicus* leads him to overemphasize the political components of stratification in society, but he is well aware of the economic and social components that determine class (1923:115–21). This constant of Western culture survived the Dark and Middle Ages and is picked up in more systematic form by scholars beginning with Machiavelli.

More significant sociologically, and for our purposes here, is the conception that derives from Aristotle's projective definition of aristocracy, glimmers of which appear as early as the second century B.C. and subsequently in the writings of Roman scholars, particularly Terence, Caesar, Cicero, Seneca, and Tacitus (Laurand 1925). When Aristotle defines aristocracy as the rule of the best, he is either making a projective, ideological statement to the effect that society should be governed by a class of the most able, virtuous, and honest men, or he is expressing the fact that the aristocracies known to him regarded themselves collectively as the best and therefore deserving the right to govern.[1] Both interpretations lead to the same sociological consequence. To define aristocracy as class rule of the best is not sociologically sound, that is, it may or may not be empirically verified synchronically (at a specific cross section of time) and almost invariably is not true diachronically (say, throughout three or more generations). Rather, the definition of aristocracy as the "rule of the best born" makes eminent sense sociologically and empirically. It is empirically conceivable that a society could emerge that, in fact, was molded and coalesced as the result of a class of individuals that could be regarded as "the best." For psychological and sociological reasons, however, no society could possibly sustain the original quality of the class "as the best to rule" over more than three generations. Thus, "the rule of the best" becomes a rationalization of the "rule of the best born," as the descendants of the original ruling class become entrenched in their position and seek to buttress their exalted position with various social, economic, and even religious subterfuges. Aristotle, or for that matter any idealist social or political philosopher, could say that the rule of the best means the constant and systematic renewal of those most qualified to occupy positions in the ruling class. This stand indeed resembles Plato's notion of a monarchy of the philosopher king as the ideal form of government. But how can one ensure the right recruitment to maintain the rule of the best? How can one ensure a succession of philosopher kings? These questions have plagued scholars for more than two thousand years, and no idealist solution has ever succeeded, except for short periods of time. Inevitably, aristocracy as the rule of the best evolves into aristocracy as the rule of the best born. Thus, at least in Western culture, we may grant that aristocracy has something to do with excellence but a great deal more to do with lineage, antiquity of origin, particular kinds of behavior, and wealth, as well as ability to rule. This study defines aristocracy as the best born and explores the social, economic, and political implications of this denotation.

Modern scholars since the Enlightenment have observed that the ruling and political attributes of class are not exclusive. For more than two centuries, scholars as various as Vico, Montesquieu, Adam Smith, Miller, and Marx have emphasized the economic aspects and organization of class within the context of the global society. More recently, Marxist and social scientists have made economics almost an independent variable in the explanation of social phenomena, and within the past generation or so the social, behavioral aspects of class and kindred structures have acquired some prominence. In this last quarter of the century, then, the concept of class may be said to entail political, economic, and social components. As far as I am aware, however, no social scientist has established their correct conceptual interrelationship.

The Greek Stratification System

From the sixth century B.C. to the fall of the Roman Empire in the fifth century A.D., Western society was, strictly speaking, stratified into two estates: free-born and slave. For a thousand years, freeborn citizens and slaves composed the multitudinous polities of the Greek city-states and Republican and Imperial Rome. If we discount slavery, however, another picture emerges: polities stratified by estates, polities in transition, and polities ranged in economic "classes" (Hammond 1958:315–87). Briefly, the fundamental distinction between estate and class stratification rests on social, economic, and symbolic privileges, accrued mostly to the superordinate group; inequality before the law and political predominance of the superordinate group; and low social mobility from the subordinate to the superordinate group. There was a generally low incidence of despotism and religious strictures in the organization of classical society. The notion of the divine right of kings, for example, did not begin to assert itself until after the fall of the empire and is unquestionably the effect of the oriental elements in Christianity.

By the time the Homeric epics were codified in writing, perhaps as early as 750 B.C., kings were on the wane among Greek-speaking peoples. Kings, never absolute, divine rulers among Western Indo-European peoples, survived until the second century B.C., but until the second century B.C. most Greek city-states were organized primarily into aristocracies, oligarchies, plutocracies, "democracies," and tyrannies (Andrews 1982:360–91). The definitions of these types of government differ very precisely, but the sociological differences are nebulous, for one could regard all aristocracies and plutocracies in the Greek world as oligarchies, since the best (or best born) and the rich are always the few. Furthermore, long-standing plutocracies virtually always evolve into aristocracies. Sociologically, then, most city-states appear to have been governed by powerful, long-standing aristocracies that emphasized antiquity of lineage, controlled certain forms of social behavior, and possessed most of the wealth. What varied from city-state to city-state was whether the local polity was organized into "classes" or estates. The evidence is not conclusive, but evidently the majority of Greek polities were organized into two estates: the aristocracy (eupatridae) and the commonality (thetes) (Fustel de Coulanges 1963:224–34). Even more confusing is the composition of commoners: were they all freeborn citizens (freeholders) or was there still a separate estate of serfs? In Homeric times the serfs, as an estate, constituted the bulk of the Achaean polities, and they survived as a segment of the commonality until the fourth century B.C., but, with the rise of slavery as the bulk of the labor force, they persisted in greatly reduced numbers (Momigliano 1955:231–65). (Equivalents of Spartan helots, or similar populations, were common in the city-states of the Greek world. These were conquered peoples reduced to serfdom.) This question need not be emphasized here. The ruling aristocracies of most city-states appear to have been close-knit groups, though undoubtedly they accommodated a certain amount of mobility from the higher sectors of the commonality. How much mobility these aristocracies allowed is difficult to say; a good guess is that they were not as close-knit as early medieval aristocracies in Europe and that nobility was more easily attained.

It is interesting to note that classical aristocracies were more egalitarian than the feudal aristocracies of Europe, insofar as neither the Greeks nor the Romans developed a system of ranked titles. The eupatridae and the patricians were undifferentiated bodies of aristocrats. Rank was not fixed by honorific titles but by recognized antiquity of lineage and service to the state. It is tempting to say that titles of nobility are exclusively associated with monarchical systems or other forms of centralized power, but in fact other considerations must be taken into account. For example, before the fall of the Roman Empire and their incorporation into Western Civilization, the petty monarchies of northern and eastern Indo-European peoples did not have a titled nobility, whereas Near Eastern monarchies, notably the Achaemenid Persian Empire, did. Perhaps, then, ranked titles of nobility appear as a sufficient but not necessary aspect of monarchy. The necessary conditions appear to be a low degree of centralization, high administrative complexity, and, above all, a pervasive belief in the divine right of the king to rule. Thus, in the case of the West, ranked titles of nobility appear with Feudalism, developing as a consequence of the inheritance of administrative and territorial positions. The process experienced a long period of gestation, of course, beginning with the orientalization of the West by Alexander the Great, the development of the principate (primarily the concept of the Roman emperor as a supreme ruler), and the triumph of Christianity, which shortly after the fall of the empire undoubtedly precipitated the concept of divine right.

Evolution of the Roman Stratification System

The development of the Roman Empire is well-known, well-documented, and of great significance for the formation and development of Western stratification until modern times. Until the late sixth century B.C., the Romans and other Italic-speaking peoples of the central part of the peninsula had monarchical forms of government. The small Roman state under the kings, three of them of Etruscan origin, was tightly centralized and divided into patrician (aristocratic) and plebeian (commoner) estates (Boak 1943:39–44). Like tribal Indo-European monarchies, the ancient Roman aristocracy was an undifferentiated body with no titles of nobility. Two other factors that must be taken into consideration are the unilineal kinship organization of the people and the tribal division of the state. The evidence suggests that originally all Indo-European peoples were patrilineally organized into some form of clan or sib structure (Paul Friederich, pers. comm.). The ancient Greek deme, for example, was a nonlocalized exogamous clan, which probably by the early fifth century B.C. had evolved into a bilateral or ambilateral kinship group. The social organization of the Romans, on the other hand, remained unilineal well into the principate. The Romans were organized into patrilineal nonlocalized exogamous clans (*gentes*), subdivided into lineages (*stirpes*) and sublineages (*familiae*) (Nutini 1961:18–29). The Romans were also divided territorially and administratively into tribes. From an original three mythic tribes, the roster had grown to thirty-six by the time of Caesar. Tribes framed the political, administrative, and military organization of the Roman state: the *comitia,* the *curiae,* the *centuria,* the *comitia curiata,* the *comitia centuriata,* and other units and mechanism being its operational units (Nutini 1961:12–18). This type of organization worked well when Rome was still a small conquest state, but when the Romans became masters of Italy and began to expand into the western Mediterranean, the tribal organization and its attendant institutions became increasingly obsolete. By the end of the Republic, they had become largely symbolic (Frank 1927:369–91; Heitland 1923:43–67).

THE PATRICIAN AND PLEBEIAN ESTATES UNTIL THE END OF THE REPUBLIC

The unilineal kinship system was, however, the fundamental structure that determined the stratification of Romans into patricians (*patres, patricii*) and plebeians (*plebs, humiliores*). No scholar has ever satisfactorily explained the origin of the patrician-plebeian distinction, but two main opinions have emerged. One group posits that separate patrician and plebeian *gentes* had existed from the beginning of the Roman city-state; another group maintains that the *gentes* included both patrician and plebeian segments. There is no conclusive evidence to support either of these assertions, but the second assertion appears more logical and economical. I suggest the following possible reconstruction: The term *patrician* derives from *patres* (forefathers), meaning evidently that the Roman aristocracy regarded itself as the collective descendants of the original founders (apical ancestors) of the Roman *gentes*. In this exalted position the patricians claimed all political power and many social and economic privileges, making themselves an aristocracy as powerful as any that has ever existed. Within the *gentes* there were patrician and plebeian lineages and sublineages bound by religious and social rights and obligations but constituting separate estates. Just as patricians constituted the overwhelming superordinate estate, plebeians constituted the subordinate estate. They lacked access to political participation, they were thoroughly dominated by the patricians, and in the early absence of slavery, they performed all labor (Nutini 1961:21–24). The dynamics of patrician-plebeian interaction within the *gentes* and the details of their social covenant are unknown, but they appear to have centered in a common worship of ancestor and certain rights of clientship (cf. Last 1969:370–406; Stuart Jones 1969:436–84). In any event, this state of affairs persisted into Republican Rome, when plebeians began the long struggle for political recognition that so greatly transformed the structure of Roman society (Boak 1943:65–220; Nutini 1961:2–11).

The monarchical, early Republican patriciate was a small body, perhaps never more than 5 percent of the Roman estate. Endogenous status and rank were primarily achieved by political participation and service to the state. The Roman senate was an exclusively patrician body, and membership conferred hereditary rank. The main avenue for achieving status recognition was by election to high magisterial and religious offices, namely, those of dictator, censor, consul, praetor, quaestor, and high priest (*pontifex maximus*) (Ferrero 1958:301–36). Nevertheless, families and stirpes were greatly concerned with antiquity of lineage, above and beyond the cult of the ancestors. There are well-known examples of leading patricians claiming descent from mythological figures or relating the apical ancestors of their *gentes* to mythical or legendary events, as in the case of Julius Caesar claiming descent from Aeneas. In sum, the patriciate of Rome, from the foundation of the city until the beginning of the late fourth century B.C., was the undisputed social, ruling, and political estate of the city. Over more than three centuries, until approximately the reign of the emperor Claudius, the Roman aristocracy evolved into a new configuration of elements, having lost political power and considerable wealth, challenged on the one hand by the plebeians and on the other by a class of new rich (Greenidge 1973:265–81). Nonetheless, the Roman aristocracy remained the ideological model of upper-upper-class stratification in the West for a thousand years, until the apogee of Feudalism. Throughout the darkest, most obscurantist period of European history, the patriciate remained a model of appropriate aristocratic behavior.

How exactly did the aristocracy evolve as the result of being challenged by other segments of Roman society? Let us take the case of the plebeians first. From the foundation of Rome to the beginning of the third century B.C., the status of plebeians was low but not quite in the category of serfs, for they had certain minimal rights of representation and formed the backbone of the Roman army. Their clientship to the patricians assured them a stable if completely subordinate position. No one doubts that slavery existed in Rome from very early times, given that from the beginning the city was a conquest state. As one of the most important economic institutions of the state, however, slavery probably did not establish itself until the early third century

B.C., perhaps even later, when Rome began the expansion that ended in the domination of the entire peninsula late in that century. Unquestionably, the plebeians' success in achieving political and social recognition is intimately related to the initiation of slavery in grand scale after the conquest of Italy, the later establishment of Rome as the dominant power in the Mediterranean, and, finally, the formation of the Roman Empire (Cary and Scullard 1975:113–37). Throughout the monarchy and for the first two hundred years of the Republic, Rome was a limited conquest state, a situation that required as much defensive as offensive warfare and offered little opportunity for plundering and taking slaves. Under these conditions, the plebeian citizen-soldiers were easily dominated by the patricians, since there was not that much wealth to be disputed by the dominant and subordinate estates. Fortified by the symbolic right to vote in the *comitia* (always subject to the senate's veto) and certain magisterial obligations, the plebeians, without undue protest, did most of the work and fought courageously for the city. The social ambiance fostered the fundamental belief that, just as the *pater familias* had undisputed authority and power of life and death over the household, so did the patriciate over the entire Roman state (Stuart Jones 1916:187–211).

By the end of the fourth century B.C., the plebeians were no longer docile. The main factor that triggered collective action was the accumulation of wealth, mostly in land and slaves, generated by the conquest of central Italy and subsequent expansion toward the northern and southern parts of the peninsula. By the time of the second Punic War Rome was a powerful and wealthy state, and slavery was an important factor in manufacturing and agriculture. As slavery replaced plebeian labor in the country and the cities and citizen-soldiers became increasingly aware of their crucial role in the conquest of so many lands and peoples, the plebeians steadily acquired a collective consciousness of their wealth and demanded more and more political recognition and a bigger share of the spoils (Greenidge 1960:176–284). By the time of the third Punic War, the plebeians had most likely coalesced into a political class (estate) with a fairly high degree of class (estate) consciousness. Even before this period, the patricians and plebeians had engaged in political contention and had organized the first political parties, in the modern sense of the term: the patricians' *optimates* and the plebeians' *populares* (Cary and Scullard 1975:560–64). By the end of the Republic, the plebeians had nearly attained political equality with the patricians, but by that time the Roman political system had been faltering for more than two generations, and further developments were cut short by the establishment of the principate and the organization of the empire under Augustus. However, in that crucial period of Roman history from the early first century B.C. to the battle of Actium, the fluidity of the Roman political system attests to the great gains of the plebeians. It was a time when a patrician such as Julius Caesar could become the leader of the *populares* and a plebeian such as Cicero could become a prominent member of the *optimates* (Cary and Scullard 1975:222–330).[2]

THE RISE OF THE KNIGHTLY CLASS AND THE MEDITERRANEAN CONQUEST

Perhaps as early as the second Punic War a new estate appeared in Roman society, namely, the *equites* or equestrian order. This knightly order had strictly military significance, and its origins went back to monarchical times. The infantry had always predominated in the Roman army, but the earliest centuries and, later, the classical legions invariably had a cavalry detachment. These mounted legionnaires never amounted to more than 10 percent of the legion's strength and were organized into small squadrons (*alae*) designed to protect the wings of the legion in combat. The equipment of the knights, including the horse, was more expensive than that of the infantry legionnaires (*pedites*). Though there were undoubtedly many patricians who fought on horseback, the main contingent of knights was actually plebeian (Boak 1943:85–88), drawn from the most affluent sector of that estate. In time the *equites* came to be known collectively as the equestrian order. From the time of the monarchy, the *equites* enjoyed certain privileges and emoluments, thus reflecting whatever upward mobility existed until the first century B.C. Probably by the middle of the third century B.C., the equestrian order had ceased to be exclusively military, acquiring increasingly the configuration of a class within the plebeian estate. The equestrian order played a prominent role in the plebeians' struggle for political and social recognition, and by the middle of the second century B.C., they had already spawned distinguished lineages of politicians and leaders of the *populares* (Ihne 1937:167–93).

The equestrian order, however, really came into its own after the conquest of Greece and other lands inhabited by Greek-speaking peoples in the middle of the second century B.C. This period, lasting until the reign of Augustus, witnessed the unprecedented growth of Roman wealth and power, and the equestrian order played an important role in the economic development that took place. Unconstrained by the beliefs and practices of patricians, whose wealth had been mostly in land, the equestrian order became a class of great plutocratic magnates that followed the path of conquest and empire. The fortunes of *equites* counted among the greatest fortunes in Rome. They appear to have excelled in every avenue of economic activity as Rome expanded throughout the Mediterranean world: urban speculation, land, manufacturing, commerce, and trading (Rostovtsev 1926:210–301). Cicero (1928:126–32) describes this class of *novi homines* at some length, as a class of very rich men who are politically powerful as well.

From the turn of the first century B.C. until the reign of Augustus, the equestrian order had an uneasy relationship with the patriciate. Patricians regarded *equites* as dangerous to their political and economic interests. At the same time, however, during the difficult period of the civil wars and the early principate, the patricians regarded the *equites* as allies in their attempt to arrest further deterioration of Republican institutions, by now in great disarray. Throughout the civil wars, encompassing the first and second triumvirates, patricians and knights almost invariably made a common cause in defense of Republican institutions against the forces of change (epitomized first by Caesar and then Augustus), whose proponents claimed the dying Republic was unable to cope with the problems and administration of the Mediterranean world (Ferrero 1958:167–72).

We do not know the size of the equestrian order, but, like all elites, it was probably small, certainly not much bigger than the patriciate. More significant are the equestrian order's configuration and its relationship to the patriciate. Was it a class or was it an estate? Strictly defined, throughout most of its existence the equestrian order was an estate, for most *equites* were recruited among the plebeians. More loosely, it may be considered a class within the plebeian estate, even though they appear to have had some privileges that the plebeians as a whole did not enjoy. By the reign of Augustus, at any rate, the equestrian order was clearly a separate estate, distinct from the plebeians and patricians. The wealth they had accumulated allowed them to

vie successfully for the social and economic privileges that separated
them from the plebeians, but it did not make them part of the patriciate (Rostovtsev 1926:287–91). Structurally, the patriciate, in terms
of privileges and social status, occupied the same position as the English peerage in modern times, whereas the equestrian order is roughly
equivalent to the Spanish *hidalguía* (gentry). Moreover, the equestrian
order is unquestionably the prototype of the lesser nobilities that
evolved in most European countries in medieval and modern times. As
a military order, the *equites* are the symbolic model of the infatuation
with and mythologizing of the horse that characterizes all Western
aristocracies, in literature and in actual social affairs, from the knight
errant to the Knight of the Garter.

The situation changed rapidly under the Julio-Claudian emperors,
and by the late first century A.D., the equestrian order had stabilized as
a distinct unit of social stratification. Perhaps from the earlier part of
Augustus's reign, the equestrian order can no longer be regarded as a
separate estate. It had entered a significant state of flux that within two
generations would transform it into a class. The patriciate had been
undergoing significant changes more or less coterminously, but they
were not quite drastic enough to transform this ancient social unit from
an estate to a class (Ihne 1937:216–31).

To a large extent, the relationship between the patriciate (essentially the senatorial order) and the equestrian order must be regarded as
one of the first well-documented situations in which a traditional
aristocracy came into intimate social, economic, and political interaction with a new plutocracy. In traditional Republican times, the equestrian order offered hope for elevation to the patriciate, a jealously
guarded privilege of potential mobility. The patricians monopolized
the great fortunes, at most regarding the *equites* as possible political
allies and occasional social partners. This relationship of unquestion-
able subordination changed when the equestrian order came into its
own, and its fortunes began to rival and even surpass those of the
patricians. What really brought patricians and *equites* together, however, were political conservatism and the desire to preserve Republican
institutions, particularly throughout the protracted period of the civil
wars. At this time, social interaction between these two orders became
basically egalitarian, as the patricians relaxed their exclusivity and
allowed more *novi homines* to join the patriciate and the senate through
adoption and intermarriage (Cicero 1928).

FLUIDITY AND MOBILITY DURING THE PRINCIPATE

From Augustus onward, the fates of the patriciate and equestrian order are further intertwined as the result of the demise of Republican institutions and the absolutism of the principate. Although Augustus scrupulously kept the form of most Republican offices and institutions, their value became largely symbolic, and with subsequent rulers, the rock-bottom principle of Roman authority and legislative power (SPQR, *Senatus Populusque Romanus*) became ever less subject to the will of the senate and the Roman people, ever more reflective of the will of the *princeps* (*Imperator,* the emperor). Thus the patriciate, through the senate, lost virtually all political power. As the principate became somewhat orientalized, the senate became little more than an ornamental court. The same fate, of course, befell plebeian institutions, and the tribunate was retained in name only (Boak 1943:288–458; Cary and Scullard 1975:507–58). It is difficult to generalize about four hundred years of Roman history, but the basic social stratification that characterized the political system was remarkably stable and may be outlined as follows. All Republican estates effectively ceased to function, and none of them survived as a political or ruling class. The patriciate-equestrian order persisted as an aristocracy-plutocracy, a kind of Roman social upper class with estate overtones. In any event, the patriciate was no longer an independent class but a social entity. Elevation to the patriciate depended primarily on the will of the emperor, who usually used his power to reward sycophantic friends or to pursue political ends. During the last decades of the Republic and the early principate, plutocratic magnates and prominent political figures of the equestrian order eagerly vied for positions in the patriciate and the senate. By the end of the early second century A.D., however, the patriciate was a rather motley conglomerate of people of mixed extraction and had de facto ceased to be an exalted body (Ihne 1937:246–59).

From the second century A.D. onward, the descendants of the old patriciate and the remnants of the traditional equestrian order, no doubt invigorated by many *novi homines* of imperial extraction and including ennobled provincials and foreign personages who had been made members of the senate, constituted the upper-upper stratum of Roman society (Rostovtsev 1926:295–321). Whether this new imperial aristocracy was an estate or a class is open to question. Strictly speaking, it was a social estate. It was, to be sure, the arbiter of appropriate behavior, but remained nonetheless an extension of the imperial establishment. It also acted as a ceremonial body to buttress the pomp of the imperial court. In provincial cities and regional metropolises, however, it is quite likely that local patriciates did function as true estates, that is, wielding significant political and ruling clout (Greenidge 1960:368–87).

The absolutism of the principate and the orientalization of the imperial court go hand in hand, making their appearance under the Julio-Claudian emperors. The fluid stratification that characterized more than three centuries of imperial society owes to the absolutism of the emperor, the role of the army in confirming the sovereigns, and the ethnic diversity that characterized the empire. The fluidity described above, whose main characteristic was a stratification that fit somewhere between an estate and a class system, was probably in place until the division of the empire by Constantine into east and west. At this point, that is, in the first half of the fourth century, a momentous change, namely, the designation of Christianity as the official religion of the Roman Empire, began to transform society (Boak 1943:438–73). Christianity in its fundamental tenets was an oriental religion, and it fostered the oriental elements that had been present in the principate almost from the beginning.[3]

Transition to the Dark Ages

By the middle of the third century the imperial system was in disarray and stagnation had set in. The empire, however, was reinvigorated during the reigns of Diocletian and Constantine, roughly two generations (285–337) of administrative, economic, political, and territorial reforms and improvements, without which Rome would not have withstood internal and external pressures for nearly another century and a half of continuous decline. When the Roman Empire ceased to exist, that is, when the last territory it controlled in Italy was overrun by Germanic invaders, most of the western provinces (Gaul, Spain, Britain, and Africa) had been conquered by various Germanic peoples (Visigoths, Ostrogoths, Franks, Suevi, Alans, Vandals, Saxons, and Angles), leading to the establishment of variously Romanized monarchies.[4] The stratification system of the principate did not change much throughout the empire's century and a half of decline (Ferrero 1958:301–19). But a number of developments did take place essential to understanding the organization of the Western monarchies and the feudal system.

PROLIFERATION OF DIGNITIES DURING THE AUTOCRATIC EMPIRE

With the abolition of Republican institutions, most of the old magistracies and administrative offices ceased to exist. From Diocletian on, the autocracy of the emperors and the imperial court demanded a new organization of the administration, and a variety of new offices sought to accommodate the increasing orientalization of the palace and the growing bureaucracy. Perhaps the most important factors contributing to the transformation of the imperial government and the creation of new offices were the loss of provincial control, the inefficiency of administrative management, and the increasing regional isolation (cf. Ferrero 1958; Gibbon 1913; Ihne 1937; Mommsen 1898; Rostovtsev 1926). These changes in the administrative and political organization of the empire contained the seeds that, fertilized by the Germanic invasion of the West, bore massive fruit in the reorganization of Christian culture.

Until the middle of the third century, the magisterial and administrative positions that, based on Republican models, had been developed during the early principate worked reasonably well in governing the empire, with occasional modifications to fit changing conditions. By the end of the century, the system was seriously faltering, however, and the empire seemed ungovernable. The political vision of Diocletian and Constantine led to radical changes that may be viewed both as effects and causes of decline and disintegration. Diocletian's tetrarchy (two co-emperors, the Agustii, and two lieutenancy emperors, the Caesarii) sharing the imperial power and Constantine's division of the empire into east and west temporarily strengthened the political and administrative system but ultimately fostered regionalism, divisiveness, and lack of control. Compounded by the breakdown in communication, the new system was directly instrumental in creating provincial autonomy, local bureaucracies, and a breed of local proconsuls with a significant degree of independent power. Gone was the centralized network of governors of the principate (Momigliano 1955:201–7).

Decentralization characterizes the administration and organization of the last 150 years of the Western empire. Regions and provinces became increasingly more autonomous from the central government, and local elites acquired unprecedented social, political, and economic power. By the time of the massive Germanic invasions, beginning in the first decade of the fifth century, such regions and provinces as Gaul and Spain had become largely independent of the central government. Imperial authority was nominal, and the empire was tenuously held together by occasional shows of force and the military ability of exceptional commanders to keep the frontiers in check. The idea of the emperor as the symbol of centralized power remained, but it was locally discharged by imperial officers who had grown aware of their independent power in a precarious balancing act of concessions, appeasement, and military action.

To approach the new stratification system of the Dark and Middle Ages we do best to focus on the development of dignities and honorific titles during the principate and the division of social classes during the Autocratic Empire. Let us take the latter first. Throughout most of the principate, perhaps until the middle of the second century, the people had been divided into the estate-classes of the senatorial order, the equestrian order, and the plebs or commonality. The orders in this classification were probably closer to estates than to classes, but, paradoxically, as the empire became more autocratic, the stratification system developed greater mobility and fluidity. By the time of Constantine or a generation later, the stratification of the empire may be characterized as a two-class system: the *honestiores* (the more important, honorable people) and the *humiliores* (the more humble, plebeian people). The *honestiores*, however, may be classified into several ranks, including the social aristocracy of the old senatorial order, imperial senators, various segments of the old equestrian order, and manifold plutocracies throughout the empire (Boak 1943:438–57). The upper ranks of the *honestiores*, primarily the senatorial and equestrian orders, must actually be regarded as estates because of entailed privileges and emoluments. Moreover, the *patricii* and the *equites* of ancient, proven lineage extending to the early Republic had survived the upheavals of the principate and constituted a social aristocracy of two ranks independent of the senatorial order periodically created by the emperors beginning with Trajan (Greenidge 1960:241–67).

Honors, dignities, and rank in the traditional patrician-equestrian system were assigned by antiquity of lineage and achieved by the discharge of military and administrative office. This long-standing tradition altered little until the reign of Hadrian, when the untitled Roman aristocracy began to evolve into a titled one in which honors and dignities were conferred by the will of the emperor. The oldest dignity can be traced to Hadrian: the title of *comes* (count, *comites* in the plural), meaning companion or follower. From this time onward the emperors would choose distinguished individuals as attendants and advisors who in time became a kind of permanent council of state (*comites principis*) known also as the *comitiva*. By the beginning of the third century *comites* had acquired a number of administrative and military functions, and by the time of Constantine they had become a permanent and important feature in the organization of the empire. There were several kinds of *comites,* but their most significant functions were to carry out military commands and to govern the most critical provinces of the empire, particularly along the northern frontier. The title *comes,* though definitely an honor and a dignity and implying a personal, intimate relationship to the emperor, was not hereditary, and several centuries passed before it became so (Luchaire 1938:163–87).

The institutional framework of the early principate had evolved periodically. In addition to strengthening the *comitiva,* the emperor Constantine created the title of patrician as the highest dignity of state. But the dignity of patrician did not survive long, apparently replaced by various ranks of *comites.* By the fall of the empire *comites* had spread across the entire military, administrative, and judicial branches of government. During the latter part of the fourth century another honorific title appeared: *dux* (duke, *duces* in the plural). This title, which can also be traced to the first half of the second century, originally meant leader, particularly military chief or commander, and it retained this connotation until well after the organization of the Germanic monarchies. The Roman title of *dux* was not as important or honorific as that of *comes,* and by the end of the empire some *comites* were also *duces,* but most *duces,* or military commanders, were not *comites.* With the establishment of the Germanic monarchies, however, particularly among the Franks, *dux* surpassed *comes* in dignity and honorific importance, and the title acquired great administrative and territorial importance. The *duces* became civil and military magnates, often controlling large territorial divisions and heading several *comitatus* (countships), particularly in border regions. Like *comes,* the title of *dux* did not become hereditary until much later, but with the decline in royal authority, the importance of dukes increased significantly and they may be regarded as petty kings in their own right (Stuart Jones 1916:387–403).

ORIENTALIZATION OF SOCIETY AND HARDENING OF THE ESTATE SYSTEM

The classical simplicity of the Roman stratification system during the early principate (the unranked division of the three Republican orders) evolved by the end of the empire into a complicated system of ranked positions buttressed by a proliferation of dignities and honors. The imperial court, and by extension all of society, had become orientalized, as evidenced by nonclassical ritualism and an elaborate ceremonialism foreign to the more egalitarian spirit of classical Greece and Rome. The Christian concept of the divine right of the king to rule merely elaborated a notion already present in the last years of the principate. The new religion fostered a society in which nothing was conceived outside the kingdom of God, and the state was subordinated to the church in theory if not always in practice.

The orientalization of society, perpetuated in the Dark and Middle Ages, had a strong foundation in the stratification and ranking of the last decades of the empire. Particularly in the upper sectors of society, an outlandish proliferation of ranked dignities demanded a fixed order of precedence: *spectabilis* (respectables), *illustres* (illustrious), *illustrissimi* (most illustrious), and *gloriosi* (glorious) (Boak 1943:444–49). This classification is significant not so much for its artificiality, but for the fact that from the beginning the ranks were called *dignitates* (dignities) and entailed a ranked order of privileges and emoluments later embodied in territorial, political, and administrative officials and ultimately in the system of titles of nobility that emerged in the twelfth and thirteenth centuries. A direct line of development thus leads from Republican Rome, to the principate, to the Autocratic Empire, to the establishment of Germanic monarchies, to the development of Feudalism, and finally to the rise of modern absolutism.

The final contribution of the Roman Empire to Western stratification was the transformation of the original equestrian order into the model for the lower ranks of the nobility. It represented a kind of middle ground between the nobility and the commonality in the later

Middle Ages and the rise of the bourgeoisie. From monarchical times, the Roman army had been an infantry force (*pedites*) barely complemented by a small cavalry force (*equites*). The strength of the legion lay in heavily armed infantrymen supported by skirmishers (*velites*) and complemented by a small body of cavalry, mostly for wing protection and communication. As we have seen, this superb military organization also provided the criteria for discriminating an elite class among the plebeians, the *equites*. By the middle of the third century, however, the Roman army was faltering, and farsighted commanders recognized the need to improve the quantity and quality of cavalry in order to counteract barbarian encroachment. But more than a century passed before the conservative Romans reorganized the army into a basically cavalry force. This change finally came with the battle of Adrianople in 378 in which the emperor Valens lost his life and his legions were totally destroyed by the cavalry force of the Goths. This defeat shocked the empire and led to radical changes in the composition of the Roman army in the east, but not such radical changes in the west (Boak 1943:435–37). In the Eastern empire, the legion quickly ceased to exist, to be replaced by cohorts (regiments) of mailed archers-lancers (*cataphractarii*), and a new military organization came into being. In the Western empire, however, the military reorganization of the army was not nearly as successful; though the army became a more balanced force of infantry and cavalry, the legion never disappeared completely. But under the leadership of such able generals as Stilicho and Aetius, the much more mobile cavalry contingents supported by the legions were able to keep the massive penetration of barbarians at bay for another two generations. These historical facts are not in themselves especially important, but within the larger context of Western Civilization they signal a momentous transformation: for a thousand years infantry cedes primacy in battle to cavalry. Sociologically, the ascendancy of cavalry revitalizes the equestrian order, as conceived militarily under the Republic, as an important segment of society under the Germanic monarchies, permanently marking the development of Feudalism in structuring the lower ranks of the nobility. The mythologization of the horse, as the main instrument of battle, has important consequences for restructuring the stratification system in feudal times, a system that may be regarded as a syncretic result in which Roman elements of law and interpersonal relationships blended with Germanic notions of kinship and a more decentralized worldview.

In the millennium that elapsed between the fall of the Roman Empire of the west and the rise of modern absolutism, new institutions emerged, including a new system of social stratification. Most new institutions, however, had classic, particularly Roman, antecedents; indeed not a few of the most characteristic elements of Feudalism can be traced to the Republican period. Classical roots are particularly apparent in the threefold division of society into nobles, knights, and commoners, in which knights as a class or estate occupied a rather ambivalent, indeterminate position. Though the stratification system of Western Civilization changed and developed occasionally intricate elaborations, it basically preserved this three-tiered composition in which the intermediate order functioned as a bridge. Throughout the Roman phase of Western Civilization, roughly from 250 B.C. to A.D. 450, there was a tendency toward blurring the basic estates of the system. Under this condition the equestrian order emerged as a distinct class. By the end of the fifth century, Western society was no longer fluid, whatever class stratification had developed in the previous four centuries was vanishing, and a rather rigid system of estates was moving into place. The more mobile class systems that had developed during the principate survived only rarely in urban environments; the West as a whole adopted an unwieldy estate system that lasted for a millennium.

The Germanic Monarchies in the Western Roman Empire

BARBARIAN SOCIETY AND STRATIFICATION IN THE FIFTH CENTURY

Whatever the initial causes of the fall of the Roman Empire in the West, it was effectively destroyed by Germanic peoples in the fifth century. Although the empire had encompassed some Indo-European peoples in its northern frontier along the Rhine and Danube, the Germanic tribes existed independently of the empire for many centuries and remained peripheral until the empire fell. Nevertheless, to different degrees, between the first and fifth centuries A.D. the various Germanic nations had been influenced by Roman civilization and by the end of the empire had achieved a significant degree of acculturation. It is difficult to pinpoint the stage of acculturative development the Germanic nations had achieved by the fall of the empire, but judging by the speed with which they acquired and internalized Roman institutions, they had arrived at the threshold of civilization. By the end of the fourth century there were probably more barbarians than citizens of the empire serving in the forty-odd legions guarding the various frontiers, including the *foederati* (entire allied legions under barbarian commanders) as auxiliary forces. In addition, the Germanic people had for centuries maintained close commercial and trade relations with the empire. Subjected to Christian missionization from the east during the last century of the empire, a good many tribes, including their kings, had already been converted to Arianism by the time they began their massive migration in the early fifth century. By the middle of the fifth century, having established kingdoms on the rubble of the empire of the west, the Germanic peoples were sufficiently civilized to blend their own institutions with those of the Romans as they settled in most of Western Europe. This momentous transformation is particularly significant for understanding the new stratification system it triggered.

In the nine centuries during which the Germanic peoples had been known to the Greeks and Romans, they never constituted a united nation but a conglomerate of many tribes. These groups were occasionally denoted by higher tribal denominations such as the Alamanni, Cimbri, Teutons, Helvetii, and Marcomani, all well-known during the principate, and, in the last days of the empire, by the larger tribal confederations of the Franks, Goths, Suevi, Burgundians, and Lombards. These and other mixed tribal groups such as the Alans and Vandals were ruled by kings whose characteristics appear to have varied. Though some of the tribes had hereditary kings, most Germanic monarchies were elective, the king chosen from among the members of a "royal family," as Tacitus (1961:107) puts it. Tacitus adds that these royal families were of divine descent, meaning perhaps that ancestors included mythological or godlike personages, thereby investing members of these kinship groups with the right to rule over the tribe. This crucial contribution of Germanic monarchies came to reinforce the divine principle of the king to rule already implicit in the concept of the Roman emperor and further consolidated by Christianity.

With a certain degree of variation, Germanic society was stratified into two estates, nobles and commoners, the former divided into classes of royal lineages and warriors, the latter constituting a freeman-freedman order. The Germanic tribes had slaves, but their status was apparently better than in most of the empire. The cleavage between nobles and commoners was less pronounced than among the Greeks and Romans, mobility higher, and on the whole the entire stratification system was more fluid, as befitted a society in the last stage of tribalism. The Germanic peoples were polytheists, and their religion was essentially the same as that of the Greeks and Romans. The Germanic peoples had, however, been influenced by Christianity for at least a century before they overran the empire. Thus some tribes were still pagan, some were partly pagan and partly Christian, and some had been converted to Christianity by the time they established monarchies in imperial territory. By the end of the seventh century only what are now the Scandinavian countries had not been converted to or missionized for Christianity. The rest of western Europe had become Catholic monarchies with increasingly close ties to the bishop of Rome. In sum, a somewhat Romanized Germanic nation became the ruling race of the empire's heartland. The several monarchies did not destroy the existing Roman institutional framework of the provinces, instead blending many disparate elements into the foundations of the modern nations of Western Europe.

Three examples will give the reader a proper perspective on the variation and extension of the Germanic conquest. From the first decade of the fifth century, Gaul was in turmoil. The Roman legions withdrew from the banks of the Rhine, and several Germanic tribes began to settle in the province. The Franks occupied the north, including the areas of Cambrai and the Somme; the Burgundians inhabited the basins of the Rhône and Saône rivers; and the Visigoths, whose powerful dominion extended from the Loire river to Andalusia in Spain, spread throughout most of Gaul. The barbarians established independent kingdoms, but occasionally the tribes were regarded by the Romans as *foederati*. They fought for a last time as auxiliaries under Aetius in 451 at the battle of Châlons against the hordes of Attila. So great was the reverence of the barbarians for the empire's aura of civilized living and its principles of political authority that even after they had established sovereign states in most of France and Spain they sought to legitimize their conquests with ratification from Rome. Thus they set a precedent for the millennium to come, when imperial Rome was replaced by the papacy, and the German emperor and the pope became the central political equation throughout the Middle Ages (Pfister 1967:148–51).

THE FRANKS AND VISIGOTHS IN WESTERN EUROPE

Under King Clovis (with whom the Merovingian dynasty begins), the Franks conquered most of Gaul and set up the most powerful kingdom in western Europe. The conversion of this king and the entire Frankish nation to Christianity ensured the monarchy's close ties to Rome. For three generations or so before their conversion, the Frankish nation destroyed Roman Civilization and imposed its own language on the territories they controlled (Fustel de Coulanges 1899:235–301). But after conversion and the unification of Gaul by the conquest of Burgundy and Provence, Roman institutions re-emerged, Mediterranean civilization revived, and Latin and Germanic languages and cultures blended successfully into a distinct entity. For nearly two centuries, the Merovingian kingdom experienced maladministration, division, and chaos under weak monarchs and suffered the virtual control of the court and the nation by ambitious officials (mayors of the palace) who became de facto rulers.

The Franks under Charles Martel rendered a great service to Western Civilization by repelling the Moslem invasion at the battle of Poitiers (732). His son Pippin the Short further strengthened the ties of the kingdom to the papacy, resulting ultimately in the temporal power of the latter that persisted until the nineteenth century. But it was Charlemagne, Pippin's son, who brought the power of the Franks to a zenith by reconstituting the almost legendary Roman Empire of the west, providing thereby the immediate model of the Western monarchy for many centuries to come. His work died with him. When he was buried at Aix-la-Chapelle, the edifice of the centralized monarchy that he had worked so hard to erect was tragically undermined by the legislative and administrative means he had devised to accomplish his ends (Lot 1948:276–312).

It appears that, unlike most Germanic tribes, the Franks had a hereditary monarchy. Shortly after Chlodio, Meroveus became king, and from then on throughout the Merovingian and Carolingian dynasties, the office passed from fathers to sons. The stratification system of the Franks at the time they established monarchies in Roman territories is not well known. There are indications, however, that they conformed to the typical model of Germanic stratification in which the royal lineages and a class of warriors and court officials composed an aristocracy that dominated an undifferentiated commoner estate. By the middle of the seventh century, the Franks had undergone several generations of acculturation with the conquered Gallo-Roman populations and had developed a modified stratification system (Luchaire 1938:176–231).

The most important aspect of this development was the relationship between the conquering Franks and the conquered Gallo-Romans. By right of conquest, the Franks constituted themselves as a ruling aristocracy, but the ensuing stratification system reflected a blending of classes and estates in the interacting societies. The stratification system of the Franks until the Carolingian period may be reconstructed as follows: The royal families or lineages preserved their Germanic integrity, while the noble estate incorporated most of the Gallo-Roman *honestiores,* particularly the families and descendants of *comites* and *duces* and other territorial and administrative magnates. The commoner estate, on the other hand, experienced no such blending, and the Franks ranked higher than Gallo-Romans in the class system that ensued. Thus, below the royal lineages, the superordinate estate was composed of a two-rank Frankish–Gallo-Roman nobility, whereas the commoner estate was composed of the Frankish freedmen, Gallo-Roman freedmen, and slaves (Viollet 1948:218–37). This classification is based on the wergeld (the monetary payment, or its equivalent in kind, to which individuals belonging to different classes and estates were entitled as compensation for murder and various injuries). In the case of early Frankish law, for example, the wergeld for officials in the king's service was 600 solidi (the solidus was a Roman gold coin the value of which at the time equaled two oxen) for a Frank and 300 solidi for a Gallo-Roman; while the wergelds for a Frankish freeman, a Gallo-Roman freeman, and a freedman were respectively, 200, 100, and 50 solidi. Individuals with wergelds of 600 and 300 solidi most likely held the rank of *comites* or *duces* (mostly Frankish, as these Roman titles were quickly incorporated into the military-administrative system of the conquerors) and lower-ranking posts (mostly Gallo-Romans), respectively.

Frankish laws provide good evidence for the stratification system, which is incomplete only in not discriminating between Frankish and Gallo-Roman freedmen. Below the level of *comes* and *dux* (the magnates or peers of the realm), there were clearly two ranks of nobles, the lower of which might have been the equivalent of the Roman *equites* and the progenitors of the medieval knights (Chadwick 1963:378–411). Of all Germanic conquerors of the Roman Empire, the Franks in Gaul most successfully combined their own institutions with those of the Romans. This achievement, together with their occupation of the most fertile agricultural area in western Europe, made Franks central to the rise of Feudalism and subsequent political developments.

The earliest Germanic tribes to disturb Hispania were the Suevi and the Vandals. The Suevi entered Spain as early as 409, settled in Galicia, and then spread to Lusitania and Boetica. They were ultimately absorbed by the Visigoths before the turn of the century. The Vandals, on the other hand, after a number of engagements with the Romans, Suevi, and Goths, moved on to Africa in 428 to found a kingdom in Carthage, now Tunisia. The Visigoth presence in Spain went back to the first two decades of the fifth century, when as Roman *foederati* they fought against the Suevi and Vandals. But large-scale migration of Visigoths into Spain did not occur until the last decade of the century, during the reign of Alaric II, when perhaps as many as two hundred thousand Visigoths settled in the peninsula. This host, which included warriors, priests, and commoners, settled in several areas of Spain, though concentrating mostly in what is today Old Castille. According to Saint Isidore of Seville (1954:98–109), writing before the middle of the seventh century, the Visigothic conquest of Spain was relatively benign and did not unduly disturb the Hispano-Roman population and its institutional configuration. The Visigoths were Arians, and the Hispano-Romans were Catholics, which prevented intermarriage between the two races and perpetuated their respective law codes. Not until the conversion of King Reccared to Catholicism (595) did the entire kingdom become Catholic and assimilation proceed rapidly (Pérez Pujol 1947, 1:176–215).

From the first, the Visigoths in Spain were not only politically weak but seriously hampered by the Visigothic nobility, bent on maintaining at all costs the custom of the elective monarchy that they had brought from their ancestral homeland. As a consequence, for the nearly two and a half centuries of Visigothic domination, Spain was plagued by instability, frequent rebellions, and political upheavals invariably generated by powerful and ambitious nobles intriguing for primacy. Nonetheless, by the middle of the seventh century, Visigoths controlled the whole of Spain, but the state, politically decadent and militarily weak, finally disintegrated even before the Arab invasion from Africa in 711. By 725, almost all of Spain fell into the hands of the Arab invaders, and many powerful nobles accepted the suzerainty of the conquerors. Most regions of Spain had no choice but to accept the benevolent overlordship of the invaders, although by the middle of the century a few small states were established in the mountains of Asturias, initiating what is known as the Reconquest, the long struggle to expel the Arabs from the peninsula that lasted until the second half of the fifteenth century (Castro 1948:28–96).

The stratification system of the Visigoths was perhaps the most rigid of all Germanic tribes that invaded the Roman Empire in the fifth century. It consisted of an aristocracy composed of two ranks, the nobles (*primates,* as they are called in the Latin sources) and the clergy, and a commoner order (*ingenui*) of freemen, both estates supported by a large slave population (*servi*). Though the terms are clear, the actual organization of the estates is not. The aristocratic estate offered no clearly distinct royal families or lineages; many ranked equally, and the clergy appears to have ranked lower. This horizontal structure explains the jealous contention among nobles and the survival of the elective monarchy until the Arab conquest. Moreover, the nobility as a whole did not mix with its Hispano-Roman equivalent, and the tradition persisted that only nobles of pure Visigothic origin could be elected to the throne. Commoners, by contrast, mixed quickly and well with the native population, though they retained a very large number of *servi,* few of whom were allowed to become freedmen. By the early eighth century the Visigothic kingdom in Spain probably had more *servi* than any other Germanic kingdom in western Europe (Altamira 1967:158–93). A caveat is necessary. The Visigoths were perhaps the most atypical of Germanic tribes. Still, their *servi,* like those of other Germanic tribes, were not really slaves but serfs, particularly in Spain where the local population was large and the conquerors few. Moreover, perhaps more than in any other area of western Europe, the fact of Christianity in Spain had significantly ameliorated the status of slaves, and chattel slavery was disappearing even before the Visigoths entered Spain for the first time. Because of their rather intimate contact with the empire since the second half of the fourth century, the Visigoths were among the most Romanized of the Germanic tribes. Indeed, the Visigothic council of state (*aula regia*) and provincial government headed by *comites* and *duces* and *judices* almost replicated the late imperial system. Whether these institutions had been present in the native social system, or had approximate equivalents, is open to question. In any event, whether because they had been corrupted by Roman political and administrative decadence or for other reasons, the Visigoths and the ineffectual and divisive monarchy that they created were unable to withstand the Arab onslaught. Ironically, however, the memory of the weak but legendary state that they had created proved strong enough to sustain the ephemeral Visigothic states in the mountains of Asturias and to launch them to the reconquest of Spain that lasted for more than seven centuries (Pérez Pujol 1947, 2:65–98).

THE ANGLII, SAXONS, AND JUTES IN BRITAIN

In roughly 400, the Roman legions left Britannia, ending imperial domination. At the westernmost part of the empire, Britannia was probably the least Romanized of the imperial provinces, and the Celtic population retained a good deal of its native culture. Roman institutions had been imposed on the Britons, and there was a significant absorption of Latin culture by the population at large, but it is difficult to determine the degree of civilization that the legions left behind. Germanic tribes conquered Britain in a stream of invasions rather than in a single massive one, and their conquest was accomplished roughly by the last quarter of the fifth century. The Anglii, Saxons, and Jutes belonged to the western division of the Germanic stock. Their homeland had been in and south of the Jutland peninsula on the North Sea just before their invasion of Britain (approximately 430). Mentioned for the first time by Tacitus (1961:129) and Ptolomy in the second century, they were undoubtedly the least acculturated of all the Germanic tribes mentioned above. By the end of the seventh century, there were at least seven kingdoms (Kent, Essex, Sussex, Wessex, Mercia, East Anglia, and Northumbria), similar in social and political organization but apparently exhibiting two distinct ethnic affiliations. The Anglii, Saxons, and Jutes had been polytheists until they conquered Britain and remained so until their conversion to Christianity by Irish missionaries before the middle of the sixth century and, more effectively, by continental missions at the turn of the seventh century (Palgrave 1921:32–121).

We know little of the Anglo-Saxon invasion, but apparently many more people migrated from the continent to Britain than did Franks to Gaul or Visigoths to Spain, and they were much more numerous proportionally to the people they conquered, for Britain at that time was less densely populated than most other areas of the empire. The main consequence of this demographic situation was that the Anglo-Saxon kingdoms in Britain were composed mainly of the conquering Anglii, Saxons, and Jutes, supported by a rather large slave or serf population of conquered Britons (Chadwick 1963:400–411). The election principle must have been strong in the Anglo-Saxon monarchies, for often a monarchy had more than one royal family or lineage, and at times there was more than one king, usually two brothers governing together. In a few instances a petty kingdom had a supreme king with a number of underkings, presumably from the same royal lineage. Sometimes a kingdom was divided in two, and what sources call kingdoms and kings resembled more closely principalities and their respective officials, as in the kingdoms of France and Spain (Palgrave 1921:148–56).

The social organization and stratification of the Anglo-Saxons are better known than those of the Frankish and Visigothic nations. The principles of kinship and personal allegiance governed all strata of society, as the institution of the wergeld reveals. At the upper echelons of society, the "thenghood" (*comitatus* as it is called in the early sources, from the original Roman *comitiva*) regulated participation in public office; admission to the king's retinue ensured, therefore, upward mobility. Although thenghood seems to have been a preserve of the noble estate, it did accommodate other individuals of unusual ability and hence allowed for a modicum of mobility from the middle ranks of society.

Discounting the slaves of Briton origin and perhaps a few of Germanic origin, in total a very large population that some authorities estimate at more than half a million, Anglo-Saxon society was divided into three classes: *twelfhynde, sixhynde,* and *twihynde,* that is, those whose wergeld amounted respectively to 1,200, 600, and 200 shillings (Chadwick 1963:306–62). This classification evidently corresponds to the classic division of Germanic society into the nobility and the commonality. The noble estate, at times generically referred to as *thengas* (*theng* in the singular), included the *twelfhynde* and *sixhynde,* and the commoner estate included the *twihynde.* The two ranks or classes of the commonality present no difficulties and may be regarded respectively as freemen and freedmen, the former including almost exclusively Anglo-Saxons and the latter including mostly Britons. The two ranks of the nobility, on the other hand, are not clear-cut, for they varied from kingdom to kingdom. But it is safe to say that the *twelfhynde* corresponded to landowning nobles and ranked higher, while the *sixhynde* corresponded to *thengas* who did not own land and ranked lower. The noble estate also included the royal lineages, whose members' wergelds amounted from twice to as many as five times that of the *twelfhynde,* including the wergelds of the king or kings themselves. In addition, and beyond the estate division of society, some of the original sources give the wergelds for administrative and territorial officials as well as for the members of the king's council.

If we compare Anglo-Saxon society and stratification with those of the Franks and Visigoths, some significant differences emerge. First, due to the sizes of the conqueror and conquered populations, the Anglo-Saxons in Britain were perceptibly influenced neither by the local Celtic population nor by any Roman institutions that had survived the imperial withdrawal from the island; they fashioned their own society. The dominated population took centuries to be effectively incorporated into the framework of an emerging English nation. The Franks and Visigoths, by contrast, were smaller hosts within much larger conquered populations, and although they remained the ruling power, they were reasonably quickly assimilated to native culture and society. Second, isolation and lack of local input kept Anglo-Saxons simpler, more tribal, and truer to their Germanic roots than the Franks and Visigoths, who perhaps two and a half centuries after their conquests had shed many of their Germanic institutions and had been effectively Latinized. Third, there is no indication that the stratification systems of the Anglo-Saxons, Franks, and Visigoths were different at the time of their conquests: all three shared the same degree of fluidity as compared with the civilized Romans. In this respect, the Frankish and Visigothic systems were not unduly changed by contact and assimilation of the Roman class-estate system, and for four centuries appeared to have remained relatively fluid. The Anglo-Saxon system, on the other hand, apparently hardened after the conquest of Britain, for the earliest sources indicate that the nobility and the commonality had become strictly hereditary, castelike structures by the beginning of the ninth century.

I have sought here to impress upon the reader the import of the Germanic conquest of the Roman Empire. Almost all ruling aristocracies of western Europe at the beginning of the sixteenth century were of Germanic origin, and the European concept of nobility and rank until modern times betrays a mythological concern with the exploits of the last conquerors, whether Goths, Franks, Saxons, Lombards, or Normans. Indeed, the concept of *the last conquerors* in Western society has been a powerful symbolic and mythological devise in stratifying society, particularly in strengthening the effective aristocracies in most parts of Europe. Briefly stated, the concept establishes a claim to social, economic, and political privilege and excellence by tracing descent, real or imagined, from the last conquerors of the land. Thus, individuals and groups legitimize position in the stratification system by right of conquest and by mythologizing the original conquerors. For example, as late as the sixteenth century, conquering Spaniards would call themselves *godos* (Goths), evoking the memory of the Visigothic kingdom that had sustained them in the reconquest of Spain from the Moslems. Among the titled nobility and gentry, well into modern times, Visigothic descent was almost a prerequisite to exalted social position, and even *cristianos viejos* (old Christians) of all stations would be symbolically ennobled by claiming descent from those great warriors of the past. This theme is present in various degrees throughout Western society since the fall of the Roman Empire, and it constitutes an important element in the formation of monarchies, the nobility, and aristocracies in general.

CHAPTER 2

Predominance of the Estate System throughout the Middle Ages

Feudalism and the Fragmentation of Western Society

The gestation of Feudalism in western Europe began shortly after the foundation of the first Germanic monarchies and continued until the reign of Charlemagne. By the middle of the ninth century, Feudalism was well in place in the Frankish Empire and it spread rather quickly to the rest of Europe, including eastern Europe. This section first summarizes the changes in the stratification of western Europe from the fall of the Roman Empire until the time of Charlemagne, then examines how Feudalism structured a stratification system, a few aspects of which survived well into the nineteenth century. It covers roughly the period from 800 to 1200, when Feudalism developed, reached maturity, and began to decline.

ROMAN ANTECEDENTS AND THE NEW ORDER

Perhaps syncretic stratification is the best way to describe the two hundred years from the middle of the fifth century to the middle of the seventh century. The Roman and Germanic systems both contributed to the emerging formation. The relatively fluid Roman class-estate system of the early Autocratic Empire had become significantly hardened by the time of the barbarian invasions, particularly in the periphery of imperial dominion. It is not clear what each system contributed, nor is it possible to reconstruct in detail how the syncretic process proceeded, for most of the earliest sources were in Latin, and many concepts got lost or were distorted in translation. Take, for example, the institution of "companionage" or "following retinue" of the old Germanic kings, which Tacitus, not more than two decades before he wrote *Germania,* translated as *comitatus,* meaning the Roman institution established by Trajan (Perret 1962:78–81). Quite likely the Roman *comitatus* and its Germanic counterpart were essentially the same in the middle of the second century, but it is by no means certain that they were the same three hundred years later.

The status as a conquered population affected the commoner classes or estates more than it affected the noble or aristocratic classes or estates of the empire. Indeed, the Roman class-estate patriciate of the provinces accommodated well to the noble system of the Franks and Visigoths, perhaps already influenced by the imperial administrative aristocracy of *comites* and *duces.* Moreover, in Gaul and Spain powerful local aristocracies in the early decades of the fifth century were on their way to a rigid estate configuration. In this milieu the Germanic monarchies in the West developed a noble estate that was more rigid, powerful, and encompassing than its original contributing parts. Lest the reader misunderstand, it is not that many Gallo-Roman and Hispano-Roman members of local patriciates were incorporated into the Germanic conquering aristocracy: some probably were; most were not. Rather, the Germanic nobility remained the ruling estate, with some mixture, to be sure, but quickly adopting and internalizing many attributes and forms of local Roman patriciates (Boak 1943:372–432).

The most important input of the Germanic monarchy was the sacred nature of the institution, that is, the belief that the king had been empowered by the gods to rule, and complementarily, the concept of the king's lineage as being of mythological or supernatural origin. These symbolically powerful ideas reinforced the existing notion of the divine right of the emperor to rule. Two aspects of this juncture are important both to the rise of Feudalism and the configuration of stratification. On the one hand, the fundamental principles of civilized government of the Germanic monarchies, above and beyond their ancestral contributions, were based on Roman principles of authority, administration, and control. From the early Frankish and Visigothic kingdoms until after the reign of Charlemagne, the aim of the monarchy was to structure a centralized form of government on the model of the principate and the Autocratic Empire. That more often than not they failed is primarily a reflection of the fractious nature of the Germanic nobility and the barbarous milieu of the conquerors, which took more than three centuries to change but ended ultimately in decentralized Feudalism. The Roman concepts of monarchy and empire never disappeared, and the actual and symbolic presence of the *princeps-imperator* became a necessary element of Feudalism. On the other hand, the Germanic-Roman concept of the divine right of kings to rule became the ideological cornerstone of Western society: it welded church and state into a single, indivisible entity; and under Feudalism, the king became the ultimate tenant-in-chief to whom God had given the land to grant to others in fief (Fustel de Coulanges 1899:342–421). The sacred conception of the king persisted in Europe until the last absolutist monarchies were abolished in the nineteenth century: under Feudalism the concept provided sacred justification for land tenure; in the later Middle Ages, it persisted as the symbolic raison d'être for hereditary titles of nobility; and in modern times, it appeared as the rationalization of absolute power. The divine right of kings also consecrated the division of the population into fixed orders or estates that could only be transcended by the symbolic or de facto action of the sovereign.

By the middle of the eighth century, the stratification of western Europe had evolved into a rigid hereditary estate system. Mobility, after the comparatively early amalgamation of conqueror and conquered populations, had become minimal and society in the country and depopulated urban centers had become provincial and isolated. The important factor to consider, however, is how the actual configuration of the superordinate estate had changed. The patriciate, and the aristocratic class in general, was a social-economic but not a ruling class, for it held no political power independent of the administrative or military positions that certain members occasionally occupied: all political power emanated from the center, and, at least in theory, the emperor was the ultimate dispenser. In the systems that followed the establishment of the Germanic monarchies, the noble estate not only included the socially exalted and the great plutocratic magnates but it gradually acquired political functions. By the beginning of the ninth century it had become a ruling estate, the basic form that it retained for nearly seven centuries, until the rise of the first national states. The gradation of the nobility was configured by Feudalism and, in the later part of the Middle Ages, by the rise of a titled aristocracy. Stratification in Western society for more than one thousand years (from the end of the fourth century to the end of the fourteenth century) displayed the increasing rigidity of an estate system, at times abated by particular local developments and the incorporation of barbaric nations, such as the Scandinavians and the Slavs, to Western Civilization.

A common misconception charges Feudalism with having destroyed the empire and Charlemagne's attempt to revive it. In fact, the barbarism of the Germanic peoples, particularly the tribal love of independence and personal liberty of the nobility, impeded the continuation of centralized government. As late as the ninth century, the conquering society had not entirely assimilated the principles of civilized living. Feudalism basically reflects the inability of the monarchy to curb the fractious nature of the noble estate that plunged European society into centuries of instability and decentralization. What saved European society from disintegration were the symbolic presence of the Roman concepts of law, authority, and empire and the universality of the Christian church, which upheld the principles of social and civil behavior within a universal state (Fustel de Coulanges 1899:218–31).

Fundamentally, Feudalism represents the breakdown of the concept of citizen, as it was understood socially and politically in the Roman state well into the fifth century. This concept, forged in the Greek city-states and involving a contract between the individual and an abstract notion of polity devoid of personalized and supernatural underpinnings, found fertile ground in Republican Rome and was given universal significance during the empire. Without citizenship no large state organization is possible, as the feudal age reveals. Throughout nearly all of Europe, including Scandinavia and the newly established Slavic monarchies, the concept of citizenship almost vanished, and local and regional society was organized instead on the basis of kinship, friendship, and propinquity. One is tempted to say that feudal society represented a devolutionary phenomenon from *civitas* to *societas,* to use Sir Henry Maine's analogy, in that territoriality and the effective boundaries of the state did not extend beyond the system of contractual relationships between ranked superordinate and subordinate estates within the local fief. Europe was fragmented into thousands of seigneuries, each with virtually absolute sovereign lords occasionally grouped into higher territorial lordships under counts and dukes; ulti-

mately all paid vassalage to the king (Bloch 1940, 1:1
principle, the king was not only the ultimate tenant-in-c
embodied supreme authority. In practice, he could not a...
ized government and authority except under extraordinary conditions,
and uniform royal justice, administration, and control could not be
enforced, or were minimally enforced, in the domains of knights,
barons, and tenants-in-chief. Europe became an isolated patchwork of
regions and provinces, and kingdoms and duchies became de facto
paper tiger political and territorial entities with symbolic value in
preserving minimal standards of civilized government but that fundamentally upheld the framework of Feudalism (Ganshof 1952:63–96).

THE ORIGINS, CONSTITUTION, AND DEVELOPMENT OF FEUDALISM

Scholars agree that Feudalism was initially adopted as a system by the
Frankish kings. Charles Martel was the first ruler who, because of the
Moslem threat, expropriated large tracts of land from the church and
granted them to noble magnates, to allow them to wage war and to
equip contingents of foot and horse independent of the revenues of the
Crown. From the middle of the eighth century the Carolingian kings
began systematically to grant royal as well as ecclesiastical land to important nobles. At this point, the fundamental principle of Feudalism
was formulated, namely, the understanding that land grants to individuals in tenure involved two provisos: possession of the land entailed recognition of a debt to the grantor, and the grantee could in turn become
a grantor. In this form, Feudalism spread to most parts of western and
eastern Europe from the ninth century on (Stephenson 1942:1–14).

The Roman antecedents of Feudalism were three institutions that
went back to Republican times and acquired their most extensive and
elaborate expression during the last days of the empire in the isolation
and turmoil of frontier provinces: the *patrocinium, precarium,* and
beneficium. Patrocinium was basically what we call today patron-client
relationship, wherein men or groups of men of lesser power, wealth, or
influence (*clientes*) place themselves under the protection of powerful
magnates (*patroni*). *Precarium* was a form of land tenure. A great landowner granted land conditionally, mainly in friendship or to secure a
debt, for a number of years or for life. *Beneficium* refers to land dis-

pensed to individuals for cultivation when the grantor himself could not do it, a type of conditional land tenure employed by ecclesiastical owners as early as the end of the fourth century, when the first lands were assigned to the church under the later emperors. These interrelated institutions pervaded the empire, particularly the frontier provinces, from the second half of the fourth century onward.

The Germanic nations, meanwhile, contributed institutions that were remarkably similar to Roman counterparts, which fact supports the assertion that Feudalism had syncretic origins. Two institutions are particularly worth mentioning: the *Gefolgschaft* and a Germanic form of *precarium*. The *Gefolgschaft*, which is most commonly translated as companionage and which Tacitus (Perret 1962:715–16) translated as *comitatus*, identified those devoted warriors who attached themselves to a powerful war leader, not necessarily a king, in exchange for favors and protection. Many scholars see in *Gefolgschaft* an early form of vassalage, directly incorporated into the early feudal system by the oath of fealty. The Germanic kings also had a form of *precarium*. Gifts of land, cattle, and goods were granted in exchange for political and military service. All these Roman and Germanic elements influenced the gestation of Feudalism (Stephenson 1942:15–39).

It took nearly two centuries for Feudalism to mature. By the beginning of the eleventh century this social order and form of government predominated in Europe, having achieved a hierarchy of integration from family plot to kingdom and from serf to sovereign. The basic institutions of Feudalism were vassalage and the fief. Vassalage was an extreme form of clientship sanctioned by custom as well as sacred beliefs; it contractually tied a lord (*dominus, senior*) and a man (*vassalus,* a word of Celtic origin with various Latin alternatives, *miles,* soldier, *fidelis,* faithful) who had received a benefice from the former. At the beginning (in the eighth century), the benefice was only a means to ensure loyal and exclusive service of vassal to lord; a man could be the vassal of only one lord. This state of affairs did not last long, however, and by the late tenth century a man could be the vassal of several lords. Soon a distinction emerged between the ordinary lords of a vassal who had many fiefs and the principal lord, to whom he paid allegiance above all others. Thus the concept of the liege lord (*dominus ligius*) came to structure the hierarchy of the mature feudal system, in which the vassal of several fiefs becomes the liege fief (*feudum ligium*). Most vassals acquired or were provided with fiefs that they themselves exploited, whereas a minority had no fiefs and lived in the court of their lords as attendant knights (Ganshof 1952:133–51). The king was absolute liege lord, and a descending hierarchy of vassals gave the feudal system a pyramidal structure, in theory if not always in practice. Those vassals who received their fiefs directly from the king were called tenants-in-chief and constituted the most august feudal group. Tenants-in-chief could grant fiefs to their own tenants, thus creating a second echelon in the feudal aristocracy. More modest knights who received their fiefs from counts, dukes, and other territorial magnates were called vavasors, to distinguish them from the king's barons. Counts and, especially, dukes were more often than not vassals of kings, though occasionally they were independent sovereigns and liege lords in their own right (Stenton 1961:205–19).

The fief, then, is the central institution of Feudalism. The term comes from the Frankish word *fehu-od,* meaning a valuable movable property, and was translated into Latin, first as *beneficium* and from the tenth century onward as *feudum.* The fief was one of two basic kinds of land tenure that characterized the Dark and early Middle Ages, and it can be defined as the means by which a vassal made his living as provided by his lord. The other form of land tenure was the allod (*allodium*), or freeholding—land held in absolute ownership. From the beginning of the fifth century to the end of the eighth century, freeholding had been the most common type of land tenure throughout western Europe, and the essence of Feudalism may be characterized as the progressive elimination of allodial lands in the establishment of ever larger and more powerful fiefs. In short, protection and defense are the main causal antecedents of the disappearance of allodial lands and the growth of the fief. With the breakdown of central authority and the inability of the Germanic monarchies to reestablish political and territorial control, local freeholders had but one choice: to relinquish rights to allodial land, receiving back the land as a *precarium* and thereby placing themselves under the protection of a liege fief or a liege lord. As Feudalism matured and ruled the land, freeholders, except perhaps in some urban centers and rural regions where they could muster their own forces for protection and defense, continued to relinquish their allodial lands, a process enhanced by the failure of the monarchy to enforce local authority and control (Vinogradoff 1968:458–84).

The fief was normally an estate in land, but it might be any source of income, and money-producing fiefs were not uncommon. A land fief could be as large as a kingdom or as small as part of a village; the rank and dignity of the liege lord, the liege fief, or even the vavasor depended on the size and number of his fiefs. Everyone who held a fief, from the king to the lowliest knight, was a vassal, and the condition of vassalage was the only thoroughly dignified and honorable condition, that is, it defined the noble estate. Within his fief, the vassal was the master and lord of the nonfeudal population: he ruled over them, and they paid him rent in money, kind, or services, but they were not truly part of the feudal system. The status of the nonfeudal population, that is, the great majority of the population, is ambiguous: in theory they were not vassals, but in practice they had a vassal-like relationship to vavasors, to liege fiefs, and, in the case of urban populations, to such great liege lords as the king's barons, counts, and dukes. The nonfeudal population included burghers, freeholders (they never entirely disappeared, even at the zenith of Feudalism in the eleventh century), villeins, and serfs. Bound peasants (villeins and serfs) were attached to the fief and were required to support the vassal. From this context arose the notion of the knight's fee: the amount of money required for the maintenance of a mounted horseman and his family in order to secure his services to the lord of whom he was a vassal, that is, of whom he held a fief. The amount varied significantly from kingdom to kingdom, and sometimes from province to province, but estimates suggest that in most of western Europe twenty to forty peasant families were required to support the smallest household of a single knight. Larger fiefs of dozens, hundreds, or thousands of knights, the vassalage of barons, counts, and dukes, configured huge concentrated or dispersed estates, provinces, and subdivisions of kingdoms (Vinogradoff 1948: 98–167).

Feudal government, as I have indicated, meant decentralized government, that is, the fragmentation of public authority that during the Roman Empire was in theory vested in the concept of citizenship but that in practice emanated from the autocratic emperor. In the feudal state, authority and administration were vested in and controlled by local territorial magnates; it became privatized. The Roman concepts of law and justice were essentially maintained, though often modified by Germanic law and customs, and the feudal state was not entirely disruptive. Feudalism's most pervasive and characteristic drawback was the concentration of power in private hands at the expense of the public administration of justice, territorial control, and the organization of production and consumption (Ganshof 1952:141–51).

Feudalism was by no means uniformly distributed throughout Europe, and in different periods—between the ninth and twelfth centuries, for example—it varied significantly from kingdom to kingdom. France displayed the most decentralization, at least during the two centuries following the reign of Charlemagne; but from the middle of the eleventh century the power of the king increased gradually, and by the late fourteenth century the monarchy resembled an incipient absolute state. England, on the other hand, was the most centralized monarchy in Europe after the reign of Alfred the Great, and Feudalism, according to most historians, was introduced only after the Norman conquest, although equivalent forms of decentralization and land tenure had existed since shortly after the Anglo-Saxon conquest. Spain is a rather special case, for the protracted struggle against the Moslems prevented extreme decentralization in the three or four Christian monarchies of the peninsula, despite the religious and militaristic strength of Feudalism. Germany followed England as the most centralized feudal area of western Europe. The king had more real power than his counterparts on the continent, and royal officials held their offices independent of vassalage. In addition, the Holy Roman Empire, claiming symbolic continuity with the Roman Empire, catalyzed Germany's fragmentation into many small states and cities. Thus, of the major areas of Europe, Germany was the least feudalized, though indeed, strictly speaking, Italy was even less feudalized, for although the fief as a type of land tenure was important, freeholding appears to have predominated (Stephenson 1942:75–96).

The distribution of Feudalism varied significantly, often within the same kingdom or large province. In England, the commoner estate probably fared the best, for England had a seigneurial system rather than Feudalism. The most exploited victims of Feudalism were to be found in central and eastern Europe, where the institution arrived late but survived longest. In France, Spain, and parts of Germany the treatment of peasants was likely relatively temperate, with significant local variations. In the countries where the nonfeudal population was largest—the Netherlands, parts of Germany, and Italy—the power and abuses of Feudalism were undoubtedly the least significant (Calmette 1938:190–218).

VASSALAGE AND THE STRATIFICATION SYSTEM

Arising from a Germanic-Roman class of military men, administrators, and territorial magnates, the mature superordinate estate of Feudalism is best characterized as a warrior aristocracy. The dignity, power, and importance of its ranks were determined by the extent of land (fiefs) that individual members controlled. As an estate, the warrior landed aristocracy was not monolithic—a case can be made that knights were a subordinate estate—but entailed significant mobility into the higher echelons of the vassalage system. At no point was Feudalism a caste system, and there was even a modicum of mobility from the commoner estate into the knightly class. The main avenues of mobility apparently were distinction in battle and cooptation of freeholders with large tracts of land into the feudal system. The feudal stratification system was an irregular pyramid with gentle and sharp breaks, particularly in the middle. The base and midsection included all different classes of the commoner estate; in the midsection two classes of commoners predominated that do not accord well with the essential tenets of Feudalism. Whereas the top of the pyramid included all ranks of the warrior aristocracy, the bottom part may be considered a class with quasi-estate attributes. The superordinate positions of ranks in the three sections of the pyramid are as follows: king, duke, count, king's baron, baron, vavasor, knight; burgher, freeholders; villein, serf, slave(?). Let us briefly elaborate on these three categories.

The aristocratic estate is defined by vassalage, and its ranks by the extension of the fief. The feudal system, from knight vassal to king, is an irregular pyramid in that the various ranks are not arranged in a series of symmetrically ascending levels. Rather, the vassalic system irregularly confirmed dignity and prestige in terms of personal achievement in war, administration, and economic activities. From the political and territorial viewpoints, the structure of the feudal estate does not conform to intrinsically ranked positions; it more closely resembles a patchwork of hereditary offices and dignities conditioned by antiquity of lineage and success in warfare and fief acquisition. Thus, barons, counts, dukes, and even kings constituted loose networks governed at the levels of region, province, and monarchy by ties of kinship, conflicting or coinciding interests, and relatively ranked positions. In this context was war waged, territory reconfigured, and economic life pursued. From the sociological viewpoint, the worldview of Feudalism stipulated that the entire vassalic estate, from knight to king, was a single domain of marriage, exchange, and social interaction. The general privatization of most domains of human interaction made kinship more important than it had been during the autocratic Roman Empire, and it colored the political, religious, and economic domains. The fundamentally martial ideology of Feudalism made it possible (though highly unlikely) for a poor but battle-honored knight to marry the king's daughter; realistically, right of conquest and honors gained in battle could take the knight a long way to a barony, or the count to a kingdom (Calmette 1938:121–37).

Feudal knights were a class within the aristocratic estate but with estate-like attributes of their own. Indeed, analogously if not homologously, the Roman knight and the feudal knight were essentially the same: an intermediary order between the commonality and the nobility, but together with the latter making up a social order that can be properly called an aristocracy (Genestal 1911:56–72). Enjoying a higher degree of mobility (from the upper echelons of the commonality) than the rest of the feudal aristocracy, and being by far the largest class of the vassalic estate, the knights had a foothold in the two estates. Expressively and sociologically, there is no doubt that the Roman *equites,* the knights of early Feudalism and of the late Middle Ages, and the modern gentry or lesser nobility have always been part of the higher aristocracies of these periods, for they provided a group of equals large enough to absorb the need of the socially exalted for exhibition and display and also numerous enough to support political and economic action.

The middle section of the pyramid is the most difficult to fit into feudal society. Many historians view burghers and freeholders as essentially outside Feudalism, in the social and productive domains. Some historians regard many urban and freeholding populations more realistically as an integral part of feudal society but not necessarily as part of the vassalic system, a position that offers the most adequate understanding of European society during the Dark and early Middle Ages. Even in a society as warrior-oriented as Feudalism, success in business enterprises offered a modicum of mobility, particularly in the later days of Feudalism and in the bustling commercial cities of the Low Countries and northern Germany. But it was probably in Spain, where the exigencies of the Reconquest entailed almost constant warfare, that exploits in battle afforded the surest means for advancement into the lowest ranks of the nobility. The origins of the bourgeoisie are to be sought in the urban centers of the Roman Empire, but one can speak of a reestablishment of this traditional social class in the later part of the feudal period, beginning in the second half of the twelfth century and well-entrenched in European society two centuries later (Pruité-Orton 1968:208–41).

The bottom of the feudal pyramid encompassed the great masses of the population tied to the land and the knightly manor: villeins, serfs, and slaves. The position and number of slaves are not clear. That they existed there is no doubt. Indeed, they survived Feudalism and persisted well into the early sixteenth century. In Europe proper they were probably scarce but likely were more numerous in European possessions in the Near East during the Crusades and in Spain during the Reconquest. Chattel slavery, however, never existed in Europe throughout feudal times. Most historians do not discriminate between villeins and serfs; sociologically, however, they are separate classes in the feudal system. Villeins and serfs were both unfree populations, the difference being that the latter were more unfree than the former. The origins of these populations varied, but probably the majority of villeins were descendants of free peasants who had been brought into the feudal system, whereas serfs were descendants both of unfree peasants before the institution of Feudalism and of populations brought into the fief as the result of warfare. Villeins held their land from the lord of the manor, working other lands of the fief and performing certain personal obligations; but though they were not free to claim and defend civil rights against the lord, they were free in matters concerning the criminal and political law of the realm. Serfs, however, had no land privileges and were tied body and soul to the manor in all matters of the law (Stenton 1961:152–71).

The twelfth century marked the last period of Feudalism as a global institution; by the end of the fifteenth century, it had disappeared. As a specific form of land tenure, however, Feudalism persisted much longer, some of its institutions surviving until the twentieth century. The decline of Feudalism coincided with the rise of the bourgeoisie, and these developments must be regarded as two sides of the same coin. In several parts of Europe, but particularly in England and Spain, the decentralized monarchy evolved into a significantly more centralized parliamentary monarchy in which the rising bourgeoisie played a part in governing the kingdom together with the church and the nobles. The economic aspect of these developments is crucial. In the cities and parliaments of thirteenth- and fourteenth-century Europe, the bourgeoisie was being taxed to support not only the established monarchies but also the new city-states that had come into existence. With this newly acquired wealth, princes and kings were able to generate centralized armies that did not depend on feudal warriors, creating also independent administrative bureaucracies. Equally significant, fundamental changes in the methods of warfare disabled the feudal estate. The development of artillery and firearms, the return of infantry as the queen of battle, and the recruitment of national militias made the heavily armored horseman obsolete (Douglas 1939:128–43).

At no time in the long trajectory of Western Civilization, from Homeric times to the present, was society more stratified than during Feudalism. Though perhaps large-scale slavery made classical antiquity more cruelly stratified, it was not so in terms of all other social classes and estates. With its emphasis on warrior honor, chivalry, and highly formalized behavior, the worldview of Feudalism belittled those who pursued other avocations. Briefly, the feudal aristocracy was a global social, ruling, and political estate, which in terms of exaltedness, power, and relative wealth has never been equaled.

Seigneuralism and the Rise of a Titled Nobility

Feudalism did not stop abruptly at the beginning of the thirteenth century. Rather, its gradual demise affected European society differentially, both in terms of its strength as a global social system and its distribution in the continent. In terms of the survival of specific elements and complexes and in ideological pervasiveness, Feudalism left a lasting impression on European society. Its most undesirable or oppressive effects disappeared gradually, while its innocuous, even beneficial, mostly ideological survivals (virtue, honor, homage, opposition to centralized government, institutional loyalty, and so on) have shaped modern democratic society and are still with us (Bloch 1940, 2:240–60). As Feudalism waned and the dominant form of government gradually evolved toward the centralized kingdom, stratification and the social system evolved even more gradually. Not until the last decades of the fifteenth century did the bourgeoisie establish itself as a distinct class of the commoner estate. The transition implies the growth of freeholding, but in fact the majority of the population remained tied to the landed states as villeins or serfs. Though the rise of the bourgeoisie affected the demise of Feudalism, it was not fully significant as a class until the sixteenth century and should therefore be analyzed as an important component in the rise of absolutism. Overall, the stratification system of the thirteenth, fourteenth, and fifteenth centuries maintained its rigidity, though it began to soften gradually in the fifteenth century in response to the increasing strength of the bourgeoisie and changes in the noble estate itself (Stephenson 1942:97–107). These changes centered on the transformation from the feudal state to seigneuralism as the landed base of the aristocracy and on the increasing centralization of power, reflected in a new system of noble titles focused on the king. For the present study, the most significant development was, of course, the inception and growth of titles of nobility as a hereditary system.

STRATIFICATION CHANGES IN THE TRANSFORMATION TO SEIGNEURALISM

The transition from Feudalism to seigneuralism was gradual, but by the beginning of the fourteenth century most of the great and small landed states were held under seigneurial tenure. What did this mean socially, politically, and economically? Let us first explain the transition from Feudalism to seigneuralism and clarify what the latter stood for as a social and land-tenure system. The decline and ultimate disappearance of Feudalism meant that vassalage as a means to acquiring a fief rapidly became obsolete. From roughly the first half of the thirteenth century the main source of land became the king, who conferred property on individual nobles in recognition of distinction in warfare, political and judicial administration, and other services to the Crown. Another source of the nonvassalic landed estate was the transformation of the great vassalic territorial magnates into direct officials of the Crown. Barons and counts began to hold their great estates not as vassals but as representatives of the central government. Thus marches, countships, and even dukedoms became in a sense administrative subdivisions of the kingdom, interdependent, existing in a territorial and administrative ambiance that emphasized standardization and uniformity to a degree much higher than had ever existed under Feudalism (Stenton 1961:218–37).

Another important development in the transition from Feudalism to seigneuralism occurred in the knightly class. For most of the feudal period, the knight had been a professional soldier, a vassal of higher vassals, and the mainstay of the early medieval armies. Again, due to the centralization of government, the knight's fee, either in land or any other usufructuary prebend, disappeared as a means for royal government to avail itself of new soldiers and local administrators. Beginning late in the twelfth century, the knight became an elite soldier and local official linked directly to the king, who provided the knight with bookland in exchange for civil and military functions. From a slightly different perspective, the knight was aristocratized by becoming a sizable landowner with local judicial, administrative, and/or political functions. The aristocratic landed knight of the later Middle Ages, as contrasted with the professional feudal knight, occupied a socioeconomic position similar to that of the *equites* during the Roman Republic. Thus, the knights of the later Middle Ages must be regarded as the early formation of a class within the aristocratic estate, known eventually in England as the gentry, in Spain as *hidalgos,* and in France as *petite noblesse* (Bush 1984:38–42). The aristocratization of the medieval knight made him an unambiguous part of the noble estate, a class unto itself, to be sure, but ideologically, socially, politically, and economically allied to nobility by multiple ties.

Seigneuralism was Feudalism without vassalage: the seignory may be regarded as a fief that is not contingent on military or other services rendered to higher lords—except the king, who increasingly embodied the public domain. Politically, seigneuralism was different from Feudalism, and as a social system at the local level, it allowed for a more open society; in other words, it represented an improvement to the extent that there were fewer conflicts between the interests of local lords and the standardization of the king's justice and administration. Nevertheless, the paramount maxim of Feudalism, "Nulle terre sans seigneur" (no land without its lord), continued to configure seigneuralism, and most of the social, economic, and judicial rights and obligations that obtained between the feudal lord and the population of his fief also persisted: the status and general treatment of villeins and serfs probably did not change appreciably. The change from feudal fief to seignory is not just terminological, for the king became, de jure and de facto, the lord paramount, ensuring that no land was without a lord, and more important, creating new seignories in order to enhance his control over the kingdom and the great territorial magnates. In this sense, centralization produced more fluid societies in the fourteenth and fifteenth centuries.

The end of serfdom and the improvement of the villeinage in the fifteenth century followed peasant uprisings and the realization of the titled nobility and gentry that agricultural production and profits would increase by transforming their seigneurial possessions into land rentals and indirect forms of sharecropping (Bush 1983:169–85). From a slightly different perspective, the transition from Feudalism to seigneuralism may be characterized as the change from castle to manor as the focal point of the landed aristocracy. Castles, the strongholds of great territorial magnates, were not only indefensible against artillery, but were destroyed or abandoned as the king asserted his authority over unruly nobles. Meanwhile, the proliferation of smaller landed estates secured the predominance of the manor as the rural base of the titled nobility and gentry. Some castles undoubtedly survived as symbols of royal authority and residences of the king's high officials in regions and provinces. The manor survived as the last bastion of Feudalism, but it underwent important transformations, and in the late fifteenth century the manor acquired the basic form that, at least in England, it retained until the end of the nineteenth century: a farming system of land rentals or sharecropping, in which the bonded family units owed varying duties and obligations to the lord or esquire (Powis 1984:67–76)

The Inception and Development of Titles of Nobility

The Greeks and Romans did not have titles of nobility, and the superordinate aristocratic estate was configured in terms of achieved status and rank. During the second century of the principate the first antecedent of titles of nobility made their appearance: the *comitiva* or companionage of the Roman emperors who were chosen on the basis of merit to accompany and advise the *princeps*. Thus derives the title of count (*comes*): an achieved, nonhereditary position appointed by the sovereign; it became the model for conferring honor and dignity as emanating from a prince. The title of duke (*dux*) entered the scene in the last century of the empire not as a dignity but as a designation of high military commanders. The Germanic monarchies adopted many Roman institutions, particularly those relating to military and civil administration (Stuart Jones 1916:390–401). Later, the conquerors transformed the dignities of *comes* and *dux* into civil and military officers of the monarchy. By the beginning of Feudalism, the offices of count and duke had become standard designations for the administrative and political subdivisions of the kingdom. Early in the feudal period, the offices combined political, military, and administrative functions, the highest ranks in the feudal system. Most significantly, counts and non-sovereign dukes became hereditary offices, not by the will and power of the king but by the growth of the feudal system and the ability of individuals to expand their fiefs and concentrate power. Although these were hereditary positions of honor and dignity, they were not in fact titles of nobility; they were essentially no different from other ranks in the vassalic hierarchy. The denominations of baron and vavasor are nothing more than lower ranks of counts and dukes in the vassalic system (Luchaire 1938:318–47). From the last century of the Roman Empire to the thirteenth century, then, count and duke stood for politico-administrative and military positions that, originally elective, had become hereditary offices as central authority diminished.

To avoid possible confusion, let me add that all ranks of the vassalic system under Feudalism became titles of nobility of sorts when administrative and territorial offices became hereditary. But a "system of titles of nobility" means something different. In the modern sense, titles of nobility came into being when a sovereign bestowed honor and dignity upon a person by conferring a title: he could confirm or create new ranks for reasons that could range from personal to political to administrative. Given this definition, titles of nobility are not present in European society until the king acquired reasonably strong central power. The system of titles of nobility, as it coalesced in most European countries by the end of the sixteenth century, took at least two centuries to achieve maturity. The modern titled system is, however, firmly based in the feudal aristocracy, and there is no sharp break in the transition from Feudalism to seigneuralism to absolutism. Indeed, the higher ranks of the vassalic system were generally confirmed, but new titles were created by the increasingly powerful king, who established his favored subjects not as vassals but as peers (*pairs,* in French) of the realm, the most distinguished nobility by the beginning of modern times. In other words, the higher ranks of the feudal nobility, by virtue of their paramount position in the vassalic system, were recognized as the most exalted aristocracy, while new titles created by the king, although of equivalent rank, did not have the same prestige unless they belonged to members of the royal family (Chaussinard-Nogaret 1975:136–201).

The nobiliary system developed in western Europe from the thirteenth to the sixteenth century was as ranked and complex as the vassalic system of Feudalism out of which it arose and which it closely paralleled in terms of prestige. By the late seventeenth century the newer system had become almost universal in western Europe, but with variations in ranking order and extension. The ranks, in terms of relative superordination, were (and are): duke, marquess, count, viscount, baron, baronet, knight, and esquire. The titles of knight and esquire are intrinsically somewhat ambiguous, and that of baronet is absent in most countries, but on the whole the system is fairly consistent. Underlying the system—in modern times configuring it—are sovereigns, those empowered to confer titles of nobility: emperor (*Kaiser, empereur, emperador*), king (*König, roi, rey*), pope (*papem, pape, papa*), and prince (*Fürst, prince, principe*). The term *prince*, de jure and de facto, may denote an independent sovereign and a title of nobility. From the late Middle Ages until the present, there were sovereign princes of small states or principalities who could grant titles of nobility in their own right. Also since the Middle Ages, the term *prince* has been used as a term of address for male members of royal families, and as a title of nobility, particularly in France and Italy, it has been bestowed by king and pope on the highest nobles of the realm. Not counting the pope, who has traditionally granted titles of nobility as a temporal ruler and not as the head of Roman Catholicism, sovereigns in Western society are Roman and Indo-European in origin and configuration, with essentially political and military connotations. Prince, from Latin *princeps,* was the title taken by Augustus as the first citizen of the state and ultimately meant the elite, veteran soldiers of the Roman legion; emperor comes from Latin *imperator,* that is, the high officials (usually consuls and praetors), who, by the will of the senate and Roman people, could exercise *imperium,* the power to command and make military, political, and administrative decisions; and king is rooted in most Indo-European linguistic families (*rex, rajah, shah*) from India to Ireland.

RANKING OF THE HIGHER OR TITLED NOBILITY

The title of duke (*Herzog, duc, duque*) is the highest title of nobility, but it is also used to designate minor sovereign princes. We are not concerned with the latter, and I have already outlined the evolution of the former from its Roman origin to its feudal usage. It should be reiterated, however, that a minority of dukes became sovereign rulers, whereas the majority emerged from Feudalism as great landed magnates whose status was confirmed by the king and who thereby retained the title as an honor and dignity bestowed by the sovereign. The earliest of these dukes appeared in France late in the thirteenth century. In Spain the title of duke was uncommon until the fourteenth century, when the title of duke was bestowed for highest services rendered to the Crown and for special merit in warfare and politics. This practice, initiated by France, was followed in most countries of Europe from early modern times. In England, however, ducal titles were initially associated with members of the royal family and their close kinsmen; only later was the title bestowed for extraordinary merit as in the rest of Europe. The highest rank in the nobiliary system, the title was generally bestowed on already titled individuals and almost never on commoners or even members of the lesser nobility (Bush 1983:131–37). For example, the achievement of Hernán Cortés, the conqueror of Mexico and of *hidalgo* (lesser nobility) rank, certainly warranted a dukedom, but because he was not already a high noble, he was awarded only a marquisate. After the sixteenth century the title became increasingly rare.

The title of marquess (*Marquis, marquis, marqués*) is the only rank in the modern nobiliary system already present in the early Middle Ages that is not of Roman origin. The title of marquess, undoubtedly related etymologically to margrave, is of Carolingian origin, dating as far back as the early ninth century. The title originally denoted a count or a duke at the head of a march (mark), that is, a frontier region or province that required special attention. In other words, the office of *marchiones* (those royal or imperial officials who held a march) or margraves from the beginning had the same functions as those of counts and dukes, and evidently they were fashioned on the Roman model of the latter. During feudal times, *marchiones* or margraves often held critical provinces at the frontiers of kingdoms and the empire. They had, therefore, more power and authority than counts and hence more honor and dignity. They often ranked as high as dukes, as exemplified by the German usage of *Markherzog* (margrave duke) rather than *Markgraf* (margrave count). Again, however, like counts and dukes, though marquesses were hereditary offices, they were not titles of nobility in the modern sense until roughly the same time as fourteenth-century nobiliary dukes. The office denoted by the term *marchiones* under the Carolingians spread to Germany and then to England. As early as the thirteenth century the term was applied to the earls of the Welsh marches, where apparently marquesses did not rank necessarily above other earls. But from the late fourteenth century onward, the title of marquess, by now a nobiliary title, ranked above that of count (earl) and just below that of duke. In Italy and Spain, perhaps because of the former's fragmentation and the latter's Reconquest, the title of marquess appears slightly later and, since the sixteenth century, has had a rather uncertain status. In the systems of other European nations, marquess appears rather infrequently—in some cases not at all—and in systems where it is common, the term is most ambiguous in terms of absolute ranking.

Terminologically, in the nobiliary systems of Great Britain and Ireland, the Old English term *earl* has always stood for count (*Graf, comte, conde*), but the Latin feminine, countess, found its way into the English language. Ever since the sixteenth century, the wife of an earl has been a countess, and so has a female who holds an earldom. As a rank and nobiliary dignity, distinguished from purely vassalic lords, count (henceforth including the earl) is the earliest hereditary title, dating back to the twelfth century. Before this time the title of count was ambiguous and equivocal. In the middle of the thirteenth century the title of count acquired more fixed attributes of a rank in the nobiliary system of France and subsequently in all countries of Europe, becoming thus the most commonly awarded title as European nobilities entered modern times. In absolute ranking, entailing corresponding honor and dignity, count ranks below duke and enjoys a status similar or just slightly lower than marquess. In terms of relative ranking and the range of individuals holding the title, the honor varied greatly from royal counts to grandee counts to counts of noble provenance and to counts of commoner provenance (Luchaire 1938:296–309). Of great importance in the evolution of the high nobiliary system was the ability of the Crown to create titled nobles whose origin and function had no direct connection with old vassalic obligations or affiliation with the royal family. These developments began late in the fourteenth century, continuing through the fifteenth and early sixteenth centuries. Thereafter, the strict connection between noble title and a fief was discontinued, though the intimate association between land and nobility or aristocracy persisted. But by the middle of the nineteenth century, most European nobles had lost their great landed base, and titles had become little more than social dignities. In France, the title of count was much more liberally conferred on distinguished public servants, a process that led in modern times, particularly after the sixteenth century, to important discriminations based on social origins, circumstances of granting the title, and the proven nobility of the holder, with the predictable consequence that the title of count *qua* title ceased to have intrinsic social prestige. This devaluation of the title of count pervaded the continent after the French Revolution, and all other lower nobiliary titles suffered a similar fate. In Germany and Italy, particularly, where there was no primogeniture concerning the inheritance of titles, and all the sons of a count inherited his title, titles quickly lost their shine (Montagu of Beaulieu 1970:21–120). Perhaps Spain is the one country besides England where the title of count has retained its social exaltedness. This survival was due to primogeniture, the extensive use of the entail (*mayorazgo*), and the apparent desire of the monarchy not to cheapen this or any other title. Undoubtedly, and this observation applies to all nobiliary titles below duke, the proliferation of titles and the loss of entailed honor and dignity must be attributed to the increasing democratization of European society during the past two and a half centuries.

The title of viscount (*Vicomte, vicomte, visconde*) was the last to be introduced into the nobiliary system. Its origin, however, goes back to early Carolingian times, and its development from political and territorial office to hereditary office and title paralleled that of the count. In the early days of Feudalism, viscounts were the deputies or lieutenants of counts, and when the latter became hereditary in the tenth century, the former followed suit. Apparently the office of viscount did not imply possession of a landed estate, but as Feudalism became more pronounced, viscounts had to qualify their office with the name of their most important fief. This development took place toward the end of the eleventh century, and a century later viscount was on its way to becoming a nobiliary title. Before the end of the fifteenth century, the title had spread to most European countries, though outside France, England, and Spain it was relatively rare and overall it is the least common of all titles of the higher nobility. In England it joined the peerage by the middle of the fifteenth century and became fairly common. Since then viscounts have outranked all barons (Selden 1937:87–96).

The title of baron (*Freiherr, baron, barón*) is the lowest rank of that sector of the European aristocracy known variously as "upper nobility," "higher nobility," "titled nobility," and, in Great Britain, "the peerage." In Great Britain and Ireland (but not on the continent), the noble estate includes only the peerage, that is, all those individuals holding titles from baron to duke, while the rest of the population, including baronets and knights, are commoners. From the standpoint of the social stratification system, this breakdown is artificial. *Aristocracy* is therefore a more encompassing term than *nobility,* for even in Britain the peerage, baronetcy, and gentry were all regarded, by themselves and others, as aristocrats tied by kinship, social practices, and expressive behavior of long standing. At any rate, the term *baron* is of Germanic origin, meaning man or freeman, and it developed as a title in the vassalic system of Feudalism in the ninth and tenth centuries. It spread from France to most countries of western Europe and to England with the Norman Conquest. In the transition to the nobiliary system, barons occasionally outranked counts, but by the time baron became established as a title in the sixteenth century, it had acquired its present position at the bottom of the higher nobility (Selden 1937:56–75). Baron as a title of nobility was first granted in the late thirteenth century in France. Nearly a century later, England invested the title with noble status, more or less conterminously with the investiture of the first dukes. In Italy, Germany, and Austria the title became common in the fifteenth century. Until the seventeenth century, the distinction could be borne only by holders of a territorial barony, but thereafter it was bestowed upon individuals regardless of landholding. In these countries, particularly in Italy, the title of baron proliferated so much that thousands of them were in existence by the beginning of the twentieth century. In Spain, baron, like viscount, was a rather rare title.

RANKING OF THE LESSER NOBILITY OR GENTRY

The title of baronet (*Baronet, baronnet, baronet*) appeared last in the European nobiliary system, or, more exactly, in the nobiliary system of the British isles—for the baronetcy is an exclusive development in Great Britain and Ireland, where only the peerage constitute the noble estate. The title of baronet is one of the two titles of the nonpeerage aristocracy of Great Britain and Ireland, and it has no equivalent in the lesser nobility of continental Europe. As a dignity between baron and knight it was instituted by James I in the first decade of the seventeenth century, and like some of the middle-range titles of the nobiliary systems of England and the continent, the title was created to generate revenue for the Crown. This practice had precedents in most European nobiliary systems, going back to the early part of the six-teenth century, but by the end of the seventeenth century it had become quite generalized and increasingly abused, including not only middle-range titles but those of count and marquess. Like the titles of nobility of the peerage and *haute noblesse,* baronets are hereditary and have the right to bear coats of arms, a privilege dating from the inception of the title. Like knights, baronets are entitled to the terms of reference and address of "Sir" and "Lady" (or "Dame"). From the last decades of the nineteenth century, the title of baronet, with that of knight and, later, that of baron, has been used by the British govern-ment to reward public achievement, thereby initiating life dignities, that is, nonhereditary (Perrot 1968:69–88).

The title of knight (*Ritter, chevalier, caballero*) is the most difficult dignity to place in the contemporary setting, nor is it easy to trace its evolution from the feudal period. Fundamentally, the dignity of knight is the same in all aristocracies of Europe: some of its attributes may vary from country to country, but as an honorific title it denotes the same rank. Although knight in English and *chevalier* (horsemen) in French came to signify the same right after the Norman Conquest, they were not the same etymologically and signified quite different referents before the middle of the eleventh century. Knight comes from Old English *cniht* meaning originally youth (alternately, attendant), and in Anglo-Saxon times *cnihtas* were fighting corps of elite youth attached to great territorial magnates. But Anglo-Saxons, from king to com-moner, fought on foot, and after the Norman Conquest and the intro-duction of chivalry in England, the English term for *chevalier* should have become *rider,* as it was the case when chivalry spread to Germany, and the term for *chevalier* became *Ritter.* When the rank of knight was achieved, the individual had to be made a knight by king, territorial magnate, or, in the early stages of Feudalism, by another knight (Baldwin 1897:76–107). The social rank that went with knighthood, however, was hereditary, and in time, as we have seen, it constituted a significant class in all countries of Europe. It should be noted that chivalry and some military aspects of knighthood did not disappear with the demise of Feudalism and the end of the crusades; it survived in the many orders of knighthood created by monarchies and republics in modern times to reward merit and service. Over the centuries, the knight in England, the *chevalier* in France, the *Ritter* in Germany, and the *caballero* in Spain became important locally and regionally, particularly when their landed status was enhanced by political and judicial functions delegated to them by the king or higher nobility, a practice that in Britain survived until the end of the nineteenth century (Powis 1984:81–95).

The term *esquire* (*Landedelmann, ecuyer, escudero*) is not really a title but a designation of social status that has become connotative of one of the upper sectors of the modern European class system. Historically part of the lesser nobility, or at least its most likely postulants, squires were of feudal origin; the term *squire* stood for attendant to and arm bearer of a knight, ranking immediately below him. The status of esquire was regarded as apprenticeship to knighthood, and from the beginning it implied an individual with the social and personal potential to become a knight. From this standpoint, the status of esquire was largely hereditary (Selden 1937:103–17). Most commonly esquires were first-born sons of knights, sons of vassalic tenants, or recipients of royal patent for gallantry in battle or for services rendered to the Crown or great territorial magnates. As Feudalism disappeared and warfare changed in the later Middle Ages, the rank or appreciation of esquire also changed, losing its preeminent military connotation and acquiring a local judicial and administrative configuration. Throughout modern times, perhaps even more than the rank of knight, the esquire personified the social middle ground that nurtured the aspirations of the rising bourgeoisie, particularly throughout the fifteenth and first half of the sixteenth centuries. This characterization of the esquire in modern times applies mostly in Britain, but to a considerable extent it also applies in France, Spain, and Italy, which are best described in the context of the gentry. Today, as a title of address and reference, esquire has been vulgarized beyond its traditional application to such an extent that it has become meaningless, except perhaps in Great Britain and Ireland, where it survives in the countryside (Perrot 1968:156–63).

The gentry (*Landadel, gentilhommerie, petite noblesse, "hidalguía"*), finally, is a difficult concept to elucidate, because although originally centered in the milieu of knights and esquires, its ranks eventually became accessible to the bourgeoisie. Once an exclusive sector of the superordinate noble estate, the gentry was from the sixteenth century on a mixed segment of a class in the process of formation. All over the continent no distinction separates peerage (titled nobility) from gentry (nontitled nobility): they are both noble and aristocrats; in Great Britain and Ireland, however, both are aristocrats but only the former are noble. The continental distinction between *haute noblesse* and *petite noblesse* is of course structurally the same as that between the peerage and gentry in Great Britain and Ireland. In terms of functional status, however, the continental *petite noblesse* entails substantially more privileges than the gentry in Great Britain and Ireland and, despite the significant degree of variation, the continental aristocracy, *qua* nobility, was substantially differently placed vis-à-vis the commoner estate (Perrot 1968:165–87). By contrast, *gentilhommerie* and *hidalguía* denote the status and condition of nobility (titled and nontitled) as well as of gentry or lesser nobility. All aristocracy had the same origin (Lira Montt 1976:811–917). Gentry, gentleman, *gentilhomme*, *gentilhombre*—all derive etymologically from the Latin term *gentiles* (*gens* members), which becomes *generosus* in Middle Latin, meaning well-born or of noble origin. As early as the thirteenth century, a class of *generosi* emerged in several European countries; it was an aristocratized knightly esquire class with hereditary privileges. From the middle of the thirteenth century to the middle of the fifteenth century, the hereditary gentry and the gentleman, and their equivalents on the continent, had been hereditary landowning classes. Beginning in the late fifteenth century, the concept of the gentleman began to change, and by the eighteenth century, from its original denotation of *noblesse* and its landed base, it had acquired a place in the evolving class system (Bush 1983:122–39). Most dictionaries and encyclopedias in French, Italian, and Spanish translate and define gentry as *petite noblesse–haute bourgeoisie, piccola nobilità–alta borghesìa, pequeña nobleza–alta buerguesía;* occasionally in French and Spanish the equivalents *gentilhommerie* (archaic) and *hidalguía* are employed. This profusion of terms quite accurately captures the evolution of the concepts of gentleman and the gentry class in the context of the rising bourgeoisie and the decline of the nobility as a privileged estate.

The main themes, then, in the transformation of social stratification in the West from 1200 to 1500 were the development of a system of titles of nobility centered mostly on the Crown, the solidification of hereditary principles, the formation of a distinct lesser nobility, and, in the last decades of the period, the rise of a powerful bourgeoisie.

CHAPTER 3

Realignment of Society and the Transition from Estate to Class in Modern Times

Decline of Noble Privilege and Rise of the Bourgeoisie

Seigneuralism did not disappear abruptly from Europe; it lingered, fading, for two centuries after the discovery of the New World, the conventional marker of the beginning of modern times. In the nearly three hundred years until the French Revolution, seigneuralism did not play a determinant role in the rise of the bourgeoisie and class stratification. This period witnessed an unavoidable interaction between the noble estate and an increasingly conscious and wealthy haute bourgeoisie. The former steadily experienced the loss of privilege, while the latter learned the uses of political and economic power. These changes signified the gradual decline of the estate system and the emergence of stratification based on social classes (Domínguez Ortiz 1974:32–98). To an extent, the conditions that characterized this period on into the twentieth century resemble those that existed in Rome from the second century B.C. to the end of the second century A.D. Without exaggerating the parallelisms, I would note that both periods exhibited the following sociocultural conditions and processes: First, both periods display a more naturalistic, less supernaturally conditioned *imago mundi,* initially constrained and ultimately suppressed by the triumph of Christianity. Second, we can discern a concerted revitalization of the plebeians' struggle for political, economic, and social recognition, in which classes rather than estates constitute the basic social building blocks. The decline and abolition of the estate system and its replacement by a class system that, centered on the bourgeoisie and particularly on its upper ranks, compare to the protracted struggle of the plebeians, aborted by the principate but resulting nonetheless in the eventual rise of the *equites* and a more fluid stratification. Third, both eras reflect the dwindling control of religion and the overall secularization of society. The important effect here for the change from estate to class stratification was desacralization of the political domain. These processes fueled the return of societal control to the public domain and the reaffirmation of the concept of citizenship. Another variable that must be considered in the gestation of the change from estate to class stratification is the rise of absolutism, which, again, parallels the rise of the principate in classical times (Doucet 1948:107–21).

ROYAL ABSOLUTISM AND THE CHANGING STRATIFICATION SYSTEM

The isolation of the Dark and early Middle Ages produced much cultural and linguistic diversity, and most regions and provinces of kingdoms were ethnic entities unto themselves. In other words, Feudalism perpetuated the isolation into which western Europe had been plunged after the fall of the Roman Empire, and to a significant extent the late Middle Ages represent the end of isolation. The tendency toward absolutism and the formation of the national state involved a confluence of variables: improved means of communication, extension of trade, increased economic productivity, technological innovation, and the growth of education. At the end of the period, the invention of the printing press and the beginning of exploration and European expansion hastened the major countries of Europe on their way to centralized monarchy, and within a century several countries had become absolute monarchies. Though Germany and Italy did not become national states until after the middle of the nineteenth century, this generalization also applies to them, for their component parts were either small national states or under the domination of the great European nations (Goubert 1973:78–83).

In the development of continental monarchies, sovereign absolutism and the rise of national states went hand in hand, leading to the erasure of regional-ethnic boundaries and the rise of a national vision. The standardization of justice, uniformity of administration, and the birth of pan-provincial institutions of trade and commerce unified kingdoms into indivisible entities symbolized by the sovereign. The implementation of public administration required large bureaucracies, the like of which had been unknown since the division of the Roman Empire. This important development permitted a degree of social mobility unheard of since the fall of the Roman Empire (Doucet 1948:165–73). Beginning in the early sixteenth century and with increasing intensity in the seventeenth century, the state bureaucracy swelled with men of ability who had either arisen from humble origins to the rank of bourgeois or who had been recruited from the established haute bourgeoisie. To be sure, royal bureaucracies were not entirely staffed by the rising bourgeoisie of meritocratic extraction—but as the traditional connection between noble status and land began to collapse, significant numbers of the *haute* and *petite noblesse* enlarged bureaucratic rosters.

As early as the fifteenth century, bourgeois businessmen had become rich and powerful enough to buy landed estates, the first step toward ennoblement, the aspiration that has characterized most members of the haute bourgeoisie ever since. The already substantial bourgeoisie at the beginning of the sixteenth century constituted the superordinate class of the commoner estate: rich and influential enough to compete for social recognition with the lesser nobility and to vie successfully for bureaucratic appointments. This context provided for the emergence in the following centuries of a haute bourgeoisie that, regardless of estate affiliation, became practically indistinguishable from the lesser nobility. From that point on, the upper reaches of European stratification were significantly governed by antiquity of lineage and new great wealth (Lucas 1973:84–89).

The transition from centralized monarchy to absolutism and a national state relates directly to the decline of the seigneurial aristocracy and the disintegration and demise of the nobiliary system. An example will place the main issues in perspective. Given the peculiar constraints of the Reconquest and the concerted action of two sovereign leaders, we can describe Spain as perhaps the first national state. By the middle of the fifteenth century the Christian kingdoms of the Iberian peninsula had managed to reconquer most of their land, and only the small kingdom of Granada remained in the hands of the Moors. Within a generation of the marriage of Isabella of Castile and Ferdinand of Aragon, Spain became unified, the kingdom of Granada reconquered, and the feudal-seigneurial nobility brought under control. When King Ferdinand died in 1516, even his most rebellious and despotic Aragonese nobles had been brought to heel, and the Spanish monarchy was well on its way toward the absolutism achieved by Philip II in the 1560s (Domínguez Ortiz 1970:43–76). Most significantly, beginning with Ferdinand and Isabella, the great nobles were encouraged to leave their estates and become courtiers. Spain's acquisition of a great overseas empire and involvement in many European ventures provided ample opportunities for noble courtiers and royal officials, as well as for meritorious and ambitious members of the bourgeoisie. In particular, the administrative, military, and judiciary bureaucracies of the New World bred great fortunes and social advancement; second- and third-born sons of the titled nobility, *hidalgos,* and bourgeois commoners vied for position and status in a new nobiliary system in which a rising haute bourgeoisie staked a significant claim (Domínguez Ortiz 1955:210–17).

Although traditionally regarded as the epitome of absolutism, France experienced this extreme form of royal control later than Spain. But when absolutism did arrive in the seventeenth century, as encoded in *le roi soleil*'s dictum, *l'état c'est moi,* it acquired its greatest expression. Louis XIV was the absolute European monarch par excellence. More than any other sovereign, he curtailed the political independence of the *haute noblesse;* and more than their Spanish counterparts, the French grandees became courtiers attached to the king to enhance the glory of his palace and his image as the grandest ruler in Europe. Having brought the higher nobility under control, the French kings shared the distrust of the Spanish kings for employing great noble magnates. The French bureaucracy was as extensive and more elaborate than that of Spain, and the king made greater use of the rising bourgeoisie; indeed, many of the highest officials of the realm were meritorious commoners. Nowhere in Europe did the bourgeoisie make more gains than in France during the seventeenth and eighteenth centuries. During the reign of Louis XIV a distinction arose between *noblesse de robe* and *noblesse d'épée,* that is, those elevated to the nobility for civil service and for military service, respectively. But the distinction also denoted the inferiority of the *noblesse de robe,* those who had been elevated for civil service and who were mostly of commoner origin, to the *noblesse d'épée,* those who had been elevated for military service—and who were, for the most part, members of the traditional seigneurial aristocracy. The French nobility put up a strong but ineffectual resistance to absolutism. Deprived of most of its political and judicial privileges, the nobility finally retreated, seeking to safeguard its fiscal privileges and pursuing the excessive exploitation of its still de facto seigneurial domains, which ultimately triggered the French Revolution (Goubert 1973:104–42). Undoubtedly, absolutism, first in Spain and then in France, contributed to the formation of the bourgeoisie and its coalescence into a distinct social class. (For reasons that are not clear, the early burst of bourgeois activity in Spain waned by the middle of the seventeenth century, as the nobility to some extent reasserted itself, while the bourgeoisie lost wealth and prestige.)

Great Britain offers one of the most intriguing cases for assessing the rise of the bourgeoisie, the loss of noble privilege, and the rise of the constitutional monarchy, all of which were achieved virtually without absolutism. Absolutism's failure to develop in England reflects the nature of Anglo-Saxon society, the effects of the Norman conquest and its aftermath, and the fact that noble privilege in Great Britain was never as great and all-inclusive as in most continental kingdoms. Even before the sixteenth century, the British aristocracy was more receptive than its continental counterparts to the aspirations of its peasants: it dismantled the most unpleasant aspects of seigneuralism and to some extent fostered the transformation into a less exploitive tenant-farming system (Bush 1984:49–60). The relatively underprivileged condition of the British aristocracy, compared to the continental aristocracy, softened the inequities between estates. Thus Great Britain became a national state without the benefit of absolutism and undue centralization. The peerage and gentry retained most of their political and judicial privileges, which on the continent the nobility lost almost entirely to absolutism. The bourgeoisie in Great Britain, meanwhile, curtailed by the aristocracy from substantial participation in the political and administrative life of the nation, monopolized trade and manufacturing, and the British haute bourgeoisie must be counted as the main architect of the Industrial Revolution. More than in any other country in Europe since the seventeenth century, the gentry in Great Britain represented an amalgamation of the *petite noblesse* and the haute bourgeoisie, and the most outstanding members of the latter were elevated to the peerage, mostly for excellence in generating economic resources (Bush 1983:79–120). After Tudor times, the British monarchy steadily evolved toward a constitutional form, a status it achieved earlier than any other monarchy in Europe. However, Great Britain's aristocracy, particularly the peerage, as entailing significant privileges characteristic of an estate system, survived longer than all continental aristocracies.

SEIGNEURIAL AND NOBLE PRIVILEGES AND THE ESTATE SYSTEM

The fundamental distinction between estate and class stratification is inequality before the law and/or customary practices that discriminate among the constituting segments of a state, be it a monarchy, or any other form of government. Within this context the nature of privilege is of paramount importance in defining and configuring the distinction between estate and class. Concisely, noble privilege may be defined as the hereditary rights of the superordinate estate over the subordinate estate. In this fixed order of things, the rights of the nobility are many, while those of the commonality guarantee little more than subsistence, and the intensity of the belief that supports this inherent inequality is determined by the origin of the institution (Bush 1983:2–5). In the case of the Romans, for example, the patrician-plebeian distinction was accepted by the body politic on kingship grounds sanctioned by the gods; whereas in Europe throughout all the Middle Ages and much of modern times, the distinction between noble and commoner was accepted partly as a right of conquest but ultimately sanctioned on religious grounds. When belief in hereditary principle and inherent inequality of people begins to wane and ultimately disappears, ultimate establishment of a class system is indicated. By the end of the Roman Republic, for example, the plebeians hardly believed in the inherent superiority of the patricians, and a class system was beginning to emerge; that it did not ultimately materialize may be attributed to the sequential effect of the principate, the orientalization of society, and the establishment of Christianity as the official religion of the empire. In modern European society spearheaded by the bourgeoisie, however, the naturalization and secularization of society ultimately lead to class stratification, as the effective constraints of the hereditary principle become upper-class bound. Once a class system comes into being, intrinsic power and wealth take the place of hereditary stratification assorters (Cobban 1969:214–18).

In Europe since the fall of the Roman Empire, the inherent superiority of the nobility has been accepted by the dominant and dominated estates alike. Although the privileges that noble status entailed were occasionally questioned, frequently leading to violent confrontation between segments of the two estates, the belief in the inherent superiority of the noble estate was not seriously questioned until well into modern times. This development was primarily fostered by the naturalization and secularization of society, which clearly pointed to religion and the supernatural as the grounds for the belief's justification (Nutini and Roberts n.d.). The origin of the nobiliary system's privileges must be sought first in the confrontation and amalgamation of the estate system of the Romans and the invading Germanic nations and second in the ensuing feudal system.

Although most noble privileges were perhaps rooted in custom, they were ultimately almost all sanctioned juridically. Certainly by the twelfth century noble privileges had been codified, and whatever new privileges were instituted thereafter were sanctioned by law. Noble privileges applied to both individuals and property and regulated many social, political, and economic domains. The most important structural characteristic of noble privileges was that they were hereditary. The noble estate, however, was constantly invigorated by commoners joining its ranks, either by means of ennoblement or through acquisition of a noble estate. As early as the twelfth century, commoners could obtain privileges of nobility without ennoblement. This phenomenon provides a significant background to the rise of the bourgeoisie in later centuries and sets a precedent for the regular usurpation of noble privileges that characterized the formation of the bourgeoisie in modern times. Once commoners had secured privileges, particularly by royal grant or by the acquisition of landed estates, ennoblement was a short step. This sequence usually characterized the movement of bourgeois into the noble estate, at least from the thirteenth century onward (Powis 1984:8–23).

There were two types of noble privileges: corporate and noncorporate. Corporate privileges were those enjoyed by the entire noble estate, regardless of position in the hierarchical order. Corporate privileges were the overall attributes that defined and characterized the noble estate as against the commoner estate. Noncorporate privileges, by contrast, were enjoyed exclusively by certain segments of the nobility in ways that varied greatly from kingdom to kingdom. The most salient discriminating factors in this respect were the distinction between *haute noblesse* and *petite noblesse* (peerage and gentry) and the rank conferred by titles (from knight to duke). The privileges of the higher nobility far surpassed those of the lesser nobility, and were located primarily in social and economic domains. Meanwhile, not every title of nobility entailed specific privileges; rather, privileges of rank roughly discriminated between the higher and lower titles of the system, and privileges generally concerned political participation and precedence. The privileges themselves were seigneurial and general (noble). Seigneurial privileges, going back to Roman times, focused on the land tenure and regulated the landlord-tenant relationship, although in certain instances these privileges were held independently of landownership (Bush 1983:6–25). Noble privileges, in general, are of feudal origin and represent the political and economic adaptions of subsequent centuries (Mackrell 1973:47–79).

Seigneurial privileges are nearly synonymous with feudal rights, at least as far as land tenure is concerned. Under Feudalism, most of the nobility enjoyed these privileges, since the land rested overwhelmingly in the hands of the warrior aristocracy. Beginning in the thirteenth century, however, as commoners acquired sizable amounts of land and the king created many landless nobles, seigneurial privileges became increasingly restricted in most parts of Europe. Seigneurial privileges regulated the relationship of the lord to his villeins and serfs, and, later, to his freer tenant farmers; they also obtained in certain contexts and situations not directly tied to land tenure (Bush 1984:27–33). Seigneurial privileges covered a wide range of categories, the most common of which were the following: (1) Dues, private taxes, and services rendered to the lord (titled noble or gentry). Tenure of the land was posited on the payment of dues or rents that the lord received in cash or kind and that constituted one of the peasant's heaviest burdens. Occasional direct taxation (tallage), which after the thirteenth century became annual levies, was used for such purposes as to wage war, to finance the lord's ransom, to provide hospitality to strangers, and so on. (2) Local justice. Insofar as seigneurial courts of law administered local justice beyond the king's justice, fines, adjudications, and all forms of litigation were income-producing activities for the lord. (3) Local administration, rights of jurisdiction, and conscription. Gathered under these rubrics were several seigneurial rights that were not only income producing but that served to control the lord's latifundia and adjacent communities. (4) Monopoly of commercial activities, rights of extraction, and usufruct, the most common of which were: monopoly in the production of oil, wine, and other spirits; exclusive rights of fishing and hunting; and exclusive rights to mineral resources. (5) Public rights of preemption and first sale. Under this category the most common items were taxation on the sale of alcohol and dues extracted for access to pasture land and water use. (6) Rights of precedence and preeminence in public gatherings: to have special pews and sit in front of the church, to be first in all processions, to command special respect and deference at social and political gatherings; and so on. (7) Social and economic control over the tenant population. This privilege embraced a rather wide range of contexts and situations, including the right to move freely, to migrate, and to marry (Bush 1983:144–69; Slicher van Bath 1963).[1]

General noble privileges were the property of the entire noble estate, or, in a restricted sense, of one of the two main divisions of it, the higher or lesser nobility. General noble privileges overlapped seigneurial privileges to a large extent, since most nobles possessed landed estates, but the overlapping diminished in modern times as the number of non-landed nobles increased (Bush 1984:81–93). General noble privileges regulated the relationship between the noble and commoner estates, and as such they included the free and unfree peasant populations as well as the urban populations from which the bourgeoisie originated. They include: (1) Tax exemptions, fiscal concessions, and private taxation. These privileges were the most troublesome for the nobility. (2) Rights of political participation, promotion, and special functions. These privileges secured exclusive or preferential membership in parliaments, diets, and other representative bodies. (3) Honorific privileges and rights: titles of nobility, coats of arms and other bearings, special forms of address, bearing arms, wearing sumptuous dress, and preferential or exclusive access to military orders, educational institutions, and religious orders. (4) Exclusivity of land ownership. This category embraces rules of inheritance, entailment of property, power of alienating certain categories of property, and so on. (5) Indemnity from judicial obligations and services to the state, a privilege that protected the nobility from many obligations required from the commonality. (6) Trading concessions, covering a variety of monopolies, ranging from the manufacture of spirits and cloth to the distribution of items of primary subsistence. These privileges placed segments of the nobility in direct competition with the rising bourgeoisie. (7) The right to hunt and fish. This privilege guaranteed the exclusive right of nobles to hunt and fish in lands and forests in the "public" domain (Bush 1983:27–143; Lewis 1974; Duby 1968).

It is impossible to do justice to the variation and strength of noble privilege in European society from the late Middle Ages to the twentieth century, but I hope with the following few generalizations to put noble privilege in structural and diachronic perspective as a concomitant aspect of the decline of the noble estate and the rise of the bourgeoisie. Seigneurial privileges in western Europe in the late Middle Ages and early modern times changed and ultimately disappeared not because of government centralization but for economic reasons relating to the more efficient use of land and rational employment of labor by the end of the seventeenth century. Nonetheless, the privileges of judicial and civil administration and the rights of precedence and preeminence persisted until the nineteenth century. And, indeed, in Great Britain both the gentry (at the local level) and the peerage (at the provincial or district level) monopolized judicial and civil administration until the twentieth century (Bush 1984:99–132). By contrast, in France, Spain, and Germany the overall survival of seigneurial privileges was more extensive and lasted longer than in Great Britain. Seigneurial privileges affected the higher and lesser nobility equally, inasmuch as these privileges were held by virtue of land ownership and not because of noble status. In Great Britain, for example, as early as the sixteenth century there were members of the gentry who owned as much land as the greatest titled magnates, but on the whole, particularly from the nineteenth century on, peers owned much more land than the gentry. In political terms this situation meant that until well into the twentieth century the influence of peers extended to the district, whereas that of the gentry was strictly local (Montagu of Beaulieu 1970:138–58).

General noble privileges, both corporate and noncorporate, are more difficult to characterize, given the cleavage between higher and lesser nobility and the fact that they both served to stratify and define the noble estate as a whole. The different ranks (from baron to duke) of the higher nobility varied significantly in the degree that privileges accrued to them. On the one hand, the corporate privileges that defined the noble estate, regardless of rank and the higher-lesser distinction, were rather low and centered mostly on honorific privileges (coats of arms, other armorial bearing, forms of address) and a few judicial rights (exemptions from certain military duties, trial by special tribunals). On the other hand, the configuration of privileges enjoyed by the higher and lesser nobility was more pronounced, and on the whole the higher nobility was much more privileged than the lesser nobility in most countries of Europe (Bush 1983:186–99). The distribution of noble privileges by kingdom also varied greatly, sometimes within the provinces of the same country. In a rough scale of noble privileges, England, northern Italy, and The Netherlands had the least privileged nobilities; France, Spain, and Austria had the most privileged nobility; and the nobilities of Germany and eastern Europe fell somewhere in between (Spring 1977; Bush 1984).

Unlike seigneurial privileges, general (corporate and noncorporate) noble privileges were directly related to the rise of absolutism, the centralization of government, and the overall liberalization of national states. In this sense noble privileges constituted an integral part of the general restructuring of European society that began in the sixteenth century and came to a head at the end of the eighteenth century, namely, the rather slow evolution from a strictly estate-organized society to a class-organized society in which stratification was not based on hereditary advantages but on "natural" constraints. Until the mid-seventeenth century, all privileges described above were discharged in most parts of Europe. Thereafter, however, noble privileges began to decline rapidly. As in the case of seigneurial privileges, the noble privileges that had to do with fiscal matters, taxation, and general economics changed more quickly, and by the end of the eighteenth century several fiscal privileges had disappeared entirely and most had been much diminished. Honorific privileges, conversely, survived almost unchanged until the French Revolution, and political or administrative privileges survived in significantly modified form. Loss and modification of privileges did not, however, wholly disrupt the noble estate, and until the French Revolution and its aftermath the European aristocracy maintained its identity as a distinct superordinate estate (Thompson 1977). In sum, the 250 years that elapsed from the middle of the sixteenth century to the end of the eighteenth century must be regarded as the evolution of the social stratification of Europe from a monolithic estate system to an incipient class system in which the bourgeoisie, or more exactly, the haute bourgeoisie, spanned the lower sector of the noble estate and the upper sector of the commoner estate.

USURPATION OF PRIVILEGES AND BOURGEOIS UPWARD MOBILITY

The roots and economic force of the bourgeoisie go back to the early fifteenth century, but the social presence and ideological underpinnings of this incipient class were shaped by the rationalistic and naturalistic worldview of European society after the Renaissance and during the Enlightenment. By the beginning of the Industrial Revolution, the bourgeoisie had a firm place in politics and the state bureaucracy, and the haute bourgeoisie had become a distinct plutocracy, well placed to vie successfully for social recognition. The model of social exaltedness remained the aristocracy until the twentieth century, but from the middle of the eighteenth century, the plutocratic haute bourgeoisie defined the canons of upward mobility and inevitably modified the ancien régime conception of aristocracy by the ennoblement of large numbers of plutocrats (Powis 1984:81–102). From the late seventeenth century onward the plutocratic haute bourgeoisie slowly forced changes that ultimately redefined the concept of aristocracy as entailing not only ascribed attributes (ancient lineage and heredity) but also achieved attributes such as economic power and wealth. Intellectual liberalism led to political liberalism, and, in some countries peacefully, in others by force or revolution, the commonality forced concessions from monarchies, further sapping the political and economic preeminence of the noble estate. At this point, a class system emerged that spanned the entire society.

The ascendancy of the bourgeoisie is most expressively illustrated by the usurpation of noble privileges. Usurpation applied entirely to general noble privileges, since seigneurial privileges were not exclusively entailed by noble status but were a function of owning landed estates, which the most successful commoners began to acquire as early as the fourteenth century. What did usurpation mean? Commoners appropriated specific privileges of the nobility without due royal or official sanction. By modern times, usurpation had become commonplace, gathering momentum in the sixteenth and seventeenth centuries. By the eighteenth century and until the demise of most nobiliary systems in Europe by the end of the nineteenth century, usurpation had become second nature to the upwardly mobile sectors of the bourgeoisie. Customarily, the usurper appropriated a noble privilege and secured it through subsequent legal subterfuge, ultimately parlaying the privilege into noble status (Bush 1983:123–30).

The most common of noble privileges usurped by commoners were honorific rights, especially coats of arms, armorial bearings, forms of address, and carrying arms. Indeed, the haute bourgeoisie of modern times so much abused these honors that by the nineteenth century it was impossible to discriminate accurately between the lower sectors of the nobility and the upper sectors of the commonality. From the beginning of centralization, the acquisition of wealth had become the main avenue of upward mobility in Europe, and the exclusivity of landownership and trading concessions became targets of usurpation as early as the fifteenth century. The acquisition of a landed estate was perhaps the surest means available to a commoner for elevation to noble status, and in England and to some extent in western Europe, many rich commoners had become gentry through this subterfuge, buttressed by the manipulation of honorific privileges (Bush 1983:131–40). Until late medieval times, the extreme concern with pedigree had been an exclusively noble preoccupation, but the rising bourgeoisie quickly grasped its utility in the usurpation of honorific privileges.

Usurpation of rights of political participation was also, however, a significant avenue of upward mobility that appeared roughly at the end of the sixteenth century. This phenomenon was related to royal centralization, which led to increasing numbers of commoners holding offices of state. By the middle of the nineteenth century, political participation of commoners had become generalized throughout Europe. From the sixteenth century to the de jure abolition of the estate system (roughly between 1789 and 1850), perhaps every privilege detailed in the preceding discussion was a target for usurpation by upwardly mobile commoners. This drawn-out struggle characterized the transition from estate to class stratification in European society (Domínguez Ortiz 1955).

Customary and judicial inequality characterized Western stratification until the abolition of the estates and the establishment of equality of all citizens before the law. The earliest, sporadic manifestations of class elements and of cracks in the estate system appear in the late Middle Ages, and incipient classes appeared in the seventeenth century. During the following critical 200-year period, the concept of class took shape as a manifestation of the more rationalistic and naturalistic approach to the world triggered by the Renaissance. These two centuries, particularly the eighteenth century, may be characterized as laying the foundations of class stratification. Revolutionary action or enlightened self-interest forced the noble estate, from king to knight, to make concessions that resulted in the establishment of republics or constitutional monarchies in which by law most privileges were abolished and, at least theoretically, all citizens became equal before the law. At this point, the class system de jure came into being, although de facto it took longer to coalesce into its contemporary form. The United States was probably the first national state to be truly stratified in terms of class, although purists may rightly argue that the presence of slavery negates the case. By the middle of the nineteenth century, most of western Europe had a class system in place (Kamen 1971).

To sort out causes and effects in the evolution of European society after the Renaissance is a monumental task. The problem of explaining the change from estate to class stratification is particularly vexing. It is simple enough to describe the transformation, as I have done in this section, but quite another matter to clearly trace the multiple causal factors of the process. For example, many scholars have affirmed that the rise of a class system in modern European society is directly related to the ideological change toward an increasingly more rational and naturalistic worldview. But how this new imago mundi became specifically efficacious, and, more fundamentally, how it came to predominate and what material and techno-environmental conditions produced it, is a problem that no social scientist has yet solved. It seems likely that the desacralization of society produced a society that from the early sixteenth century on questioned and ultimately changed radically the established social order. Yet no one has formulated a theory that explains the transformation from estate to social class while still preserving the fundamental attribute of stratification, namely, the division of society into segments characterized by an unequal distribution of influence, economic well-being, and social prestige.

Class Stratification, the Haute Bourgeoisie, and Aristocratic Decline

With the demise of the ancien régime, usually traced to the French Revolution and its aftermath, we enter the domain of classical sociology. Given the scope of the present study and the dearth of studies on upper-class stratification, I limit my analysis to aristocratic and plutocratic interaction. I outline the decline of the European aristocracy, its ultimate demise as a significant political and economic force, its survival as a social class, and its increasing association and ultimate amalgamation with the plutocracy. This entity came to include elements of aristocratic as well as plutocratic extraction and for lack of a better term has been designated as *haute bourgeoisie*. As long as the term is understood to include the most exalted segments (social, ruling, political) of a social system, haute bourgeoisie is an appropriate designation for the superordinate class of the stratification system. A word of caution: Although structurally and ideologically the transformation of European society from estate to class was fundamental and most certainly ameliorated social and economic interaction and redounded in more egalitarian societies, it did not significantly minimize stratification.

END OF THE ANCIEN RÉGIME AND BEGINNINGS OF CLASS STRATIFICATION

The concerted liberalization of society that occurred in the eighteenth century challenged the fundamental assumptions of the estate system. Enlightened self-interest and concrete social and economic pressures and constraints had been fueling changes in the privileges of the nobility for most of the century, but evidently not as fast as the bourgeoisie and the commonality as a whole expected. The explosion came with the French Revolution, which shocked all European nobilities, and the estate system was never the same again (Bush 1983:78–120). The ancien régime (the estate system in its changing but still classically oppressive form) began its rapid disintegration with the French Revolution and the Napoleonic Wars, which brought the successive demise of economic, political, social, and symbolic privileges of the nobility. The French Revolution did not establish representative democracies, and the Napoleonic interlude ensured that two generations would pass before such an end was achieved. The great importance of the French Revolution—and indeed of the American Revolution—was ideological; it emboldened the commonalities of Europe to push the nobility toward a more egalitarian society (Myers 1975:37–65).

By the middle of the nineteenth century, a class system was in place in most countries of Europe, and estates had effectively ceased to exist. Political power and wealth were no longer primarily determined by birth and heredity, though social prestige remained for much longer the realm of the dying aristocracy. By the early twentieth century, the nobility had vanished as an organic component of Western society, although in most countries titles of nobility were still very much in vogue. From 1900, then, it is more appropriate to refer to the vanishing nobility as an aristocracy by virtue of their still undisputed claim to social exaltedness. The political, economic, and social lives of most

European countries were thereafter dominated by an upper class that included a rising plutocracy and new political class, members of the titled nobility, and significant numbers of the gentry or lesser nobility. The titled nobility still factored into the stratification equation, as titles were the last privileges to have operational significance. Meanwhile, the gentry either merged with the haute bourgeoisie or led a marginal existence, becoming practically indistinguishable from what sociologists later referred to as the upper and upper-middle classes. By the middle of the twentieth century, the transformation was complete, and the aristocracy was essentially an expressive concern or locus of realization. The last of the symbolic privileges and dignities of the titled nobility stood now only for a stubbornly unrealistic concern with the past (Bush 1983:79–103).

Despite bourgeois-led revolutions and the struggle of the commonality for political and economic recognition, the aristocracy, that is, the titled nobility and gentry, exhibited surprising staying power and enterprise not only in the social but in the political, administrative, and economic domains. Here again the British aristocracy led the way, but even in countries such as Austria and Hungary, the titled nobility managed to stay at the top until the First World War, partly because of their dominance in the armed forces (Anderson 1974:69–107). Centuries of institutional advantage and the traditional occupation of this former warrior caste explain the preponderance of the European aristocracy in the officer corps of national armies and navies until well into the twentieth century. Indeed, beyond the domain of manners and expression, the armed forces were the last bastions of real aristocratic power (Montagu of Beaulieu 1970:67–86).

Though the European aristocracy engaged in trade and commercial activities as early as the late Middle Ages, by far their main source of wealth and revenue was land. With the Industrial Revolution and the great mining and manufacturing enterprises that accompanied it, landed wealth was quickly displaced by industrial wealth, and by the middle of the nineteenth century many a plutocratic haut bourgeois was richer than most landed aristocrats. There were exceptions, of course, but for the most part aristocratic plutocrats did not join the industrial and manufacturing establishment nor the banking and financial establishment that in the nineteenth century grew out of the Industrial Revolution. The traditional aversion to accumulating wealth by any means other than those directly related to land prevented the aristocracy from competing successfully with the rising plutocratic haute bourgeoisie (Powis 1984:23–37).

Throughout the Middle Ages the nobility neither monopolized appointment to high church offices nor unduly controlled ecclesiastical administration, and religion in Western society remained the most democratic domain to which commoners could aspire. In modern times, particularly after 1600, law and scholarship attracted new interest. In France, an inordinate number of scholars during the Enlightenment were of aristocratic extraction. In the nineteenth century, however, England took the palm, and a great number of its scientists and philosophers were established members of the gentry. Possibly due to the establishment of universal education and more intellectual opportunities for the middle and lower classes, the preponderance of aristocrats in scholarship ended with the onset of the twentieth century (Perrot 1968:93–109).

Titles of nobility, armorial bearings, and coats of arms have always been the validating symbols of nobility. Armorial bearings and coats of arms have been the main attributes validating the status of the gentry, the nontitled nobility from baronet down, and since the Middle Ages the most difficult to regulate, despite the efforts of monarchies and the various colleges instituted for this purpose. Indeed, by late modern times armorial bearings and coats of arms had become largely unregulated and the easiest trappings of noble status to usurp. For this reason, most upwardly mobile plutocrats have availed themselves of these instruments in the quest for status recognition. Titles of nobility, on the other hand, were more strictly controlled, at least in most European nations until the turn of the century, and have retained their potency as a symbol of aristocratic affiliation. With the establishment of republican government, titles of nobility were abolished in most European countries and came to have strictly honorific connotations. In countries with constitutional monarchies, titles of nobility were recognized by the state, and in most cases the nobiliary system continued to be regulated by officially appointed bodies (Bush 1983:130–40).

By the mid-twentieth century, however, titles of nobility had become largely customary, except in Britain. Although nobiliary titles had been abused before the end of the ancien régime, from 1800 onward titles proliferated as a result of royal patronage, political expediency, and changes in the inheritance system away from primogeniture to a system in which all children of a noble inherited his title. These pervasive trends vulgarized nobiliary titles to the point that nowadays it is often difficult to discriminate between genuine traditional titles and those acquired deviously or by association or proliferation. As a social phenomenon, aristocratic affiliation in Europe is still very much treasured, but interest in titles has waned. It is enough to know that one belongs to a distinguished family, that one can document an ancient aristocratic lineage, but to flaunt titles in public has become the mark of insecure bourgeois behavior. Perhaps it is only in Great Britain, where the general public still accords the aristocracy an inordinate degree of deference and respect, that actual titles perpetuate an ambiance of traditional aristocratic values and behavior (Perrot 1968:254–71).

From 1500 onward, there was a steady proliferation of titles generated by royal favoritism, the need for more revenue, and the continuation of the traditional practice of rewarding excellence in government and military service. The new wealth generated by colonization, the intrinsic growth of the European economy, and the Industrial Revolution created a new class of plutocrats of both bourgeois and gentry origin that vied successfully for royal patronage and titles of nobility. Though undoubtedly the growth of the nobiliary system resulted significantly from venal royal policy, it primarily reflected the liberalization of the stratification system and the increasing economic and political power of a haute bourgeoisie. In the eighteenth century, the majority of titles in most European countries were being awarded to the new capitalists, successful government bureaucrats, and administrators close to the Crown (Warner 1960:47–59).

The British constitutional monarchy, however, went beyond conferring noble titles simply to stabilize the upper sectors of the social system and to provide a symbol of upward mobility. First, from the eighteenth century the British monarchy, more than any continental monarchy, consistently awarded titles of nobility to public servants. Distinguished service to the Crown was certain to be rewarded with a baronetcy, a viscountship, or an earldom, regardless of social provenance. Thus, throughout the nineteenth century scientific and scholarly excellence and creative generation of wealth, in addition to the traditional political and military pursuits, were consistently rewarded by the Crown with the by now largely symbolic and honorific award of a knighthood, baronetcy, or title of nobility. Second, knighthoods, baronetcies, and titles for life have been awarded to hundreds, perhaps thousands, of commoners who have excelled in most professions and disciplines, tending to perpetuate the notion of the British aristocracy as unique, as an abode of excellence, and as preserving some of the values of the old system. In reality, the Crown and the hereditary aristocracy of Great Britain bear no resemblance to the new system of titles for life, and profound class differences persist in this society as compared to those of most continental countries (Mingay 1976:107–31).

EMBOURGEOISEMENT OF THE ARISTOCRACY AND ARISTOCRATIZATION OF THE BOURGEOISIE

Since the French Revolution, the European aristocracy has been dwindling in the face of growing social classes and the steady democratization of society. If the aristocracy has been undergoing a slow but steady process of decline for more than two hundred years, however, the decline has been considerably slowed by traditional constraints that have prolonged the visible life of the aristocracy. The progression of the decline is the roughly as follows. Until the French Revolution, the aristocracy was the ruling, social, and, to some extent, political class (or estate) of all European countries. By the middle of the nineteenth century, it was no longer the undisputed ruling class, for its wealth had been diminished by the powerful enterprise of the bourgeoisie. By the turn of the century, the aristocracy was definitely not a ruling class, and as a political class it was in its last stage of disintegration, the power of which was lost after World War I. By the middle of the twentieth century, the aristocracy was nothing more than a social class, still at the top of the stratification system, but sharing honors with the very rich haute bourgeoisie (Powis 1984:81–101).

Aristocratic life has been characterized since medieval times by great consumption and much pomp and circumstance—in short, a style of living that demanded armies of servants and many resources. From great titled magnates to local gentry, the maintenance of aristocratic behavior demanded the expenditure of much revenue, and aristocrats have always been notorious for spending beyond their means. From the French Revolution onward, this pattern of expression began to change for two main reasons. First, fear of attracting hostile attention to their wasteful and conspicuous consumption forced the aristocracy to lead a more circumspect lifestyle as it became the foci of revolutionary action during the first half of the nineteenth century. Thenceforward the great palaces, mansions, and establishments of the aristocracy shrank steadily. Second, landed wealth was no match for industrial and banking wealth, and therefore the aristocracy steadily lost economic power. By the turn of the century, most continental aristocracies lost much of their land; only in Great Britain did the aristocracy retain its land wealth. The years between 1850 and 1914 were hard ones for the European aristocracy; they experienced economic hardship from which most of them never entirely recuperated. Aristocrats not only lost most of their land but they had to sell much of their great art in order to survive. Thus, fear of public opinion and loss of wealth meant not only a drastically scaled-down expressive life for the European aristocracy, but the dismantling of the great establishments that for centuries had been the most ostensible symbols of its once undisputed power and wealth (Powis 1984:89–105).

Perhaps the best term for this process of downward expressive mobility is *embourgeoisement* (Bush 1984:158). Becoming bourgeoislike is exactly what the aristocracy has been doing since the middle of the nineteenth century; the process has accelerated since World War II. Embourgeoisement has been a common aristocratic pattern of decline in most European countries. Some of the great titled nobles retain a significant place, though most titled nobles have come down a few notches; some of the gentry are still recognizable, but most of them are now part of the upper-middle class. Great palaces have been transformed into state museums; landed estates have become country retreats for the weekend. Once great public figures and personalities, aristocrats today have almost gone underground; once notable political actors and statesmen, great plutocrats, and reputable scholars, most aristocrats today engage in low-level politics, work as middle-level businessmen or industrialists, or even join the liberal professions (Perrot 1968:130–41).

Let us finally turn our attention to the other side of this equation: the haute bourgeoisie. From the decades preceding the French Revolution to the end of the Napoleonic Wars, the haute bourgeoisie had coalesced into a definite social class of plutocrats involved in business, banking, and manufacturing and including an array of high-ranking politicians and illustrious members of the professional sector. They were undoubtedly the first limited social class, sociologically defined, to emerge from the ashes of the ancien régime. From now on, however, the core driving force of the haute bourgeoisie was very rich plutocrats and high government officials. It is with this group of the haute bourgeoisie that the aristocracy entered into a relationship of acculturative interaction. Throughout the following 150 years the haute bourgeoisie steadily wrested power and wealth from the aristocracy, but in the accompanying acculturative transfer, they acquired much of its emerging expressive array of manners and behavior (Montagu of Beaulieu 1970:138–63).

Up to the end of the ancien régime, bourgeois plutocrats and other commoners who had risen high in government aspired to ennoblement, and those at the top achieved their goal. From the expressive perspective, the aristocratic model of manners and behavior was the only one available that satisfied upwardly mobile aspirations. This basic equation remained unchanged until the end of the nineteenth century. In the early stages of development particularly, distinguished members of the haute bourgeoisie sought ennoblement, assiduously cultivated the aristocracy, and lavishly copied its patterns of expression and behavior. The first phase of intense and sustained plutocratic haute bourgeoisie–aristocratic interaction, lasting roughly from the beginning to the end of the nineteenth century, entailed upwardly mobile members of the bourgeoisie vying for aristocratic affiliation, securing this distinction by ennoblement or, most commonly, by close social interaction with the gentry or titled nobility. The primary qualification for attaining aristocratic status was full control over the expressive and behavioral code of the aristocracy, still the undisputed model of appropriate conduct. Over this four-generation period, original plutocratic postulants became bona fide members of the aristocracy (Montagu of Beaulieu 1970:93–107).

The character of the basic equation began to change subtly in the twentieth century, particularly on the continent, where titles of nobility had not been granted since the early twentieth century. From this time onward, the haute bourgeoisie began to assert themselves, propelled by their increasing confidence and generations of learning and the rapidly decreasing power and wealth of the aristocracy. For the first time the haute bourgeoisie fashioned their own ambiance of social and expressive realization independently of the aristocracy. This process so accelerated after the Second World War that many aristocrats began to identify more and more with the distinct haut bourgeois worldview that was beginning to emerge. Until shortly before the Second World

War, the overall interaction of the aristocracy and the haute bourgeoisie had been characterized by the aristocratization of the latter. With increasing rapidity after the war, the surviving aristocracy became more and more like the aristocratized haute bourgeoisie (Montagu of Beaulieu 1970:61–80).

This process of honorific usurpation began in the sixteenth century, gathered momentum in the seventeenth century, and became generalized in the eighteenth century. As European society became more fluid, there was a general loss of respect for the nobility. The bourgeoisie, in particular, felt that achievement and excellence should be rewarded regardless of lineage and heredity. As early as the seventeenth century a new sense of self-respect, of the individual's intrinsic worth, appeared, or rather reappeared, in the more affluent and dynamic sectors of the commonality. Quietly at first but with increasing firmness, they demanded to be treated respectfully by the nobility. This trend represented a return to the public concept of the citizen that had nearly vanished with the Germanic destruction of the Roman Empire. It had, however, survived for more than a thousand years in the small urban environments that had escaped Feudalism. The first century of modern times was still a period of effective control by the European nobility, but the first well-documented cases of usurpation of honorific terms of address can be traced to the sixteenth century.

In the seventeenth century, honorific terms of address applying to the nobility began to change rapidly and to include increasing numbers of the bourgeoisie who had become rich and important (Lefevre 1970:46–78). Two examples are illustrative. Most of the everyday terms of address that are used today in English ("master," "mistress," "mister," "misses," "miss"), and their equivalents in most European languages, were originally honorific forms of address entailed by noble or customary privilege. As late as the end of the Middle Ages, these forms of address were enforced by custom and local law, and though upwardly mobile commoners occasionally appropriated these and other terms, there was no mass usurpation that concerned the noble estate. During the sixteenth century, however, usurpation of terms of address became common. The evolution of the Spanish term *don* (feminine *doña;* from Latin *dominus*) provides a more precise example. Originally, probably until the end of the fifteenth century, *don* was used exclusively to address nobles of high rank, lords of seigneuries, and titled nobles in general. From the beginning of the sixteenth century the term was extended to members of the gentry and knightly classes, and it is in this sense that Cervantes named his hero Don Quijote de la Mancha. From the eighteenth century onward, the term *don* was progressively vulgarized, and by the nineteenth century it had become a term of respect for any person of some consequence regardless of status and rank. In the New World particularly, *don* had lost all noble or genteel connotations, and newly arrived Spaniards were shocked at the vulgarization of the term (Durand 1953:31–39).

The other example concerns the development of the concepts of gentleman and gentility. The term gentleman derives from the Latin *gentiles* (gens member). Until the middle of the sixteenth century, gentlemen and their equivalents in continental countries were regarded as noble individuals who were generally members of the gentry, although most of them were no longer landowners, forming instead an urban segment of the lesser, untitled nobility. Although the term *gentleman* as a social category has quintessential British connotations, it finds equivalent expressions in continental countries, and I use it as a comparative concept. By the sixteenth century, gentlemen in Britain were no longer a distinct category of the nobility, to say nothing of the aristocracy, which by that time was already firmly structured in terms of peers and gentry (Fox-Davis 1895:32–43). On the continent, however, all individuals entitled to the appellation gentleman were still regarded as members of the lesser nobility. As upwardly mobile new plutocrats and government officials of commoner origin and members of the gentry and nobility interacted increasingly during the seventeenth century, the concept of gentleman underwent its first transformation: it ceased to denote an exclusive category of the lesser nobility and acquired its first achieved attributes, namely, an upgrading of status due to proper behavior and accepted social and economic interaction with members of the nobility. By the end of the eighteenth century, the term *gentleman* had lost most of its exclusive hereditary attributes. By the middle of the nineteenth century, probably the majority of gentlemen were of commoner extraction, but the achieved status of gentlemen implied the acquisition of a coat of arms, which by then it was not difficult to obtain. This development exemplifies the second transformation: although "gentleman" had ceased to have an exclusive aristocratic association, and the majority, perhaps the great majority, of gentlemen were of haute bourgeoise extraction, they still felt compelled to buttress their status with a symbol of aristocratic association. From the middle of the nineteenth century onward, and particularly after the turn of the century, the designation of gentleman lost all aristocratic attribution. Thus arrived the final transformation: the concept of the gentleman now implied breeding, "culture," honorability, good manners, and, in a residual sense, noblesse oblige, as befit a category of original noble affiliation now with variable meaning to each class of society.

Arisocratic Survival and Bourgeois Dominance

The evolution of gentility is the collective correlate of the evolution of the gentleman as a social category. Gentility may be defined as the adoption of appropriate manners by the haute bourgeoisie, who learned from the nobility and the gentry the correct behavior and expressive mechanisms that would bring them social acceptance and ultimate amalgamation with the superordinate stratum. In the early stages of this process, gentility was an individual asset, but as the power and influence of the haute bourgeoisie grew, and its numbers increased after the middle of the nineteenth century, gentility became a collective phenomenon. The appropriate behavior for successful upward mobility was based on an aristocratic model and manners of the nobility, but the haute bourgeoisie also modified these expressive and behavioral patterns. In the final stage of this creative process of acculturation from the turn of the century to the present, the plutocratic haute bourgeoisie assumed firm control of the stratification system, and the aristocracy came to play a rather small role. In short, gentility in the second half of the twentieth century is as much a part of the aristocratic worldview as it is the creation of the powerful haute bourgeoisie (Wiener 1981:193–98).

Indeed, not only has the aristocratic *imago mundi* survived, though modified, but the aristocracy as a social class itself survived until the second half of the twentieth century, despite the downward mobility of the higher and, especially, the lesser nobility. Insofar as the various European aristocracies were able to engage successfully in public life— many aristocrats competed successfully as professional administrators, soldiers, and politicians—they survived as more than mere social classes. Nevertheless, the demise of the ancien régime initiated a drastic change in the social stratification of Europe. Until the end of the eighteenth century, the superordinate estate constituted a united, fairly monolithic political class, ruling class, and social class; from then on, the aristocracy consecutively lost its monopoly as a political class, ruling class, and, now in the second half of the twentieth century, it is on the verge of being superseded as a social class by a haute bourgeoisie, of which it forms a significant but no longer the most salient part. Power has lost its aristocratic associations, heredity and rank have ceased to structure the social order, but the tendency to aristocratize power and wealth and to make them hereditary whenever possible has not disappeared (Powis 1984:101).

The survival of the aristocracy was essential for the growth of the haute bourgeoisie, for the former provided the fundamental model of expression and a worldview that furnished a new identity for the latter. The haute bourgeoisie was configured by the survival of the aristocracy as a social class, and indeed these two sectors coalesced as a fairly distinct social order by the beginning of the twentieth century.

Finally, a few words on the ethos and ideology of the European aristocracy. With a degree of national diversity, the aristocracy exhibited a remarkable consistency and continuity in values and behavior as it evolved from its classical roots to the Dark Ages, the Middle Ages, and modern times. In its various evolutionary forms of warrior caste, civilian ruling class, and declining social class, the aristocracy's fundamental values have changed in response to economic, political, and material realities, but have nonetheless retained an ideological core: deep concern with honor and dignity, perpetuation of family and lineage, conspicuous consumption and a passion for exhibition and display, aversion to manual labor and active pursuit of pleasure, and a distinct preoccupation with etiquette (Bush 1983:71–77).

The term *haute bourgeoisie,* as it has been used in the foregoing account, denotes two complementary groups. From the end of the ancien régime to the turn of the twentieth century, the haute bourgeoisie denoted the most upwardly mobile members of the economic, political, and social elites of the various European national states. These various elements of middle-class extraction were *la crème de la crème* of the European plutocracy and political establishment; the aristocracy, though rapidly evolving, still constituted a separate sector in the higher stratification of European society. From the turn of the century onward, the haute bourgeoisie denotes the rising ruling class that became established after the Second World War as the uppermost sector of the European stratification system. The surviving aristocracy, as a minimally identifiable class, still has a place in this new equation, but increasingly as a function of nontraditional aristocratic involvements. Thus, the contemporary haute bourgeoisie in most European national contexts may be regarded as being composed of an aristocracy with modest claims to social exaltedness, a plutocracy of the richest of the rich, and a political sector (Pirenne 1966:103–5).

The three preceding chapters outline stratification from the beginning of Western Civilization until the present, emphasizing the upper classes and estates. The main objects of this exercise were twofold: first, to analyze the concepts of aristocracy, nobility, and gentility and their adaptation to changing economic, political, religious, and social milieux; second, to trace the evolution of estate and class, alone and in relation to one another, and the roles they have played in the structure and configuration of Western Civilization. I also wished here to provide a context for the analysis of the Mexican aristocracy until the Revolution of 1910.

PART 2

Evolution of the Mexican Aristocracy
from the Spanish Conquest to the
Present (1519–1990)

CHAPTER 4

The Conquest of Mexico and the Formation of a Landed Aristocracy in the Sixteenth Century

Early modern times were most distinctly characterized by the expansion of western European peoples throughout the world. By the end of the eighteenth century, European national states had conquered or colonized the New World and much of Africa, Asia, and Oceania. More than any of the great Colonial powers, Spain fashioned conquered lands and their peoples in its own image. When the Spanish possessions in the New World became independent in the first quarter of the nineteenth century after more than three centuries of Colonial domination, they were veritable extensions of the mother country, except in the political domain, for, at least in theory, most Latin American states became representative republics. Throughout Colonial times, and to a significant extent until today, the social, religious, urban, and intellectual life of Latin American nations closely reflected that of Spain, despite the survival and influence of ethnic diversity. One may classify nations as more European (Argentina, Chile, Uruguay) or more Indian (Bolivia, Mexico, Peru), but all Latin American countries share a common Hispanic heritage, most intensely and universally centered on the domains of social and religious interaction. The domain of social stratification and the general organization of society, particularly, reflect a worldview that is quintessentially Spanish, modified of course by local (national) traditions and constraints. Subjected to the same institutions of domination and exploitation throughout the sixteenth, seventeenth, and eighteenth centuries, all subdivisions of the Spanish Empire, from

California to Tierra del Fuego, developed similar social systems underlined by basically the same stratification system (Madariaga 1963:121–47). After over 170 years of existence as national states, the class system of these former colonies still betrays many elements of Spanish origin linked directly to specific institutions dating from the sixteenth century. This phenomenon is most noticeable in the upper sectors of the stratification system. Thus, in order to understand and explain upper-class stratification in most Latin American countries today, we must analyze several institutions employed in the conquest, colonization, and exploitation of the New World: the land tenure system, the organization of the conquered population, tribute paying, and the foundation of cities.

The next four chapters describe the inception, formation, development, and maturity of an aristocracy in the most valued possession of the Spanish Crown in the New World. I analyze the social, economic, political, and other variables that structured this Colonial aristocracy throughout nearly four hundred years. My account emphasizes the structural entailment and expressive configuration of the Colonial aristocracy. Its relationship to the other sectors of Colonial stratification will be explored only to illustrate processes of domination and control over the subordinate population and political accommodation to the imperial political class.

The Conquest: Antecedents, Execution, and Personnel

The Conquest of Mexico is generally understood to refer to the fall of the so-called Aztec Empire (the Triple Alliance) in central and southern Mexico, and particularly the destruction of Tenochtitlán, its most important capital city. This episode took place within four years, but accustoming the land and its people to domination and exploitation took longer. By the middle of the sixteenth century, however, most of what came to be known ethnologically and archaeologically as Mesoamerica had been incorporated into the Spanish Empire. A generation after the establishment of the viceroyalty of New Spain in 1532, Colonial society had acquired its characteristic traits, and the institutional framework for exploitation and control was implemented. By the end of the century, the social system of New Spain had crystallized, and it remained basically unchanged until the end of Colonial times (Weckmann 1984, 1:101–75). I do not mean to suggest that from 1600 to

1820 the system remained static, only that the society did not undergo any fundamental transformations.

SPANISH CULTURE AND SOCIETY AT THE END OF THE MIDDLE AGES

Under the Catholic kings, Spain became a centralized state, the independent power of the nobles was broken, and the nation initiated the trend toward absolutism in western Europe. These developments did not signal the end of seigneuralism, but they did soften the estate system and release forces and personnel of the commoner estate, effects that had significant consequences for the conquest and colonization of the New World.[1] More directly relevant to the Spanish imperial enterprise was the end of the Reconquest. For more than seven centuries, the Spanish kingdoms, originally founded by the Visigoths, had struggled against the Moorish occupation of the peninsula. In the last decade of the fifteenth century, under the leadership of Ferdinand and Isabella, they managed to conquer the kingdom of Granada, the last Moslem stronghold. More than any other western European country, Spain emerged from the Middle Ages a nationality forged by military struggle, a fact that undoubtedly affected the personnel, social constitutions, and general configuration of the conquest and colonization of the New World (Altamira 1969). No other country in Europe was in a better position to undertake this momentous enterprise.

In short, the fifteenth century was the dress rehearsal for the conquest and colonization of the New World, initiated by the discovery of the continent and the establishment of colonies as part of an enormous overseas empire. The almost constant state of confrontation that characterized Christian-Moslem relationships, punctuated by short-lived periods of accommodation, engendered a nationality forged in combat. All levels of society shared the belief that new horizons offered glory and social and economic advancement (Weckmann 1984, 1:139–52).

The institutions developed in Spain in the late Middle Ages were very important sociologically and stratificationally, and several of them played a leading role in the settlement, exploitation, and organization of New World colonies. Among them were the *cabildo* or *ayuntamiento* (city or town government), the foundation of new cities, and the organization of reconquered territories by rewarding participants in the enterprise. Even such Colonial institutions as the *encomienda* and *repartimiento* systems can be traced to late medieval Spain. Though most experts agree that the *encomienda* and *repartimiento* acquired their basic form in the Antilles and were then introduced into Mexico and the rest of the continent (Zavala 1973:13–39), antecedents can be found in Spain of the late Middle Ages in the *mercedes* (grants) awarded to important participants in the reconquered lands (Muñoz 1793:43–61; Solórzano Pereyra 1930). The other three institutions, however, are of distinct Spanish origin, and again they were by-products of the Reconquest and its system of rewards and incentives, or they were shaped by inputs from Moslem culture and society.

The *cabildo* is a quintessential Spanish institution of local government that prospered throughout the late Middle Ages. Similar forms of local government developed in northern Italy, the Low Countries, and other parts of western Europe as Feudalism began to wane at the end of the early Middle Ages. But the *cabildo,* as an integral institution of reconquered lands, towns, and cities, is originally Spanish, apparently evolving from the thirteenth century, when the pace of the Reconquest accelerated. The *cabildo* system involved the organization of a newly founded town in reconquered territory or the reorganization of an existing town or city that had been taken from the Moors. In both cases the *cabildo* acquired the same form: local government by a number of officials (*alcalde, regidores, alguaciles,* and so on) appointed by the commander of the conquering host, who was empowered by the king to select from among the most illustrious, able, or worthy participants in the successful enterprise (Casariego 1946:40–65). Given the strength of the estate system, membership in the *cabildo* was generally monopolized by the titled nobility and *hidalgos* (a contraction of "hijo de algo" [son of something], denoting the hereditary rank and economic status of the lesser noble), as were the spoils of conquest (Rodríguez Arzúa 1947). (The principle of ennoblement by right of conquest and by the performance of military exploits never completely faded in many regions of Spain, for entire communities in the Basque country and Asturias, the cradle of the Reconquest, considered themselves *hidalgos* even though they were not so recognized by the courts of nobility that existed in Spain as early as the beginning of the fourteenth century. It is this search for glory and personal recognition that motivated many of the New World conquistador and settlers.)

Equally important were the legal foundations of the *cabildo* system. Organized by their leader, the participants in the reconquest of land

and settlements had the right to become members of the founding charter of the new Christian polity. Juridically, this was a most important act, for the participants had exclusive or preferential rights to the spoils, land, and other assets of the new polity. Undoubtedly, nobles received the lion's share, but there were well established procedures to reward individuals according to rank and relative contribution to the success of the enterprise, so that from the highest noble to the lowest commoner participant, individuals were rewarded in reasonably equitable fashion. Another juridical aspect of great importance in the establishment of a new *cabildo* was the legal control that this event conferred upon those, particularly the leader, who had participated in the conquest of new territories. Immediately upon arriving in the Gulf Coast of what is today the state of Veracruz, for example, Hernán Cortés established the *cabildo* of the Villa Rica de la Vera Cruz, a political move that set the foundations for his independence from the governor of Cuba, Diego Velásquez, and established himself as a new Captain General (Diaz del Castillo 1967:37–49). For more obviously mercenary and utilitarian reasons, founding new *cabildos* became standard operational procedure after the conquest or discovery of new lands and a means to organize the exclusive exploitation of human and natural resources as the Spanish Empire expanded throughout the New World.

Moslem culture and society in Spain were essentially urban, which undoubtedly influenced the configuration of the Christian kingdoms. Well into the fifteenth century, Spain was one of the most urbanized areas of Europe, and the centers of royal and seigneurial power had become cities and towns. Noble and commoner alike gravitated toward the urbs, and the superordinate estate ultimately developed a country-city dichotomization of living that became an important aspect of its social character. This characteristic in turn became important in the formation and development of Colonial society in the New World (Rascher 1904). Briefly, the landed aristocracy that emerged after the Conquest was urban-based but with a strong rural component. By the end of the sixteenth century, the *encomendero* class that dominated the landscape of New Spain had become equally at home in the country and the city.

The Spanish Crown aimed at the spiritual conquest of the great masses that populated the colonies. This goal required inland colonization and the foundation of cities and towns from which Catholic religion and Spanish culture could be imparted to the Indians. Spanish colonization, then, was not simply trade and the wholesale exploitation of native population, but the thorough conversion of the people to Catholicism and to Spanish culture as much as local conditions permitted (Gil Munilla 1955). In this context Colonial institutions coalesced; and exploitation, conversion, and cultural transformation became a focused process.

By the end of the Middle Ages, and well into modern times, Spanish society was a complex mosaic of ethnicities and regional variations. But the Christian struggle for religious and cultural unification had created a nationality possessing a number of traits that were not necessarily present in comparable western European nationalities. There are, for example, indications of a less rigid seigneurial system as compared, say, with France and Germany. I do not mean to suggest that the Spanish nobility at the end of the Middle Ages was significantly more open and less jealous of its privileges than the French or Italian nobility, but there is a certain element in the Spanish estate system, if one can generalize from the diverse kingdoms of the peninsula, absent from the estate systems of other western European countries. This subtle development reflected a "national character" that made the breakdown between the lesser nobility and the commonality less abrupt and fostered a less subservient attitude among the latter. When one compares the haughty demeanor and proud countenance of Spaniards of all stations to their social superiors (from the assertive, almost insulting oath of fealty of Aragonese nobles to the king to the amused disrespect of *villanos* toward poor *hidalgos*) with the respect and subservience of the commonality toward the nobility in Great Britain, or with the traditional Italian cynicism toward rank and status, one suspects that the Spanish estate system was somewhat more fluid than those of other western European countries. Furthermore, the origin of this peculiarity of the Spanish estate system must undoubtedly be sought in the feats of arms and the almost religious fervor that characterized the Reconquest (Altamira 1969).

Spain emerged from the Middle Ages with a warrior aristocracy very much aware of being the leader of a holy crusade and a commonality that fully participated and shared in the glory and spoil. The Spanish nobility did not, however, stand apart from other Western aristocracies because of more punctiliousness about its role as a warrior class or more concern with the laws of derogation. This fact is important, for in the Conquest of Mexico and its aftermath, nobles and *hidalgos* alike performed jobs and engaged in activities that they presumably would have shunned in the mother country. The Spanish aristocracy's much-vaunted aversion for manual labor and, indeed, activity besides that of a military, political, or religious leader is probably an exaggeration, or it may be a characteristic developed in the seventeenth and eighteenth centuries (Montagu of Beaulieu 1970:118–32). Certainly, thrown together in a great enterprise and sharing the same religious and economic goals, nobles and commoners behaved in the same fashion. Far away from the mother country, less constrained by tradition, the amalgamation of *hidalgos* and commoners proceeded smoothly, a process that probably could not have occurred in Spain. Thus, while there were a few higher nobles, many *hidalgos,* and, of course a majority of commoners that participated in the Conquest of Mexico and were rewarded with land and Indians and other privileges, one cannot make too much of these social distinctions; the Conquest became a great upward social leveler, and after a short three generations in the new land, the *encomenderos,* descendants of nobles and commoners alike, constituted a budding aristocracy.

In assessing the formation of Colonial Mexican society in general, and of stratification in particular, we must distinguish the private aims and concerns of conquistadors and settlers from the official aims and concerns of the Spanish Crown, particularly as concerned religion. Spain emerged from the Middle Ages as the champion of Catholicism by virtue of having forced the inhabitants of reconquered lands to convert or to leave the country. This near fanaticism was a relatively new phenomenon; for several centuries, Christians, Moslems, and Jews had lived side by side. By the time of Ferdinand and Isabella and the discovery of the New World, however, the Spanish Crown had become the champion of an orthodoxy that led to the expulsion of the Jews from Spain and the active conversion of the Indians (Castro 1948:73–97). In the New World, the Crown had to modify its ideal, for it was faced with exigencies and constraints that it did not face in the peninsula. The Crown apparently made every effort to ensure that all personnel coming to the New World were Christians of old standing (*cristianos viejos*). Nonetheless, conquistadors and settlers by no means completely shared the Crown's concern with converting the Indians and organizing them in congregations under the leadership of the Mendicant friars. Throughout the sixteenth century in New Spain, Indian congregations were under the supervision and control of the Mendicant friars, who became veritable defenders of Indian rights against the voracious hunger of the *encomenderos* and other Spaniards for land and labor (Weckmann 1984, 1:418–32). In principle, the Crown supported the efforts and general policy of the friars, but it was constrained to compromise because of the alleged rights of *encomenderos* to Indian labor and land as a sort of payment for being the sole defenders of the country and its own interests in exploiting the gold and silver mines that required large numbers of Indian laborers. This mixed policy somewhat curtailed the excessive greed of *encomenderos* and settlers, but not enough to stifle the growth of a powerful landed class. Not until well into the seventeenth century, when the Indian congregations were secularized, did the landed class gain the upper hand; but by then the Indian population had acquired the marginal demographic and territorial position that it still occupies (Nutini and Bell 1980:27–309).

The effect of Spain's political transformation under the Catholic kings on the social and stratification systems of New Spain may be summarized as follows. During the long reign of Ferdinand and Isabella, Spain became a single nation, although the rebellious Aragonese nobles were not brought entirely to heel until the reign of Charles V. The establishment of a centralized police force (*santa hermandad*) and the concerted efforts of the sovereigns to centralize administration ultimately broke the local and regional power of the nobles and launched the kingdom onto an absolutist course. Notwithstanding these political developments, seigneuralism probably remained as strong in Spain as it did in France until the nineteenth century (Altamira 1969). The nobles became a courtly class—or royal bureaucrats—setting a pattern in western Europe that reached a peak under King Louis XIV of France. These political developments had a twofold effect on Colonial stratification. First, the cash-poor Crown instituted the *encomienda* and *repartimiento* systems to reward conquistadors with Indians and land. But the Crown had no intention of perpetuating or initiating another seigneurial system that endowed great landowners with independent power. Nonetheless, the *encomendero* class did develop into a sort of seigneurial system, and a de facto estate system regulated the social, economic, and political relationships of a large sector of the population. Second, the Crown organized the colonies under strict royal supervision. The Spanish Creole population were allowed a measure of local (city, town) control, but all higher officials, from the provincial to the viceregal levels, were always *peninsulares* directly appointed by the Crown. This policy relaxed somewhat in the seventeenth and eighteenth centuries, but though the Creole *encomenderos* and, later, *hacendados* developed into a powerful Colonial ruling class, it never became a political class. This unswerving policy of the Crown curtailed the development of the local aristocracy and was bitterly resented by the conquistadors and their descendants in the sixteenth century, becoming a source of constant complaints in the following centuries (Domínguez Ortiz 1970:108–34).

No obvious population pressures compelled people to migrate to the New World, nor did the economic conditions in the peninsula warrant emigration. Spaniards chose to try their luck in the New World for personal economic and psychological reasons, in pursuit of a vision that had been forged in the struggle of the Reconquest (Weckmann 1984). We should be careful, however, not to under-emphasize the local inputs (unique conditions of the Conquest) that configured this version of Western aristocracy differently from the Spanish and other European aristocracies. (The reader should consult Foster [1960] for the wider, ethnologic understanding of Spain on the eve of the Conquest.)

THE NATURE OF THE CONQUEST AND ITS IMPLICATIONS

Carrasco (1976:287–88) puts matters in perspective when he says: "It can be said that Mesoamerica, given the conditions of the XVI century, was an eminently conquerable country for the Europeans. It was suffi-ciently civilized to attract the interests of Spanish expansion, but not advanced enough militarily and politically to offer the kind of resis-tance that the peoples of North Africa and the Orient had offered, that in the same century defeated Iberian attempts at conquest and coloniza-tion. Therefore, Mesoamerican population and culture were a funda-mental antecedent and component in the formation of the Mexican nation" (my translation). This statement in no way diminishes the ingenuity and generalship exhibited by Cortés and his men in the roughly seventeen years they took to subjugate most of Mesoamerica. When one reads the original account of this momentous enterprise (Díaz del Castillo 1967), the saying that "truth surpasses fiction" comes alive in the wondrous description of the land and its people. The Conquest of Mexico brought Europeans into contact with the most advanced civilization of the New World, and as news of the wonders of the land reached Europe, the European conception of the New World changed forever, and its peoples and cultures never ceased to amaze and hold the interest of scholars (Weckmann 1984,1:33–88). New Spain became the Crown's most prized possession by virtue of its riches in silver and gold and privileged geographical position. The extension of the land, the density of its population, and its relatively easy overseas access made New Spain a magnet for migration and a staging area for the conquest and colonization of other lands. New Spain retained its preeminence until the end of Colonial times, and Mexico City, its capital, became the largest, most populous, and most important city in the New World.

Legend tells us that Queen Isabella pawned her jewels in order to finance Columbus's voyage of discovery. There is no truth in this legend, but it does underscore the fact that in 1492, after more than a decade of political struggle and the reconquest of the kingdom of Granada, the Spanish Crown was none too affluent. Ferdinand and Isabella authorized and empowered Columbus to undertake the voyage and allowed him to contract the necessary crews. Largely, however, the discovery of the New World was undertaken as a private enterprise: the association of Columbus with the Pinzón brothers from the port of Palos made it possible to outfit the three ships for the enterprise (Haring 1953:27). This arrangement established the basic pattern for voyages of discovery, conquests, and colonizations for more than a century: royal permission and sponsorship were necessary requirements, but the actual journey was undertaken on the basis of private individuals risking their own property.

The histories of the conquest of Mexico and Peru are well known, and they set the pattern for similar enterprises that characterized most of the sixteenth century. Groups of leading would-be conquistadors formed an association to explore and conquer an area where gold and silver were to be found (Zavala 1943:41–46). The details of the constitution and general modus operandi of expeditionary forces are not directly pertinent to the present study, but the following outline is necessary for understanding certain aspects of early formation of Colonial society. After securing royal authorization and sponsorship for the expedition, either directly from the Crown in Spain or through its representatives in the New World, a leader or several leaders emerged upon whom fell the economic and military organization of the enterprise. The general principle regulating this aspect of the expedition was the future reward to participants (at first, almost exclusively in precious metals discovered) in proportion to their original material contribution to the enterprise. Legal agreements (*capitulaciones*) drew together all members of the expedition and stipulated the basic principle of economic reward: of all riches found, one-fifth went to the royal treasury, another was divided among the leaders of the expedition, and three-fifths were distributed proportionally among the rank and file (Prescott 1973, 1:144–262).

There were variations of this basic pattern, to be sure, usually concerning the circumstances and constraints of time and place, but none were so determinant as outstanding military leadership. Even in cases of collective leadership, the actual conduct of military affairs was vested in a single leader—one designated from the beginning, like Cortés, or one who by the force and cunning of his personality emerged in the course of the enterprise, like Pizarro in the conquest of Peru (Haring 1953:57–71). Whatever the case, the leader of an expeditionary force of conquistadors or discoverers was empowered to reward members of the host before the land was organized as a colony and thereby became subject to direct Crown control. The Conquest of Mexico and the early organization of New Spain exemplify this state of affairs.

The Conquest of Mexico has been well documented by sixteenth-century and contemporary scholars (see Díaz del Castillo 1967; Gómara 1971; Solís 1968; Prescott 1973). I shall, therefore, only briefly mention five features of this event essential to understanding the inception and early configuration of the Creole aristocracy that became the ruling class of New Spain by 1600. First, born in Cuba and operating under the sponsorship of the governor Diego Velásquez, Hernán Cortés, the leader of the expedition, quickly disassociated himself from his sponsor. In trying to regain control, Velásquez sent more than nine hundred soldiers to the mainland to subdue Cortés. This action facilitated the Conquest, for by defeating a force four times larger than his own, Cortés enlarged his original host to more than fifteen hundred soldiers; within a year this number increased again, augmented by new arrivals from Cuba and Spain who were attracted by the rumors that there was great wealth to be gained. The actual Conquest of Mexico thus was achieved by some twenty-three hundred Spaniards. Second, this great feat would have taken much longer, resulted in many more Spanish dead, and proved much more costly without the assistance of Indian allies—mainly Tlaxcalans and Zempoalans—seduced by Cortés's great diplomatic skills. Third, the travails of the Conquest united the disparate social elements that constituted the conquering host, forging a social awareness of their worth and of what they had accomplished for the Spanish Crown that any less dramatic deed would not have accomplished. This sense of self-worth was one of the ideological foundations of the Creole aristocracy and one of the main sources of future economic and social claims. Fourth, the actual and legendary feats of the Conquest created a worldview that, based on the ancient concept of the last conquerors, configured the claims and aspirations of the budding ruling class of the colony throughout the sixteenth century. Fifth, and finally, the foundation of the city of Veracruz almost immediately upon the arrival of the Spanish host in central Mexico set the juridical foundations of the new colony in the classic Spanish tradition. Socially and symbolically, the *cabildo* of Veracruz provided the model for future cities and towns in New Spain, setting up the pillars which supported Colonial society and stratification. Reinforced by the fact that the Conquest was an achievement of private enterprise, the original conquistadors claimed the rewards of the land for themselves and their descendants. The conquistadors presented these claims repeatedly to the Spanish Crown trying to safeguard their interests against later arrivals (*pobladores*), who were rewarded with Indians and land by virtue of royal or viceregal patronage (Gómez de Cervantes 1944:98–108). The last two points are the fundamental considerations in explaining the formation of the Creole aristocracy of New Spain, and their repercussions affected the evolution of this social class for much of Colonial times.

Immediately after the fall of Tenochtitlán, Cortés began to organize the colony in what had been the area of effective control of the Triple Alliance. By the time Cortés returned to Spain for the first time in 1527, Guatemala had been brought under control and most of the land from Michoacan to Honduras had been reasonably pacified and was being organized into municipalities. Seven years after the first viceroy of New Spain, Antonio de Mendoza, took up residence in Mexico City in 1535, Spanish control had been established as far north as Culiacán, in what is today the state of Sinaloa (Haring 1953:348–92). Thus, for Mesoamerica and some distance beyond its northern frontier, conquest and pacification were over by around 1545.

In October 1522, Cortés was ratified as governor, Captain General, and Chief Justice of New Spain, positions that he held until he returned to Spain for the first time (Prescott 1873, 2:234). After his return from Spain in 1530, and until 1535 when he began to collide with the viceroy, Cortés exerted a great deal of influence and was instrumental in protecting the interests of fellow conquistadors. Indeed, even those who opposed him during the early years of the Conquest saw him as a defender of their interests against royal bureaucrats, who lost no time in favoring their own interests and those of members of their entourages. First- and second-generation conquistadors saw these bureaucratic interests as encroaching on their own rights of conquest that, as they never ceased to point out, had been won with such dedication and suffering (Zavala 1948:102–43).

Conditioned by the rather narrow demographic and geographic situation of the Antilles, most conquistadors signed up with Cortés in search of gold and other immediate, tangible rewards. In this context, the *capitulaciones* specifying the redistribution of booty worked well, as probably most conquistadors planned to return to Spain as soon as they had secured enough silver and gold. Things did not work out that way, however. After the so-called treasure of Montezuma had been distributed and most of it lost during the retreat from Tenochtitlán (*Noche Triste*), the rank and file were very disappointed and many wanted to go back to Cuba. They quickly reconsidered, however, apparently realizing that the real richness of the country lay not in gold and silver but in the land and its people, and many may have stayed because of sheer love of adventure and fame. Shortly after the fall of Tenochtitlán, Cortés began to distribute land and Indians to individual conquistadors, thereby establishing the first *encomiendas* in New Spain, and before the arrival of the first viceroy, the *repartimiento* was already in place (Zavala 1973:40–73). The first to benefit from these institutions were the captains and important people in Cortés's army, but the rank and file also partook of these rewards. During this critical decade the transition from immediate riches to the lasting rewards of the land and its people was made, and by 1530 the great majority of conquistadors had decided to stay in New Spain, and many of them were actively engaged in seeking land and Indians. By the end of the following decade, many conquistadors had made the transition to *pobladores* (settlers), either as members of original *cabildos* (that is, those that had been founded before 1527) or as *vecinos* (charter members) of new *cabildos*, as effective Spanish control expanded to the north and south from the central highlands.

These two decades established the economic base of a new superordinate class and shaped the fundamental ideology of the future *encomendero* class. The conquistadors' struggle for what they considered due compensation from the Crown made them lords of the lands and Indians they had conquered and generated an ambiance of exclusivity and a worldview that was markedly aristocratic. Undoubtedly, the many *hidalgos* among them provided the model, but *hidalgos* and *villanos* alike behaved as conquerors in the best tradition of the Reconquest, for the latter came to believe that their deeds entitled them to *hidalguía,* whether the Crown ennobled them or not (Durand 1953, 1:45–65).

SOME SOCIAL AND DEMOGRAPHIC CONSIDERATIONS CONCERNING CONQUISTADORS AND EARLY SETTLERS

Given the peculiarly unifying effect and ideology-creating context of the Reconquest, the populations that conquered and settled New Spain during the first fifty years were highly homogeneous in orientation and motivation. This conjunction of historical circumstances made Spain especially well suited to initiate the age of European imperialism (Ots Capdequí 1934:107–48). Despite the ideological uniformity that characterized the Conquest of Mexico, it is important to have an overview of the demography, provenance, and social composition of the conquistadors and *pobladores* that shaped the first generation of Colonial society.

First- and second-generation conquistadors of New Spain (that is, those who were in the land at the fall of Tenochtitlán, and those who undertook the conquests of Guatemala, Yucatán, and other areas of Mesoamerica between 1522 and 1545) came from all provinces of Spain. Undoubtedly the majority were from the southern provinces of Andalucía and Extremadura. These were perhaps the poorest provinces of Spain; being closer to the last Moorish strongholds, these areas kept alive the martial spirit that had fueled the Reconquest; and, most significant, more than any other area on the peninsula, southern Spain was closer to Seville and Cádiz, the city and port most intimately tied to the New World. This tradition has been somewhat romanticized (see Madariaga 1958), but there is no denying the notable role of Extremeños and Andaluces in the Conquest of Mexico and other areas of the New World. Cortés and Pizarro are the best-known examples, but many other discoverers and settlers came from the south as well. During the first critical generation (1519–45) in New Spain, however, conquistadors and *pobladores* came from practically all provinces of Spain; some were even Italian and Flemish. In descending order of numbers from southern Spaniards came Castellanos, Leoneses, Vascos, and Gallegos. Surprisingly, there were few conquistadors and *pobladores* in this early period from Asturias, Valencia, Navarra, and other provinces of northern and eastern Spain, and Catalanes were conspicuous for their absence (Boyd-Bowman 1964:20–217; also see Foster 1960:29–33). One might explain the few participants from these provinces in terms of their greater affluences relative to southern Spain, but there may have been other factors involved. Oddly enough, from the middle of the seventeenth century onward most of the migration to New Spain and other Spanish colonies in the New World came from middle and northern Spain, particularly Asturias, Aragon, and Valencia (Davis 1957:43–77).

More central to the present study is the social provenance of conquistadors and early *pobladores*. The Black Legend, that painful thorn in Spanish history, asserts that the conquistadors were a band of cruel and unscrupulous cutthroats from the dregs of society. This is a maligning, dishonest characterization, for the Spaniards were no more cruel than the English (the inventors of the Black Legend) or the French, nor were they more self-serving and avaricious. Indeed, in terms of social position, the conquistadors as a whole, as compared say, to the English colonists anywhere in the world from the seventeenth to the nineteenth century, were of higher social standing. A brief analysis of first- and second-generation conquistadors indicates that they included a few members of the higher nobility, many *hidalgos,* and a majority of commoners, including many individuals with specialized occupations, from physicians and apothecaries to professional soldiers to carpenters and masons. There has been a consistent tendency in twentieth-century historiography to downgrade the social background and standing of conquistadors and early settlers by emphasizing their lowly origin and lack of education and refinement and de-emphasizing the significant presence of *hidalgo* elements. Both U.S. (Gruening 1928; Priestly 1926; Meyer and Sheridan 1979) and Mexican (Cué Canovas 1946; Covarrubias 1953) historians have taken this stand, which may perhaps be attributed to the late effects of the Black Legend in the case of the former and to the rather senseless practice of denigrating all things Spanish, latent since Independence and exacerbated since the Revolution of 1910, in the case of the latter (Simpson 1967:23).

The ranks of conquistadors and early *pobladores* included members of all subdivisions of the noble and commoner estates. At the top were a few individuals related to distinguished noble families: don Tristán de Luna y Arellano, Mariscal de Castilla, Andrés Dorantes de Carranza, Alonzo Hernández Puertocarrero, Gonzalo Hernández de Palos, Leonel de Cervantes, Pedro de Ircio, Rafael de Trejo, and several others. None of these noblemen were titled, but they belonged to the main or cadet lines of well-known titled families. Just below this group were *hidalgos* of high standing, including Cortés himself, most of his captains, and those who came with Narváez, Garay, and participants in subsequent, less important conquests (Dorantes de Carranza 1970:99–360). It is also possible that there were members of this category among the rank and file, but the information is sketchy. By *hidalgos* of high standing I mean those members of the lesser Spanish nobility who had proved their standing (submitted *probanzas*) before nobiliary courts, were everywhere recognized as bona fide members of this nobiliary rank, and were commonly referred to as *nobles a fuero de España* (nobles according to Spanish nobiliary law). It is difficult to say how many *hidalgos* in this category participated in the Conquest of Mexico, but a conservative guess is several dozen. At the bottom of the lesser nobility were those who in Spain were referred to as *hidalgos de gotera* (lesser-known *hidalgos*), that is, gentry who were known as such only locally and who had not, or could not, prove their *hidalguía* officially (Lira Montt 1976:900–905). It was common in early sixteenth-century Spain for entire communities or even regions to claim *hidalguía* by virtue of some feat of arms or heroic deed during the Reconquest. Cervantes portrays this tendency lovingly in his *Don Quijote,* but later it was satirized by Spanish novelists, particularly in the nineteenth century. How many conquistadors claimed to be or can be regarded as *hidalgos de gotera* is even more difficult to tell, but again a conservative guess is that they numbered well over one hundred.

In a list of 1,385 conquistadors and *pobladores* of New Spain for the decade following 1540, roughly 80 can without a doubt be regarded as having been *hidalgos* of the categories described above. However, allowing for individual exaggerations, but reading between the lines (the use of honorific terms of address, offices held, and so on) and correlating the list with other accounts, at least another 150 individuals were *hidalgos* when they arrived in New Spain (Dorantes de Carranza 1970). By all accounts, this is a representative list of the conquistadors and early *pobladores* of New Spain by the middle of the sixteenth century, and if the calculation of 230 is reasonably accurate, then nearly 17 percent were nobles and *hidalgos*, while 83 percent were commoners (Icaza 1969; Zavala 1973:229). This proportion of the upper and lower nobility in New Spain was considerably higher than in Spain at the time; indeed, no European country had a noble estate constituting more than 10 percent of the population, at least not until the second half of the eighteenth century, when in France it went up to 12 percent.

The great majority of conquistadors and *pobladores* of early New Spain were commoners; many probably came from *behetrías* and had developed specialized occupations by the time they arrived. There is every indication that most *hidalgos*, particularly those *a fuero de España*, were from the beginning more amply rewarded in land and Indians than commoners were, if nothing else because they generally occupied the more important positions in the conquering army and in the many *cabildos* that were established immediately after the fall of Tenochtitlán. Indeed, almost all officials of the original *cabildo* of Veracruz were *hidalgos*, setting the pattern for future municipalities (Solís 1968:82–87), at least until the viceroyalty was established, and commoners were favored for public office. This pattern was much resented by the commoner rank and file, for it restricted their access to land and Indians. No wonder, then, that the conquistadors of humble commoner stock were the most active in their quest for economic rewards and social recognition, namely *encomiendas* and patents of *hidalguía*. Their social and economic positions secure, *hidalgos* in New Spain provided the ideological rallying point and model for the *imago mundi* that characterized the birth of the Creole aristocracy, while commoner conquistadors anxious to receive official sanction of *hidalguía* and acquire more access to economic rewards were the most vocal and persistent in lobbying before the Crown (Peña 1983:181–233).

To sum up, then: roughly 83 percent of conquistadors and early settlers were commoner would-be *hidalgos*, while the remaining 17 percent (230) were distributed as follows: about 20 were related to titled noble families; perhaps as many as 60 were *hidalgos a fuero de España;* and roughly 150 were *hidalgos de gotera* (Konetzke 1951:329–57). Some sources (Las Casas, Durán, Dorantes de Carranza) indicate that the conquistadors of New Spain may have included nearly twice as many *hidalgos*. These figures do not include later *pobladores* who became *encomenderos* by virtue of viceregal or Crown connections, which is another aspect that must be considered.

Do other variables or considerations impinge on the composition of conquistadors and early settlers in New Spain? Two aspects of Spanish society come to mind. First, many conquistadors were professional soldiers, inasmuch as this term can be applied to a period when there were not yet professional armies, at least not in the modern sense. The final episode of the Reconquest, that is, the fall of the kingdom of Granada, created a class of professional soldiers, and Spain became the preeminent political and military power in Europe. As knowledge of new lands to discover and conquer reached Spain during the early part of the sixteenth century, this martial spirit found expression in the men who flocked to the Antilles, the first staging area for further conquest and exploration in the New World. This hypothesis explains the high quality of Cortés's troops, for it is difficult to believe that most of them, particularly officers, became effective soldiers without extensive prior military experience (Lohmann Villena 1947:21–92). Second, and more significant, was the institution of *mayorazgo* (entailed property vested on the firstborn) and siphoning second- or third-born sons into the military. The *mayorazgo* applied exclusively to the nobility, but commoners may also have encouraged sons to join the military. Certainly the *mayorazgo* prodded younger sons to seek fortune elsewhere, and the New World was a natural magnet for this familial excess population (Clavero 1974). All these variables informed the Conquest of Mexico and other major conquests during the first half of the sixteenth century, and this is reflected in the army's generalship and leadership and the superb combat performance of the rank and file. For generations, the conquistadors' accomplishments sustained the claims of their descendants and were a significant element in the formation of the Creole aristocracy (Gómez de Cervantes 1944:77–127).

By 1521, at the fall of Tenochtitlán, there were roughly 2,200 Spaniards in New Spain, including Cortés's original host, the men who came with Narváez, and other reinforcements that had come from Cuba before the siege of the city. Accounting for the dead of the *Noche Triste* and various other engagements, there were at that time roughly 1,800 conquistadors, while the remaining 400 Spaniards were immigrants from the Antilles who had come as the news of the new land reached the islands (Prescott 1973, vols. 1 and 2). At this stage, conquistadors constituted the great majority of the population. By 1530, the situation had almost completely reversed. By that time there were roughly 7,000 Spaniards, but no more than 2,100 conquistadors, that is, the original 1,800 plus another 300 that had participated in the conquests of Guatemala and other provinces of the colony. By 1545 or so, the population of New Spain was roughly 15,000 Spaniards, of which only 2,500 were conquistadors, that is, another 400 had participated in assorted conquests and voyages of discovery (Dorantes de Carranza 1970:99–361). Accounting for the dead, in 1541 there were probably no more than 2,000 conquistadors who could rightfully vie for honor and economic rewards. When the viceroy Mendoza tried to implement the *Nuevas Leyes* (New Laws, the de jure but not de facto abolition of the *encomienda*), 1,385 Spaniards gave information as to their status and condition in the colony (Zavala 1973:229–43). Of these no more than 1,000 were conquistadors; the rest were *pobladores* of note who had been awarded land and Indians directly by the Crown or viceregal authorities. These figures give a fair idea of the drop in conquistador claims, and consequently of downward economic and social mobility, a process that began with the foundation of the city of Puebla in 1531 as a refuge for displaced conquistadors. By the end of the sixteenth century, perhaps another 500 or 600 Spaniards could have attained the status of conquistadors, as the viceroyalty expanded well beyond the confines of Mesoamerica. By then the Spanish (Creole and *peninsular*) population of New Spain was perhaps 70,000, of which roughly 5,000 were descendants of conquistadors and *pobladores* who had received *encomiendas*, constituting no more than 900 families (Meyer and Sheridan 1979:207–11). After 1550, the situation becomes muddled demographically, but it is clear that in this two-generation period until the turn of the century, a local, colonial ruling class came into being. This class was composed of descendants of conquistadors, descendants of early *pobladores*, and some Creoles of non-*vecino* status: they were the great landowners, possessed all the *encomiendas*, and controlled the cities and towns that their ancestors had founded or in which they had made their fortunes. This ruling class was small, never larger than 7 percent of the total Creole population, a tiny fraction of the total population of the colony, and it remained small until the twentieth century. Indeed, by Independence this ruling class was much smaller, perhaps less than 2 percent of the Creole and *peninsular* population of more than a million, and at the onset of the Mexican Revolution of 1910 it was probably less than 0.3 percent of a total population of nearly 14 million.

The most difficult elements to handle in this equation are the *pobladores* who acquired *vecino* status between 1530 and 1560 but were not conquistadors or descendants of conquistadors. Quantitative and descriptive information about them is difficult to obtain. What we know for certain is that they received their grants of land and Indians through viceregal or royal patronage. Some of them were former royal officials who decided to stay in New Spain after their tour of duty, and others apparently came to the colony from Spain with the understanding that they would receive land and Indians. From the beginning this was an important element in the formation of the Colonial ruling class, as many *pobladores* were quick to adopt the sometimes unreasonable expectations of original conquistadors. But we do not know their relative strength, nor exactly how they were incorporated into the conquistador-*encomendero* class.

Key Institutions that Precipitated Colonial Stratification and a Creole Aristocracy

In the foregoing section I discussed the main institutions that structured early Colonial society and stratification, namely, the *encomienda* and *repartimiento* systems, the *cabildo* or *ayuntamiento,* and the foundation of cities and towns as an intrinsic aspect of the latter. The interplay of these institutions was of special significance for the structuring of the ruling class that developed throughout the sixteenth century. A fourth institution should be considered as bearing indirectly on the problem at hand, namely, tribute paying by the Indian population. These institutions were interrelated and, during the three generations after the fall of Tenochtitlán, converged to give birth to a Creole ruling aristocracy that dominated the agrarian sector of the colony and, later on, the mining sector as well.

A SYSTEMATIC OUTLINE OF INSTITUTIONAL EFFICACY

The Spanish colonization of New Spain had two main purposes: economic exploitation of the Indians and their conversion to Catholicism. In pursuing these goals, the Spanish Crown relied primarily on the establishment of cities and towns and on the *encomienda* system. As far as the exploitation of the Indians, these institutions succeeded impressively at exploiting Indians, but failed to achieve their conversion and catechization, tasks assumed by the Mendicant friars and their wide-ranging system of missions and congregations.

Since the Crown did not have cash, the usual method of rewarding conquistadors was to give them land in trust, an *encomienda,* which included a corresponding number of Indians. The possessor of an *encomienda* was termed an *encomendero.* Briefly, the *encomendero,* through the *repartimiento,* or periodic reallotments, was given the responsibility of civilizing the Indians, that is, of indoctrinating them into the Holy Catholic faith, teaching them elements of Spanish culture, and protecting them. In turn, the Indians were expected to work on the *encomendero's* landed estate and to serve in his home. The system never worked well, for the *encomendero* enforced his rights but generally ignored his responsibilities. It is very difficult to assess the impact of the *encomienda* on the Indian population. A fair assessment probably falls somewhere between the position of those who regarded the *encomienda* system as an exploitative institution without redeeming value and that of those who viewed the institution as necessary to secure the safety of the colony and posited on the goodwill of *encomenderos* (Nickel 1988:42–46).

The establishment of cities and towns did more than the *encomienda* system to hold and exploit the territories of New Spain. The Crown was acutely aware of the importance of towns and cities as centers of trade, mine exploitation, manufacture, and administration, and it took every opportunity to instruct the conquistadors and, later, Crown officials and private entrepreneurs to identify propitious locations on which to establish towns and concentrate Indian populations. The insistence on the manifold importance of cities and towns was not confined to the capital of the viceroyalty and provincial centers but applied equally to more circumscribed regions or *corregimientos.* The Crown aimed to integrate its vast domains in New Spain in a network of administrative and commercial centers reaching from the highest to the lowest levels of the colony (Garretón 1933).

Spain pursued its urbanization policy in inland settlement as well, hoping to open the American continent to its Colonial ambitions. A series of ordinances, beginning with those of Philip II in 1573, were issued concerning the foundation of new towns (Nuttal 1922). The first half of the sixteenth century witnessed the real birth of the great cities of New Spain, either on pre-Hispanic Indian sites (for example, Mexico City) or on new sites (for example, Puebla de los Angeles) strategically selected by leading conquistadors or viceregal authorities for exploitation of circumscribed demographic regions (Nutini 1971).

Establishment of the *encomienda* system and foundation of new towns went hand in hand. After a territory had been secured for the Crown, one of the first official acts of the leader (*adelantado, capitán general, gobernador*) was to found a municipality and establish the town council (*ayuntamiento* or *cabildo*). Usually, all able-bodied men of the expedition signed the founding charter, thus acquiring the status of "citizens" or *vecinos* (neighbors) of the town and accepting clearly established privileges, rights, and responsibilities. The concept of *vecino* is important in the study of Colonial urbanization, for *vecinos* and their descendants constituted the central core of the economic, social, and political life of cities, due to original rights of residence granted by the founder of the municipality (Moses 1898).

What really made the original *vecinos* the nucleus of the Colonial city, however, was the *encomienda*. After a municipality was founded, the leader of the expedition often had the right to grant *encomiendas* and allot *repartimientos* to the members of his group or army according to rank, merit, and the prior agreement (*capitulaciones*) signed by the members of the expedition. But the exigencies of holding a newly conquered territory made this model of granting *encomiendas* and allotting *repartimientos* rather difficult and generally favored those of high military and social rank. Thus, recompense to the average conquistador for his services to the Crown usually came later, from royal emissaries. The *vecinos,* then, became *encomenderos* by virtue of having first rights of exploitation of the land, Indians, and natural resources falling within the jurisdiction of the new town or city of which they were charter members (Navarro 1930).

Eventually, many Spaniards migrated to the cities and towns of New Spain, which rapidly increased in population. These late arrivals, usually traders, merchants, and specialized craftsmen, were referred to as *habitantes* or *moradores* to distinguish them from the *vecinos* or *encomenderos,* and they did not enjoy the rights and privileges of the original settlers (Moore 1954). Despite its small numbers, however, the *encomendero* class was the driving force in Colonial urban life and agrarian affairs. In 1572, Philip II decreed that all descendants of *vecinos* would enjoy the full status of *encomenderos*, underscoring the great importance of this group in Colonial society.

An important aspect of Colonial urban development was the Crown's policy of segmenting the Indian population into manageable political units that facilitated exploitation and conversion. The policy of *reducciones*, sometimes referred to as *congregaciones*, was instituted by the Crown not only to exploit and convert the Indians, but also to protect them against the excessive rapacity of *encomenderos* and other Spanish settlers. In theory, the Indian communities that were not part of *repartimientos* were under the political and economic control of officials known as *corregidores*, directly responsible to the Crown. In practice, however, the Spaniards of both *encomendero* and *morador* classes usually contrived to exploit the Indian *reducciones*, either by bribing *corregidores* or by legal subterfuge (Castañeda 1929:456). Therefore, large numbers of Indians whom the Crown had originally intended to leave as independently organized peasants were, in fact, transformed into city-dwelling mine workers, domestic servants, and artisans.

This brief overview of the main institutions that shaped the formation and sixteenth-century development of New Spain's society may be regarded as the matrix in which stratification was structured. The interrelationship of these institutions reveals the source of power and wealth of the emerging ruling class in relation to the subordinate Indian population as well as to the great majority of the colony's Creole population. The *encomendero* class, augmented by a class of *vecinos* of nonconquistador origin, managed from the beginning to obtain exclusive access to land and Indians, the colony's most valuable assets. Thus were they the nucleus of the ruling class of New Spain, the Creole aristocracy, that had been firmly established by 1600 (Liss 1975:109).

The Interrelationship of Land, *Encomienda*, and *Repartimiento*

The *encomienda* system matured in the Antilles and was brought to New Spain by Cortés and his conquering army. Cortés (1963) began the distribution of *encomiendas* shortly after the fall of Tenochtitlán. In his third and fourth *Cartas de Relación* to the emperor Charles V, Cortés specified the conditions for granting *encomiendas*, the necessity of recompensing his soldiers, the justification of the system, and the general procedures. He said nothing, however, about the quantities of Indians awarded in *encomienda,* the discriminating procedures applied to officers and rank and file, and the *mercedes* (grants) of land. There is considerable information about the first two points, but little information concerning the land that made the original *encomenderos* agrarian magnates. What we know for certain may be summarized as follows. In most regions of central and southern Mesoamerica, where the *encomienda* system began, Indians left a good deal of agricultural land uncultivated. By the 1540s, when the concentration of Indians in nucleated congregations depopulated indigenous communities, even more land became available to the Spaniards. To complete the picture, as the Indian population diminished dramatically during the second half of the sixteenth century, land was never a problem; indeed, Indians to work the land, who for the first generation after the fall of Tenochtitlán were available in great numbers, now became extremely scarce (Serrano y Sanz 1918:67–108).

Since Indian tribute paying in kind or cash was organized after the arrival of Viceroy Mendoza, initially most of the Indians in *encomienda* worked the land of the *encomendero,* which presupposes that land grants or unlawful appropriations were an aspect of the granting of Indians. *Mercedes* of land throughout the sixteenth century were apparently always available to *encomenderos* and often to other Spaniards who did not fall into this category, even in choice regions close to important urban centers. As the Indian population decreased, the vying for more land decreased as well, but the competition for Indians became fierce (Meyer and Sheridan 1979:204–36). By the end of the sixteenth century, New Spain was dotted with great landed estates that were undercultivated because of the serious shortage of Indian labor.

The *encomienda* conferred no landed property, and *mercedes* of land constituted a separate process (Gibson 1964:58). Shortly after the first *encomiendas* were granted, the *encomenderos* began to lobby hard for *mercedes* of land and actively engaged in wresting pasture and arable land from the Indian communities that had been granted to them. By the middle of the sixteenth century, several large landed estates provided a model for the proliferation later in the century and the growth of the classical *hacienda* by the middle of the seventeenth century (Peña 1983:52–54). In his excellent study of the formation of landed estates in the sixteenth and seventeenth centuries, Chevalier (1952) analyzes the relation between land and labor and their connection to the *encomienda* system and viceregal patronage. These aspects of the agrarian economy, impinging directly on the configuration of the Creole aristocracy, are best described in the context of the birth of the *hacienda* system (Nickel 1988:48–51).

The details of the *encomienda* and *repartimiento* systems are analyzed in Silvio Zavala's (1973) monumental study, *La Encomienda Indiana*. Since as early as 1525 the Crown tried to curtail the *encomienda,* seeking to avoid reduplicating the disastrous experience in the Antilles. But the Crown was well aware of the needs of the conquistadors, the constraints of organizing a new colony, and the requirements of generating royal revenue, and was forced to compromise. Zavala (1973:49) puts matters in perspective: "The possibility was now [1525] admitted to perpetuate the *repartimientos.* . . . The solutions given in the instructions to Ponce de León [resident judge sent to New Spain]— *encomiendas* according to the manner initiated by Cortés, seigneuries with vassals as they existed in Spain, feudatories paying certain dues to the Crown, and tribute paid to the king which he could partly assign to individual Spaniards—tended to harmonize, as far as it was possible, Indian liberties, the economic needs of Spaniards, the sovereignty of the king, and his fiscal revenue" (my translation).

Between 1522 and 1542 nearly six hundred *encomiendas* were first awarded by Cortés, then by various royal authorities, and finally by Viceroy Mendoza, who regularized the procedures by which conquistadors and other worthy persons could petition for land and Indian grants. During this generation, more than during any subsequent period of the sixteenth century, *encomiendas* were awarded to individuals of non-*encomendero* origin by royal and viceregal patronage. These upstarts displaced conquistadors and incurred much resentment. Though as early as ten years after the fall of Tenochtitlán, plenty of conquistadors were already dropping out of the system of superordinate (*hidalgo*) aspirations into which the Conquest had cast them, settling instead for merchant, business, or small farming existences (Chevalier 1948), more than half of conquistadors spent these years actively securing *encomiendas* and assuring themselves of *repartimientos,* either as Indian labor to work their estates or to secure the tribute that went with it (Nickel 1988:42–46).

The New Laws (abolishing the inheritance of *encomiendas*) exploded in New Spain like a veritable bombshell. The situation was well managed by the viceroy, and after a few years there was peace in the colony, primarily because of the Crown's spirit of compromise. In 1546 the

New Laws were revoked, and by the end of Mendoza's administration, the *encomienda* system was essentially the same as it had been before 1542 (Chevalier 1963:45–46). In the end, the New Laws had the beneficial effects of securing better treatment for the Indians and forcing the *encomenderos* to be less exploitative. On the whole, they redounded in a better accommodation between Indians and Spaniards. Moreover, from then on, viceregal authorities were more selective, less willing to grant *encomiendas* and *repartimientos* to conquistadors and their descendants; still, the process of granting Indians and land continued, albeit at a slower pace. By the middle of the sixteenth century there were more than six hundred *encomenderos* in New Spain, a number that increased by perhaps another five hundred by the turn of the century (Zavala 1973:40–91). This growth reflects the large-scale mining exploitation that made New Spain the principal supplier of gold and . silver in the Spanish Empire, a role requiring a steady supply of Indian labor that was primarily generated by the *repartimiento* system. Significant, too, is the fact that members of the *encomendero* class did become miners, thereby enhancing their economic base as the undisputed ruling class of the colony after the turn of the seventeenth century. From the last quarter of the sixteenth century until the end of Colonial times, the ruling class of Mexico was a mixture of agrarian *encomenderos* and, later, *hacendados* with a significant base in mining, business, and trade (Gómez de Cervantes 1944:77–91; Peña 1983:181–233).

The perpetuity of the *encomienda* also reflects the Crown's concern to balance the conflicting interests of generating royal revenue, guarding the welfare of the Indians, and supporting the economy of *encomenderos*. From the early days of the *encomienda* in the Antilles the conquistadors had aimed to make it hereditary. The Crown never acceded, but it did compromise, and for nearly a generation of litigation the question of perpetuity was settled by granting life possession of the *encomienda* to original *encomenderos*. Possession then passed down a direct line of descent, but it could not be disposed of in any other way. Direct inheritance of *encomiendas* led to the *mayorazgo* system that became prevalent in New Spain among the Creole aristocracy (Peña 1983:219–23). This policy persisted until the demise of the *encomienda* system beginning in the middle of the seventeenth century. The *encomienda*'s perpetuity was linked to the mining enterprise, for the *repartimiento* system survived longer in mining cities and areas (Zavala 1973:74–91).

At least until the end of Viceroy Mendoza's administration, the conquistadors-*encomenderos* constituted the sole army of New Spain, the almost exclusive force that could be mustered against insurrections in not yet pacified areas. This situation was a powerful argument in favor of maintaining the *encomienda* system, and it had been advanced by Cortés himself in his ordinances for the good government of the colony promulgated in 1524. Moreover, convinced by the experience of the Antilles that it was not a good idea to place Indians in *encomienda* with individuals who were not strongly tied to the land, Cortés ordered that the *encomenderos* of New Spain had to reside for at least eight years in or near their lands, under penalty of losing whatever fortunes they had amassed if they left earlier (Zavala 1973:40–51). The martial duties of conquistadors remained in effect for roughly two generations, until most of them had died and no more conquests remained to undertake. The warrior ideology coalesced in their role as *encomenderos,* which they viewed in a seigneurial light: the warrior accepting active responsibility in times of need. The descendants of the conquistadors cherished this myth-reality even after *encomenderos* had ceased to constitute the main body of the army of the colony, which was no later than the turn of the seventeenth century, when the viceroyalty began to organize independent armed forces. For example, in a text compiled by Zavala (1973:727–28) for 1541, the Spanish army was composed of some 2,200 men: nearly 1,900 horse and 300 foot, and the *encomenderos* were regarded as a military class for as long as the colony could not organize a regular military. By the first decade of the seventeenth century, the situation had become more myth than reality, as New Spain was well organized politically and demographically, and manifold groups of Creoles and *peninsulares* engaged in various economic pursuits (Durand 1953, 1:31–45).

The Spanish Crown never allowed *encomenderos* criminal and common jurisdiction over *encomienda* Indians. This prohibition extended to holding the office of *corregidor* or any other office of regional or provincial rank relating to the administration of Indian justice, the collection of tribute, and other administrative matters (Gibson 1964:58). Thus, the *encomenderos* never developed into a de jure political class, neither at the highest viceregal level nor at the Indian administrative level. De facto, however, the *encomenderos* exercised seigneurial rights and privileges in their landed domains under the indifferent or bribed eyes of *corregidores* (Zavala 1973:209–11). The *encomendero* class did, however, have firm control of town government, which to some extent counter-balanced the political monopoly of high office exercised by *peninsular* royal officials. In other words, while *peninsulares* dominated the most important *cabildos* of Mexico City and Puebla, Creole *encomenderos* pre-dominated in most other *cabildos* of New Spain. From the beginning, centralization was a fact of Colonial political life, and Mexico City, tied closely to viceregal administration, was always the preeminent *cabildo*. Nonetheless, the *cabildos* of several other important cities were con-trolled by *encomenderos,* both Creoles and first-generation *peninsulares* (Liss 1975:66, 97, 135). In this political context, the Creole-*peninsular* distinction is not entirely significant. For example, even in the *cabildos* of Mexico City and Puebla, most of the *alcaldes* and *regidores* of peninsu-lar extraction had a stake in the land and businesses of the colony, and their children almost invariably became first-generation Creoles (Peña 1983:153–71).

It should be emphasized that the political dimensions of the Creole aristocracy are important in assessing its position as a social and ruling class within the context of Colonial and later Republican society. Most patterns of political participation, as we have seen, emerged within two generations of the Conquest. Though they changed little for the next three centuries, careful assessment of the precise political domain must inform our inferences about the Creole aristocracy, how it was structured, and the evolving circumstances to which it had to adapt throughout the centuries (Priestley 1926:176–85). In New Spain and independent Mexico, what was legislated often differed significantly from actual practice.

The size of *encomiendas* and their accompanying landed estates var-ied in place and time. The most densely populated area of the New World, New Spain had the largest *encomiendas,* which, during the first decade after the fall of Tenochtitlán, included thousands of Indians and occasional large landed estates, for a single conquistador could hold the lands of several communities that were not under cultivation. At this stage, of course, the donation of an *encomienda*'s land came directly from Indian communities. Only later did *encomenderos* begin to appropriate more land from the Indians and legalize it as private property, for the *encomendero* was entitled only to the tribute assigned to him by the Crown (Weckmann 1984, 2:422–31). Beginning with Viceroy Men-doza, land grants were awarded profusely (Chevalier 1963:121–25). As the size of the landed estates increased, however, the *encomiendas* and *repartimientos* decreased in direct proportion to the dramatic diminution of the Indian population. If before 1530 there were five or six million Indian tributaries, this population had been more than halved by mid-century. The information for the last decade of the sixteenth century is less accurate, but there were probably no more than 600,000 or 700,000 tributary Indians in New Spain, not counting Guatemala. If one considers that the number of *encomiendas* increased throughout the century, original conquistadors, at least in theory, were more affluent than their descendants three generations later (Zavala 1973:71–90). Furthermore, the tribute of *encomienda* Indians was rich and undoubtedly a source of capital accumulation for original conquistadors that could have been used for agrarian and commercial diversification. A considerable number of *encomiendas* were not attached to a landed base, that is, the *encomendero* simply received the assigned Indian tribute. In the early mines of Taxco and Cuahutepec *repartimiento* Indians did the labor, a practice that became universal as the great mines of New Spain began to be exploited later in the century. This mixed economic strategy of *encomenderos* probably accounts for the most affluent members of the class at the turn of the century (Carreño 1961:10–35). Peña (1983:189–205) offers an excellent analysis of this process in his discussion of the economic formation of an aristocratic nucleus that, out of mixed conquistador-*encomendero* and mining-merchant origins, coalesced shortly after the onset of the seventeenth century.

Individually, the size of the *encomienda* in 1522–30 ranged from the enormous estates of Cortés, the Marquisate of the Valley of Oaxaca, which included at least thirty medium-size and large Indian communities, several million acres of land, and about thirty thousand tributaries—producing an annual income of more than seventy thousand gold pesos, an enormous sum that few, if any, grandees of Spain could equal—to small *encomiendas* of two hundred to three hundred Indians, constituting perhaps part of a community (*calpulli*), covering a few thousand acres of land, and producing an annual income of five hundred or six hundred gold pesos (Zavala 1973:217–20). By the end of the century, the population of Mesoamerica, the heart of New Spain, had dropped from probably 12 million to no more than two million. This demographic factor dramatically affected every agrarian aspect of the *encomienda*. Writing during the last decade of the sixteenth century, Gómez de Cervantes (1944:117–25), a leading *encomendero*, complains that the countryside is depopulated and that large tracts of land remain uncultivated for lack of Indian laborers. If we discount those who worked in the mines and paid tribute but did not work as agricultural laborers, probably fewer than three hundred thousand Indians worked on the estates of the *encomenderos*. Again, details are unknown, but from 1530 to 1600 the number of Indians working on the estates of *encomenderos* had dropped more than ten times, while the number of individual *encomiendas* had increased perhaps three times. The revenue of the *encomienda* dropped, but not nearly as much as the Indian population, which explains the mixed economic strategies pursued by *encomenderos*. If by the seventeenth century the Indian population had been reduced to one-sixth of its 1519 size, that of Creoles, Mestizos, and *peninsulares* had grown many times, populating mainly the cities and towns of New Spain. There were a few thousand *peninsulares*, perhaps as many as eighty thousand Creoles, and maybe two or three hundred thousand cultural and biological Mestizos living in urban areas (Meyer and Sheridan 1979:208–19). In addition, the Indian population had been sufficiently acculturated to create many needs for goods and services that required a much more diversified economy than New Spain had during the generation after the fall of Tenochtitlán (García Soriano 1954:205–37).

By the end of Viceroy Mendoza's tenure, there were more than six hundred *encomiendas* in New Spain, while fifty years later there were more than a thousand. At least one-third of these *encomenderos* were recipients of royal and viceregal patronage in 1600, a fact much resented by the descendants of conquistadors. Little information exists concerning the number of descendants of conquistadors that had lost *encomendero* status by the end of the century, but a good guess is that more than half of all conquistadors either did not receive *encomiendas* or, if they did, they were too small to have survived the hard times of the last quarter of the sixteenth century. One last consideration addresses the size of the *encomienda* and preferential treatment of *hidalgos*, for most officers in the conquering armies were also recipients of royal and viceregal patronage. It appears that the richest *encomiendas* were awarded to important people, including all three of the above categories, and practically from the beginning there developed a class of rich and powerful *encomendero* that significantly outranked the run-of-the-mill conquistadors who received Indians and land (Durand 1953, 1:65–73). This elite was never a large group, perhaps not more than a hundred or so *encomenderos* and their families, but they exercised a great deal of influence by virtue of being the leading *vecinos* of Mexico City and of the most important provincial cities such as Puebla, Oaxaca, Morelia, and Guadalajara (Peña 1983:219–33).

Three generations after the fall of Tenochtitlán, this crème de la crème of the *encomendero* class included only a tiny fraction of the descendants of the most distinguished conquistadors. It was composed of a few descendants of average conquistadors of *hidalgo* extraction and a few members of the rank and file, but mostly of *pobladores* that became prominent by virtue of royal and viceregal patronage. From the seventeenth century onward this core increased in direct proportion to the growth of the Creole population, but never was it more than 2 percent of this population until the end of Colonial times. There was a significant degree of upward and downward mobility as individuals were drafted into or dropped out of the system, but a consistent core maintained the integrity of this ruling class, members of which for more than three centuries managed to monopolize the greatest fortunes and epitomize social exaltedness (Ortega y Pérez Gallardo 1908).

URBANIZATION AND THE POWER BASE OF THE *ENCOMENDERO* CLASS

Urbanization in New Spain reflected the Spanish tradition of urban living going back to the early Middle Ages. The juridical implications of the *cabildo* made urbanization not only the intimate complement of the *encomienda* system but its prerequisite in the formation and development of Colonial society. Thus, throughout the sixteenth century, New Spain became connected and interrelated by a network of cities and towns. As the century progressed the urbs discharged different functions, and the *encomendero* class played a very important role. First, with the exception of the sui generis foundation of Veracruz, administrative cities (Mexico City, Tlaxcala, Oaxaca, Morelia, and so on) were established whose main functions were to organize the pacified territories and to furnish the seat of the viceregal and provincial bureaucracies. Next came the foundation of agricultural cities and towns, sometimes coterminously with administrative cities, and inevitably associated with the growth of the *encomienda*. Mining towns soon sprang up, often associated with the production of goods for general Colonial consumption. Finally, as the frontiers of New Spain expanded, primarily to the north, military and religious towns were established for controlling and converting new Indian populations (Nutini 1971).

The earliest towns controlled by conquistadors were, of course, administrative centers, primarily Mexico City, Veracruz, and Coyoacán, whose *vecinos* became the earliest *encomenderos*. As *encomiendas* proliferated, new administrative-agricultural cities came into being, first in the heartland of what had been the Triple Alliance and then to the north and south. Thus emerged the important *encomendero* cities of Querétaro, Morelia, Guadalajara, Oaxaca, and a few less important towns. In the heartland of New Spain, several other new cities shortly became *encomendero* centers, such as Puebla, Jalapa, Coatzacoalcos, Toluca, and so on (Nutini 1971). The *vecinos* of Mexico City and Veracruz should have had the greatest claims to *encomiendas* awarded within the more circumscribed areas of these latter cities. It did not happen according to plan—probably because of a natural process of fission and the greater convenience to *encomenderos* to have in their *encomiendas* a city closer to the Indians as a base of operation. By the turn of the seventeenth century, there were many administrative *encomendero* cities from Guatemala to Sinaloa. Some of these cities were little more than medium-size towns, never quite becoming important, and from the middle of the seventeenth century *encomendero* towns began to consolidate into larger, more powerful cities. To judge by the provenance of aristocratic *hacendado* families that migrated to Mexico City from the provinces after the Mexican Revolution of 1910, the leading *hacendado* cities basically had not changed in two and a half centuries. They remained Puebla, Guadalajara, Morelia, Guanajuato, Querétaro, San Luis Potosí, Veracruz, Jalapa, Oaxaca, Chihuahua, Durango, Zacatecas, and Mérida. Smaller concentrations of the agrarian ruling class may be regarded as satellites of these principal centers (Nutini 1986).

The situation is complicated by the distance to Mexico City and provincial capitals, types of agrarian enterprises, size of *encomiendas* and landed estates, and geographical features. A few examples may clarify matters. First, the central Mexican highlands and the coastal and inland areas of Veracruz were the first areas of New Spain where the *encomienda* flourished, and the *vecinos* of Mexico City and Veracruz were the first to be awarded Indians and land. Such, likely, was the state of affairs until the arrival of the second Audiencia, when the awarding of *encomiendas* proceeded faster (Liss 1975:95–125). In the meantime, new municipalities (*cabildos*) were founded in this vast territory (Coatzacoalcos, Tepeaca, Toluca) and new *vecinos* became *encomenderos* who appeared in the original grants as residents of these municipalities. Most new settlements, however, did not become *encomendero* towns, meaning essentially permanent urban residences for the large establishments characteristic of this class (Kubler 1942). Only on the northern fringes of New Spain did new *hacendado* towns come into being, but they never had much importance in the development of the Colonial ruling class, for they came late in the eighteenth century, were far from the centers of political and administrative power, and remained frontier areas until nearly the twentieth century (Nutini 1971).

Second, the case of the city of Puebla is illuminating. Some of the earliest Indian communities to be placed in *encomienda* (1521–23) were in the valley of Puebla, a rich agricultural land extending from the Sierra Nevada in the west as far as Orizaba and Tehuacán in the east. Many *encomiendas* were awarded in this area, among the recipients some of the most distinguished conquistadors such as Andrés de Tapia, Diego de Ordáz, and Leonel de Cervantes. But these *encomiendas* were rewarded to these and other conquistadors qua *vecinos* of Mexico City after the fall of Tenochtitlán. With the foundation of Puebla, the city became the center of craft production and manufacturing, for it harbored many Spaniards, both conquistadors and *moradores*. The great majority of conquistadors, although *vecinos* of Puebla, did not receive *encomiendas,* but engaged instead in craft production in the city itself, many opting for small-scale farming in the cultivation of the mulberry tree and cochineal, mostly with free Indian labor (Zavala 1973:231–37). In time, however, as early as 1570 or so, the city became an important *encomendero* center whose *encomiendas* included Indian communities from the Valley and far beyond. By the early decades of the seventeenth century, Puebla had become an *encomendero* city par excellence, combining a large population of Indians, Creoles, and Spaniards with a thriving craft and production establishment (Pérez de Salazar 1939). Until the twentieth century, Puebla was the second city of the land and an important *hacendado* center boasting a large array of old aristocratic families, some of whose mansions, a few of them still standing, date to the second half of the sixteenth century (la Casa del Mayorazgo de los Pérez de Salazar, la

Casa del Dean, the oldest standing private residence in Mexico, circa 1575). The earliest *encomenderos* in the area, prior to 1531, retained their Indians and land, but most of them continued to reside in Mexico City after Puebla was founded. One may assume that the attraction of being close to the viceregal authorities must have outweighed other considerations (Fernández Echeverría 1931:78–131). More significant is the fact that by the last decade of the sixteenth century, *encomenderos*, no longer constrained by the requirement of maintaining an inhabited residence where their *encomiendas* were located, could and did have several *encomiendas*, often distantly separated. Gonzalo Gómez de Cervantes, third-generation descendant of an original conquistador, had *encomiendas* in the Valley of Puebla, in the Valley of Mexico, and near Michoacán (Zavala 1973:692–95).

Third, as mining operations expanded from within a radius of one hundred miles from Mexico City toward the north and northwest, they added a new dimension to the *encomienda* and *repartimiento* systems. Near the turn of the century, when large mining operations began in New Spain, original *encomenderos* and small mining operators who had become reasonably rich participated jointly in the enterprise that made Spain the richest country in the world in silver and gold. This development modified the *encomienda* system, or rather the budding *hacienda* system, beginning shortly after the onset of the seventeenth century (Peña 1983:72–83). Owners of large mines from the first decade of the seventeenth century onward were among the most powerful members of the Colonial ruling class; if they were of *encomendero* extraction, they pursued a double economic strategy that combined mining with agrarian operations, and they were usually among the largest landowners in New Spain. If they were not, and had made their fortunes strictly as miners, they soon became *hacendados*, that is, acquired landed estates. It was an unspoken requirement for all upwardly mobile individuals of non-*encomendero* origins, whether miners, businessmen, or merchants on a large scale, to acquire a landed estate in the process of becoming bona fide members of the Creole aristocracy (Carreño 1961:31–42). At this stage, of course, the mining *repartimiento* was the structural equivalent of the *encomienda*, even though the former was more often than not awarded to individuals who were not descendants of conquistadors. This fact alone ensured that the miners of New Spain would occupy an important niche in the ruling class, particularly after 1700 (Ladd 1976:141–50).

The power base of *encomenderos,* and later of *hacendados,* rested not only in their agrarian and mining base but also in their control of the cities and towns where they lived and where their agrarian and mining operations were located. The concept of *vecino* meant fundamentally enfranchisement in a town or city, and in time, at least after the last original conquistadors had died, it referred to individuals who had become enfranchised by virtue of having been granted an *encomienda* within the community's sphere of influence and/or control. Thus, not all original *vecinos* became *encomenderos,* though foreign *encomenderos,* mostly recipients of royal or viceregal patronage, frequently became *vecinos.* Whatever the origin of *encomenderos,* they consistently monopolized the most important offices of the local *cabildo,* assiduously supported the church and sponsored religious constructions, and not infrequently engaged in business, trade, and manufacturing. The *encomendero* class was always small, never including more than 10 percent of the local Spanish and Creole population, and as the century advanced it became much smaller (Miranda 1947). By the middle of the seventeenth century, for example, the *encomendero* and *hacendado* class in the city of Puebla was less than 3 percent of the Creole and Spanish population of perhaps 15,000, that is, roughly eighty nuclear families that dominated the social, economic, political, and religious life of the city (Pérez de Salazar 1928).

As I have indicated, *encomenderos* were required to maintain *casa habitada* (inhabited house) in or near their *encomiendas.* Eventually, these modest abodes grew into large establishments, and by the middle of the seventeenth century they had become impressive constructions accommodating many people, storing varied agricultural products, and providing facilities for animal husbandry (cattle, horse, sheep, goat, and pig raising). Nothing in four hundred years of Mexican social and economic history is more telling than the *cascos de hacienda* (the fabric of elaborate establishments), manors that in various stages of disrepair dot the countryside of the central and southern states of the country. The earliest of these establishments have their roots in the last two decades of the sixteenth century. Most of the *haciendas* (this ambiguous term denotes both the manorial establishment and the lands it exploited), however, date from the late seventeenth century through the nineteenth century; some of them are elaborate and huge, with significant architectural merit. The *hacienda* became a symbol of aristocratic identification, a fountain of renewal, and a source of servants and many of the other amenities that sustained *hacendados* in the city (Pérez de Salazar 1928).

In the towns and cities that *encomenderos* and then *hacendados* controlled, the most ostensible measure of power and wealth were the mansions where they resided most of the year, another example of outstanding civic architecture. Town mansions—some of them in the eighteenth century approached the category of palaces—are not quite as old as country *haciendas,* although a few examples from the last decades of the sixteenth century can be found. Most of the mansions noted for architectural excellence are in Mexico City, Puebla, Morelia, and two or three other important Colonial cities that date from the last quarter of the seventeenth century to the end of the eighteenth century. Even today, eighty years after the Mexican aristocracy lost its great wealth, provincial cities remember these mansions. If the *hacienda* (rural mansion) represented the ostensible validation of the land and genealogy, the city mansion represented the continuous renewal of an aristocratic style of living. City mansions were complex and elaborate establishments designed for ostentation and social manipulation and conceived to distinguish their owners from the rest of the population. The Mexican aristocratic mansion in the city required large spaces, many servants, and an abundant supply of goods and services that every family of the class strove hard to satisfy to the best of their economic abilities. (Ovando n.d.).

Probably by the last decade of the sixteenth century the country-urban axis described above had appeared, but not until the middle of the seventeenth century do we have some concrete information concerning its role in the social life of the class. Though the aristocratic family had its permanent residence in the city, perhaps once a year the family spent a few weeks to a few months at a nearby *hacienda,* generally within fifty to one hundred miles at most. Most *hacendados* had more than one *hacienda* and generally had one close enough to the city for this kind of arrangement. *Hacendados* whose *haciendas* were hundreds of miles from the city, as in the case of some landed potentates of the north who resided permanently in Mexico City, either had a country place or visited the nearby *haciendas* of kinsmen and friends (Gage 1978:127–46). The country-city axis and the associated seasonal variation were important aspects of aristocratic living that changed little in hundreds of years and are still of residual importance for the dying aristocracy.

We should note here two aspects of the Spanish sociopolitical system and the ruling class it created: centralization and absentee land-lordship. At the viceregal level, Mexico City was the center of political power and all branches of the Spanish administration. From the beginning, New Spain was a centralized colony. The provinces, smaller replicas of the viceroyalty and provincial capitals, were invariably *encomendero* and *hacendado* cities where the second echelon of political and administrative control was concentrated. The Creole ruling class naturally gravitated toward these centers of power for social and cultural reasons as much as for political and economic reasons. The relatively brief interludes in the country were both respites from city life and mild efforts on the part of landed magnates to exploit their enormous estates more efficiently. This situation meant an urban ruling class of absentee landlords with few agrarian roots, except, of course, the ideological value of owning land and lording over the *encomienda* Indians and, later, the peons tied to the *hacienda* (Priestley 1926:270–94).

Of the more than one thousand *encomenderos* in New Spain at the turn of the seventeenth century, probably one-third resided in Mexico City, either as original *vecinos* or as *vecinos* of other cities who kept their main residence in the capital. As original *vecinos* of Mexico City, *encomenderos* had land and Indians not only in the provinces adjacent to the capital, within a radius of 150 miles or so, but also commonly in faraway provinces, and they generally also kept residences in provincial cities. Many of the remaining *encomenderos* (and, later, *hacendados*), who kept their main residence in the city to which their *encomienda* or *hacienda* was tied, also kept a residence in Mexico City where they spent a good deal of time (Carrión 1897:276–83). By the end of the seventeenth century only such large cities as Puebla and Guadalajara were complex and attractive enough to deter their *hacendados* from maintaining a residence in Mexico City. Centralization, then, concentrated an inordinate number of members of the *hacendado* ruling class in the capital, perhaps as many as 40 percent at any given time. Particularly from the late fall to the beginning of spring, when it reached its highest concentration of Creole aristocracy, the city bustled with social and economic activity. Even *hacendado* families from nearby cities who did not therefore keep a residence in the capital (cities such as Puebla, Querétaro, and Guanajuato, all within two to five days travel) converged on the capital for extended periods, particularly for the Christmas and New Year celebrations (Ovando n.d.).

Note that in the preceding discussion *encomenderos* are occasionally equated with *hacendados*. These categories are structurally different, but very similar in terms of personnel, that is, *encomendero* families became *hacendado* families when the *encomienda* was finally abolished and no more *repartimientos* were awarded. New *hacendado* families did arise after the abolition of the *encomienda*, but the bulk of them, and certainly the most prominent landed magnates, had been *encomenderos* of prominence. Despite much downward and some upward mobility in the structure of the Creole aristocracy, there is an unbroken continuity in the transition from *encomienda* to *hacienda* and on to the twentieth century (Zavala 1948:54–59).

Social Configuration of the Creole Aristocracy at the Beginning of the Seventeenth Century

The first two decades of the seventeenth century witnessed the crystallization of a Colonial ruling class that I characterize as a Creole aristocracy of *encomendero* origin. It included descendants both of conquistadors and recipients of royal and viceregal patronage. The more than one thousand *encomendero* families in New Spain during this period were concentrated in the capital and some twelve provincial cities throughout the viceroyalty. Mexico City was the hub of the Creole aristocracy, with more than a third of its total families, while every provincial nucleus contained anywhere from thirty to as many as eighty families. In terms of power, wealth, and social standing, however, this group was not uniform. From the beginning, the Creole aristocracy exhibited considerable differentiation. The *encomendero* class, which in about 1600 numbered less than 10 percent of the Creole and *peninsular* population, had a core of roughly three hundred families concentrated in Mexico City, Puebla, Guadalajara, and perhaps one or two more provincial capitals. They led the aristocracy by virtue of wealth, and power, and connections to the viceregal establishment (Baudot 1927:108–431).

The foregoing description may give the impression that as Colonial society entered the seventeenth century a number of independent provincial ruling classes, associated with the great agricultural and mining enterprises, dominated the social, economic, and political life of the major cities in New Spain. In fact, a national Creole aristocracy spanned the breadth of the colony, and, if not structurally uniform, it shared a worldview, it adopted the same values and orientation, and it used the same symbols and means of self-identification to ascertain its position as the superordinate class of the colony. Three main arguments buttress this assertion.

First, extrapolating from contemporary ethnography, we discern in the three generations after the Conquest a nucleus of Creole families centered in Mexico City and *encomendero* cities within a radius of about three hundred miles. The genealogies of a dozen families going back to the second half of the sixteenth century clearly demonstrate the kinship and social interrelationship among members of this nucleus and their intimate ties to the *peninsular* establishment, that is, high-ranking royal officials from the viceroy down to provincial governors (*alcaldes mayores*) (Ortega y Pérez Gallardo 1908). Except in terms of political functions, the precise segregation of Creoles from *peninsulares* is spurious. There is no specific information available concerning the number of *peninsulares* who returned to Spain after their tour of official duty. My guess is that, except for viceroys, the majority of Crown officials remained in the colony, their descendants hereby becoming Creole after a generation. In other words, the Creole aristocracy was constantly renewed by *peninsular* blood of the Crown bureaucracy (Ovando n.d.). From the standpoint of kinship and stratification, there was never any distinction between the Creole aristocracy and the elite bureaucracy. In any event, by 1600 a powerful, small, and rather close-knit Creole aristocracy had emerged in close social and matrimonial alliance with the viceregal bureaucracy. This nucleus of the Creole aristocracy remained fairly constant throughout Colonial times, but it was periodically reinvigorated by peninsular elements and local plutocratic, upwardly mobile elements (Pérez de Salazar n.d.).

Second, by as early as the last two decades of the sixteenth century, intermarriage among descendants of conquistadors of *encomendero* status was becoming very common. This phenomenon again is revealed in contemporary genealogies and in the accounts of historians (Ladd 1976; Israel 1975; Gómez de Cervantes 1944). When the missions were secularized and when the *hacienda* system began on a large scale, the Creole aristocracy was an essentially endogenous class, whose social life was discharged within an essentially endogenous ambiance (Chevalier 1952). It is possible to document marriage alliances among *encomenderos* and, later, *hacendados* in the centrally located cities, particularly Mexico City, Puebla, Guadalajara, Morelia, Querétaro, Oaxaca, and Veracruz. Prominent families from Mexico City, Puebla, and Morelia were related by marriage alliances that continued uninterrupted until the end of Colonial times. These families had been started by some of the founders of these cities, a few of the largest original *encomenderos*, and a sprinkling of later arrivals, recipients of royal or viceregal patronage (Pérez de Salazar n.d.). They were the richest sector of New Spain, and a decade into the seventeenth century, members of this elite of the elite were the first Creoles to receive titles of nobility. By that time, however, the *encomienda* was already decaying and this magnate group had significantly diversified its economic interest, including cattle raising and commercial agriculture in lowland areas, mining operations, and commerce. Landed estates after the middle of the seventeenth century often changed hands, for there was a good deal of downward economic mobility. There was also, however, stability in the highest ranks of the landed aristocracy, and this subclass within a class had an unbroken existence until the Mexican Revolution of 1910, as attested by the survival of some one hundred families today that can demonstrate social and landed continuity to the middle of the seventeenth century (Castillo Ledón 1932). Even the peripheral component of the aristocracy was drawn into the core networks of kinship and marriage, and by the beginning of the seventeenth century, the *encomendero* class as a whole considered themselves *hidalgos*, whether they were descendants of conquistadors or of *pobladores* who had arrived later (Ovando n.d.). It is tempting to make a distinction between a higher and a lower Creole aristocracy. Such a distinction actually became a jural reality by the middle of the eighteenth century, when New Spain featured several dozen titles of nobility. Even at this early time, however, the four main variables that configured and stratified the aristocracy were at work: antiquity and distinction of lineage, and power and wealth. Descendants of original conquistadors with small *encomiendas* on the fringes of the system could contract advantageous marriages with magnate aristocrats or with powerful upcoming plutocrats, while many poor *encomendero* families were dropping out of the system (Perrot 1968:76–84). This pattern recurred until after the Mexican Revolution of 1910: a significant number of upwardly mobile plutocrats become aristocrats, while an even more significant number of aristocrats drop out of the system. This process of upward and downward mobility is the single most important perpetuator of the Creole aristocracy and, after Independence, the Mexican aristocracy at a fairly constant level for more than three hundred years: one thousand families, give or take one hundred (Fernández de Recas 1965).

Third, above and beyond the multiple regional and colonywide ties of kinship and marriage that configured the most salient sectors of the Creole aristocracy, this ruling class was further united by a network of social ties, which included the gamut of personal and family interaction such as *hacienda* visiting, invitations to important events, participation in secular and religious celebrations, games, and so on. These patterns of social interaction were, of course, the rule at all levels of Colonial society, but particularly among all sectors of the aristocracy (Weckmann 1984:641–58). These expressive patterns were most accentuated at the core of Creole aristocracy, and to a large extent the segment enfranchised in Mexico City set the tone for the rest of New Spain. The Creole aristocracy enfranchised in cities far from the capital paid periodic visits to the capital to renew old friendships and acquaintances, visit friends and kinsmen, acquire the latest fashions, participate in elaborate entertainment, and perhaps most important of all, survey the marriage market. In addition, this peripheral aristocracy engaged in the same activities at the regional level, and a provincial city often functioned for the region as Mexico City did for New Spain as a whole.

The lists of original conquistadors (from 1519 to 1542) and the original *cabildos* of which they became charter members show that surprisingly few could be counted among the magnate *encomenderos* or other rich and powerful people by the onset of the seventeenth century. To begin with, the descendants of the two main dramatis personae of the Conquest of Mexico were never really part of the social life of New Spain: the descendants of Montezuma moved to Spain at the end of the sixteenth century, and the descendants of Cortés never lived in New Spain for any length of time. Perhaps more significant, the descendants of only two of Cortés's distinguished officers and important men in the conquering army were prosperous, important families in 1600: Andrés de Tapia and Diego de Ordáz, both of them original *encomenderos* in the Valley of Puebla. Pedro de Alvarado, Cristobal de Olid, Gonzalo de Sandoval, and a few others died before 1536 and left no descendants, although the brothers of Alvarado prospered in Guatemala (Dorantes de Carranza 1970:435–91). Even accounting for the dead, the survival and adaptability of the descendants of distinguished conquistadors were very low, perhaps as low as the descendants of rank-and-file conquistadors. Separating reality from myth, one may hypothesize that conquistadors were superior warriors but mediocre managers. Genealogical information, published and in private archives, indicate that only a handful of descendants of distinguished conquistadors, notably those of Leonel de Cervantes, were members of the elite nucleus of the Creole aristocracy in 1600 (Ortega y Peréz Gallardo 1908). In short, there was a high degree of downward mobility among the descendants of original conquistadors (Conde Diaz Rubín n.d.).

Though the recipient of an *encomienda* earned this distinction by service to the Crown, thereby becoming a member of an elite group, the possession of an *encomienda* guaranteed neither permanent social distinction nor economic success. Indeed, as we have noted, the majority of *encomendero* families of conquistador extraction had dropped out of the system by the turn of the century, moving downward to the level of the Creole population concentrated in cities and towns (Ortega y Pérez Gallardo 1908). Who, then, were the elite aristocratic nucleus by the turn of the century? The majority of this group were descendants not of conquistadors but of recipients of royal and viceregal patronage. These were later arrivals who did not participate in the Conquest, but who managed to acquire *vecino* status in some of the *encomendero* towns already in existence (1530–50) in the choice *encomienda* regions in the heartland of New Spain. Significantly, these nonconquistador elements engaged more actively in business; they became the leaders in the manufacturing and trade that characterized the second half of the sixteenth century (Peña 1983:112–34). This group also included founders of new *cabildos,* and thus *vecinos* in their own right, as the frontiers of New Spain expanded, particularly to the north, and large areas were effectively controlled. Another very important component of the aristocratic nucleus were high-ranking royal officials, whose descendants were handsomely rewarded with Indians and land (Ovando n.d.). First- and second-generation Creoles, recipients of the earliest titles of nobility, formed the core of the Creole aristocracy, and by virtue of their multiple kinship and ritual kinship interrelationships, they became the arbiters of social life until the end of Colonial times (Ladd 1976:13–23).

The discussion would not be complete without reference to the native Indian aristocracy. As part of the policy of "indirect rule" (that is, employing native rulers as intermediaries between royal authorities and the Indian masses), the native nobility was recognized by the Crown and acquired a place in Colonial society. Pre-Hispanic society was basically stratified into a noble and a commoner estate, and the former in turn was further divided into three ranks: *tlatoani* (king or petty king), *teuctli* (lord), and *pilli* (nobleman) (Carrasco 1976:192–98). Many high-ranking nobles, mostly *tlatoanime*, were incorporated into the upper ranks of Spanish society. By the end of the sixteenth century, however, most of the Indian nobility had reverted to commoner (that is, peasant) status. There were exceptions, of course; the nobility of the Tlaxcalan Confederacy, for example, survived as a native aristocracy until after Colonial times.

A significant amount of intermarriage occurred between conquistador-*encomenderos* and Indian women of the highest rank, though very few Indian nobles married Spanish women of rank. This pattern of intermarriage was established at the beginning of the Conquest when two Tlaxcalans princesses, Luisa Xicohtencatl and Leonor Maxixcatzin, daughters of the two main lords of the Confederacy, were presented to Cortés; they eventually married distinguished conquistadors (Nutini and Bell 1908:288–91). Within a generation of the fall of Tenochtitlán, a significant number of noble Indian women had married conquistadors or later arrivals from Mexico City, Texcoco, Huejotzingo, and several other cities that had been centers of the most important pre-Hispanic principalities. One explanation of this relatively frequent practice is that it provided well-placed conquistadors with another avenue of securing more Indians and land, for noble Indian women provided these commodities as dowry. There was another element that facilitated these marriage alliances during the first two generations, namely, the upward aspirations of some conquistadors and the allure of the refined nobility and civilization that they had destroyed. Three generations later these incentives were gone, and the Creole aristocracy became highly endogamous. By 1600, marriages between Creole aristocrats and Indian women no longer occurred, for the native nobility had disappeared as a viable social class, and its most prominent members were incorporated into the *encomendero* ruling class (Israel 1975:60–63). Throughout the remainder of Colonial times, pride in lineage and race dominated the superordinate class.

I do not intend to slight the function of merchants, trading, and manufacturing in the formation of the Creole ruling class of New Spain. I am well aware of the important role of these nonagrarian, nonmining elements. Their significance is well demonstrated by Peña (1983), particularly with reference to the various economic strategies employed by *encomenderos* and *pobladores* alike and to the configuration of powerful oligarchical nuclei of mixed provenance, including merchants who amassed fortunes without the benefit of mines, land, or, perhaps, royal or viceregal patronage. Moreover, from the start *encomenderos* and early *pobladores* (recipients of royal patronage) engaged in mercantile activities, but the most successful merchants often surpassed the wealth of those engaged exclusively in agrarian enterprises, given the inefficiency of agriculture and the inadequacy of *encomienda* income as the century progressed (Peña 1983:109–10; 134–43). In this fluid ambiance, plutocratic merchants and budding aristocrats interacted socially, and by the turn of the century they had contracted crucial matrimonial alliances. The inability of most conquistadors to establish lineages (*mayorazgos*) and the aristocratic pretensions of merchants of nonconquistador extraction were further significant inputs in the formation of the Creole ruling class (Peña 1983:234–38).

By 1630, then, there was a well-established Creole aristocracy fashioned in the same pattern as that of the mother country, including an incipient nobiliary system (the first titles were being awarded to Creoles). This fledgling aristocracy numbered about a thousand families centered in the capital and main *encomendero-hacendado* cities, and it was roughly stratified into three ranks: a small group of no more than three dozen families—related by multiple ties of kinship and marriage—who possessed the five titles of nobility at the time (the highest oligarchical nucleus identified by Peña [1983]); an elite group of some three hundred families enfranchised in the capital and three or four centrally located cities; and a more numerous peripheral group distributed in nine or ten cities throughout the viceroyalty. Though the Creole aristocracy did not participate politically at the viceregal and provincial levels, its members controlled or played prominent roles in local (*cabildo*) politics. They were prime movers in the most important cities associated with agriculture, cattle raising, and mining. Thus, the Creole aristocracy was a powerful ruling class by virtue of its landed, mining, and commercial wealth; and it was the dominant social class by virtue of its multiple kinship ties and its control of the "cultural" and expressive life of the cities.

CHAPTER 5

Ideology and Expressive Configuration of the Creole Aristocracy as a Social and Ruling Class

In Spain, as in all European nations, many medieval institutions and a seigneurial ideology survived until the nineteenth century. But it was in the colonies of the New World that the inheritance of the Middle Ages not only survived but thrived for more than three centuries. Several scholars (Durand 1953; Weckmann 1984; Liss 1975; Chevalier 1952) have discussed Mexico's medieval inheritance, rightly emphasizing that it shaped many social and cultural domains of the nation, that it fashioned a polity whose ideational and ideological framework was still somewhat rooted in the fifteenth century, and that it was, in fact, affected very little by the Renaissance or the Enlightenment. The century following the Conquest of Mexico witnessed the formation of a distinct polity: an essentially medieval ideology and conception of society configured a new system that sometimes confronted and sometimes accommodated to somewhat modern notions and constraints imposed by the political and economic realities of the Spanish Crown. This basic equation colors practically every aspect of Colonial life, and the institutional, social, and cultural foundations of the colony often became combinations of arcane and modern elements. The realities of Spanish imperialism and demographic constraints modified the expectations of conquistadors and later arrivals, configuring an ideology and *imago mundi* that were both antecedent conditions and consequent realizations of a ruling class vested in a Creole aristocracy (Chevalier 1952:245–87).

Inception and Structuring of the Conquistadors'
Imago Mundi

SCHOLARLY BACKGROUND AND SCENARIO OF THE
SPANISH CONQUEST

Until quite recently, it has been difficult for most historians, Mexican
or not, to write objectively and impartially about the Conquest of
Mexico and its aftermath. The works of Durand (1953), Chevalier
(1952), Liss (1975), Peña (1983), Weckmann (1984), and Zavala
(1973), to name a few of the most outstanding scholars who have dealt
with these problems, rise above the insidious effects of the Black
Legend or the subtle influence of misplaced nationalism and class
preconceptions, to write balanced, objective accounts of this important
episode in the formation of classes and nationalities in the New World.
From different perspectives and with different goals, these scholars
construct accurate, comprehensive accounts of the formation and implications of an estate-class system.

Given the nature of the Spanish Conquest of Mexico, the contradictory aims and expectations of conquistadors and of the Crown and
religious authorities, and the great rewards available, it is not an easy
task to assess myth and reality, rightful claims, and spurious exaggerations. In the new land, ancient European institutions forged during the
Middle Ages not only survived the mother country but actually experienced a vigorous revival. Underlying the birth of the new society was a
blending of medieval principles and ideas and immediate expectations
borne out of the economic fruits of the Conquest. Behaviors and proclivities that in Europe were being constrained or obliterated by modernization and royal absolutism were reinvigorated in a milieu that
provided new opportunities and the material conditions of millions of
Indians and vast expanses of land. Thus ensued the tug of war between
conquistadors, the ideological shapers of a medieval revival, and the
viceregal government, the defender of Crown control and centralization
(McAlister 1963:349–70).

The mistaken notion that the worldview of conquistadors differed
from that of the warrior class of Spain as it emerged in the Middle Ages
can be traced to the early part of the twentieth century. In truth, the
imago mundi of the superordinate class (estate) remained basically unchanged. Differences do exist, however, in the economic and demo-

graphic conditions of New Spain, which permitted continuation of the medieval model, but only as constrained and stunted by the centralized, quasi-modern model of the Spanish Crown. The Crown was never entirely successful in preventing the growth of seigneurialism, but neither did the *encomienda* system and the formation of landed estates in New Spain become the seigneurial system that existed in Spain before Ferdinand and Isabella. Durand (1953) does an excellent job of presenting the myth and how it was constrained by reality. Weckmann (1984) ably discusses reality and how it was shaped by the myth. In this chapter I seek to bring these elements together.

In order of efficacy, the following ideological and structural inputs shaped the formation of the *imago mundi* of New Spain's ruling class: (1) The time-honored right of conquest of the Christian host as Spain emerged from the last episodes of the Reconquest. (2) The warrior ideology of conquistadors, also conditioned by centuries of fighting foreign domination of the peninsula. (3) An estate conception of society in which all Indians were *pecheros,* all Creoles *hidalgos,* and all conquistadors and their descendants a sort of higher nobility. (4) The private-enterprise nature of the Conquest of Mexico in securing vast possessions for the Spanish Crown. (5) The military "feudal" duties of *encomenderos* in holding the land for the Crown until the establishment of regular militias late in the sixteenth century. (6) A relentless pursuit of honor, fame, and personal advancement in the service of the Crown. (7) The ambition of nobility, the usurpation of noble privilege, and the foundations of *mayorazgos* as a means to perpetuate lineage.

IDEOLOGICAL INPUTS AND STRATIFICATIONAL VARIABLES

Conquistadors cherished the fundamental medieval belief that the profession of arms was the noblest pursuit. Spaniards had nurtured this deeply ingrained belief for centuries of fighting the Moors, and it had its roots in the conquest of Spain by the Visigoths. The belief-myth was fully alive during the Conquest of Mexico, as conquistadors often referred to themselves with pride as *godos* (Goths). After the Conquest of Mexico the term became archaic, but it was renewed and metamorphosed graphically the word conquistador. During the century following the Conquest this myth-reality was embellished and acquired attributes suitable to the changing times (Durand 1953, 1:73–77).

Right of conquest pervades the writings of conquistadors, their legalistic maneuvers and agitations to secure Indians and land becoming in time exaggerated statements of what they achieved. The deeds of the Conquest become almost impossible accomplishments, and the feats of the Spanish host come to resemble the works of Hercules (Weckmann 1984, 1:55–88). Ultimately, the embroidered myths of conquest became counterproductive to the goals of conquistadors and their descendants, who sought above all just recognition of their deeds in terms of honors and economic rewards. Conquistadors and their descendants achieved some of their goals but never became the ruling or the political class of New Spain. The conquistadors and their descendants nonetheless created a powerful *imago mundi* that became the cornerstone of a local aristocracy that combined social, ruling, and political functions indivisibly constituted, the likes of which had ceased to exist in Spain and most of Europe.

After the fall of Granada, many "professional" soldiers made their way to the New World and continued to arrive even during the wars in North Africa and Italy. These seasoned soldiers were attracted by the opportunity of gold and adventure promised by each new discovery and by the fabulous descriptions of the land and its people. Astonishing vistas opened invitingly to the restless Spaniards of that time (Weckmann 1984, 1:55–70). Soldiers or peasants, *hidalgos* or *villanos,* the conquistadors of New Spain overnight became a warrior class. They conquered in the name and glory of king, country, and the Holy Catholic Church, but what they conquered, they felt, was theirs to reap as an inalienable right. To a man, the conquering host shared this conception of itself, and regardless of station its members demanded to be treated as befitted this status. Cortés (1963) himself fueled these pretensions in his dispatches to the emperor by describing the Conquest as an unparalleled feat of arms that had won the Crown vast lands and potentially untold riches, by exalting the bravery of his soldiers, his generalship, and by emphasizing the great sufferings with which the land had been won.

The composition of Cortés's army, as near as we can establish from the incomplete and somewhat indeterminate data presently available, included about 17 percent *hidalgos*. This estimate may be too low. Las Casas, no friend of conquistadors, says that in Santo Domingo there were many *hidalgos*. Dorantes de Carranza, at the beginning of the seventeenth century, concurs, as does Zavala among modern scholars.

Durand (1953, 1:80–82) even states that in the period of the great conquests (Mexico, Peru, and New Granada) *los hidalgos segundones* (second-born sons of *hidalgos*) predominated in the conquering hosts. Moreover, the high number of *hidalgos* among the conquistadors became a significant acculturative element, playing a determinant role in homogenizing the *imago mundi* of conquistadors: the distinction between *hidalgo* and *pechero* blurs and ultimately disappears by virtue of the former serving as the model for the latter. That the initial configuration of conquistadors' attitudes, behaviors, and distinct worldview was a kind of *hidalgo-pechero* acculturative process is attested by Díaz del Castillo (1967).

The conquistadors' assertion of right of conquest and the conception of themselves as a warrior caste reflected the belief that after their feat had been accomplished they were ipso facto elevated to a superordinate rank: *pecheros* rightfully became *hidalgos* entitled to traditional privileges; and *hidalgos* could rightfully vie for titles of nobility. Again, material and demographic conditions supported this ancient claim and gave credence to the conquistadors' allegations: in New Spain, as in all other lands of the New World, Spaniards were not required to pay tribute, making them de facto *hidalgos* according to ancient custom; and *hidalgos* of high standing, most of Cortés's captains, felt they deserved no less a title of nobility than that which Cortés received from the emperor (Díaz del Castillo 1967:267–71). Thus, all Indians became tributaries, that is, *pecheros,* while all Creoles and *peninsulares,* regardless of their original social standing, became *hidalgos* since they did not pay tribute. The situation was significantly more complicated, however, as a large class of Mestizos had come into existence by 1600, who also did not pay tribute but who by no stretch of the imagination could style themselves *hidalgos* and be so recognized by the Creole population (Liss 1975:109–22). The same more or less applied to the great majority of the approximately seventy thousand Creoles residing in New Spain by the turn of the seventeenth century.

Original conquistadors of commoner extraction assumed the status of *hidalgo* not only as a right they had earned but with the tacit approval of the Crown. Though it never officially sanctioned the practice, on several occasions the Crown stated that original conquistadors had the right to *hidalguía,* which was later on extended to *pobladores.* It is not clear whether this meant that with due *limpieza de sangre* (status of a Christian of long standing), commoner conquistadors could present *probanzas* (genealogical proof) and officially be elevated to *hidalgo* rank, or simply that the Crown bestowed the status of *hidalgo* as a customary courtesy. Judging by the high incidence of downward mobility during the second and third generations after the Conquest, most commoner conquistadors, when their reward in Indians and/or land never came or was too small to make a significant social difference, gave up hope, though their descendants may have kept the myth-reality alive. In the end, *hidalguía* conveyed little more than an honorific status, for most conquistadors never achieved that legal standing, though bona fide *hidalgos* among conquistadors did manage to establish *mayorazgos* or become part of the ruling aristocratic nuclei of New Spain (McAlister 1963).

In New Spain, estate stratification never existed de jure among the Creole and *peninsular* population, not even after a local nobiliary system came into existence beginning in the seventeenth century and greatly augmented during the eighteenth century. The titled nobility of New Spain became an essentially ceremonial aristocracy, enjoying honorific privileges and rights of precedence, and few if any significant economic privileges vis-à-vis the Creole population (Liss 1975:134–35). But from the beginning, and until the end of Colonial times, an estate system of stratification existed between those who paid tribute, the Indians in their communities, and those who did not, Creoles, *peninsulares,* and the growing Mestizo population. Thus, the estate system of New Spain had a strong ethnic component nonexistent in Spain that de jure and de facto deepened stratification into two near castes. In this respect, the rather ambivalent position of the Spanish Crown fostered the growth of a landed aristocracy and ruling class that its express policy intended to curtail (Peña 1982:76). The ethnic component, given the great demographic imbalance between Indians and Spaniards, ultimately defeated the stated aims of the Crown, and New Spain was dominated by a seigneurial system that not even Independence could dislodge.

We must differentiate between the customary and the juridical aspects and implications of the Colonial estate system in order to understand the role of *hidalguía* and the Spanish (Creole)–Indian (Mestizo) cleavage in forming the Colonial ruling class and its world-view. The concept of a lower nobility was not as significant in New Spain as in Spain, since it had nothing to do with the ethnic distinction between Europeans (Creoles and *peninsulares*) and Indians and peoples of mixed parentage. Thus, tribute paying juridically defined the two estates, but custom defined Mestizos as members of the subordinate estate and minimally discriminated between the *hidalgo* and non-*hidalgo* population of Creoles and *peninsulares*. *Hidalguía* in New Spain was never as important and as extensive as in Spain, and it may very well be the case that the *hidalgo*-commoner ratio was much higher at the time of the Conquest than a century later, since subsequent migrants from Spain throughout the sixteenth century were mainly of commoner extraction. Again, the customary dimensions of *hidalguía* stem from the deeply felt belief of conquistadors and their descendants that the Conquest had ennobled them (Lira Montt 1976). It was enough to know that one's ancestry included a conquistador to consider oneself *hidalgo*. The number of genuine juridical *hidalgos* in New Spain by the first half of the seventeenth century had probably dropped below 10 percent of the population, less than the percentage in Spain at the time. They were the descendants of *hidalgo* conquistadors, a few rank-and-file conquistadors who were ennobled, and Crown officials and recipients of viceregal patronage who were *hidalgos* when they arrived in New Spain or were ennobled after having achieved economic success. Thus, by the first half of the seventeenth century many Creoles could claim customary *hidalguía,* while probably the majority of the *encomendero-hacendado* had become juridical *hidalgos* (Durand 1953, 2:31–53).

In summary, *hidalguía* was a source for as well as a result of the right of conquest of conquistadors, who with a warrior *imago mundi* created a society that discriminated on the basis of ethnicity (Creole and *peninsular* versus Mestizo and Indian), while it served as a mechanism of validation among ethnic equals in the quest of upward mobility (Creole and *peninsular*). The juridical quest and acquisitions of *hidalguía* were almost exclusively associated with the upward mobility of a rising plutocracy that acquired rank by virtue of power and wealth, or upon being integrated into the ruling nuclei that constituted the Creole aristocracy. In this context, juridical *hidalguía* was prized as a validation of acquired status and as a means to acquiring the ultimate honor, namely, a title of nobility. Customary *hidalguía,* on the other hand, was little more than an expression of the fluidity of a new society, as contrasted with a vastly more numerous subordinate population, and an usurpation that was tolerated because it entailed few social and no economic consequences (Lira Montt 1976).

Juridical Inputs and
Sociopsychological Determinants

If the right of conquest was the necessary condition for the conquista-dors' claim to the land and its exploitation, the sufficient condition is to be sought in the way the Conquest was undertaken. Conquistadors' petitions for grants of Indians and land repeatedly emphasized not only that they had risked their lives, worked ceaselessly, and suffered many privations but that their deeds had been accomplished with their own resources. They claimed that *encomiendas* and grants of land were a just recompense for risking life and fortune for king and country, occasion-ally exaggerating the importance of the Conquest and their outstand-ing contributions. This reasoning constituted the most persistent and cogent argument of conquistadors in defense of their rights well into the seventeenth century. The argument was most forcefully stated by Gonzalo Gómez de Cervantes (1944:91–94). Whatever the merits of Cervantes's spirited defense of the rights of *encomenderos,* whom he implicitly equates with descendants of conquistadors, he vividly ex-presses resentment, probably universal among this social group, over not having been properly rewarded and over the favoritism of the Crown toward Spanish-born bureaucrats, sentiments echoed by future Creole writers for generations to come. For example, early in the seventeenth century Baltasar Dorantes de Carranza (1970:235–37) bit-terly complains that many conquistadors have abandoned the land for lack of Crown support and that parvenus have taken their place to the detriment of all; a few years later, Juan de Solórzano Pereyra (1930, vol. 1) maintains that the *encomiendas* given to conquistadors are noth-ing more than rightful stipends for their labors in conquering the land.

In describing Mexico's medieval inheritance, Weckmann (1983, 1:31–121) emphasizes the conquistadors' "feudal" conception of their feat of arms and the tremendous deeds they had accomplished. Early chroniclers and modern scholars almost unanimously describe the con-quistadors as marveling at the vast panoramas of the new land and at the strangeness of customs and peoples. Myth and reality must have been ever present to conquistadors, if we are to believe the primary and secondary accounts of the Conquest (Díaz del Castillo 1967; Gómara 1971; Solís 1968) and the research of modern scholars (Durand 1953; Liss 1975; Verlinden 1954; Weckmann 1984), who have reconstructed the social and psychological ambiance of the Conquest of Mexico.

After the entrepreneurial nature of the Conquest, the military, feudallike duties of conquistadors reinforced their claims to Indians and land and their right to political office. The exigencies of establishing the colony and the task of maintaining the peace constituted a real claim to honors and rewards. The Crown had to rely on the original conquistadors and their *encomendero* descendants. They were the only military force that could be called upon in emergencies, as it happened on a few occasions, particularly the Mixton War (1541–43). That the Crown could have established a military presence in New Spain independent of conquistadors after the arrival of the first viceroy in 1535 is not likely, entangled as it was in fighting the Counter-Reformation and in the military operations in Spain's several European possessions. As it developed, the viceroy relied on *encomenderos,* most of whom until the latter sixteenth century were not landed proprietors and were therefore free to engage in the military operations to expand the northern frontiers of New Spain (Weckmann 1988, 1:3–9). For two generations after the Conquest, until roughly 1575, the *encomenderos* and many conquistadors who had not received *encomiendas* made up the army of New Spain. Furthermore, until well after the arrival of Viceroy Mendoza, *encomenderos* performed duties similar to those of the Santa Hernandad in Spain: to enforce justice, to provide protection for travelers, and to maintain orderly civil life in the *cabildos* they controlled and in the Indian communities that had been granted to them. Though they had no juridical functions, *encomenderos* could be called by *corregidores* to help in the manifold judicial and administrative aspects of controlling Indian populations. During the last quarter of the sixteenth century, the raison d'être of conquistadors as a military force disappeared, as regular militias were being organized under the direct control of the viceregal government (Weckmann 1988:415–17). By then, of course, the martial conception of conquistadors and *encomenderos* was firmly entrenched and had played a significant role in the worldview of the group, which thenceforth rationalized their configuration as a social class.

Much has been made of the unbounded desire of conquistadors for honor and fame, or as Durand (1953:45–51) puts it, *ir a valer más* and *el afán de honra.* These appetites are certainly important considerations in assessing the character of conquistadors and the reasons that impelled them to join conquering hosts. But what these variables mean sociologically and how they became significant inputs in the configuration of the *imago mundi* of the Creole aristocracy in New Spain are difficult questions to answer. Spaniards came to the New World, for the three generations after Columbus's discovery, to search for gold and other riches. There is no question that in the Conquest of Mexico, as in many other similar enterprises, Spaniards were motivated primarily by greed for gold and recognition. The conception of themselves as paladins of a new crusade for king and faith is a later development, a rationalization, if you will, for the purely personal achievement of honor and fame. There is little doubt that significant numbers of original conquistadors, perhaps the majority of *hidalgos,* were motivated solely by a quest for honor and fame, not by a desire for wealth. To be sure, the original evidence is scanty and ambiguous, either self-serving (Cortés 1963; Díaz del Castillo 1967; Gómara 1971) or written generations after the Conquest (Solís 1968; Dorantes de Carranza 1970; Torquemada 1969). It is almost impossible to address these problems sociopsychologically; nonetheless, the concepts of honor and fame must be made sociologically more explicit.

I suggested that, due to the Reconquest, the estate system in Spain was less rigid than in the rest of western Europe. But if the Reconquest had to some extent liberalized the estate system, and upward mobility was more easily attained by commoners, the ideology of stratification remained more conservative and traditional than in most of western Europe (Pike 1972:22–51). In classical feudal fashion, only those who waged war and ruled were entitled to honor and fame; in Spain, these were prerogatives that belonged and accrued only to the nobility. If we define honor as "the respect and accompanying homage that a man deserves and universally receives because of his personal qualities, lineage, power, or wealth" and fame as attained only by practitioners of the honorable professions (warfare, statecraft, and literature), only the titled nobility and *hidalgos* were in principle honorable men and could aspire to various degrees of fame (Durand 1953, 1:45–51). These were the behavioral, psychological privileges of the nobility, and they were part of Spanish society until well into the seventeenth century. It seems likely, therefore, that the majority of *hidalgos,* commoner soldiers, and *pecheros* who came to the New World were motivated not only by the quest of wealth but by the prospect of attaining honor and fame: *hidalgos* set on becoming higher nobles; commoners desirous of attaining a measure of honor and fame through military exploits, the most accessible means of upward mobility. Conquistadors of commoner extraction must have been particularly motivated to escape a difficult situation of social and ideological subordination and to achieve recognition in the new land that opened itself bountifully to them in the astonishing accounts that had circulated in Spain since Columbus's original voyage (Chevalier 1970:309–14).

It is doubtful that many merchants and peasants participated in the Conquest of Mexico. The last two categories of conquistadors were in fact minimally represented, as befitted perhaps the least adventurous segments of the Spanish population of the time. The configuration of conquistadors in terms of estates and professions is important to consider, for the ideology and *imago mundi* that were developed by subsequent generations were most likely created by a rather homogeneous group with a strong warrior orientation. Though conquistadors did change, perhaps greatly, after the Conquest and in the process of becoming or seeking to become *encomenderos*, their actions were those of a warrior class with a high sense of mission and a definite self-conception as rulers of the new land (Simpson 1967:22–51).

The *hidalgos* constituted the centerpiece of the initial configuration of the conquistadors as a determinant group in forming Colonial society and in developing an aristocratic worldview, for they provided the expressive model and the patterns of upward mobility for the rank and file. The changing perception and structural configuration of conquistadors, as they evolved into *encomenderos*, then into a Creole ruling class, and ultimately into a titled aristocracy, may be regarded as a case of acculturation. *Hidalgos* provided the basic superordinate ideology, while the rank and file among conquistadors and subsequent personnel of *poblador* and merchant extraction contributed numerical strength and a solid economic orientation. Though the majority of conquistadors participating in the conquest and consolidation of New Spain (1519–45) were undoubtedly motivated by the desire to return to Spain rich, most of them stayed in the New World and became acutely aware that the land and its people constituted the real wealth of the colony, thereby undergoing their first transformation and became *encomenderos* or actively and persistently lobbied the Crown for Indians and land. The effect of the Conquest itself was determinant. When conquistadors found themselves masters of a vast domain and entrusted with the economic control of enormous numbers of Indians, all wealth became means to the ends of honor and fame. The final, definitive transformation is a consequence of the fact that, in the ideology of conquistadors, the acquisition of honor and fame was the same as being ennobled: the official acquisition of *hidalguía*, titles of nobility, and the perpetuation of one's lineage (Durand 1953, 2:7–30).

By 1575, first- and second-generation conquistadors had acquired a basically medieval vision of themselves as the lords of the land, a vision soon shared by *encomenderos,* recipients of royal and viceregal extraction, and powerful plutocrats. They assumed a preeminent position vis-à-vis the Creole population with a claim to high political office and seigneurial domain over the Indian population and in the landed estates that they had managed to acquire. Perhaps all conquistadors and their descendants regarded themselves as *hidalgos* by right of conquest. Successful conquistadors—that is, those who had received sizable grants of Indians and land—were not content with this customary usage and eagerly sought juridical *hidalguía,* while those who were juridical *hidalgos* to begin with became the prime candidates for titles of nobility. A parallel process applied to all nonconquistadors with pretensions to *hidalguía* and higher nobility, namely, *encomenderos* and assorted plutocrats by virtue of royal and viceregal patronage (Weckmann 1984:102–17).

The preceding variables may be roughly placed in the following context: The right of conquest, the warrior ideology of conquistadors, and their conception of society as an estate system vis-à-vis the Indian population constituted the structural-ideological matrix that legitimized the conquistadors' claim to the land and its people and the organization of a new society in the image of the traditional society out of which Spain was emerging. What propelled conquistadors and gave definitive form to the matrix I describe was the relentless pursuit of honor and fame and the desire for ennoblement and perpetuation of lineage. Within the boundaries of a somewhat more fluid estate system, the conquerors saw themselves as actors in a drama that, given the aims of the Crown, could not possibly be validated entirely. Nonetheless, conquistadors cast themselves in a superordinate role, alleging that they had conquered the land with their own resources and that they were the sole guarantors of security.

The Aristocratic Expressive Array and Its Implications

The worldview and ideological underpinnings of a well-bounded social group are nowhere more clearly manifested than in the group's expressive array. Particularly in the case of estate and class stratification, whatever the determinant structural variables (economic, political, religious) may be, the most immediately visible components are behavioral configuration and expressive array, spelled out in specific patterns and domains. Thus, in the inception and formation of the Creole aristocracy, local ethnic, demographic, and even ecological considerations restructured the medieval estate system, modified also by the economic, political, and religious aims of the Spanish Crown. From this perspective, the *imago mundi*—expressive array of the Mexican aristocracy, which by the beginning of the seventeenth century had acquired a definitive form, is but a variant of the Spanish aristocracy. The new land and its people, to say nothing of isolation, were the most significant variables in the transformation, but the processes of syncretism and acculturation affected several aspects of the expressive array of the aristocracy, as they did most aspects of the formation of the Mexican nation.

EXCLUSIVE SOCIAL AND ECONOMIC DOMAINS

The land as a value in itself and as a validation of lineage. This fundamental expressive value colors several other domains of the array in manifold subdomains of realization. For the classic aristocracies of Greece and Rome, essentially urban in values and orientation, the land, though important, had a primarily economic value, as the polity dominated the cultural and social life of the superordinate estate. With the fall of the Roman Empire, the fragmentation of society, and the decline of urbanization during the Dark Ages, the aristocracy of western Europe became essentially rural, with a corresponding change in values and orientation. During the Middle Ages the land acquired an expressive value above and beyond economics and politics, very much like that of the urbs of the Greek and Roman aristocracies: an institutional source of strength, a fountain of social validation, and a mechanism of continuity (Perrot 1968:146–83). The rise of modern capitalism may be explained partially by the fact that it was created by urbanites who were unencumbered by the ideological conception of the land that, in one degree or another, governed all Western aristocracies. Since the early stages of modern capitalism in the fifteenth century, Western aristocracies have been notoriously conservative. As a class, they adapted with difficulty to the economic changes that accompanied the passage from seigneurialism to capitalism, perhaps precisely because they could not think in economic terms independently of the land. The aristocratic expressive array has consistently conspired against any economic activity and source of political power that was not based primarily on possession of land. The land became the central ideological focus for Western aristocracies, coloring every sociocultural domain more than a thousand years ago and still part of the expressive array of the new superordinate class created by capitalism. This aristocratic ideology and expressive array were brought to New Spain when they were perceptibly beginning to decline.

The *encomienda* did not satisfy *hidalgo* conquistadors and the more upwardly mobile members of the rank and file. Indian tributaries undoubtedly gave the semblance of a seigneurial system but not the permanence required to properly found an aristocratic society. Soon after 1540, when the colony was reasonably well pacified and organized, the race for land began, or as Chevalier (1963:134–47) puts it, "the land grabbers" began to accumulate land to form the great estates. By the end of the century many great landed estates existed. After the *encomienda* and *repartimiento* system declined and ultimately disappeared by the second half of the seventeenth century (at least in central Mexico), and with the establishment of the *hacienda* system, the evolution was complete (Zavala 1973:201–39). From as early as 1570, when the first *encomenderos* of nonconquistador origin began to accumulate property, land became partly an end in itself and partly a way to validate upward mobility. Thus, rich, upwardly mobile merchants and miners with *hidalgo* aspirations invariably acquired landed estates as a sort of admission fee to the rank to which they aspired (Peña 1983:214–17).

In Western culture, at least during the past twelve hundred years, peasants and aristocrats have valued the land beyond its economic value, and I do not say this metaphorically. In my experience, the feeling for the land as a source of identification and a feeling of belonging are not essentially different for Mexican aristocrats and Indian peasants. This is a worldview that most of Western society no longer shares, and even in Mexico, where important changes have occurred during the past generations, most of the population of the country shares the same position. This love affair with the land has been an impediment to the economic development of aristocrats, and perhaps of peasants as well, throughout the capitalist transformation of modern times. Mexican aristocrats are among the last groups to have been violently forced into a totally different socioeconomic niche by the total loss of their landed estates, thereby significantly altering their expressive array. But though aristocrats owned a vast portion of the country's land, their expressive array derived significantly from the city-country axis, a pattern that came into existence during the crucial formative period in the second half of the sixteenth century (Durand 1953:32–40). Considering that for three centuries the *hacienda* was the locus of several expressive domains, one should not underestimate the function of the land in the overall expressive life of the Mexican aristocracy. Under the *hacienda* are included the Indians and Mestizos who, with their masters, commuted between the country and the city—all the many household servants, nannies, wet nurses, footmen, and other personnel required by aristocratic life. The culture of the horse and of hunting, combined with the love of individual and collective display and ceremonialism, earned the *hacienda* its place as the structural and expressive sine qua non for the realization of the aristocratic worldview (Benítez 1953:20–32).

A deep-seated belief in the perpetuation of lineage and the continuation of descent. In this domain, the Creole aristocracy followed the Spanish and European model. Fundamentally, individuals and groups tend to perpetuate superordinate social, economic, and political position by any means available. Upwardly mobile individuals are quick to learn from members of the group to which they aspire, and they are the most assiduous practitioners of the methods available to ensure their position for their descendants. Thus, every well-documented method that has been devised by aristocracies perpetuates status and rank as well as configures domains of expression that serve as means of self-identification, mechanisms of exclusivity, and standards of selection, such as genealogy, heraldry, and other more visible signs of status and rank. What varies from one society to another are the methods themselves, which, in the case of the Mexican aristocracy from its inception, are all of Spanish-European origin. The most salient of them are the following: a high concern with genealogies; much interest in heraldry; displaying coats of arms and other symbols of noble rank; establishing *mayorazgos* or entailed property; vying for membership in military orders; questing for titles of nobility; usurping privileges and dignities (Powis 1984:23–80). These subdomains may be regarded individually as fairly well circumscribed contexts of realization that played a significant role in the overall configuration of the expressive array of the Creole aristocracy.

The usurpation of privileges and dignities. Usurpation of privileges has been common in Western society since the late fourteenth century, and it is associated mostly with the rise of the bourgeoisie. In New Spain, usurpation assumed much larger proportions because of the bourgeois elements of Colonial society and the general fluidity of Creole society. Rather harshly, Durand (1953, 2:44–53) characterizes this syndrome as "aseñoramiento de los plebeyos," or the uppitiness of commoners behaving like lords. This natural result of the Conquest and the establishment of the Creole estate had implications for the entire polity. New arrivals were shocked by the easiness with which viceregal authorities tolerated the usurpation of privileges, the improper use of dignities, and the laxness of address and behavior. In the new land a new expressive game developed in which even the Indians participated, to some extent liberated from ancient social and religious constraints. But it was in the middle and upper sectors of the stratification system where the usurpation of privileges and dignities was most extensive, most noticeable, and most consequential. Thus, rich and not so rich Creoles with pretensions to *hidalguía* usurped the privileges of this noble rank, while juridical *hidalgos* and the Creole ruling class of *encomenderos* and associated extraction behaved as if they were grandees of Spain (Benítez 1953:150–69). Usurpation in this particular domain acquired the semblance of a mostly utilitarian manifestation of upward mobility, but it did entail a most significant expressive component. Two examples of the most common usurpations will place matters in perspective.

Usurpation in New Spain began shortly after the Conquest, but specific, long-standing antecedents in Spain went back to the early fifteenth century. In addition to isolation and the fluidity of a new society, usurpation resulted to a significant extent from the frustration of conquistadors who felt they had not been properly recompensed by the Crown with honors and dignities. This frustration fostered a social ambiance that filtered down to the Creole population at large. Usurpation, then, reflects the conquistadors' decision to do themselves justice, although those who came after them usurped a right that they had not earned. The first usurpations were the sumptuary privileges of the higher nobility that rich *encomenderos* exercised with abandon in the absence of viceregal control. Indeed, the viceregal court itself led the way, becoming a replica of the Spanish court, and even rivaling it in luxury, elaboration, and sumptuousness of display (Weckmann 1983:557–68).

The second example also had its inception in Spain and falls under the general rubric of bourgeois usurpation characteristic of perhaps all Western aristocracies in the fifteenth century. In New Spain this usurpation acquired epidemic proportions. I am referring to the term *don,* an honorific privilege and the equivalent of a nobiliary title granted by the king. Both as a term of address and reference it had a rather wide range of application, from the king himself to prominent knights. As late as the early sixteenth century in Spain it was not usurped lightly, as the risks were ridicule and even legal sanctions (Pike 1972:22–34). In the New World, the great captains in the conquering hosts assumed the *don* from the beginning, and by the second half of the sixteenth century it had become generalized among *hidalgos.* By the beginning of the seventeenth century, *don* had become generalized as a term of address for all prominent, and sometimes not so prominent, rich, and powerful Creoles. By the end of Colonial times, and certainly during the nineteenth century, the *don* had become meaningless and denoted little more than the democratization of society, a process that in Spain, and most European countries, did not occur as quickly. The Spanish Creoles of the New World led the way, thus, in the willful usurpations of noble privilege.

A related aspect of this usurpation is the proliferation of exaggerated and contrived forms of address and courtesy formulas that begin to appear in New Spain shortly after the Conquest. Formulas such as "muy noble señor" (most noble sir), "muy ilustre señor" (most illustrious sir), "vuestra excelentísima persona" (your most excellent person), "vuestra señoría" (your lordship), and other even more elaborate forms were common in Spain for noble personages of the highest rank. In New Spain, by the second half of the sixteenth century, they had become vulgarized and part of the general patterns of intercourse among Creoles. Abuse of such courtesy formulas filtered down to the middle levels of society, thereby rendering these exalted forms of address and reference meaningless as markers of social differentiation. Here again, the conquistador *imago mundi* played a determinant role in this form of usurpation (Rozas de Oquendo 1964:30–65).

PRIMARY INCLUSIVE BEHAVIORAL DOMAINS

An inordinate concern with ostentation and display in individual, social, and material affairs. Sociopsychologically these expressive traits stem from a concern with demonstrating one's status in the face of inadequate recognition. These expressive traits entail a significant acculturative component; they are present in both traditional Spanish culture and Indian pre-Hispanic culture, but forged in the context of the reaction of conquistadors and other Creole personnel against specific policies of the Crown. By the second half of the sixteenth century, ostentation and love of luxury were important aspects of Creole aristocracy (Domínguez Ortiz 1970:38–67). They were apparent in many aspects of the social, material, and religious life of the rich and powerful and they affected the expressive life of an even wider segment of Creole society. Furthermore, Mexico, after the conquest of the Philippines, became a crossroad of the European-Asiatic trade routes. Porcelain, fine silks, spices, and other oriental products fostered the psychological need for an ostentatious and luxurious life, which continued unabated until the end of Colonial times (Ots Capdequí 1934:127–49).

Luxury and ostentation manifested themselves primarily in dress, residence, household appointments, and associated patterns of living, and secondarily in sponsoring great secular and religious ceremonies. Sumptuary laws and regulations, still in effect in Spain in the sixteenth century, were absent or had no effect in New Spain, except perhaps that they regulated some aspects of Indian life by prohibiting horse riding and sword carrying. Chroniclers of the time describe a veritable orgy of personal ostentation in the form of jewelry, the finest clothes, and furnishings that rivaled the lifestyles of the highest born in Spain (Benítez 1953:54–72). By contrast, events in the life and religious cycles almost invariably acquired a public ceremonial component, for burials, weddings, and even birthdays of important people attracted large numbers of the populace. The sponsoring of processions, special masses, and other religious activities were also part of the ostentation-luxury complex, for thus the Creole aristocracy validated its power and social standing. Sponsoring public games of various sorts, usually having to do with horses and races, was yet another manner of ostentation for the rich and powerful. Mexico City and, to a lesser extent, the five or six most important cities of New Spain in the sixteenth century were lively centers of social and popular activities fueled by the desire for display of the ruling class of the colony (Peña 1983:160–63).

Creole refinement and the growth of courtesy and politeness. Américo Castro (1948:32) says that upon coming to the New World, Spaniards lost spontaneity but gained refinement and courtesy. This characterization aptly captures one of the main expressive domains of the Creole aristocracy in particular and of the Creole population in general. An associated element should be mentioned in this connection, namely, "la dulzura de expresión y la suavidad y donaire en el trato" (the gentleness of expression and the delicacy and gracefulness of manners and behavior) that became a hallmark of polite society in New Spain. After Spain became the dominant European power early in the sixteenth century, Spaniards were at once regarded as extremely courteous and ceremonious and noted for their bluntness and directness. These traits of national character were transplanted to the New World (Durand 1953, 2:84–95). In the new land an important transformation took place that may be characterized as follows: the Creoles retained and enhanced courteousness and ceremoniousness, but divested themselves of bluntness and directness. This transformation constitutes another case of syncretism in which similar expressive patterns, particularly courtesy, politeness, and ceremonialism, were present in the Spanish and pre-Hispanic cultural traditions (Motolinía 1903; Sahagún 1956). Although the period of Spanish-Indian interaction on more or less the same footing was short, the culture and society of the Indians were still more or less intact and viable concerns, and the Spaniards had ample opportunity to observe their behavioral characteristics, particularly those of the nobility, from which some Spaniards took wives.

More specifically, the syncretic matrix that shaped this aspect of the Creole ruling class was the institution of nannies and wet nurses, an inseparable aspect of the city and country life after conquistadors had been transformed into *encomenderos* and well-established families had come into existence. This process took a while, for few Spanish women came to New Spain before the arrival of the first viceroy, but by around 1560 one can discern the beginnings of the aristocratic household complete with its large retinue of mostly female servants. The role of servants—particularly of nannies—in the enculturation of children is significant. The city-country axis configured the culture of the household and the personnel that staffed it, for the *encomienda* provided virtually unlimited numbers of servants, eventually on a regularized basis as a function of the *hacienda,* a pattern that has remained virtually unchanged to the present day. From the seventeenth century onward, the *hacienda* became the purveyor of long lines of lackeys, servants, nannies, and other personnel to the aristocratic household. In this environment, nannies became a determinant factor in the early enculturation of aristocratic children, for their influence was usually prolonged and intensified by the tender attachment established between child and nanny. From the age of two or three, right after weaning, the child was provided with a personal nanny. Generally young and not necessarily well acculturated, nannies were chosen for their appeal and loyalty to the household. Nannies were directly responsible for the well-being of children, playing with them, feeding them, and spending an inordinate amount of time with them. The close and tender relationships that developed between nannies and their charges outlived childhood and became lifelong attachments. After nannies ceased to function as such, generally at the time of marriage for girls and shortly before for boys, they not infrequently remained in the household in some other capacity, traveling with the family and attending their former wards. This relationship was thoroughly reciprocated by ladies and gentlemen, and nannies and former wards turned to each other in times of trouble and gave each other unqualified support. This institution often achieved its ideal form, judging by its persistence even after the *hacienda* system came to an end. (I am indebted to Solange Alberro for this discussion [Alberro 1990].)

The social ambiance of the child-nanny relationship was the main context in which the first generation of Creoles internalized those aspects of interpersonal behavior, manners, and demeanor that distinguished them from *peninsulares*. Nannies were perhaps the most influential syncretic brokers in the behavioral and expressive transformation of Creoles. Through their agency, Spanish bluntness and directness diminished, while Spanish courteousness and ceremoniousness were enhanced and given a gentler and more delicate balance. In this process of syncretic transformation, the Creoles became more like the Indians. The transformation, however, went beyond the domain of interpersonal behavior and affected the cadence and accent of language (it became softer and more circumlocutory), the manifestation of personal demeanor (it became more elaborate and artificial), the configuration of communication and social presentation (they became more precious, less spontaneous, and laced with euphemisms), and other domains of social interaction.

Though syncretic components in the transformation of Spaniards in New Spain were important, they should not be overemphasized. The courtesy, refinement, and politeness of manners and behavior that came to characterize the Creole aristocracy, and Creole society in general, stem also from the unwavering aim of conquistadors and their descendants to achieve high social recognition and, ultimately, noble status. As in the case of other groups seeking upward mobility, their insecurity caused them to overshoot the mark. By the middle of the seventeenth century, a Creole aristocrat had emerged who possessed a worldview and expressive array significantly different from those of his Spanish counterpart. Furthermore, the social, economic, and political role into which the Creole ruling class had cast itself differed from that in which the Crown had cast it. This discrepancy created a latent tension that heightened the differences that divided Creoles and *peninsulares* and reinforced stereotypes. Thus, *peninsulares* considered Creoles vain, lazy, unreliable, and pretentious; while Creoles regarded *peninsulares* as coarse, vulgar, arrogant, and greedy. These stereotypes, by the way, still color the mutual perceptions of Mexicans and Spaniards. There was some truth to the charges of both parties in this somewhat jocular but serious controversy, a controversy that had different consequences on both sides of the Atlantic. In Spain, Creole aristocrats were regarded as parvenus. In New Spain, Creole aristocrats were always the socially exalted, despite the viceregal authorities and the constant recycling of *peninsulares* in high bureaucratic positions. The glory of the Conquest was very short-lived. Cortés was received in Spain as a conquering hero and paladin of old by the most exalted nobility, but such a reception was never to happen again, and the Creole ruling class centered its life in the colony, to some extent disconnected from the mother country (Weckmann 1983:569–85). The Creole aristocracy developed its own arrogance, love for pomp, and conspicuous display, establishing a seigneurial style of living that approached that of the mother country but never equaled or surpassed it.

Family, household, and the city-country axis. These domains have long been part of the aristocratic expressive array, and the conquistadors of *hidalgo* extraction introduced them in New Spain. The nuclear family, beyond its biological and sociological functions, was for conquistadors and their descendants the starting point in the quest for honors and aristocratic status. Thus, successful conquistadors almost invariably made marriages of convenience, that is, acquired wives of higher social standing than their own. Cortés himself set the precedent by marrying a lady of the highest noble standing, and conquistadors followed his lead until perhaps the last quarter of the sixteenth century (Manuel Quintana, pers. comm.). By the seventeenth century, when Creole society became almost exclusively centered in the colony, the original model was modified by inputs from the rising plutocracy and considerations such as large dowries.

When the aristocratic Creole family crystallized as a local institution—that is, when there was a pool of Creole women large enough for most marriages to occur endogamously—it was seldom constituted as an independent nuclear family. From 1560 or so until the end of Colonial times, most aristocratic families were extended households, often of very large proportions. The household included primary kinsmen, collateral kinsmen, nonkinsmen attached to the family, and always many servants. Aristocratic households included several categories of personnel: married sons and daughters who had not yet become economically independent; some poor collateral relatives; friends in need; occasional hangers-on; business associates of subordinate standing; and, at times, patronized artisans—not counting servants, lackeys, and other menial personnel (Carlos de Ovando, pers. comm.). The institution of *mayorazgo* contributed to the size of the household by vesting most of the property on the primogenit; this institution deprived younger sons of a completely independent residential and social life. From the beginning, city and country mansions were large, designed as seigneurial establishments, and could often accommodate dozens of people in addition to many servants and attendants. The seigneurial establishment included coachmen, lackeys, footmen, running footmen, and most of the panoply of peninsular noble households. The whole retinue, from kinsmen to kitchen help, was part of the public persona of the family and served to enhance the prestige of the head of the family.

The city-country axis is another aspect of the expressive complex of the household. The Creole aristocratic household was invariably large and prominently located, and while it did not achieve the great proportions of the French chateaux or so-called stately homes of the British aristocracy, it could accommodate a hundred people or more. In the city, the aristocratic household always lay within a few blocks of the central square. As cities grew, mansions became small palaces with associated commercial activities, and aristocratic households were built farther away from the central square (Durand 1953:35–41). Occasionally occupying half a city block, these residences were imposing two- or three-story buildings with dozens of high-ceilinged rooms clustered around several consecutive patios and prominently displayed coats of arms on elaborate façades. The size and excellence of aristocratic residences reached their peak in the eighteenth century, as attested by more than one hundred well-preserved palatial establishments that survive in Mexico City, Puebla, Guanajuato, and a few other cities. These were the centers of the social, ritual, and ceremonial activity that played such an important expressive role in the life of the Mexican aristocracy until the twentieth century.

From 1600, when the *hacienda* or suburban retreat became increasingly complementary to city life, the aristocratic household cannot be understood without reference to the country. Beyond the ideological and economic value and attachment to the land discussed previously, the country, as respite from the city, constituted a complementary expressive domain: a retreat from the hustle and bustle of the social and recreational world of the urbs and a source of variation in the world of games and entertainment. Most aristocratic families were absentee landlords, and the typical pattern of multiple holdings allowed them the luxury of a *hacienda*, not too distant from the city, to which they could repair periodically throughout the year or for a block of some months. The great country mansions that by the end of the seventeenth century had become widespread in New Spain were not just agricultural centers or cattle-raising operations but extensive and elaborate residences (Romero de Terreros 1956). The *hacienda* or suburban retreat developed its own expressive style: the games and entertainments were more subdued, more intimate, but, just like the city, it drew large numbers of personnel.

SECONDARY INCLUSIVE DOMAINS AND IMPLICATIONS

The horse complex and associated domains. Since antiquity, the horse has been a symbol and expressive instrument of the Western aristocracy, particularly since the fall of the Roman Empire until the onset of modern times. During the early episodes of the Conquest of Mexico, the horseman of the Spanish host was not only a valuable instrument of war but a psychological weapon that inspired terror among the Indians. The sixteen original horses of the conquistadors are lovingly remembered in fact and legend, and Bernal Díaz del Castillo (1967) left us an indelible account of their physical characteristics and the military feats of their owners. By the turn of the seventeenth century, there were millions of horses in New Spain, and the horse complex had matured to become an important element in Colonial society. For the great majority of the population, including Mestizos and some of the Indians beyond Spanish control, the horse was little more than a utilitarian object, but for the Creole aristocracy it became an instrument of expression (Benítez 1953:55–57).

The expressive importance of the horse developed immediately after the Conquest as conquistadors in general, and *encomenderos* in particular, were urged to keep horses and arms and be ready to take to the field in case of emergencies. To be sure, the horse complex also became a domain of expression for the population of the colony at large, but it was the Creole aristocracy in the *haciendas* and in the context of the city-country axis that made it a salient expressive domain. From the very beginning equestrian games were the most popular form of entertainment in the city life of New Spain. These games entailed private (aristocratic) and public (communal) components that in varying degrees brought together the different strata of Colonial society. The most important equestrian games in Colonial times, all of which had their origin in the first half of the sixteenth century, were the following: *juegos de cañas* (also known as *zoiza* or *quintana,* a kind of jousting); *torear a caballo* (also known as *alancear,* lancing bulls on horseback); *juegos de sortijas* (lacing rings at the gallop); *juegos de alcancias* (mock confetti fights on horseback); several types of horse racing; and hunting on horseback. These games were introduced shortly after the Conquest, were practiced throughout Colonial times, and a few survived until the twentieth century. Some of them were restricted to the Colonial nobility, while others became popular at all levels of society. For example, *juegos de cañas* was a privilege of *hidalgos a fuero de España,* and as late as the first quarter of the eighteenth century it was forbidden even to rich members of the bourgeoisie (Chevalier 1970:301). The game was a mock combat in which participant knights, organized in *cuadrillas* (troops) of ten or twelve, threw at each other fragile twigs or reeds two-and-a-half meters long. *Juegos de sortijas,* however, soon became open to all, assuming several forms and becoming one of the most popular games. Even Indians participated. Though *juegos de cañas* and other games accessible mostly to the nobility disappeared by the end of Colonial times, *juegos de sortijas, juegos de alcancias,* and horse races survived as popular events until the twentieth century; indeed, *juegos de sortijas* is still practiced by Mexican *charros* (cowboys) today, though they use machetes instead of lances (Weckmann 1983:153–68). With the exception of hunting, these equestrian games were not only good private and public entertainment but an inseparable aspect of the ritual and ceremonial life of New Spain's cities throughout nearly three hundred years of Colonial life. The Creole aristocracy played the leading role as the main actors, sponsors, and patrons of the various games.

The *hacienda* and *estancia* contributed significantly to the horse complex, for extensive breeding operations were tied to these rural estates. In addition to breeding horses for the various specializations of the complex, the *hacienda* developed its own expressive subdomains. Partly utilitarian and partly expressive, the *hacienda* horse complex evolved within an elaborate ensemble of activities in which the *hacendados* played a leading expressive role. The foremost of these activities evolved from entertainment and display: horsemen, finely attired, paraded and engaged in games of dexterity for the entertainment of urbanites. Throughout Colonial times the horse complex changed and adapted to new conditions; in the nineteenth century it was modified by the diffusion of equitation and polo, while in the twentieth century *charrería* (the Mexican cowboy complex) survived as an expressive spectacle no longer tied to the land.

Religious sponsorship and church activities and institutions. The conquest of New Spain was regarded by conquistadors as a crusade for the conversion of the Indians. The *encomenderos* and the Creole population at large, however, were apparently not directly interested in the conversion and catechization of the Indians. In fact, the Catholicism of the Creole population and the urban Catholicism that evolved throughout Colonial times and persisted after Independence were significantly affected by Indian religious inputs, or if you will, by the adaptations of orthodox Catholicism of the sixteenth and seventeenth centuries to the constraints of Colonial society. Briefly, Mexican Catholicism became more ritualistic, ceremonial, and pragmatic than peninsular Catholicism, reflecting a general orientation and worldview that retained several medieval characteristics. Catholicism in Mexico retained from the Middle Ages (or acquired after the Conquest) a certain magical aspect and a pragmatic-ritualistic component absent in peninsular Catholicism, certainly after the eighteenth century (Nutini 1988:276–83). The Creole aristocracy that emerged from this milieu was religiously undifferentiated from the Creole population at large and the urban Catholicism of the colony.

There is one significant religious component that should be conceptualized as an independent expressive domain: sponsorship. The Creole aristocracy developed a sponsorship system similar to the Indian *mayordomía* (stewardship) system, not as elaborate and well structured but with similar functions. Sponsorship of religious events and occasions in the yearly cycle became an important mechanism of expressive gratification, as it was contracting collective and individual relationships of ritual kinship within the religious sphere. The most important collective events included such special events as masses, processions, morality plays, and various ceremonial activities. These activities were generally centered on permanent and formal associations such as brotherhoods (*hermandades*) and sodalities (*confradías*), associated with particular events such as the Christmas cycle, Holy Week, All Saints' Day and All Souls' Day, and so on (González Obregón 1900:132–46). Many of these activities were formal, brilliant affairs offering much opportunity for personal display and public ostentation.

More subtly constituted, the establishment of *capellanías* (chaplaincies) provided another expressive aspect of the religious domain. Essentially, these chaplaincies were endowments for the support of an ecclesiastic or an amount of capital of which the interest served the same purpose. The establishment of chaplaincies was fundamentally an expressive activity, a symbol of social achievement, and ultimately an indicator of rank. Another related practice was providing dowries for aristocratic women entering conventual life. Many aristocratic women became nuns during Colonial times, and the practice continued well into Republican times. Though the practice may to some extent be explained by the fact that it was cheaper to provide dowries for nuns than for brides, particularly those who married hypergamously into the higher peninsular nobility, it was fundamentally an expressive activity that blended endearment to the church with social approval.

Exclusivity, endogamy, and purity of blood. From the first, conquistadors and their descendants engaged in concubinage, first with Indian women, and then with Black, Mestizo, and Mulatto women, but they almost invariably married Spanish women. It is a fact that a considerable number of original conquistadors married Indian women of high noble rank, but the practice had ended before the first generation of Creoles came to maturity. By the time the demographic balance of the Creole population had stabilized, perhaps shortly before 1600, the emerging aristocracy was essentially an endogamous group. The situation remained unchanged until the end of Colonial times; aristocrats apparently became extremely conscious of *pureza de sangre* (purity of blood) and took considerable pains to marry their own (Durand 1953, 1:35). Ethnic admixture was never significant, as the Mexican aristocracy today (1990) is somatically European, basically of Spanish stock with a modicum of French, German, Anglo-Saxon, and Italian admixture. For most of its existence, the Mexican aristocracy was highly exclusive ethnically, culturally, and racially.[1]

Aristocratic exclusivity, and its associated patterns of endogamy and endogeny, created from the beginning an ambiance that fostered expressive realization. Dress, personal behavior, etiquette, and modes of entertainment were influenced by the exclusivity that characterized the Creole aristocracy and defined it vis-à-vis all other segments of Colonial society. Lacking the clear-cut privileges and functions that characterized the *peninsular* nobility, the Creole aristocracy created its own distinguishing markers as a social group, in the process becoming at once more traditional and more open than the Spanish aristocracy from which it derived (McAlister 1963). For example, it was easier in New Spain for the haute bourgeoisie to acquire aristocratic status than it was in Spain, where the noble-commoner distinction was significantly more stringent and remained so until the nineteenth century.

This account by no means exhausts all the domains of expressive realization of the Creole aristocracy, but it does define the core expressive array. None of these domains is strictly limited to the Creole aristocracy: it shares some domains with the Spanish aristocracy, as constituting the common denominator of all Western aristocracies; it shares others with the Creole population at large. The former are the exclusive domains of the Creole aristocracy with respect to the Creole class as a whole, while the latter the aristocracy share with all Creoles, and to a significant extent they represent syncretic syntheses that were the result of Indian and Spanish expressive patterns that amalgamated under specific social and demographic constraints of the sixteenth century.

Coalescence and Configuration of an Aristocratic-Plutocratic Ruling Class

Two aspects must be examined to conclude the discussion of the formation of the Creole aristocracy: first, the policy of the Spanish Crown in fostering or impeding its development and its acquisition of privileges in the light of specific policies and expectations; second, the definitive configuration of its basic membership by the incorporation of new personnel of plutocratic extraction.

OPPOSITION AND REACTION OF THE SPANISH CROWN

As we have seen, the original conquistadors and their *encomendero* descendants firmly insisted that, because of the private nature of the Conquest and their military duties in holding the land and their ancient privileges of right of conquest, they were entitled to unqualified honors and to all the land that its people had to offer. These included three sets of rewards: permanent possession of the land, and of the Indians as tributaries, as vested in the *encomienda* and *repartimiento*—a veritable hereditary seigneurial system; honors and dignities that included *hidalguía,* membership in military orders, and access to titles of nobility; and monopoly of political offices, including the highest position in the viceregal bureaucracy. The Crown was willing to compromise, partly in recognition of the services of conquistadors, but mostly because of the constraints involved in holding and organizing the colony. But the Crown never agreed to grant universal *hidalguía* to conquistadors and their descendants nor to grant titles of nobility indiscriminately; meanwhile, the Crown resisted the continuation of the *encomienda,* divested it of all seigneurial aspects, restricted its assignation to conquistadors, and ultimately abolished it. Of greater consequence, the Crown was adamant about not endowing the Colonial ruling class with important political functions.

Within ten years of the Conquest of central Mexico, the Crown was curtailing the growth of the seigneurial system set in motion by the granting of the great *encomiendas* of the 1520s, particularly Cortés's marquisate of the Valley of Oaxaca. This basic aim of the Crown underlay the political, economic, and even religious realities of New Spain and colored most actions of the viceregal government, directly or indirectly affecting the emerging ruling class. This policy was a direct result of Spanish centralization and the growth of absolutism initiated by the Catholic Kings and pursued diligently by Charles V and Philip II. With the Caribbean experience in mind, the Crown engaged in a kind of balancing act: granting conquistadors and their descendants enough Indians and land to ensure against outright revolt, but withholding any rights of *encomenderos* that smacked of seigneurialism, such as judicial functions, corvée, and other privileges

(Benítez 1953:198–217). The Crown was not successful, however, in curtailing the growth of seigneurialism, for it became a pillar of the Creole aristocracy. Thus, despite the legal framework of Colonial society, seigneurialism became de facto a significant aspect of interethnic relations and fostered the growth of a local, powerful ruling class. The results of this policy may be summarized as follows: Though the Crown significantly modified the structure of the Creole ruling class and molded it into an officially controllable group, it did not modify the aristocratic aims of its members. The Crown, through its viceregal establishment, was perfectly willing to tolerate a Creole aristocracy that officially conformed to royal policy but unofficially became a medieval seigneurial system (McAlister 1963).

The Crown never intended to foster a more egalitarian society in New Spain as compared to the peninsula. But it did its best to make sure that the essentially estate-stratified society of the colony did not exceed certain limits. In pursuing this policy, the Crown consistently tried to limit the economic power, honors and dignities, and political participation of conquistadors and their descendants. The niggardliness of the Crown in these three domains was the bitterest complaint of conquistadors, who considered themselves betrayed. The bureaucrats and more recent arrivals favored by the Crown, however, joined the ranks of conquistadors-*encomenderos* and were quickly infected with the latter's often unreasonable thirst for honors and rewards (Durand 1953, 1:10–14). Before the promulgation of the New Laws in 1542, most recipients of *encomiendas* were conquistadors, but after 1546, when the laws were rescinded, most recipients of *encomiendas* were individuals of nonconquistador origin, namely, those favored by the viceregal authorities. With respect to *repartimientos,* for obvious reasons the Crown favored those assigned to the mines, and nearing the end of the century *repartimientos* were almost exclusively awarded for this purpose. Thus, as the *encomienda* became increasingly less important economically, the Creole ruling class began to diversify, and before the *encomienda* came to an end in most of central and southern Mexico, the *hacienda* and its system of debt peonage had become the main economic reality of New Spain (Nickel 1988:42–96).

Soon after Cortés was made Marquis of the Valley of Oaxaca, Charles V promised *hidalguía* to all participants not only of new conquests but of new settlements. In New Spain, this promise was not wholly implemented, for the local viceregal administration favored granting *hidalguía* to individuals of nonconquistador extraction. The viceroy, and to a lesser degree royal justices (*oidores*) and a few other high viceregal officials, favored their own retinues, and most highly placed royal officials were not above being bribed by rich *peninsulares* and Creoles in the quest of *hidalguía*. By 1600, therefore, there were many more *hidalgos a fuero de España* of nonconquistador extraction. By the early decades of the seventeenth century, the process of ennoblement had been regularized, and the acquisition of *hidalguía* required the normally stringent procedures employed in Spain. The granting of titles of nobility to Creole aristocrats did not happen until nearly a century after Cortés was made a marquis: another testimony to the reluctance of the Crown to foster any aspect of seigneurialism in the colony (Weckmann 1983:173–78). Not until the eighteenth century, when the policy of the Crown was significantly liberalized, did considerable numbers of titles accrue to Creole aristocrats.

Beginning with Ferdinand and Isabella, the Crown was a highly centralized power, a policy pursued stringently by the Hapsburg dynasty until the eighteenth century. This centralization explains why the Creole ruling class never occupied high positions in the viceregal bureaucracy and never dominated the most important *cabildos* of New Spain. There were always Creoles in the *cabildos* of Mexico City, Puebla, and other important urban centers, but they were generally outnumbered by *peninsulares* (Peña 1983:143–71). This uneven representation was tempered by the fact that most royal bureaucrats probably stayed in New Spain after their tour of duty, as was certainly the case with peninsular members of *cabildos,* most of whom were not professional bureaucrats but rich and powerful businessmen who had made their fortunes in the colony. Another important factor was the practice of "buying" positions in the viceregal bureaucracy, particularly the higher offices, a practice that apparently acquired epidemic proportion during the second half of the eighteenth century. This recognized fact of Colonial administration affected the Creole aristocracy, for the nominations to high office were invariably made in Spain, and only local level posts were subject to immediate viceregal control (Pike 1972:23–31). The result was jealousy and dissension between Creoles and *peninsulares*. This friction was mitigated, however, by the fact that most Crown officials eventually joined the ranks of the aristocracy and their children became Creoles. The lasting consequence of this policy had more drastic effects: having had little experience in political and administrative affairs during Colonial times, the Creole aristocracy could not overnight assume the leadership of the emerging nation after Independence, and whether out of inexperience or lack of interest, they allowed the rising Mestizo and Creole rank and file to become the main political actors.

In conclusion, it did not serve the imperial interests of the Spanish Crown to foster the formation and development of a Colonial ruling class centered on a Creole aristocracy, but specific policies of the Crown differentially affected the crystallization of the Creole aristocracy. Indeed, some of the economic restrictions ultimately enhanced the power of the Creole aristocracy as a social and ruling class, while political restrictions did not prevent a measure of local control that proved beneficial to its overall interests, as in the case of the transformation from *encomienda* to *hacienda* and the control of provincial *cabildos* by the *hacendados* throughout New Spain. Highly instrumental in the preservation of an acknowledged but unspecified status quo during the Colonial period was the constant influx of Crown bureaucrats that remained in New Spain.

PLUTOCRATIC UPWARD MOBILITY AND ARISTOCRATIC RESISTANCE: THE FIRST RENEWAL, 1550–1630

From the moment that the first conquistadors were given Indians in *encomienda,* an aristocracy was in place. The formation of this aristocratic ruling class, from inception to crystallization, may be characterized by three stages. First, original and second-generation conquistadors established the model upon being awarded large numbers of Indians who paid tribute to them and/or worked the land they had been able to acquire. By right of conquest, conquistadors were transformed into *encomenderos.* The most critical stage, it lasted roughly from 1521 until the arrival of Viceroy Mendoza in 1535. Second, beginning as early as 1530, *encomiendas* were being awarded to nonconquistadors, recipients of royal and viceregal patronage. This group of *encomenderos* became more numerous after the arrival of the viceroy, as the granting of *encomiendas* went on until well after 1570. Throughout this stage conquistadors and their descendants continued to receive *encomiendas,* but after 1580 there were more *encomenderos* of nonconquistador origin than those of conquistador extraction. Third, at least two decades before the turn of the seventeenth century, another element began to make an important con-

tribution to the developing ruling class, namely, upwardly mobile elements of *morador* extraction who for two generations had amassed fortunes in mercantile and trading activities. By the last decade of the
sixteenth century, several of these plutocratic magnates had been incorporated into the budding Creole aristocracy.

Large-scale migration from Spain began after 1535. By 1550,
there were close to twenty thousand Creoles and *peninsulares* in the
colony, and twenty-five years later the number had more than tripled.
It is difficult to pinpoint the size of the pool of Creoles and *peninsulares*
from which the plutocratic class in the cities of New Spain drew. We
know that by the third quarter of the sixteenth century every
encomendero and mining city had a plutocratic establishment monopoliz-
ing manufacture and trading. Still uncertain is the social composition
of these local plutocracies, namely, how many were *encomenderos,* and
presumably *hidalgos,* and how many were nouveaux riches. From the
beginning a considerable number of *encomenderos* engaged in business
activities beyond the various agrarian enterprises associated with Indians and land (Peña 1983:72–105). By the last quarter of the sixteenth
century, the dozen or so most important cities of New Spain were
connected by an extensive network of trade and manufacturing, and
they functioned as centers of specialized production and distribution.
From 1550, commerce with mining centers was important, and trade
was significantly enhanced when mining operations were expanded to
the north in the later part of the century (Chevalier 1970:117–228).

By the last two decades of the sixteenth century, the landowning
and Indian-controlling *encomenderos* were the richest class in the colony,
but there were also plutocratic magnates, whose fortunes had been
made exclusively in nonagrarian enterprises, whose fortunes were as
large or larger than those of *encomenderos.* Given the fluid society in
New Spain, Creoles and *peninsulares* of humble origins could and did
rise to great plutocratic wealth (Peña 1983:145–76). Thus, from the
end of Viceroy Mendoza's tenure until the turn of the century, an
important group of plutocratic magnates emerged, not tied to the land
but with increasing economic power and including some of the richest
men in New Spain.

Within just forty years or so, Creoles and recently arrived *peninsulares* had risen to economic prominence in mercantile and manufacturing operations based in Mexico City, Puebla, Veracruz, Guadalajara,
Morelia, and a few other cities and mining centers. Since shortly after

the Conquest, *moradores* in the towns of New Spain had engaged in business and trade, but not until the second generation, when these populations had become Creoles, can one speak of real wealth amassed in this fashion. By then, continuous migration from Spain had brought increasing numbers of *peninsulares* who were not just craftsmen or unskilled workers but experienced merchants. During the last quarter of the century, this sector of the Spanish population in New Spain included the richest plutocrats, who brought another important dimension to the economic life of the colony: the preponderance of overseas trade with Spain and among New World colonies, including trade with the Orient via de Manila Galleon (Nutini 1986). In this new plutocracy, the *peninsulares* outnumbered Creoles.[2]

By the last decade of the sixteenth century, half a dozen of the most important cities of New Spain had become manufacturing centers with wide networks of distribution involving long-distance trade (Ovando and Ovando 1986). Supporting these manufacturing, trading, and commercial activities was an ample supply of currency that affected all cities and towns and to a significant extent the Indians as well. These manifold economic activities created much wealth, which was mostly controlled by a powerful sector of Creole and *peninsular* plutocrats strategically located in the key cities of New Spain, but always converging on Mexico City, the undisputed social, economic, religious, and political center of power throughout the Colonial period (Chaunnu 1951).

The last two decades of the sixteenth century in New Spain witnessed the first realignment of the ruling class, which was brought about by a new plutocratic sector of non-*encomendero* origin. This was a small group, strategically located in the choice commercial centers of the colony, and its wealth rivaled that of the majority of *encomenderos.* Here we have a classic example of upward and downward mobility affecting two distinct social groups (subclasses) of a dominant class (or estate): the budding Creole aristocracy of conquistador-*encomendero* origin was restructured by most of its members dropping out of the system, but reinvigorated by the admission of new members of plutocratic-merchant origin. In Western stratification since the end of the Middle Ages, similar transformations have occurred time and again, and the catalytic elements have always been economic power and social prestige.

Downward mobility had been an important aspect of the conquistador-*encomendero* class virtually since its inception, and by roughly 1580, well more than half of the conquistadors who had received grants had dropped out of aristocratic nuclei, which were nonetheless increased by recipients of royal and viceregal grants (Peña 1983:205). The incorporation of these latter elements, however, are not part of the renewal, for regardless of the resentment that conquistadors and their descendants felt against them as not having participated in the Conquest, they were mostly *hidalgos* and thus easily incorporated, for no social differentiation separated them. Meanwhile, the merchant, bourgeois class, composed of rank-and-file Creoles and recent arrivals from Spain, had become an upwardly mobile group, the most successful among them constituting a small elite highly desirous of the social standing enjoyed by the *encomenderos*. If the downward mobility of conquistadors can be explained by their *imago mundi* as a warrior class significantly impeding the development of a business orientation, the upward mobility of the plutocratic merchants was fueled by their business acumen and drive.

The rigidity of stratification diminishes in direct proportion to the control exercised by the superordinate group over social, economic, and political resources: if the superordinate sector completely monopolizes these resources, the system is rigid, almost a caste, and entails little or no upward mobility, as in the estate feudal system of western Europe from 800 to 1200; if the superordinate sector does not entirely monopolize these resources (and there are several possible degrees of monopoly), the system is fluid or relatively fluid and offers various degrees of upward mobility, as in class systems that began to emerge in western Europe in the late eighteenth century. The least important determinant of class or estate stratification and upward mobility is control of political power, whereas social and economic monopoly or control are fundamental. In the present case, lack of political participation did not prevent the Creole aristocracy from becoming a powerful and well-structured social and economic ruling class three generations after the Conquest. Thus, upward mobility is configured by economic power and social ambition, and these two ingredients determine the nature, form, and final restructuring of elite renewal.

The first renewal of elites occurred when plutocratic merchants and businessmen joined the ranks of the Creole aristocracy of conquistador-*encomendero* extraction. With this infusion, the Creole aristocracy crystallized into a ruling class composed of several nuclei of predominant economic interests (agrarian, mining, and mercantile) but socially homogeneous. The conquistador-*encomendero* class was composed of *hidalgos a fuero de España* and included several members related by consanguinity and affinity to highly placed titled families in Spain. Even by the strict standard of the peninsula, the Creole aristocracy was a local nobility with the social, economic, and expressive attributes associated with this estate (Domínguez Ortiz 1970:217). New Spain's nobility was the exalted social class of the colony, the standard of upward mobility to which poor *hidalgos* and rich merchants alike aspired. By contrast, the plutocratic merchants, Creoles and *peninsulares,* were not *hidalgos,* but the most upwardly mobile among them possessed great fortunes, in some cases even surpassing those of aristocrats. Most significantly, they were in an economic position to learn quickly the expressive ways of the aristocracy (Peña 1983:179).

The exclusivity of the Creole aristocracy was a fact two generations after the Conquest, and it was based on descent from conquistadors, by then all of gentry rank, and on the incorporation of *hidalgo* recipients into this very small group of royal and viceregal patronage. The Creole aristocracy had diverse economic interests, but collectively they may be referred to as *encomenderos,* as the dominant nuclei were composed of the landed magnates working the land with *encomienda* Indians. It was an exclusive social class with close connections to the viceregal establishment. Creole aristocrats looked down upon the (mostly peninsular) plutocrats, whom they felt were recipients of unfair patronage from the Crown (Gómez de Cervantes 1944:121–27). Nonetheless, plutocratic merchants (the Colonial haute bourgeoisie) vied for social recognition and matrimonial alliances with Creole aristocrats.

The two basic elements in the renewal of elites, then, were the economic power of the plutocracy and the expressive receptivity of the aristocracy, conditioned by the ethnic homogeneity of the two groups and the need for expressive validation by the former and the consolidation of economic alliances benefiting the latter. Rivaling aristocrats in wealth, many plutocrats were well positioned to emulate their expressive life. In this respect, the fundamental condition for acceptance and incorporation was the willingness of plutocrats to learn to behave like aristocrats and acquire their discriminating symbols. The quid pro quo for aristocrats were mainly economic benefits, particularly for the less affluent members of aristocratic nuclei, for there were many *encomenderos* with illustrious lineages but skimpy resources (Carlos de Ovando, pers. comm.).

There is no information on the number of plutocrat merchants and businessmen incorporated into aristocratic nuclei between 1550 and 1630, but many individual cases are known, and Peña (1983:181–233) ably analyzes their rise to economic power and incorporation into aristocratic nuclei. Before the last quarter of the sixteenth century aristocratic-plutocratic alliances were rare, but before the end of the century the pace of incorporation increased significantly, and by the third decade of the seventeenth century, the Creole aristocracy had been augmented by many individuals of plutocratic extraction.

THE PACE OF CLASS RENEWAL AND ESTATE STRATIFICATION

The concept of the renewal of elites must be refined if it is to play a theoretical role in studies of social stratification and mobility. Two questions present themselves: What is the pace of class renewal? What are the changes it engenders? The period of renewal lasted from 1550 to 1630, as the historical data available indicate that throughout these eighty years many plutocrats became part of the Creole aristocracy. The frequency of incorporation is impossible to determine, except to say that before 1565 the first individuals of merchant and business extraction had not yet acquired lasting relationships to the aristocratic establishment.

During the roughly 450-year history of the Mexican aristocracy, four fairly distinct renewals of elites have taken place in which plutocratic *haut bourgeois* have been superordinately incorporated in concentrated numbers, thereby modifying the constitution of the social and ruling class. These renewals occurred during the years 1550–1630, 1730–1810, 1850–1900, and 1940–90. Each period is marked by economic developments that affected the social composition of the superordinate group, followed by periods of relative inactivity. Borrowing an analogy from biological evolution, the social evolution of the Mexican aristocracy from 1519 to 1990 may be characterized as punctuated equilibrium, that is, extended periods of upward mobility are followed by periods during which upward mobility does occur but not extensively enough to affect, in any noticeable way, the structure of the superordinate class. During the renewal periods, on the other hand, gradualism prevails, that is, upward mobility goes on all the time, although it may be more concentrated in a generational span, as indicated above.

In the present context, the renewal of elites means concentrated changes brought about by the admission of upwardly mobile elements into a superordinate class. In Mexico, the four renewals have been entailed by changes in the domains of production and distribution and the combination of the two. Regardless of the economic variables involved, the renewal has social and economic effects on both the upwardly mobile individuals and those in superordinate position. The best way to describe and analyze this process is as a case of acculturation: the personnel of both groups in close interaction contribute specific elements, which ultimately restructure the social and economic order. The upwardly mobile group contributes more economic elements but is more changed socially (that is, behaviorally and expressively), while the superordinate group contributes more social elements but is more changed economically. The four renewals of elites experienced by the Mexican aristocracy are variations of the same socioeconomic theme: plutocrats desire social validation; aristocrats see plutocratic wealth as a desirable end. The new wealth and business acumen contributed by plutocratic merchants in each renewal changed the overall configuration of the conquistador-*encomendero* ruling class without significantly altering the Creole aristocracy behaviorally and expressively.

Finally, a few remarks on the global stratification of New Spain at the beginning of the seventeenth century and the position of the Creole aristocracy therein. Historians have argued about whether the *encomienda* and *repartimiento* systems were forms of Feudalism (see Nickel 1988; Gibson 1964; Simpson 1967; Zavala 1973; Hanke 1965; García Martínez 1969). Not Feudalism but seigneurialism is really involved, although one element, the military obligation of *encomenderos,* may be regarded as feudallike. Let me reiterate: legally, the *encomienda* was not a seigneurial system, as the *encomenderos* never had fiscal, judicial, and administrative functions over the Indian population. Moreover, the Crown opposed the hereditary possession of the *encomienda,* and *mayorazgos* could not be established on its basis. The Indian tribute assigned to individuals favors the interpretation of the *encomienda* as a seigneurial system, but this is the only argument that can be adduced. In short, the *encomienda* and *repartimiento* systems, as far as the Crown and its viceregal representatives were concerned, were not seigneurial institutions. For the reasons discussed previously, however, these institutions, and the *hacienda* that came afterward, may historically be regarded as seigneurial until 1910. What is important sociologically is that de facto seigneurialism during Colonial and Republican times largely configured the Mexican aristocracy's *imago mundi* and expressive life.

In the global context of Colonial stratification, by the onset of the seventeenth century the aristocracy was part of an undifferentiated, superordinate estate as contrasted with a subordinate, tributary Indian estate, whereas Mestizos and the nascent *castas* constituted somewhat vague intermediary classes, ethnically blurred and stratificationally uncertain. As the Creole population increased, the originally fluid Creole estate hardened, the aristocracy composed entirely of *hidalgos a fuero de España* predominated, and by the middle of the seventeenth century an *hidalgo-pechero*-like distinction developed that affected the total Creole and peninsular population of New Spain. More precisely, the Creole population at large had developed a somewhat subordinate position vis-à-vis the aristocracy of *hidalgos*.

The sixteenth century was crucial for the formation of the Mexican nation, and particularly for the configuration of the stratification system. In a short eighty years, Colonial society developed a hierarchical order at the top of which stood the Creole aristocracy as the social and ruling class of New Spain. Periodically reinvigorated, the Creole aristocracy remained virtually unchanged in its basic structure until Independence.

CHAPTER 6

The Seventeenth and Eighteenth Centuries: Economic Dominance and the Growth of Honors and Dignities

The structural and expressive framework of the Creole aristocracy, the social and ruling class of New Spain, was a product of the sixteenth century. The institutional foundations of this social class did not change during the remaining two centuries of Colonial rule, nor did its economic power and social prestige in any way diminish, unlike most variants of Western aristocracy. Concentrating on the economic bases and the control of the local level politics, this chapter chronicles the adaptations of the Creole aristocracy and its increasing expressive elaboration and diversification of social roles. Given that the economic bases of the oligarchical ruling class have been well studied (see Israel 1952; Chevalier 1970; Brading 1971), I emphasize here expressive changes and the growth of honors and dignities.

Social and Expressive Configuration of the Creole Aristocracy until Independence

New Spain's medieval inheritance remained very much in evidence throughout the seventeenth and eighteenth centuries. Coupled with the ethnic and racial differentiation between Creoles and all other populations of the colony, this inheritance accounts for the survival of a de facto estate system. Whereas throughout these centuries this system may be said to have mildly or minimally obtained between the Colonial aristocracy and the Creole population at large, it certainly was an important aspect of New Spain's society as a whole, that is, as affecting the Indians and the various *castas*. Thus, the social and economic interaction between the Creole estate and the tributary Indian estate remained stringent through these two centuries, while that between the Creole aristocracy and the Creole rank and file changed. At the end of Colonial times, the titled nobility was a powerful oligarchy, and its descendants managed to retain this exalted social and economic position for another century.

CRYSTALLIZATION OF EXPRESSIVE AND SOCIAL FORMS: 1600 – 1675

After the invigorating effects of the first renewal, the Creole aristocracy acquired a definitive form as a social and ruling class. The best way to describe its subsequent evolution is as a process of increasing elaboration of rather fixed social and expressive themes. Of critical importance was the inception of New Spain's higher nobility between the first and third decade of the seventeenth century, when four titles of nobility were awarded to Creole aristocrats. These titles represented the culmination of the old conquistador-*encomendero* class. Another batch of titles had been awarded by the last two decades of the century, but they did not satisfy the hunger of the Creole aristocracy (Ladd 1976). Again, they sought to redress the injustice against them, the consequence of which was the growth and elaboration of an expressive array to suit the nobiliary image the Creole aristocracy had of itself.

For 450 years, the main urban and rural loci of the Mexican aristocracy have been in central Mexico—more precisely, in the land and cities within a two hundred–mile radius of Mexico City. Here the core nuclei of the ruling class had their social and economic beginning, although in time their members acquired far-flung lands and mines and extended their mercantile operations to the limits of New Spain. The model of gentility, the standards of expression, and the norms of social conduct were set by these core four or five nuclei, most member families of which resided in the capital and in smaller cities within two to five days' travel. The aristocratic core, however, was not the whole of the social and ruling class. It included many more families enfranchised in cities far distant from the capital, to whom the capital-dwellers extended social and expressive recognition. Throughout most of the seventeenth century, the expansion to northern Mexico was an important source of wealth for the Creole oligarchy composed primarily of members of the core nuclei. Significant numbers of miners and *hacendados*, although in one fashion or another connected to the capital, were nonetheless resident *vecinos* of faraway cities, where they replicated the aristocratic patterns of the center. Thus, the three major components of the Creole aristocracy by the middle of the century were the core nuclei, the centralized sector enfranchised in locales within two hundred miles from Mexico City, and a peripheral sector enfranchised in more distant cities. The core nuclei included the titled nobles and the most prominent oligarchs, while the centralized and peripheral sectors may be regarded as the gentry of New Spain (Chevalier 1970:148–84).

This threefold division may be justified as follows. Extrapolating from Spain, the core nuclei were most certainly a titled nobility with corresponding cadet lines, since after all they were part of the same nobiliary system, regardless of peripheral position with respect to the metropolis. I would go even further and call the nuclei that included titled members the grandees of New Spain, for economically and socially they wielded much power in the colony. As to the rank-and-file members of the Creole aristocracy, they must also be considered a Colonial lower nobility, since probably most of them were *hidalgos a fuero de España*. Regardless of the economic impermanence that modern scholars have associated with the various categories of plutocratic oligarchs during the seventeenth and eighteenth centuries, there is a social continuity to the three categories of Creole aristocrats. Within the framework of the global estate, the three rungs of the Creole aristocracy constituted a small fraction of the entire Creole population, which by the second half of the seventeenth century was probably more than 150,000. Up to that time, this population had been composed entirely of individuals of Spanish stock, racially and culturally. Perhaps until the close of the seventeenth century, the label "Creole" had not yet Mestizoized, that is, the overwhelming majority of Creoles were Spaniards born in the colony (Saravia 1941:216–33). By the third quarter of the century, the Creole aristocracy numbered probably no more than 1,200 families or roughly 7,000 or 8,000 people, that is, about 6 percent of the total Creole population.

The landed estate was unquestionably the single most important consideration that generated solidarity and consciousness of kind among the members of the aristocratic class. By the middle of the century the *hacienda* had been established as the main economic and expressive factor of the Creole aristocracy, while a small minority of its members, the oligarchical magnates, combined it with mining and mercantile operations. Given the low productivity that characterized the *hacienda,* the most affluent members of the Creole aristocracy, who usually belonged to families of the core nuclei, pursued a mixed economic strategy in which mining and mercantile enterprises frequently produced more income than agrarian ones. But the *hacienda* was the expressive glue that held the Creole aristocracy together and gave it recognizable boundaries. In other words, *hidalgo* rank was the necessary condition for aristocratic membership, while the sufficient requirement was the ownership of a landed estate. Though in the periphery of the system it might have been difficult to determine *hacienda* owners who had not been accorded recognition as bona fide members of the aristocratic group, no such ambiguity existed in the major cities of New Spain. Family name was another important mechanism of aristocratic recognition, for genealogical knowledge played a significant role in the matrimonial and social alliances that predominated in the superordinate stratum of Colonial society. Aside from the titled nobility, which in New Spain remained very small until the turn of the eighteenth century, the Creole aristocracy was a gentry that required a measure of self-definition and control, since, though peripheral, it was nonetheless an extension of Spanish *hidalguía* (Lira Montt 1976). Genealogical inquiries were conducted for postulants to *hidalguía,* and no doubt upon request when proof of *limpieza de sangre* was needed for a certain office, but they were never as stringent as in Spain.

Peña (1983) shows that the most powerful aristocratic nuclei during the first two decades of the seventeenth century had their inception during the administration of Viceroy Mendoza and achieved maturity at the turn of the century. Not only did the core nuclei establish the model of aristocratic behavior and achievement, but its component families were the most permanent, that is, their diversified wealth preserved them from the downward mobility of many families of centralized and peripheral nuclei. Indeed, of the twenty aristocratic families today (1990) that I have identified as tracing descent to original conquistadors and distinguished *pobladores* of the sixteenth century, fifteen have apical ancestors belonging to the core nuclei. Thus, permanence for the aristocratic core and impermanence for the center and periphery have been constants in the history of the Mexican superordinate class.

The core nuclei included the families and extensions of the titled nobility, four in number, excepting Pedro Cortés, the fourth Marquis del Valle de Oaxaca, whose family was enfranchised in Spain. These four families included those of the Count of Salinas del Río Pisuerga, the Count of Santiago de Calimaya, the Marquis of Villa Mayor de las Ibiernas, and the Count of Valle de Orizaba. In addition, several nontitled *hidalgo* families of the highest rank competed in power and prestige with the titled families. Among the most noteworthy were the Cervants Casaus, the Gómez de Cervantes, the de la Mota y Escobars, the Cano Moctezumas, the Sámano y Turcios, the Pérez de Salazars, the Ramírez de Arellanos, the Luna y Arellanos, the Díaz de Vargas, the Carmona Tamariz, and several other enfranchised in Mexico City, Puebla, Guadalajara, and other cities in central Mexico, again demonstrating the concentration of the Creole aristocracy in a rather circumscribed area of New Spain. The titled and *hidalgo* families of these two divisions of the aristocracy constituted a fairly tight-knit nuclei, cemented by an extensive network of social and matrimonial alliances. Their great landed estates dotted central Mexico, a particularly advantageous location close to the most important centers of distribution and consumption, and their mining and mercantile interests complemented their agrarian enterprises.

From Viceroy Gelves's administration onward, the economy of New Spain was in disarray and the inhabitants of the colony, from Indians to aristocrats, suffered from stagnation. As far as the Creole aristocracy is concerned, its off and on confrontation with the viceregal administration intensified, and it experienced a significant degree of downward economic mobility (Brading 1971:12–21). *Hacienda* and mining production declined and *mayorazgos* diminished and somewhat decayed, but on the whole the aristocracy survived. The core nuclei were less affected, and some of the aristocratic magnates even prospered, while the peripheral nuclei suffered the most, as many large estates declared bankruptcy or were abandoned. Toward the end of the period, however, conditions began to improve, and New Spain launched into another period of growth and relative political stability (see Chevalier 1970; Brading 1971).

Diversification of the Social and Expressive System until Independence: 1675–1810

During the eighteenth century the population of the colony doubled, but we do not know the details or rate of the increment, primarily because of the consistently unreliable population estimates that began with the Conquest and persisted until Independence, when estimates became more reliable. For example, Cook and Borah (1960) greatly exaggerate the population of Mesoamerica at the time of the Conquest, while Miranda (1947) is equally unreliable concerning the Indian population for the seventeenth century. In the case of the former, the population has been estimated at probably twice of what it was; in the case of the latter, it falls short by nearly half.[1] There is no question that economic conditions began to improve with significant population increases during the end of the seventeenth century. Demographic growth affected the productivity of the *hacienda* and the mining boom beginning two decades later and, of course, created bigger markets.

The most significant variables in the evolution of the Creole aristocracy during the mature Colonial period—that is, roughly from the middle of the seventeenth century to Independence—were the transition from *encomienda* to *hacienda* and the proliferation of great landed estates, particularly in the areas immediately to the north of the traditional boundaries of Mesoamerica. Mining also contributed greatly to the economic recovery and general well-being of the colony, in turn fueling manufacturing.

During the eighteenth century, the cities of New Spain experienced an unusual degree of population growth, complexity, and urban elaboration. Few new cities had been founded, but those dating from before the middle of the seventeenth century—by now numbering more than twenty—had experienced important changes in building and urban planning, as attested by Alexander von Humboldt (1966:35–159) at the turn of the nineteenth century. Though no city of New Spain, except to some extent Puebla, came close to Mexico City, there is good evidence that at least seven provincial cities had experienced unprecedented improvements and beautification. The surviving architecture of this period attests to the eighteenth-century building boom of New Spain.

The building boom took place roughly between 1720 and 1780, which, not surprisingly, coincides with the most intensive period of mining exploitation. From Oaxaca to Zacatecas, the surviving public (civil) and private (domestic) architectures of some fifteen cities of the Mexican plateau attest to this period of affluence in Mexican history. The most visible testimony of this urban renewal was public architecture, as exemplified by the many churches, squares, arcades and other buildings that adorned the late Colonial city, most of which still stand today. Not quite as visible were residences and business establishments, constituting the bulk of private architecture. Many aristocratic magnates were directly involved in the construction of distinguished buildings (Tovar de Teresa 1986).

Religious architecture is a special domain with public and private components and involving the participation of rich and prominent aristocrats. The construction of religious buildings was an important domain in the expressive array of the Creole aristocracy, and in exceptional cases, an entire church was built with funds provided by a magnate and presented to the community as a gift. More commonly, construction was a communal affair, though one or several aristocrats generally provided most of the funds. Indeed, these two methods of providing for church construction persisted until the Mexican Revolution of 1910. An associated aspect of religious architecture was the construction of chapels. Separate, independent chapels were occasionally commissioned and fully paid for by aristocratic magnates for specific occasions or in honor of a particular saint of their devotion. Many of these chapels, even in provincial cities, disappeared in the urban renewals of the late nineteenth century, but they were common sights before this period. Much more frequently, lateral chapels in old or newly constructed churches were "donated" by prominent Creole aristocrats, that is, they paid for the installment and decoration of retables and other accoutrements in the circumscribed area (Ovando n.d.).

Perhaps more immediately significant as an expressive manifestation was the construction of aristocratic urban residences. They constituted the most outstanding example of private architecture in the cities of the Mexican plateau, and many mansions have survived until the present relatively intact. Mexico City, Puebla, Guadalajara, Guanajuato, Querétaro, Morelia, and San Luis Potosí, all traditional *hacendado* cities par excellence, have today the largest number of these establishments, some of them veritable palaces. Mexico City, of course, had the most outstanding examples of these residences, many of which are today cultural and business landmarks, while Puebla and two or three of the principal Colonial cities lagged not too far behind. The aristocratic establishment was always large, often containing as many as fifty rooms sufficient to accommodate the expressive style in living of a relatively numerous titled nobility. By the end of Colonial times, the residences of New Spain's titled nobility were the largest and most elaborate expression of the New World's Creole aristocracy (Ortega y Pérez Gallardo 1908).

The economic boom that brought more wealth to the Creole aristocracy as a whole was accompanied by an expressive boom. Dating from as early as 1710, a considerable array of furniture, religious art, oil portraits and paintings, and miscellaneous articles of decoration can still be found in the contemporary aristocratic household. Aided by the significant oral tradition associated with these heirlooms, one can reconstruct the household expressive domain and some associated private and public aspects of the social life of the Creole aristocracy by the middle of the eighteenth century.

By the first quarter of the eighteenth century, Creole and Mestizo craftsmen were manufacturing luxury furniture that quite favorably compared with similar articles in the mother country. Particularly noteworthy were the tables, desks, chairs, chests of drawers, armoires, dressers, chests, and other pieces of color woods and ivory inlaid (*marquetería*) furniture from Puebla; and the lacquerwork and decorated screens of Valladolid (now Morella) and its environs. Imports from Spain and, occasionally, Italy and France were common, particularly during the last quarter of the century, and the furniture of the well-appointed aristocratic household combined domestic and foreign items. Tapestries and carpets of high quality were all imported from Europe, and the former were particularly important items in the decoration of the household. By the eighteenth century, silk, brocades, porcelain, and pottery were essential decorative elements in the aristocratic household, and they were supplied abundantly by the Manila Galleon.

Portraiture was the most important expressive element, judging by the great number of oils from the eighteenth century that still decorate the aristocratic household. Men, women, and children were mostly formally depicted individually, rarely in groups; the structure of the portrait was generally somewhat stilted, conventional, but highly expressive of the person's social station: elaborate finery, framed by coats of arms and other armorial bearings, and long descriptions of titles, positions, and accomplishments. Though some of the religious art was done by well-known Colonial artists, portraiture occupied many less-important artists. Another form of portraiture, in a very different tradition, was the depiction of nuns in their deathbeds, portrayed as the brides of Christ in elaborately Baroque garb.

Given the abundance of silver and gold, the household naturally contained a wide array of articles manufactured from these metals, such as flat silverware, trays, dishes, and many other objects. Few of these heirlooms have survived, for, beginning late in the nineteenth century, gold and silver objects were the first items to be sold by downwardly mobile families, and later on by aristocratic families most affected by the land reform of the 1930s (Carlos de Ovando, pers. comm.).[2] Many other miscellaneous household items of decoration and display do survive, and they point to an extensive array of imported and domestic ensemble of artifacts reflecting the same general characteristics as the western European aristocratic household, which until the eighteenth century had retained a rather high common expressive denominator among its several variants (Spanish, French, English, etc.). Significantly for the ethnographic analysis of the Mexican aristocracy, Western aristocracies underwent a period of expressive differentiation between the French Revolution and the First World War, and since then a new process of convergence has been taking place.

Though it is possible to reconstruct the general expressive ambiance and configuration of the household during the affluent years of the eighteenth century, one can make only tentative generalizations concerning dress, manners and mores, the aristocratic image of the city, and the wider public domains so much a part of the Creole aristocracy. It is nonetheless possible to encapsulate the expressive position of this social class in the urban context.

First, New Spain was a Colonial society not only politically but culturally as well. In the important domains of expression that configured daily, social, and ritual life, the Creole aristocracy was not innovative; at most it adapted patterns, usages, and behaviors fashioned in Spain and other European countries. Thus, the fashions and styles of the aristocracy were indistinguishable from those of Spain, except insofar as they were slightly behind the times. This point should not be overemphasized, for in country attire and accessories Creole society combined Spanish and local patterns in a novel and elegantly distinct style of dressing.

Second, the eighteenth century did not witness the inception of distinctly new expressive patterns. Rather, this period must be characterized as an intensification of patterns and domains that had crystallized by the middle of the previous century, but that now exhibited greater complexity and diversification. Affluence alone does not account for these changes; the facts that Creole society had grown greatly and that the aristocracy performed on a stage several times larger than that of its formative period must also be considered. Indeed, medieval survivals such as certain games, forms of address, and honorific privileges of *hidalgos* had become obsolete, and though certain formal distinctions remained, the distinctions between titled *hidalgo* and commoner in behavior and social functions had become more fluid. Despite its lack of political functions, the titled nobility—by the first decade of the nineteenth century including nearly one hundred counts and marquises—enhanced the visibility of the Creole aristocracy in its social and ceremonial functions.

Third, the perpetuation of the original expressive array, augmented by the appearance of new elaborations reflecting the changes in European society toward the end of the century, brought the Creole aristocracy to a pinnacle of social and expressive influence and exaltedness. This achievement was the result of the confluence of great wealth, the large scope of the expressive array, and the surviving privileges entailed by the estate system. The aristocracy became more visible than ever. They were by now the social and expressive leaders of a milieu including one million Creoles and Mestizo-Creoles.

Fourth and finally, the growth of honors and dignities was directly tied to the economic affluence that characterized the ruling class of New Spain throughout most of the eighteenth century. The motivating mechanisms have been discussed extensively, but more than ever before, the new wealth made the attainment of honors and dignities more likely than at any period before. This circumstance essentially reflects the maturity that the Colonial superordinate class had achieved by the onset of the eighteenth century, and it finds its most extensive expression in the establishment of *mayorazgos,* vying for admission to military orders, and securing nomination for titles of nobility. From the turn of the century until shortly before Independence these social and expressive activities were the main concerns of the established aristocracy as well as of upwardly mobile plutocratic magnates.

The Economic and Local Political Bases of the Ruling Class

This study is essentially a social history, and economic, political, and even religious considerations are brought to bear upon the changing process only insofar as they constitute immediate inputs into the structure and ideology of the aristocracy's expressive culture and associated patterns of behavior and action. The economic and political history of New Spain in the eighteenth century is well known, and the outstanding work of Brading (1971) may appropriately serve as background to the following account.

ORGANIZATION OF *CABILDOS* AND CONTROL OF REGIONAL RESOURCES

From the moment conquistadors landed in Veracruz, the *cabildo* was the most important representative institution of the colonists. The *cabildo* never diminished in importance, and until Independence this form of municipal government was crucial in the life of the colony, not only for Creoles and Mestizos but for Indians as well. At the beginning, and perhaps until two generations after the Conquest, the *cabildo* was a representative institution of the *vecinos,* that is, the charter members of the community. By 1590, when the cities and towns of New Spain had become a mixture of *vecinos, moradores,* Mestizos, and descendants of conquistadors, the *cabildo* was no longer a representative institution, but rather represented the interests of a plutocratic minority, including always the locally enfranchised Creole aristocracy. Membership in the *cabildo,* however representative of its constituents it might have been originally, was not really democratic. From 1519, the *cabildos* of New Spain were controlled by *hidalgo* conquistadors and later by the Creole aristocracy that came to dominate the economic and social life of cities and towns (Bayle 1952). The earliest *cabildos* of Veracruz and Mexico City attest to the monopoly exercised by the most important conquistadors, inherited by their descendants, passed on to a combination of surviving elements of conquistador extraction and *pobladores,* and ultimately vested in the Creole aristocracy that had crystallized by the turn of the seventeenth century. The control of cities and towns became the main interest of the local ruling class and was of utmost importance to its economic interests. This basic situation remained constant until the end of Colonial rule (Haring 1953).

The *cabildo* of New Spain was a transplant, one of the few Spanish institutions that did not undergo syncretic or acculturative transformations in the new land. Its composition, functions, and activities did change somewhat from the sixteenth century to Independence, but its basic configuration remained the same. The *cabildo* consisted of one or two *alcaldes ordinarios* (mayors, aldermen), six to as many as nine *regidores* (aldermen, councilmen), and a number of subsidiary functionaries: *alguacil mayor* (constable, peace officer), *alguaciles* (police officers), secretaries, interpreters, and so on. Until perhaps the middle of the sixteenth century *alcaldes* and *regidores* were elected democratically by the *vecinos*. In the course of the sixteenth century the *cabildo* adopted a rather closed system of election that favored *peninsulares* and was more easily influenced and controlled by the viceregal authorities. By the beginning of the seventeenth century, the offices of *alcaldes* and *regidores* had become heavily influenced to election by former officeholders, some were openly sold, and some had become proprietary, not infrequently for life (Israel 1975:94–101). In short, from early in the seventeenth century until Independence, *cabildos* throughout New Spain were closed, self-perpetuating oligarchies.

The specific configuration of the *cabildo,* including the number and proportion of *alcaldes* and *regidores* and the execution of specific functions, did change through time. The most notable changes, however, came in the last quarter of the eighteenth century with the establishment of *intendencias* (intendancies), part of the Bourbon reform of the overall Colonial administration, which reflected the loss of control of the Spanish Crown. The *cabildo* acquired many new positions that reflected its widening regional influence and ties to the central government: *alcalde provincial, alférez real,* and *procurador general,* to name just a few. The reform was little more than a formal recognition that the central government was not functioning well; already for several decades *cabildos* had been acquiring wider regional functions (Brading 1971:319–28).

More directly related to the evolution of the Mexican aristocracy is the social composition of the *cabildos* of New Spain—basically the Creole or *peninsular* provenance of its members—and the regional variations that composition entailed. Here again the lines of development are fairly clear. Until the arrival of Viceroy Mendoza, *alcaldes* and *regidores* were all conquistadors. From his arrival until the last quarter of the sixteenth century, the composition of *cabildos* was a mixture of a few original conquistadors, descendants of conquistadors, recipients of royal and viceregal patronage, and a sprinkling of upwardly mobile merchants. During this forty- to fifty-year period, Creoles in considerable numbers became *alcaldes* and *regidores* for the first time. Most of these first- and second-generation descendants of original conquistadors were core members of the nascent Creole aristocracy (Bayle 1952). Until the turn of the seventeenth century, however, the majority of *cabildos* had more *peninsulares* than Creoles, reflecting the patronage of the Crown. Throughout the seventeenth century, Creoles acquired increasing control of *cabildos,* in many cases outnumbering *peninsulares* in the positions of *alcaldes* and *regidores,* although the situation was not uniform throughout New Spain (Brading 1971:302–18).

We might also look at local government from the regional perspective, keeping in mind the economic enterprises associated with specific cities and towns. First, the more centrally located the cities and towns, the less control the Creole aristocracy exercised on the *cabildo.* Thus, in Mexico City and Puebla, for example, throughout most of the seventeenth and eighteenth centuries, Creoles seldom outnumbered *peninsulares* in the total number of *alcaldes* and *regidores* (Peña 1983:163–70). Second, *hacendado* cities and towns, that is, those associated with eminently agricultural regions, were dominated by Creole *cabildos,* for most of the largest agrarian enterprises were in the hands of aristocrats with long landholding traditions, and, in the seventeenth century particularly, *peninsular* entrepreneurs were generally miners and merchants. By contrast, mining cities in the eighteenth century were often dominated by *peninsulares* who occupied the majority of positions in the *cabildo.* Third, most of the peripheral, less important cities and towns were controlled by Creoles. In these municipalities Creole aristocrats had the greatest control of the *cabildo,* by virtue of being the great landowners and to some extent due to isolation from the central government.

Throughout Colonial times, local politics were important to the Creole aristocracy, both as an instrumental tool and as a domain of expressive realization. With respect to the former, holding the office of *alcalde* or *regidor* was important to protecting economic activities in the region dominated by the *cabildo.* Economics were evidently the most important motivation for local political control, namely, safeguarding the mining, agricultural, and mercantile enterprises centered in the city whose *cabildo* aristocratic oligarchs monopolized. On the one hand, mining cities, seldom very populous, were invariably very important economically. They were usually the centers for distributing food and supplies to the mining camps located within their areas of influence. Traveling and established merchants maintained warehouses in mining cities, which were, therefore, busy centers of trade. On the other hand, trading-agricultural cities became thriving centers in their own specialties. Often, too, they were important trading and mercantile centers, usually supporting extensive areas dominated by *haciendas*.

The conquistadors set the pattern of political participation by regarding the cities and towns of which they were charter members as an extension of the household, which they had the right to fashion according to their needs and inclination. This expressive attitude became deeply ingrained in the descendants of conquistadors and later *pobladores* and was perpetuated by the mature Creole aristocracy. It manifested itself in a conception of the city as a stage on which some of the most cherished expressive domains of the ruling class could be acted out, an attitude that often led to urban planning and alteration to suit the aristocratic image of the city. This aristocratic concern is closely related to religious ceremonialism, and parochial and diocesan authorities invariably made common cause with the ruling class, by consistently sanctioning salient expressive roles played by the ruling class in yearly public events and activities.

THE TRANSITION FROM *ENCOMIENDA* TO *HACIENDA* AND GROWTH OF LANDED ESTATES

In the foregoing chapters the *hacienda* was placed in proper structural and expressive perspective, namely, the role it played in the inception and early development of the Creole aristocracy. The following remarks trace the evolution of the *hacienda* from the early seventeenth century to the end of Colonial rule, again emphasizing the expressive components and how they related to the changing economic panorama of New Spain.

The *hacienda* in New Spain may be said to have begun with Cortés's ordinance that conquistadors had to keep a house near the communities of their *encomienda* Indians. However, the *hacienda*, a large landed estate with a substantial building establishment in it, did not begin until the second half of the sixteenth century. By the last quarter of the sixteenth century, the *hacienda* was established as the paramount agrarian institution in the colony. On the one hand, the rapid decline of the Indian population left many lands vacant, and *encomenderos* and plutocratic entrepreneurs wasted no time in occupying these areas by availing themselves of viceregal grants. Demographically, while the decline of the Indian population made possible the birth of the *hacienda,* it also created greater problems for the supply and distribution of labor, which ultimately led to the abandonment of the *encomienda* system. On the other hand, the accumulation of land during the second half of the century was also related to the type of agrarian enterprise that apparently yielded the most profit with rather modest investments in labor and capital, namely, cattle and sheep raising. For several decades after the Conquest, animal husbandry was the fastest growing agrarian enterprise, a phenomenon facilitated by the fact that wheat, corn, and other staples were grown by Indian populations as a means of paying tribute. The viceregal authorities encouraged, and sometimes even required, this tribute, as a means to keep the colony adequately supplied (Nickel 1988:40–63).

By the turn of the seventeenth century, in central Mexico, and to some extent in the northern and southern areas of the colony, three types of agrarian enterprises had emerged. First, relatively small landholdings surrounding or immediately adjacent to the Indian congregations, which were probably the best arable lands and the most intensely cultivated, produced staple crops for the maintenance of the cities and towns. Second, large *haciendas* located in less desirable lands, away from the main cities and towns, were dedicated to the cultivation of staple crops, commercial crops such as sugar, and some cattle and sheep raising. Third, immense *estancias* raised cattle, sheep, horses, and goats, mules, and donkeys. In fact, the Indian population had declined so much that large tracts of previously cultivated land in the central plateau had been devoted to livestock (Chevalier 1952:68–132). The great landed expanses of *haciendas* and *estancias* were the almost exclusive preserve of aristocratic magnates, while smaller landholdings were owned by Creole rank and file.

Well before 1600, labor shortages were the most serious problems facing the *hacienda,* a situation that lasted until the end of the century, when it began gradually to improve. Another consideration in assessing the growth of the *hacienda* during this period also relates to the decline of Indian population: *encomenderos* suffered greatly from loss of tributary income and were becoming less affluent than the operators of mining and agrarian enterprises, which undoubtedly forced many of them to engage in large agrarian enterprises, further increasing the size of the *hacienda* (Simpson 1934:72–106).

Of course, the *encomienda* did not entail possession of the land, and essentially the growth of the *hacienda* and labor supply represent two different developments. In an insightful analysis, Zavala (1943:93–103) refutes the idea entertained by many authorities on the Colonial period that debt peonage originated in the *encomienda*. He argues that when the *encomienda* began to decline, *encomenderos* lost control of Indian labor because *repartimientos* were regulated independently by viceregal authorities. The new legislation did not seriously affect *encomenderos;* for years they had attracted to their landed estates Indians from neighboring communities, who were known as *gañanes* or *laboríos*. Thus, instead of waiting for periodic assignment of Indians by viceregal authorities, *hacendados* already had many Indian families living on their estates as laborers. Furthermore, landowners did everything in their power to strengthen their hold on the *gañanes* by depriving them of freedom of movement. The legal means of accomplishing this was to advance the Indians money and goods, which bound the *gañanes* to the *hacienda* by placing them in debt. It was this method, and not the *encomienda*, Zavala argues, that was the true forerunner of debt peonage and the *hacienda*. Though basically agreeing with Zavala, Nickel (1988:43–46) maintains that landownership and Indian labor cannot be separated and that in fact these two aspects were intimately interrelated. Another consideration for the *gañanes* is that by attaching themselves to a *hacienda* they were protected from the labor levies of Crown and community (*tequio*), which at times could be very harsh and disturbing (Brading 1971:4–6). Furthermore, the *hacendado* granted them a plot of land for their own cultivation. Thus, despite population decline and the difficult economic depression that affected New Spain during much of the seventeenth century, the great aristocratic magnates who dominated much of the agrarian landscape of the colony managed to survive. By itself, the *hacienda* would not have been sufficient to maintain an adequate lifestyle for the Creole aristocracy, had it not been for its diversified mining and mercantile strategies. The *hacienda* system produced for an internal market, and thus the *hacienda* to an extent survived as a function of the expressive value that the land had for the Creole aristocracy (Galván 1884:78–96).

The *hacienda* proper, that is, the great landed expanses dedicated to the cultivation of staples, probably fared badly, but plantation *hacien-*

das dedicated to the cultivation of single crops such as sugar and cochineal fared fairly well, and livestock *estancias* more often than not were profitable enterprises, given minimal capital investment and the fluidity of the landed estate. Moreover, as the century advanced and the population increased, particularly in the cities, the internal market expanded, and the *hacienda* in its various forms began its slow recuperation. The *hacienda* became a world unto itself, isolated from much of Colonial life, self-sufficient in many respects, and harboring owners and peons into a rather close system (Chevalier 1952:235–60). The *hacienda* developed its own independent administration, system of justice, police force, and internal economic system in dealing with the Indian population enfranchised in the landed estate, and frequently exerted control on nearby communities. Occasionally, in order to control and protect their enormous landed estates, *hacendados* created veritable armies. A rather fixed stratification system grew out of this social milieu: the *hacendado,* his family, and a few Creole associates were at the top; a Mestizo administration occupied intermediary positions; and the Indian peons and their families scraped along at the bottom (Alessio Robles 1938:139–48).

Nickel's account of the Mexican *hacienda* is the best in the literature. He divides the growth and development of the Colonial *hacienda* into three stages: the formative period from 1530 to 1630; a consolidating phase from 1630 to 1730; and a period of classical florescence from 1730 to 1810 (Nickel 1988:66–68). This categorization accords well with the development of the Creole aristocracy as an agrarian ruling class. The first stage corresponds to the period of land acquisition embodied in the *encomienda,* during which the great landed estates in central Mexico came into existence by the combined process of viceregal grants and usurpation of the land from Indian communities. The second stage covers a period of stagnation and the beginnings of recovery of the *hacienda,* during which land was legalized, primarily by the payment of a certain amount of money to the Crown. The third stage is roughly coterminous with New Spain's century of florescence, which witnessed the recovery of the *hacienda* and, at the end of the period, its further territorial growth.

If the seventeenth century may be characterized as a century of depression, the eighteenth century was a century of economic recovery and affluence. The agrarian, mining, and mercantile sectors experienced unprecedented growth and the economy, from the second de-

cade until shortly before Independence, was almost continually up-
beat. The population began to increase more rapidly; by 1800 it had
surpassed six million people. The internal market became much
larger as new cities came into existence and old ones became larger
population centers. In this ambiance of economic well-being, the
hacienda proliferated, both as a function of the global Colonial economy and as a manifestation of regional diversification (Velasco Ceballos 1936:46–54).

In this propitious environment, the *hacienda* system experienced
important changes: it expanded, streamlined production, and became
in short an independent viable economic enterprise. The most affected
areas were in the north and south, that is, the periphery of New Spain
and the areas immediately adjacent to the central Mexican plateau. In
these areas, ownership became more stable, and *haciendas* no longer
experienced the economic downward mobility that had affected many
hacendados in the seventeenth century. Stability had been achieved, and
from the middle of the eighteenth century until the 1910 Revolution,
ownership changed little, as compared with the bankruptcies and land
resale that had characterized agrarian life until the last decade of the
seventeenth century (Ovando n.d.).

More than at any time since 1580, the size of the *hacienda* increased
during the second half of the eighteenth century. There were two
reasons for this transformation: improved and more secure means of
communication, and the expulsion of the Jesuits from New Spain.
During the last sixty years of Colonial rule, the main regions of New
Spain became more easily accessible by a network of roads and more
adequate means of transportation, which allowed the effective exploitation of faraway lands, particularly toward the north, encompassing
today's Mexican states of Sonora, Sinaloa, Coahuila, Chihuahua, Nuevo
León, and Tamaulipas. But in central and southern Mexico as well the
hacienda experienced growth that can be traced to a greater degree of
accessibility due to improved roads and transportation. Meanwhile, the
expulsion of the Jesuits from New Spain made available large amounts
of land that the order had accumulated for nearly two centuries.
Though part of these lands ultimately ended in the hands of the secular
church, most of them were sold to existing *hacendados* or miners in the
process of becoming *hacendados*. The lands of the Jesuits were highly
desirable, which is why the Count of Regla, a rich plutocratic miner
and trader recently ennobled, bought four Jesuit *haciendas* in the north-

ern part of the Valley of Mexico for more than a million pesos: a classical example of acquiring land not only as an investment but to legitimate recently acquired aristocratic rank (Gibson 1964:290).

The most significant expressive development in the century of affluence was the construction of large and elaborate establishments in the *haciendas*. In central Mexico, *hacienda* manors were already extensive by the late seventeenth century, including living complexes for the *hacendados* as well as ample facilities for processing and storing agricultural production, including silos, corrals, administration quarters, and so on. Not until the middle of the eighteenth century, however, did *cascos* acquire unprecedented extension, elaboration, and architectural excellence. The *hacienda* manor became more elegant and better conditioned to permanent habitation. Perhaps also as a function of improved means of communication, *hacendado* families now spent more time in the *hacienda* than at any other period since the Conquest. Many of the *haciendas* closer to the city became abodes for the family during most of the year. Although the aristocratic family was permanently enfranchised in the city, the *hacienda* was used for longer periods of time. This development is also related to the greater use of the *hacienda* for recreation and as the setting for such events in the life and religious cycles as baptisms, confirmations, and celebrations of saint's day (Ovando n.d.).

Mining and Trading Strategies and the Landed Aristocracy

Shortly before the turn of the seventeenth century, *encomenderos* became increasingly engaged in mining activities, and by the time the century of depression began to ebb, mining was an important aspect of the combined economic strategies of many aristocratic *hacendados*. During the mining boom that began in the second decade of the eighteenth century, however, the more conservative *hacendados* were not the richest and most outstanding miners, most of whom were more adventurous *peninsulares* and almost all of whose families became Creoles before the end of the century (Ladd 1976:125–56). Mining was not, in fact, a widespread economic interest among Creole aristocrats. It was strongest among members of the core nuclei, though many of the richest mines in the eighteenth century were in the north.

Mining meant primarily the exploitation of gold and, particularly, silver deposits. The earliest mines were located near Mexico City,

Pachuca, Sultepec, and Taxco being the most important early centers. During the second half of the sixteenth century, mining exploitation shifted to the north along the Sierra Madre Occidental, extending from the Valley of Mexico to Sonora, and including such well-known areas as Guanajuato, Real del Monte, and Zacatecas. By the end of the sixteenth century, silver mining was scattered over a large area, and the development of the *hacienda* in the north was an integral aspect of this economic activity. More than in central Mexico, the north became an area in which the various agrarian enterprises (mostly the very large *haciendas* and *estancias*) and mining were inseparable and toward the end of Colonial times it became the fountain of some of the greatest fortunes in New Spain (Brading 1971:129–68). These mining *hacendado* oligarchs, however, also owned land and engaged in other economic enterprises in central Mexico and were therefore members of the core Creole aristocracy. From the middle of the sixteenth century until the first decade of the seventeenth century, silver production increased steadily then declined precipitously and remained in a slump until the turn of the century. By 1720, silver and gold production was again on the rise, and during the last three decades of the century it experienced an unprecedented boom.

It is beyond the scope of this account even to outline the trading and commercial activities that were an important component of the wealth of the Creole ruling class during most of the Colonial period. I refer you to Brading's excellent account of merchants in Mexico in the eighteenth century (Brading 1971). I will briefly outline this economic activity only in relation to the other wealth-generating strategies of the Creole aristocracy over time. Mercantile activities were not frowned upon in New Spain, and the so-called Spanish aversion to them was never a factor in the development of the Creole aristocracy. Indeed, as Pike (1972:22–38) demonstrates for the upper and lower nobility of Seville in the sixteenth century, whatever laws of derogation had been in effect in medieval times, the aristocracy of the city actively engaged in business. From the Conquest onward, the situation in New Spain was at least as fluid as that in Spain.

Upward plutocratic mobility acculturated the core nuclei of the aristocracy to invest in trading and commerce, within the colony and with Spain and the Orient. From the second quarter of the seventeenth century, that is, after the first renewal, mercantile operations became an increasingly important part of the economic strategies of the Creole

aristocracy, together with mining and agriculture and livestock raising. Thereafter, until the end of Colonial rule, the *hacienda,* mining,
and commerce were the economic pillars of the ruling class. The extent
to which new mining and trading fortunes were made in the middle
and late seventeenth century is unknown, for the plutocratic owners
were incorporated into the established Creole aristocracy. Mercantile
operations mostly aimed to supplement income from the mining and
agrarian operations of long-established aristocratic magnates, that is,
members of the core nuclei. Large-scale commerce was an almost exclusive preserve of aristocratic magnates enfranchised in the center, but
with far-flung economic interests throughout New Spain (Arróniz
1952).

Trade and commerce came into their own with the economic recovery of the eighteenth century. Beginning in 1710, large fortunes were
made in internal and overseas trading, the distribution and sale of
livestock and agricultural production, and the manufacture of a wide
range of goods. Thus, oligarchical interest in New Spain may be summarized as control of overseas trade and internal commerce entailing
extensive networks with colonywide ramifications. The initiators of the
mercantile boom were mostly *peninsulares,* who for structural (viceregal
favoritism) and expressive reasons amassed large fortunes independent
of mining and agriculture, a phenomenon that had occurred in the past
but did not become common until the eighteenth century. The architects of the mining boom were also mostly *peninsulares.* Probably the
majority of these mining and trading entrepreneurs were commoners:
when they arrived in New Spain, that is, they were not *hidalgos a fuero
de España,* although quite likely, if they were Basques or Montañeses,
they could claim to be *hidalgos de gotera* (Brading 1971:106–14). The
great economic success of many of these entrepreneurs made them
prime candidates for the more than sixty titles of nobility that the
Crown granted to residents of New Spain during the eighteenth century, and this introduced a new element in the evolution of the Creole
aristocracy: for the first time an individual passed from commoner
status to titled nobility without the transitional step of *hidalguía* of
long standing or recent creation.

By the last fifty years of Colonial rule, the Creole ruling class, core
and periphery, was a landed aristocracy: most of its members derived
their wealth from the various forms of the *hacienda* and had only
subsidiary interests in mining and trade. The aristocratic magnates, on

the other hand, had a truly diversified economy in mining, trade, and agrarian enterprises, and very few were exclusively miners or traders. Though fewer long-established aristocratic *hacendados* engaged in other economic enterprises, when they did, they equaled or occasionally surpassed in wealth the newer mining and trading aristocrats. The most common strategic combinations were agriculture and mining, followed by agriculture, mining, and trade, and, much less commonly, mining and trade together or by themselves. Several fortunes surpassed two and three million pesos, while the average fortune was somewhere between five hundred thousand to a million and a half pesos, enough to support the social and expressive life of the core aristocracy in a grand style. The ethnic composition of this ruling class was fairly evenly divided between Creoles and *peninsulares,* but, as always, with a distinctive Creole stamp (Ladd 1976:175–87).

Entailed Property and the Perpetuation of Aristocratic Rank

In the New World, especially in New Spain, three institutions were means to aristocratic rank: entailed property, membership in military orders, and titles of nobility. From shortly after the Conquest until the end of Colonial rule, these were important components of the Creole aristocracy and the upwardly mobile plutocracy, and for more than 250 years superordinate class position was characterized by various forms and manipulations of these perpetuating institutional mechanisms. Although not necessarily determining attributes of aristocratic class membership, entailed property, military orders, and titles of nobility were an intrinsic aspect of the aristocratic model and therefore merit close scrutiny.

CONSTITUTION OF THE *MAYORAZGO* AND ITS SOCIAL AND ECONOMIC CONSEQUENCES

Entailed property is a very old institution going back to the early Roman *fideicomisos* (feoffment in trusts) recorded in Spain for the last decades of the first century A.D. During the Visigothic monarchy, the Roman institution was modified and reinvigorated, and by the time of the Moslem conquest, entailed property was a significant component of the Iberian aristocracy. With the rise of Feudalism, primogeniture became increasingly important to the superordinate estate, and thenceforward entailed property and primogeniture were almost synonymous. By the time seigneurialism replaced Feudalism, certainly no later than 1300, entailed property vested in the primogenit was perhaps the most significant characteristic of the dominant estate in western European society. In Spain, entailed property vested in the primogenit became known as *mayorazgo,* and from the end of the fourteenth century on, primogeniture and *mayorazgo* had essentially the same meaning (Clavero 1974:59–92).

By the beginning of the sixteenth century entailed property in general, and the *mayorazgo* in particular, had been widely diversified. So important was this institution of the nobiliary system that by the first decade of the century the laws and regulation of entail had been codified in the *Leyes de Toro* (Clavero 1974:51–56). In this codified form the *mayorazgo* was instituted in New Spain, and from the start it influenced the formation, development, and florescence of the Creole aristocracy.

Entailed property (*propiedad vinculada*) means that the beneficiary of the entail has the right to the usufruct but not to the property itself. Inherent in the juridical foundation of the *mayorazgo* is the prescription that primogenits will successively inherit the usufruct of the property. Thus, the term *mayorazgo* denoted both the primogenit and the entailed property. This usage has remained constant until today, as Mexican aristocrats occasionally refer to their firstborn as the *mayorazgo,* while specific items of property—primarily distinguished urban residences— are still regarded as the *mayorazgo* of a given family. Since the beginning of the Castilian *mayorazgo* in the thirteenth century, any property, movable or immovable, could be entailed, including seigneurial rents and tributes. This system was introduced in New Spain in the first half of the sixteenth century.

Mayorazgos were regulated by the Crown and could not be established at will solely on the basis of an individual's wealth. Upon petition, the Crown, through its local representatives, approved the foundation of *mayorazgos* by letters patent, and the Colonial judiciary system supervised the proper functioning of the institution, that is, the usufruct of the entail, its inheritance, and the legal successor. Apparently, as late as the end of the sixteenth century, *mayorazgos* could be founded only by the upper and lower nobility. Eventually, this rule was relaxed, and by the middle of the seventeenth century *hidalguía* was not a requirement. The size of the *mayorazgo* was an important consideration, as the Crown insisted that property be large enough to support the style and quality of life implicitly associated with the individual's rank (González Serrano 1876:137–43).

The *mayorazgo* had both social and economic functions. Just as the kingdom, the first *mayorazgo*, strove for continuity through institutionalized succession, unity through economic integration, and greatness through brilliant social and ceremonial life, so did individual *mayorazgos* of titled nobles and *hidalgos* perpetuate the high living standards of individual families. Thus, as part of an undifferentiated noble estate from king to *hidalgo*, the Crown had a vested interest in perpetuating lineage and aristocratic lifestyles commensurate with the dignity and rank of the superordinately placed. The social function of the *mayorazgo*, then, was to provide the proper ambiance for the discharge of aristocratic values with dignity and honor; and the economic function of the institution was to ensure the continuity of a lifestyle that would have disappeared if property were partially inherited.

In New Spain, almost any property could be entailed, but the most usual *mayorazgos* were in agricultural land, urban property, mines, livestock enterprises, specific agricultural enterprises (corn, sugar, wheat, *pulque*), mining shares, urban buildings, *hacienda* manors, and urban palaces and mansions. Less common *mayorazgos* included such property as books, paintings, furniture, fine coaches, horses, slaves, jewelry, suits of armor, and so on. Income-producing property was obviously the economic, utilitarian backbone of the *mayorazgo;* most other entailed property could be considered heirlooms and constituted the expressive components of the institution. Although the emphasis here is on the *mayorazgo* as primogeniture, other forms of entailed property should be mentioned. The founder of an entail had the legal power to establish the conditions for the disposition of the usufruct, who inherited, and the conditions under which inheritance took place. For example, bastards were generally disinherited, the bulk of an entail could be inherited by second- or third-born children, occasionally daughters would be favored over sons, and so on (Ladd 1976:71–75).

By Spanish standards, the *mayorazgo* in New Spain was rather limited: among the Creole population as a whole, the *hidalgos a fuero de España* were proportionately half as numerous than the *hidalgo* population on the peninsula. The configuration of the *mayorazgo* from the sixteenth century to the end of Colonial rule changed as follows. Though original conquistadors may have entailed their *encomiendas* and *reparti-*

mientos in *mayorazgos,* the New Laws and other vicissitudes suffered by these institutions throughout the first one hundred years after the Conquest prevented the situation from crystallizing into a permanent arrangement (Clavero 1974:181–207). In fact, then, the first *mayorazgos* in New Spain were established during the second half of the sixteenth century by descendants of conquistadors and recipients of viceregal patronage and probably they were mostly in land. Few *mayorazgos* existed before the turn of the century, but they increased during the first quarter of the seventeenth century. Almost all core families of the Creole aristocracy throughout the seventeenth century founded *mayorazgos;* how widespread the institution was among peripheral aristocrats is not known. Most *mayorazgos* were in land, agrarian operations, urban property, and mining (Ortega y Pérez Gallardo 1908).

By the eighteenth century *mayorazgos* flourished. By then, almost any Creole could found a *mayorazgo,* as the requirements had been liberalized and individuals no longer had to be *hidalgos* in order to entail property. This situation reflected the liberalizing trend of Spain's estate system. The new fluidity found its most characteristic expression in the direct ennoblement of plutocrats and in the *mayorazgo,* and entails in general, being available to all rich and respectable Creoles. By the middle of the eighteenth century, at least 150 families had founded *mayorazgos,* and most of them were members of the Creole aristocracy or vying for aristocratic rank (Carlos de Ovando, pers. comm.). The Crown favored *mayorazgos,* reasoning that lineages with a vested interest in the economy and the land were more likely to be pillars of the system, faithful to the sovereign, and men of enterprise benefiting the commonwealth (Ladd 1976:76–83).

The size of *mayorazgos* ranged from small ones of 30,000 to 50,000 pesos to large ones of 500,000 pesos or more, but few were more than 1 million pesos. Unquestionably, the largest *mayorazgos* were those of the core nuclei of the Creole aristocracy. These noble magnates possessed the oldest titles in New Spain but were in intimate social and economic interaction with nouveaux riches nobles. We know much more about these large *mayorazgos.* There are no known cases of a magnate's entire wealth being in a *mayorazgo;* rather, the most common strategy was to entail anywhere from one-third to one-half of one's property. Multiple *mayorazgos* were common, and a magnate could have as many as ten *mayorazgos* on behalf of his children and other masters of his or her immediate family, for females also had the right to found *mayorazgos* and entail property (Ladd 1976:74–88). Judging by the continuity of the core nuclei of the Creole aristocracy from the late sixteenth century to the end of Colonial rule, most *mayorazgos* increased in value from their foundation; even the *mayorazgos* founded near the middle of the eighteenth century had significantly increased in value when the system was abolished at Independence.

The *mayorazgo* as an institution to ensure the continuity of a lifestyle commensurate with aristocratic rank had some inherent disadvantages. The *mayorazgo* had equivalents in all Western aristocracies, and one of the characteristics that plagued the system since early feudal times were the dissension and litigation that it created in the immediate and extended aristocratic family by favoring the primogenit, sometimes exclusively, over siblings and collateral kinsmen. The *mayorazgo* system was fraught with bickering, antagonism, and lawsuits, and suffering the most were daughters, younger sons, and widows (Ladd 1976:85–86). Despite the efforts of most founders of *mayorazgos* to be fair, pride in lineage and the overwhelming desire to continue the expressive preeminence of the family often made jealousy and discontent inevitable, and often children sued parents for a more equitable distribution of property.

Clavero's assertion that the *mayorazgo* in the New World was limited in value and incidence is reasonable insofar as it applies to the ambiguous legal status of the *encomienda* and *repartimiento* systems (1974: 192–204). But his argument does not hold in cases of *mayorazgos* and entails of property beyond the control of the Crown. Throughout Colonial times most *mayorazgos* were founded by members of the core nuclei, which partly explains their much greater stability and continuity as compared to members of the peripheral Creole aristocracy. Socially and expressively, the *mayorazgo* provided concrete validation of aristocratic rank and reinforced membership in the group; meanwhile, it was a successful economic strategy for perpetuating the aristocratic *imago mundi* of ostentation and display.

MEMBERSHIP IN MILITARY ORDERS AND ITS SOCIAL AND EXPRESSIVE IMPLICATIONS

Military orders or orders of knighthood have a long tradition in Spain, dating to the second half of the twelfth century, when the three main orders were founded: Santiago, Calatrava, and Alcántara. Two other orders, Montesa and San Juan de Jerusalén, were founded two centuries later, but they were never as distinguished or as powerful as the original three. Santiago, Calatrava, and Alcántara were incorporated into the Spanish Crown by Ferdinand and Isabella and Charles V between 1492 and 1523. The Spanish orders were founded as noble brotherhoods to fight the Moslems, and throughout the second phase of the Reconquest (1200–1492) they played an important role as military forces. By the last quarter of the fifteenth century, the Spanish military orders were very powerful, possessed much landed property that had been wrested from the infidel, and constituted veritable states within the structure of the Spanish kingdoms. After their incorporation into the Spanish Crown, the military orders became essentially orders of merit, a reward for service to the Crown.

Almost immediately after the Conquest, several of the most distinguished conquistadors, such as Cortés and Alvarado, were awarded membership in military orders. By the turn of the seventeenth century many descendants of conquistadors, distinguished *pobladores,* and recipients of royal and viceregal patronage had become members of military orders. But it was in the eighteenth century that membership in military orders proliferated, and many more Creoles and *peninsulares* residing in the colony were knighted than during the previous two centuries (Lohmann Villena 1947:ix–xxxvi). Until the last decade of the seventeenth century, knighthood, like titles of nobility, was most commonly awarded for civil and military service to the Crown, and knightly awards by virtue of plutocratic achievement were relatively rare.

From 1525, when Cortés was made a knight of Santiago, until the end of Colonial rule, the Crown knighted more than 600 Creoles and *peninsulares* who were either residents of New Spain or members of the viceregal administration. Martínez de Cosío (1946) offers the following breakdown: 426 knights of Santiago, 121 of Calatrava, 66 of Alcántara, 6 of Montesa, and 11 of San Juan de Jerusalén (also known as Malta). The ratio here of Creoles to *peninsulares* is roughly fifty-fifty, although there were undoubtedly differences throughout this three hundred-year period. For example, until the late sixteenth century, all the knights were *peninsulares,* with the exception of Martin Cortés, the conqueror's son, who was made knight of Santiago at the age of seven; and throughout most of the seventeenth century, there were more knighted *peninsulares* than knighted Creoles. In the eighteenth century parity was finally achieved, and during the last two decades of Colonial rule, there were more Creoles than *peninsulares* in the military orders.

Probably most of the highest viceregal officials who came to New Spain had been knighted or had received other dignities before they took up residence in the colony. They constituted a small minority, and most recipients of knighthood were Creoles or *peninsulares* who had been residents of the colony for long periods of time. Of determinant importance was the process of nomination for knighthood (García Pelayo 1946:205–31). Before 1535, original conquistadors could petition directly to the royal chanceries by virtue of feats of arms, but after the establishment of the viceroyalty, probably no knighthoods were awarded by this method, and the viceroy became an indispensable link in a complicated bureaucratic process. Given how few knighthoods were conferred during the sixteenth century, we can assume they were genuine awards for military and administrative service to the Crown. During the seventeenth century, many knighthoods were awarded for administrative service but very few for military service. In the later part of the century, viceregal officials could be influenced or bribed for dignities, and genuine *hidalgos* and nouveaux riches vied for *hidalguía* and aristocratic recognition. Venality proliferated during the century of affluence, when most knighthoods were awarded for business acumen and the accumulation of wealth and the military orders ceased to denote distinguished service to the Crown. Magnates often obtained their knighthoods simply by donating money to the Crown, raising militias at their own expense, or, occasionally, by becoming bankers to the administration and otherwise ingratiating themselves with the Crown and its local representatives (Ladd 1976:56–58).

Strictly speaking, knighthood was not hereditary; it was conferred for the life of the recipient, much like the contemporary British knighthood. In the Spanish system, all *hidalgos a fuero de España* were *caballeros* (knights), de facto and de jure, and knighthood was an extra dignity that reflected the merits of an individual and that did not need to be perpetuated. In practice, at least in New Spain, knighthood was remembered by the descendants of the recipient and became a badge of honor and prestige (Ovando n.d.). This tradition has survived the demise of military orders for more than a century and a half, and families still point with great pride to their knightly ancestors.

Given the Spanish concern with pomp and ceremony, reinforced and augmented in New Spain, every aspect of knighthood entailed rather exaggerated elaboration and display. In the eighteenth century, for which we have reliable information, the ceremony of the investiture of a knight was a sight to behold: the elaborate uniforms, the bountiful display of wealth, and the huge number of participants. Moreover, knights led civil and religious ceremonies and events, and their presence always lent prestige to the many affairs in which they participated (Villar Villamil 1910:103–27). These important expressive activities for the aristocratic family ended with the death of the knight and his magnificent burial.

The eighteenth century also witnessed a new development related to the pursuit of knighthood, namely, loyalty to the king and active participation in military affairs. As the central power of the Spanish Crown decreased, the Creole aristocracy's loyalty to the king increased, particularly among the titled nobles and their families. This phenomenon manifested itself in two ways. More than ever before, members of the Creole aristocracy joined the military and attained high rank, something that would have been difficult in the seventeenth century. The noble magnates were particularly notorious for their outright gifts to the king, such as creating and privately subsidizing militias. From roughly 1770 to 1810, for the only time in the history of Mexico, the aristocracy made a concerted effort to control the military (Ladd 1976:71–88).

In their respective spheres, the *mayorazgo,* mainly an economic institution, and the military orders, mainly an expressive institution, had a combined expressive-utilitarian function in perpetuating and enhancing aristocratic rank. To different degrees of intensity throughout Colonial times, these institutions were inseparable from the aristocratic *imago mundi.* After Independence, when they were legally abolished, they sustained aristocratic claims and symbolically buttressed a slowly vanishing universe, particularly after the Revolution of 1910, when the Mexican aristocracy became a mere social class. The Mexican aristocracy did not end abruptly, and the perpetuating mechanisms of *mayorazgo* and knighthood unexpectedly prolonged its survival after all juridical and most economic support had vanished.

The Nobiliary System and Its Social and Oligarchical Configuration

The two-rank nobiliary system in New Spain was born when Cortés was made Marquis of the Valley of Oaxaca. It did not begin to mature, however, until the first quarter of the seventeenth century, when the first titles were conferred upon members of the Creole aristocracy. The seventeenth century may be regarded as the formative stage of a local system of titled nobility; for not until the eighteenth century were sufficient titles granted by the Crown to Creoles and *peninsulares* to warrant calling the Mexican aristocracy a two-rank system. Ladd (1976) has ably described the nobiliary system of New Spain during the last fifty years of Colonial rule, and I follow her analysis closely.

THE EVOLUTION AND DEVELOPMENT OF TITLES OF NOBILITY FROM THE CONQUEST TO INDEPENDENCE

The nobiliary system of New Spain was an extension of the Spanish system, with no structural differences, although it entailed some expressive differences conditioned by the social and political milieu of the metropolis and the colony. The present discussion is concerned with the nobility enfranchised in New Spain, whose titles had been awarded to individuals associated with the colony for a variety of reasons, regardless of whether they were Creoles or *peninsulares*. From this perspective, ignoring marginality and expressive differences, we can describe the Colonial nobiliary system as an integral part of that of the mother country. Critics and students of the system in New Spain—contemporary scholars and Republican Creoles right after Independence—have characterized it as ephemeral, little more than a ceremonial ornament, a provincial appendage that elicited the condescension and derision of the mother country's nobility (Alamán 1942; Mora 1972; Otero 1967; Brading 1971; Ladd 1976; O'Gorman 1942). These assessments, though perhaps true, offer insufficient appreciation of New Spain's nobility. On the one hand, the contrasts and invidious comparisons between metropolis and colony, between center and periphery, are universal aspects of the pecking order of all stratification systems. On the other hand, it is doubtful that the old Spanish feudal aristocracy, the grandees of Spain, perceived the petty titled nobles of Galicia or the Basque country any differently from the titled nobles of New Spain. Regardless of its marginal position, the nobiliary system of New Spain had the same functions and occupied the same position in the local stratification system as the peninsular system. Moreover, the entire span of New Spain's system fell within the period of decline of all Western aristocracies. In the eighteenth century particularly, when New Spain's aristocracy was a flourishing two-rank nobility, aristocracies everywhere were undergoing a degree of embourgeoisement. This factor has not been considered by historians (see Brading 1971; Ladd 1976; Lockhart 1972; O'Gorman 1942), who have unanimously assumed, for example, that the greater fluidity of aristocracies in the Spanish New World and the upward mobility of merchants and traders were determined by the Colonial situation. In fact, a similar process had been happening in practically all Western aristocracies since the late sixteenth century, as the rising haute bourgeoisie of England, France, Spain, and Italy became the recipients of ennoblement since early in the seventeenth century, to say nothing of the merchant princes of Italy since the Middle Ages.

Eight years after the fall of Tenochtitlán, Cortés returned to Spain and was granted the title of Marquis of the Valle de Oaxaca. This event raised great expectations among the captains who had participated in the Conquest, at least two or three of whom expected to be equally rewarded with titles of nobility. Only two titles were granted in the sixteenth century after Cortés: Mariscal (Marshall) de Castilla (1531), awarded to a member of the Luna y Arellano family, of ancient Castilian lineage; and Adelantado (no equivalent in English) de las Filipinas (1569), awarded to Miguel López de Legazpi, conqueror of the Philippines. These were not exactly titles, however; they were special dignities peculiar to the Spanish nobiliary system that were hereditary in the same manner as standard titles (Ladd 1976:187–228). No real titles were awarded to Creoles or *peninsulares* associated with New Spain until exactly eighty years later, when the title of Marquis of Salinas del Río Pisuerga (1609) was awarded to Luis de Velasco the younger, twice viceroy of New Spain.

The nobiliary system of New Spain properly begins in 1609 with the Marquis of Salinas del Río Pisuerga. During the next eighteen years, three more titles were granted: Count of Santiago de Calimaya (1616), awarded to a grandson of Luis de Velasco the younger; Count of the Valle de Orizaba (1627), awarded to Rodrigo de Vivero, captain-general of Panama and the Philippines; and Count of Moctezuma (1627), awarded to Pedro Tesifón Moctezuma, great-grandson of the Aztec "emperor" Motecuhzoma Xocoyotzin. The descendants of the two main dramatis personae of the Conquest of Mexico were never really part of the social life of New Spain: those of Moctezuma had moved to Spain by the end of the sixteenth century, and those of Cortés never lived in New Spain for any length of time, and in the fifth generation the title passed to the Pignatelli, a princely Sicilian family (Nutini, Roberts, and Cervantes 1982). The descendants of the other five original title holders became the dominant nucleus of the Creole aristocracy in New Spain; and by virtue of their multiple kinship and ritual kinship relationships, they became the arbiters of the colony's social life until the end of Colonial times (Ladd 1976:13–23).[3]

The Crown granted no titles of nobility from 1628 until 1682. In the following decade nine titles were granted: Marquis of San Miguel de Aguayo (1682); Count of Miraflores (1689); Marquis of Villar del Águila (1689); Count of la Casa de Loja (1690); Count of Miravalle (1690); Marquis of Monserrate (1690); Marquis of Valle de la Colina (1690); Marquis of Sante Fé de Guardiola (1690); and Marquis of San Román (1691). By the end of the seventeenth century there were about eighteen titles enfranchised in the colony or closely associated with it. The second issue of titles in the last two decades of the century indicates that titles of nobility were awarded to individuals who had not necessarily been administrators or military men but who distinguished themselves in the economic development of the colony. This more liberal definition of the qualifications for a noble title reflects the changing economic conditions and, as some authors have maintained (Madariaga 1963:231), was a subterfuge of the Spanish Crown, which hoped to profit by the improving economic conditions that began at the end of the century of depression in New Spain. Indeed, the writings of late Colonial and early Republican scholars (Mora 1972; Otero 1972; Lizardi 1966) commonly maintain that most of the titles granted by the Crown throughout the eighteenth century until Independence did not reflect the true principles of Spanish nobility; that rich parvenus purchased them outright, to enrich the Crown and to satisfy their own desire for vulgar ostentation. Significantly, in most western European countries since the late seventeenth century, the same trend affected the noble estate. In France, for example, and to some extent in Spain, ennoblement had vastly changed from the early sixteenth century, embourgeoisement had affected even the titled nobility, and the structuring principle and expressive *imago mundi* permitted a process of upward mobility in which the haute bourgeoisie replaced the lower nobility as the most significant pool for recruiting titled nobles.[4]

Of all the titles granted by the Spanish Crown in New Spain, more than three-fourths were awarded during the last 117 years of Colonial rule, between 1704 and 1821. Demographic considerations were undoubtedly relevant to the growth of the system, but here again New Spain faithfully reflects western European aristocracies, where the same proportional increments characterized the nobiliary systems of England, France, and Spain. In England, for example, there were roughly fifty titles of nobility at the onset of Henry VIII's reign. By the end of the seventeenth century, some sixty more titles had been created, and the eighteenth century witnessed a great proliferation of titles, which by the onset of the nineteenth had more than tripled (Bush 1984). The earlier comparative niggardliness of most western European monarchies was tempered by liberal policies for membership in the lower nobility. The proliferation of titles in the eighteenth century may be interpreted as the inability of western European monarchies to satisfy the increasing economic power of the haute bourgeoisie and their need for royal revenue (Powis 1984:56–81).

The most complete list of titles of nobility awarded to Creoles and *peninsulares* enfranchised in or associated with New Spain for the entire Colonial period is that of Ladd (1976:187–228). She offers a very good reconstruction, including much genealogical information and the names of title holders from the original grant until Independence. She compiled eighty titles, beginning with that of Cortés to the last ones awarded shortly before Independence. Carlos de Ovando (pers. comm.) maintains that there are at least another twenty titles not included in Ladd's list, eighteen of which are the following: Viscount of la Moraleda Almenas (1690); Count of Castelo (1690); Marquis of Buena Vista (1696); Marquis of las Torres de Rada (1704); Marquis of Villa de la Peña (1704); Marquis of Álamo de Puebla (1704); Count of Lizárraga (1705); Count of Santa Sabina (1708); Marquis of Ledesma de la Fuente (1710); Marquis of Torre Campo (1714); Marquis of San Felipe y Santiago (1715); Conde de Quiebra Hacha (1721); Count of San Javier (1732); Marquis of Casa de Alba Madariaga (?); Marquis of Casa Ramos (?); Count of Casa Torres (?); Marquis of la Laguna de Términos (?); and Marquis of Villa Sierra (?). These eighteen titles, awarded mostly to Spaniards who were never intimately associated with the colony and whose families returned to Spain before the wars of Independence, were not socially or economically important.

Of the ninety-eight identified titles—and there may be another ten that I have not identified—twenty were granted between 1529 and

1696, while seventy-eight were between 1704 and 1821. About twenty of these were granted during the last two decades of Colonial rule, and more than half of the total were granted in the eighteenth century, clustering between 1704 and 1735, and 1760 and 1785. It is tempting to say that the "traditional" nobiliary system ends with Philip IV, the last of the Hapsburgs, that is, that the last titles routinely awarded according to the old principles of *hidalguía* ended in 1696. Perhaps those principles were still in effect until the second decade of the eighteenth century, but thereafter a break with tradition occurs, and non-*hidalgo* plutocrats were made titled nobles. We know this change to be a fact in at least five cases, and most likely the majority of the Creoles and *peninsulares* of merchant, non-*hacendado* extraction were not *hidalgos a fuero de España*. Extrapolating from the last stage of the third renewal (see chap. 7) for which I have reliable evidence, we can assume that the gatekeepers of the traditional Creole aristocracy looked down upon the nouveaux riches titled nobles, most of whom had risen to preeminence in a short generation. Thus, despite the many matrimonial alliances that by the nineteenth century had united the core nuclei of the Creole aristocracy to parvenu titled nobles, many traditional nontitled aristocrats still regarded the latter as *arrivistas* (upwardly mobile, uppity) and not immediately their equals (Carlos de Ovando, pers. comm.). It was the economic disaster accompanying the wars of Independence that homogenized the second renewal. All upwardly mobile plutocrats, titled or nontitled, had to pay their social and expressive dues in the traditional pecking order of superordinate stratification in Western society, even after the noble estate, with a few insignificant exceptions, ended in the early twentieth century. To offer an example very much to the point: a landed nontitled gentleman in England who has been in possession of his land since before the War of the Roses considers himself more noble, and is so regarded by the British aristocracy, than many an earl of post-Elizabethan origin (Perrot 1968:159–63). This basic equation underlies the Spanish aristocratic system, and by extension that of New Spain.

The nobiliary system of New Spain boasted only counts and marquises—and one viscount. With the exception of Columbus, no Creoles or *peninsulares* received titles of duke in the New World during Colonial times, and the title of baron was conspicuously absent. The nobiliary system of New Spain featured essentially a single rank, for from the early sixteenth century, marquis and count ranked equally, unlike in France and England, where the former ranked higher than the latter. Still unclear is why the title of count was awarded at one time and the title of marquis at another. Perhaps the individual awardee could choose between one or the other; more likely, the decision was made by the chanceries that dealt with nobiliary matters (Nutini and Roberts 1991).

The contexts of recruitment for titles of nobility have been implied in the foregoing chapters, and may be summarized as follows: conquest and colonization, bureaucratic administration, economic development, and military service. For the first two centuries of their existence, titles could only be awarded to individuals of the rank of *hidalgo a fuero de España*. A meritorious commoner vying for a title had first to become *hidalgo*. This situation occurred rarely, for the overwhelming majority of candidates for titles were already *hidalgos* (Lira Montt 1976). This traditional system was in effect until the first quarter of the eighteenth century. Thereafter, commoners could be awarded titles of nobility without passing through the rank of *hidalgo*. Though this new openness persisted until the end of Colonial rule, most titled nobles were still probably *hidalgos* at the time of ennoblement. But the charge by several writers after Independence (see Alamán 1942) that commoner plutocratic magnates bought their titles is justified in light of the traditional system, in which wealth per se did not play a determinant role (Ladd 1976:13–22).

Titles were least frequently awarded for reasons of conquest and colonization; most such titles were awarded in the sixteenth and seventeenth centuries to the conquerors of Mexico and the Philippines. No distinguished *poblador* or founder of cities and towns was awarded a title in the sixteenth century, and only a few were granted for colonizing activities at the end of the seventeenth century. The last title awarded for colonization was that of the Count of Sierra Gorda, whose holder pacified Tamaulipas and founded many settlements very quickly (Ladd 1976:15).

Military service, and more specifically the organization of local provincial militias, is the second most important context for the creation of titled nobles in New Spain and is associated particularly with the last fifty years of Colonial rule. At least fifteen titles have this origin and most were granted after 1800, coinciding with the breakdown of Crown control and the wars of Independence. The militias for which these individuals were ennobled were necessary to control the provinces before Independence, and during the war they fought mostly on the side of the Crown. This limited military experience in noway ensured aristocratic control of the armed forces during the wars of Independence nor, more significantly, throughout the nineteenth century (Bancroft 1972:205–18). As in politics and administration, military experience came too late and in too small a dose to make a difference to the Mexican aristocracy as a ruling class. Indeed, the three hundred years of political and military inexperience of the Creole aristocracy was one of the worst aspects of the Colonial inheritance.

Bureaucratic administration produced nearly half of all titles of nobility from early in the seventeenth century until the end of Colonial rule. Among the recipients were viceroys, captains-general, royal justices (*oidores*), and high-ranking military officers. From the beginning of the seventeenth century, most of them were *hacendados* or businessmen who held political office, and most of them became enfranchised in the colony, thereby becoming Creoles. Ladd (1976: 13–16) correctly observes that the first aristocratic nucleus of New Spain were the families of three of the four titles granted between 1609 and 1627. During the second issue of titles between 1682 and 1696, a few were administrators, but, naturally, the great majority fell during the last seventy years of Colonial rule. Probably more titleholders of bureaucratic extraction and their families went back to Spain than ever before; nonetheless, the majority stayed in the colony and their descendants became Creoles. Titleholders of bureaucratic extraction were not generally as rich as the plutocratic magnates ennobled during the last sixty years of Colonial rule, but their influence on local affairs was significant, and they were generally highly respected (Castillo Ledón 1932:146–54).

Contributions to the economic development of the colony in mining, agriculture, and trade and manufacturing created the final context for ennoblement. In a sense, this context may be regarded as an aspect of colonization. The main characteristic of this complex of titles is that the awardees were plutocratic magnates, mostly commoners without a long history in New Spain. In other words, the issue of titles that took place roughly from 1760 to 1821 reflected the liberalization of nobility and the general embourgeoisement of the decaying noble estate. The other side of the coin was that the Crown was pressed for money and saw the new breed of plutocratic magnates as a source of revenue to subsidize projects the Crown could not afford (Frazer 1982:65–76). With three or four exceptions, the twenty or so greatest fortunes in New Spain on the eve of Independence belonged to nobles who had been titled after 1760 (Ladd 1976:184–86). Though there were probably many nontitled Creole aristocrats that were wealthy by the standards of the time, plutocratic titled nobles were the wealthiest in the land.

NOBLE PRIVILEGES, THE SUPERORDINATE ESTATE, AND THE GLOBAL CONFIGURATION OF THE CREOLE ARISTOCRACY

The nobiliary system of New Spain must be analyzed in the broader context of the evolution of Western aristocracies since the end of the Middle Ages. Some differences arose from the marginal, Colonial position of the former, but by no means did nobles in Spain serve significantly greater political and social functions. To be sure, Spanish nobles occasionally became ministers of the Crown, but so did Creole nobles become highly placed Colonial officials. What had not existed since the middle of the sixteenth century was a professional class of royal bureaucrats. Privileges also changed greatly throughout the sixteenth, seventeenth, and eighteenth centuries. The titled nobility and *hidalgos* of the New World enjoyed fewer privileges than the aristocracy of Spain, but they experienced certain advantages. The Colonial system stratified the Creole-*peninsular* aristocracy and all other populations into two quite distinct "estates." Meanwhile, the de facto situation on the great landed estates was essentially a throwback to the fourteenth-century Europe. Ladd (1976:3–8) emphasizes the limitations of titled nobles in New Spain: lack of political continuity vested in a local political class, the presence of corporate privileges, mostly those of the church and the military, and the proliferation of privileges affecting several kinds of commoner populations such as royal lawyers, military officers, and even university graduates—as if in varying degrees the same situations had not obtained in Spain as well! Ladd is right to point out the ethnic components of the stratification system, but she draws the wrong sociological conclusions.

The fluidity of the system for Creoles and *peninsulares* stemmed from the structural fact that Indians, always the great majority of the colony's population, were organized into a subordinate, tribute-paying estate and from the ideological fact that, actually or mythologically, the Creole aristocrats considered themselves descendants of conquistadors, with all the privileges accompanying right of conquest. Titled nobles, the Creole aristocracy, and the Creole and *peninsular* rank and file shared the privilege of not paying tribute, thus weakening the overall privileges of the first. A second consideration is whether any estatelike distinctions existed that redounded in specific privileges for the titled nobility. The answer is yes, small distinctions existed, fundamentally not so different from the situation in Spain at the time.

By the middle of the eighteenth century several of the corporate and noncorporate privileges discussed in chapter 3 had been abolished or were weak in the Spanish nobiliary system, and were further curtailed in the New World. Of the noncorporate privileges, particularly (1), (2), and (5) were weak or had virtually disappeared; while of the corporate privileges, (7) had become obsolete, while the other six were still in existence but somewhat weak. Extrapolating from the mother country, noble privileges in New Spain may be summarized as follows: (*a*) Exemption from taxation involving tribute, a privilege diluted by the fact that nobles shared it with all Creoles and *peninsulares*. (*b*) Some minimal privileges of local justice and administration, shared by the *hacendado* class of *hidalgo* and non-*hidalgo* extraction, but sanctioned mostly by custom. (*c*) Rights of precedence and preeminence in public gatherings, perhaps the most extensive and visible of the noble privileges in New Spain. Titled nobles shared this privilege with prominent nontitled members of the Creole aristocracy. (*d*) Customary but not juridical social and economic control over the Indian population of their estates, which they shared with all Creole *hacendados*. This intrinsic aspect of debt peonage and the *hacienda* system gave the system a distinctly seigneurial character. (*e*) Some reduced rights of political participation, promotion, and special functions, which titled nobles shared with members of the ruling class and Crown bureaucrats. This merely customary privilege allowed the Creole aristocracy inordinate participation and control of executive bodies such as *cabildos* and *consulados*. (*f*) Indemnity from judicial obligations and *fuero* or juridical privileges apart from the common system of justice: exemption from torture, from execution by hanging, and from seizure of persons or property for debt. The titled nobility shared these privileges with the church and the military in a weaker form. (*g*) Last and most significant, honorific privileges and rights. These included titles, coats of arms, armorial bearings, special forms of address, exemption from sumptuary laws, and preferential access to military orders and religious institutions. This group of privileges essentially defined the titled nobility of New Spain as a ceremonial aristocracy (Ladd 1976:3–12; Lira Montt 1976).

An individual was titled with great pomp and ceremony after payment of two taxes of ancient origin, preserved by the Crown to generate revenue: *lanzas,* a tax that paid for exemption from military service; and *media annata,* a tax to ensure the right of succession. In all other respects, titled nobles were no different from *hidalgos a fuero de España.* In traditional Spanish fashion, there was no categorical separation between the upper and lower nobility, between titled nobles and *hidalgos;* together, they constituted an estate bound by the same expressive code, a uniform *imago mundi,* and social and matrimonial exchange (García Carraffa 1919, 16:46–71). All things being equal, only wealth and distinguished service to the Crown were significant in the network structure of titled nobles and *hidalgos.* The titled nobles of New Spain, beyond the fact that their titles entailed certain exclusive privileges and forms of address, did not constitute a discernibly well bounded or coherent group. They were part of the wider whole of the Creole aristocracy (Lohmann Villena 1947:ii–xl; Ladd 1976:6–12).

Though the titled nobility of New Spain always constituted the core of the ruling and social class, that is, of the Creole aristocracy, wealth was the main catalyst in upward mobility, and the ultimate goal of upwardly mobile plutocrats was the acquisition of a noble title. Although the eighteenth century was characterized by the Spanish Crown's loss of control over the colony, it was also marked by extensive mining, import-export, agrarian, and internal trading activity. During the second half of the century, personal fortunes reached more than three million gold pesos, great wealth for the times (Brading 1971: 169–302). Although these fortunes included entailed and nonentailed mining and trade, the bulk of the wealth was in agriculture, cattle raising, and other stock. It is clear, however, that the wealth of New Spain had been diversified to include all kinds of business activities under the rubrics of mining, manufacturing, trading, and banking. Despite the fact that land remained the validating symbol of aristocratic status, a diversified economy was the preferred strategy of the rich and powerful (Weckmann 1984, 2:648–76). Shortly after 1800, the economy began to decline, and the wars of Independence dealt a deadly blow to the social and economic life of the ruling class, a blow from which it did not entirely recover until Porfirian times.

To reiterate: the titled nobility was not a discrete, self-contained sector of the Creole ruling class, not during the seventeenth century and early part of the eighteenth century, much less during the last sixty years of Colonial rule. Until the third decade of the eighteenth century, the Creole aristocracy was composed of eighteen or so resident titled nobles and their families, a wider network of *hacendados* miners, and various entrepreneurs, most of whom were *hidalgos a fuero de España* enfranchised in the capital and ten other important cities of New Spain. The core and center of the Creole aristocracy had always been a fairly bounded social group, linked by many social, economic, and matrimonial ties; the periphery, almost exclusively constituted by *hacendados* with some local business interests, was less affluent and only tangentially related socially and matrimonially to the core and center (González Obregón 1937:706–32). Clearly, the traditional and new titled nobility were in every respect part of the changing Creole aristocracy, and no structural or expressive standards set the former apart from the latter (Weckmann 1984, 1:236–73). Indeed, as I have demonstrated, antiquity of lineage and long possession of the land counterbalanced recent wealth, even recent wealth buttressed by a title of recent origin. Thus, in the time-honored fashion of Western aristocracies since the early sixteenth century, there were always *hacendados* of conquistador extraction who considered themselves superior to those who had recently been awarded titles.

THE EXPRESSIVE ARRAY OF THE TITLED NOBILITY AS THE CORE OF THE CREOLE ARISTOCRACY

In any stratification system, whether traditionally structured as an estate system or designed as a continuous hierarchy of classes in the modern sense, power and wealth stratify the component segments, but the expressive array homogenizes the strata into which a class or an estate may fall. Thus, from its inception until the end of Colonial rule, the Creole aristocracy constituted an undifferentiated expressive whole, though it was structurally (economically) stratified. Almost synonymous with the aristocratic nuclei, the titled nobility shared the same expressive array and worldview of the Creole aristocracy as a whole. Differences in the realization of the expressive array, then, arose exclusively from the economic affluence of individuals and groups and not from variations in the *imago mundi*.

Examining the diversified, highly elaborate, and extensive expressive array of the titled nobility at the close of Colonial times, one is led to conclude that the lack of institutionalized political functions beyond the local level enhanced ostentation and display in public ceremonies, in social activities, and, most spectacularly, in the discharge of several domains of religion. The titled nobility, says Ladd (1976:53–54), emphasized "God, king, and family," and in her view, nobility was preeminently a "religious characteristic." Ladd exaggerates, however, for Creole aristocrats were no more profoundly Catholic than the Creole rank and file, nor even than a large proportion of the Mestizo population, all of whom by the eighteenth century were practicing perhaps not the syncretic religion of the Indians, but one undoubtedly modified by it, that is, a slightly unorthodox Catholicism that persists today at all levels of Mexican society (Nutini 1990).

The expression of religiosity described by Ladd must be interpreted sociologically as a pragmatic activity reflecting the validation of rank, particularly among the newest titled nobles, and the realization of ostentation and display, the true ideological motivator of such activities as *capellanías* and *obras pías* (endowed charities). A slightly different argument can be made for loyalty to the king as an effective expressive domain. In part, this attitude of titled nobles and *hidalgos a fuero de España* reflected their knowledge that nobility ultimately comes from the king and is sanctioned by him; in part, the attitude reflected a self-serving, pragmatic identification with the Crown as the preserver of the status quo. In short, the worldview and the main domains of the expressive array forged by the Creole aristocracy in the sixteenth century had not essentially changed by the last decades of Colonial rule, and they framed and defined the entire expressive culture of the ruling and social classes of New Spain.

Qualified by the preceding considerations, then, the religious life of the titled nobility was indistinguishable from that of any other segment of Creole society, except, of course, in the public ostentation and pious displays of *obras pías, capellanías,* certain charities, and the expensive undertakings of religious buildings of several kinds. As to formal religious life, there is no evidence that proportionally more titled nobles or members of the Creole aristocracy than any other sector of Creole society joined the regular or secular religious orders, though certainly many bishops and other high church officials were members of aristocratic families (Pérez de Salazar n.d.). Aristocratic women, however, do appear to have joined the conventual orders in higher proportions than women of the Creole rank and file. Since the early seventeenth century, some of the richest convents were associated with the expressive life of the Creole aristocracy, a tradition that survived until the early decades of the twentieth century. The ceremonial and ritual aspects of religion afforded the Creole aristocracy vast domains of expressive realization, and rich plutocratic nobles took full advantage of the situation in all the subdomains, as specified in chapter 5 (Carlos de Ovando, pers. comm.).

The structure of kinship, marriage, and lineage in the last decades of Colonial rule had not changed much since the crystallization of the Creole aristocracy more than a century and a half earlier. If anything, the structure had hardened as the traditional aristocracy came of age and made wealthy marriage alliances. Traditional nobles, and old Creole aristocrats generally, preferred to marry their daughters to *peninsulares,* usually young men who had come to New Spain as officers or members of the viceregal bureaucracy, and, more significantly, the overwhelming majority of *peninsulares* who were awarded titles married daughters of old titled or nontitled Creole aristocrats. Conversely, the majority of titled and nontitled Creole aristocrat men married Creole women of their own class. These marriage practices were particularly characteristic of the core nuclei of the aristocracy (Ladd 1976:19–23). Similar marriage practices apparently took place in the central and peripheral sectors of the Creole aristocracy. By the end of Colonial rule, the social and ruling class of New Spain was a truly Creole aristocracy in which many original *peninsulares* had been Creolized, expressively as well as ethnically. Wider patterns of kinship among the Creole aristocracy built social and economic networks in the core nuclei, and there is evidence that the same situation obtained in the centralized and peripheral sectors. Ties of kinship, *compadrazgo,* and matrimonial alliances almost exclusively configured a colonywide aristocracy into a ruling class. Locally (regionally), the aristocracy appeared as a series of segments relatively independent of one another, but linked by social and economic ties from titled nobles to modest old *hacendados* (Pérez de Salazar n.d.).

In all other expressive domains, primarily those pertaining to behavior and to material culture, every aspect described in chapter 5 for the Creole aristocracy applied to the titled nobility at the close of Colonial times. If Creole aristocrats were characterized as a group by conspicuous consumption and love of display, titled nobles dominated these expressive domains, for they had the wealth and the local social control to shine supreme. Their palaces in the city and their mansions on the *hacienda* were the largest and most highly and ostentatiously decorated. Aristocratic families had established *mayorazgos,* but those of the titled nobles were larger and more diversified, serving as patrons to large numbers of kinsmen. Titled nobles reached a zenith of personal ostentation in the elegance and elaboration of their daily attire, military uniforms, and ceremonial garb. Most titled nobles resided in the capital and a few large cities but quite frequently occupied secondary residences in the cities of their mining, commercial, and agrarian operations, and thus they literally monopolized the civic and religious commercial life of urban environments (Carrión 1897:106–53). The titled nobility were the arbiters of the social and ceremonial life of the colony, and few important events of a civic or religious nature escaped their leading participation, and they were also the arbiters of private manners, morals, and aristocratic behavior. By extension, the Creole aristocracy of New Spain, modeled after the titled nobility, performed the same social, ceremonial, and behavioral functions that Western aristocracies had been playing since the beginning of modern times.

The titled nobility in particular, and the aristocracy in general, was never actually much admired by the population at large, particularly from the end of the Middle Ages when they began to lose power and control. Thus, when Creole insurgents and then Republican critics after Independence said that the titled nobility was a worthless institution composed of powerless, ambitious, irrelevant, and foppish men and women, they were expressing the ideological stance of a new breed of men for whom all peoples were created equal. Their criticisms echoed those of countless revolutionaries from the French Revolution on. In one respect the critics of the titled nobility are inaccurate; as an internal part of the Creole aristocracy, as it emerged from the Colonial situation, it was neither powerless nor irrelevant. The Mexican aristocracy became the social and ruling class of an independent country, retaining nearly the same position that the Creole aristocracy occupied in Colonial times: without control of direct political power, mostly as the result of inertia, the descendants of the old ruling class remained socially and economically preeminent for nearly another century. This survival was recognized by writers in the decades following Independence. They accurately assessed the situation by saying that nothing had really changed: for the country as a whole, independence from Spain did not mean that the ruling class had disappeared nor had the new order appreciably improved the lot of the nation (see Mora 1972; Weckmann 1984:619–27).

The Second Renewal (1730–1810) and the Stratification System at the End of Colonial Rule

By the end of the eighteenth century the total population of New Spain was more than six million, more than a million of whom were Creoles and *peninsulares* living in many cities and towns. The ruling class of New Spain had remained very small, perhaps no more than one thousand families, composed exclusively of Creoles and *peninsulares,* and constituting a fraction, perhaps no more than 3 percent, of the population of European origin. The main characteristics of the second renewal were the larger scale of the transformation, that is, the greater number of plutocrats that joined the ranks of the aristocracy, and the vaster economic resources that configured a more elaborate expressive style. In all other respects, the second renewal repeated the structural and expressive variables and considerations of the first renewal.

PLUTOCRATIC UPWARD MOBILITY AND ARISTOCRATIC ACCEPTANCE

By the time the second renewal began, the Creole aristocracy had existed for more than a century. It was composed of the great *hacendados,* miners, and businessmen who dominated the economic life of New Spain. Firmly anchored to the land and dominating local politics, the Creole aristocracy (core, center, and periphery) was a homogeneous social group. Hard economic times until the second decade of the eighteenth century made upward mobility more difficult and reinforced endogenous relationships. Great new fortunes began to be made in mining and trade and manufacturing in the third decade of the century. The architects of this boom included a few Creoles, but most were new arrivals from Spain who by 1770 or so constituted a powerful new haute bourgeoisie. From this milieu came upwardly mobile plutocrats who joined the ranks of the aristocracy, and by the time of the wars of Independence, a new ruling class had crystallized— a slightly modified Creole-Mexican aristocracy.

The levels of wealth and economic diversification of the second renewal were much higher than those of the first renewal, and these factors affected both the structural and expressive realization of the transformation. The wealth of the *hacendados*-miners-businessmen-aristocrats before the second renewal had been significant, the largest fortunes amounting to perhaps several hundred thousand gold pesos. During the following two generations, some of the fortunes of the ruling class increased to millions of gold pesos.

The great fortunes amassed by the Colonial haute bourgeoisie made full incorporation of plutocrats into the aristocracy easier and faster than it had been in the seventeenth century. This process obtained most strongly at the core and central sectors of the aristocracy, more weakly at the periphery. And though there were plenty of moderately affluent *hacendados* who could boast *hidalguía a fuero de España* and who regarded newly titled nobles as social parvenus (Carlos de Ovando, pers. comm.), structural (economic, political) considerations usually overrode expressive (kinship, lineage) considerations.

Greater wealth redounded in a richer, more complex, and significantly more elaborate expressive life, and many expressive domains grew at an unprecedented rate. The core aristocracy, and to some extent its central and peripheral sectors, became significantly more differentiated from the Creole rank and file, which at that time included an important bourgeois component of fairly rich merchants, manufacturers, and large-scale farmers. No doubt in the social and geographic periphery, the lesser aristocracy and the local bourgeoisie to some extent overlapped, but in the capital and certain other important cities, the aristocracy was a distinctly separate social category from the haute bourgeoisie. What differentiated these two social categories was not wealth per se but antiquity of lineage and expressive attributes, now enhanced by the controlling wealth of the aristocratic sector (Mingay 1976:112–32).

As in all variants of Western stratification, the social system became more fluid, and upward mobility, particularly from the haute bourgeoisie, became increasingly frequent and less stringent. In New Spain on the eve of Independence, wealth, as an instrument of upward mobility, could dispense with *hidalguía*. But as great plutocrats were incorporated into the nobiliary system, or became nontitled members of the aristocracy, they adopted the expressive array and ideology of the superordinate group, that is, the sine qua non for aristocratic membership. This process is well documented for the new titled nobles in the last two generations before the end of Colonial rule. As in the first renewal, but now on a much larger scale, their main structural card was great business acumen in mining and trade. Ironically, there is evidence that the peripheral Creole aristocracy was more conservative than the core of the traditional ruling class (the older titled nobility before 1730 and a close network of nontitled families) when it came to incorporating plutocrats (Ovando n.d.). Apparently the gatekeepers of the peripheral aristocracy, many of them *hacendados* of long standing, proud of being *hidalgos a fuero de España,* paid more attention to *hidalguía* and were not overly tempted by alliances with wealthy plutocrats in the inevitable process of upward mobility that characterized all three rungs of the Creole aristocracy during the last decades of Colonial rule.

While Western aristocracies shared a uniform ideology and worldview, their ranks have often been somewhat differentiated by the realization of the expressive array. Such was the case in New Spain during the period in question, when the discriminating variable was wealth. The core aristocracy, being the richest group, could discharge the expressive array to the fullest, while the peripheral sector could only assay a pale imitation of the model presented by the core. The expressive array on the eve of Independence reached a peak of elaboration and complexity in itself and in relation to the wider society, even unsurpassed by the wealthier Mexican aristocracy of Porfirian times. This situation can be explained partly by the demise of the estate system and partly by the transition from a monarchical to a republican system that significantly diminished the ceremonial, public roles of the aristocracy (Romero de Terreros 1944:32–49). The aristocracy evolved from a highly public presence in the discharge of its expressive functions into a more private domain of realization centered on the household and the confines of the *hacienda.*

Perhaps the most outstanding feature of the Creole-Mexican aristocracy has been the permanence of its numerical strength of roughly one thousand families. Since the early seventeenth century until the middle of the twentieth century this strength has remained constant, implying a great deal of upward and downward mobility in all three renewals, until its demise in the fourth renewal. The second renewal exhibited the highest incidence of upward and downward mobility: hundreds of members of the Colonial haute bourgeoisie became members of the Creole aristocracy, while an equal number of traditional aristocrats dropped out of the system (Brading 1971:13–19). Upward mobility during the second half of the eighteenth century was swifter than during the first renewal, and plutocrats occasionally became titled or nontitled aristocrats within a generation, after spectacular economic gains (Ladd 1976:25–52). By contrast, downward mobility was slower and exclusively involved traditional nontitled aristocrats, mostly of the peripheral but occasionally of the centralized sector. With remarkably few exceptions, the core of the Creole aristocracy from the late sixteenth century onward did not experience downward mobility, and indeed from the inception of the Mexican aristocracy until the middle of the twentieth century, the closer an aristocrat was to the core, the less downward mobility he could expect to experience.

Class, Race, and Estate on the Eve of Independence

Finally, how did the stratification system change from the first renewal, and what was its basic configuration at the end of Colonial times? The basic patterns of stratification in New Spain had coalesced by the end of the sixteenth century, and they remained rather constant until Independence. By the end of the eighteenth century, these patterns had been somewhat modified, largely because of demographic changes, but the principles of stratification that governed social relations remained the same. Thus, the estate system was still in place, and mild as it was, it divided the population into two great sectors: the Indians, who paid tribute, and everybody else, who did not. Discounting black slaves, who by then were few, the non–tribute-paying population included *peninsulares,* Creoles, and most Mestizos, Mulattos, and various *castas* or mixtures of the three main racial strains. Although legally, with the exception of slaves, all subjects of the Crown in New Spain were free and equal, in fact, socially and behaviorally, clear-cut distinctions separated these strata (Fisher 1951:15–137).

Creoles and *peninsulares,* regardless of the former's racial admixture, constituted the superordinate stratum, a mild estate behaviorally, and Mestizos and most *castas* occupied an ambivalent position: they did not pay tribute and could engage in any of the professional and economic activities that went on in the colony, but they constituted a separate social stratum vis-à-vis *peninsulares* and Creoles. Perhaps as many as 50 percent of the more than one million classified as Creoles were Mestizos of various somatic admixtures; this sector of the Creole population cannot be clearly distinguished from most of the several hundred thousand Mestizos that lived in the cities of New Spain. Two issues here are of fundamental importance in conceptualizing social stratification: the presence of classes and the admixture of racial (somatic) components that entered into the constitution of classes. Unfortunately, the available data are vague, impressionistic, and reflect formal categories (an elaborate framework of race classification, often pictorially depicted) that do not correspond to the actual, behavioral state of affairs (Meyer and Sheridan 1979:203–19). This inconclusiveness only partly accounts for the fuzzy picture of stratification in New Spain on the eve of Independence—just as significant is the consistent inadequacy of historical interpretations. At any rate, I offer the following reconstruction of the end of Colonial times.

An estate system did exist in New Spain throughout Colonial times, but did an estate system exist between the Creole population at large (that Creole population that was somatically Spanish) and what has been defined here as a Creole aristocracy, composed of some one hundred titled families and eight or nine hundred families with *hidalguía a fuero de España?* The answer is yes, and although marginal, with minimal privileges and no doubt less complex and elaborate than the estate system in the mother country, it was nonetheless a variant of the Western aristocratic model and displayed the same ideology and expressive array. This stratification group—and I grant that it may not be an estate but an "oligarchical class"—was modeled after the Conquest; it existed in countries of Latin America as diverse as Peru, Chile, and Cuba; and with different degrees of integrity it survived until the twentieth century. Moreover, the Creole aristocracy in New Spain never totaled more than twelve hundred families—less than ten thousand people within a total population of more than six million—creating a ratio of noble to commoner many times smaller than in all European countries in the eighteenth century. As insignificant as these marginal aristocracies might have seemed to disappointed local observers, they were nonetheless sociological variants of the Spanish aristocracy (Nutini and Roberts n.d.). More to the point, contemporary historians who have written on the stratification system of the last fifty years of Colonial rule are invariably unclear about the distinction between class and estate and have in mind a model of estate stratification that in most Western countries had not existed since early modern times. Even before the end of the ancien régime, the haute bourgeoisie had blurred the boundaries of the lower nobility, and the acquisition or outright purchase of titles went on unabashedly not only in Spain but in France, Italy, and other continental countries.

Brading (1971, 1973, 1974) is one of a handful of scholars whose work has greatly enriched the Colonial historiography of Mexico, and in my opinion he is the most perceptive historian of the eighteenth century. Yet in outlining the stratification system of New Spain during the second half of the century, he lacks the insightful understanding that he exhibits in discussing the economy of the colony:

> New Spain's society was as unbalanced, distinctive and colonial as its economy. The contemporary European class distinctions of noble, gentle, bourgeois, free commoner and serf cannot be applied in Mexico without violent distortion. True, a species of titled aristocracy existed, but for the most part of such recent creation and transitory florescence as to excite derision among a European nobility. [Otero 1967, 1:28–29]. Moreover, we seek in vain for any middle class, any bourgeoisie, mercantile or professional, conscious of a middle rank in society. Nor does the distinction between free and unfree commoners invite employment: apart from a handful of slaves, everyone in New Spain was free, in the sense that all subjects of the Crown enjoyed access to royal justice; no man at law was bound to a landowner for life. In effect, Mexico did not possess a clearly defined class system. (Brading 1971:19–20)

I disagree with almost every assertion here. First, the contemporary European distinction between the upper and lower nobility and the rest of society qua sociopsychological groupings was not one of class but of estate. Classes, in the modern sociological sense, did not come into existence until after the American and French revolutions, while it is perfectly appropriate to speak of classes within the estates. Accounting for the Colonial situation and the ethnic-racial components of New

Spain—the source of superordination for those of Spanish extraction and those somatically categorized as Creoles—roughly the same stratification system obtained on both sides of the Atlantic. The differences between Spain and New Spain were a matter of degree; in New Spain there was an upper and lower nobility proportionally much smaller than in Spain, likewise for the limited bourgeois middle class. Meanwhile, the Mestizo and *casta* populations most certainly corresponded to the freeholders of the Western world, and the Indians to the *pecheros* of the peninsula. To say that Mexico did not possess a clearly defined stratification system of classes and estates is an exaggeration that stems primarily from Brading's conception of the Western social system that mixes elements of sixteenth-century and nineteenth-century history. In fact, in sixteenth-century Spain, serfs had mostly disappeared or had been transformed into tenant farmers or small freeholders, thus corresponding to the Mestizo and *casta* rural populations; while *pecheros,* still to be found in Spain, corresponded to the Indian population paying tribute. Furthermore, the bourgeois class consciousness that Brading refers to did not yet exist in western Europe, much less in Spain, and it took perhaps two generations after the demise of the ancien régime to acquire the attributes that characterize class stratification today.

Brading takes a static view of nobility and the wider category of aristocracy. He exaggerates the downward mobility and impermanence of the superordinate estate and does not consider the expressive components of stratification. From the Conquest to the Revolution of 1910, the Mexican aristocracy enjoyed an uninterrupted existence, centered about a core of families who mostly still survive, despite the high degree of downward mobility that has characterized this social sector. How does this system differ from the British nobiliary system, when no more than 9 or 10 percent of peers today have pre-Elizabethan titles? There is no difference: the British aristocracy, just like the Mexican aristocracy, with due respect to differences in size and cultural elaboration, survived downward mobility as an uninterrupted expressive system. And what is the difference between what the Howards and Talbots in England, or the Guzmanes and Mendozas in Spain, felt about all the parvenu nobles being titled in the eighteenth century, and what the Gómez de Cervantes and the Luna de Arellanos felt about the equally parvenu titles that were being awarded to the merchants of New Spain? Again, none, once we adjust to time scale and differences in lineage (Perrot 1968:205–18; Bush 1984:217–41). Briefly, in principle, *imago mundi,* and expressive culture, New Spain's Creole aristocracy was the same as those of all Western aristocracies.[5]

Brading (1971:20–25) outlines the stratification system of New Spain much in the same way as other historians (see Fisher 1951; Meyer and Sheridan 1979; Priestley 1926), although he de-emphasizes distinct social groupings, emphasizes fuzzy class boundaries, and categorizes the system in terms of broad, intractable labels such as *gente de razón, gente decente, la plebe,* and so on, that bring to mind the ideological categorization of the global social system by Indians that still survives in rural communities. Brading asserts rightly that race as much as class determined a person's position in society, but he exaggerates the former and does not adequately conceive social categories in terms of somatic and cultural attributes. Anthropologists know that the definitions of most social categories in Mexico since the sixteenth century have been cultural, while elaborate patterns of somatic characteristics complicate the situation. Nevertheless, Brading exaggerates the racial-somatic composition of Creoles, Mestizos, Indians, and *castas.* He says, for example, that Creoles were mostly Mestizos. No doubt many Mestizos were legally and behaviorally defined as Creoles, but of the more than one million people classified as *Creoles* on the eve of Independence, there is no evidence that less than 50 percent were somatically European; indeed, evidence supports the contrary assertion. Brading quotes Lucas Alamán, a member of an old family with *hidalguía a fuero de España,* to the effect that the nobility of New Spain was distinguished from the Creole rank and file only by its wealth, and that the latter was distinguished from the rest of the population by dress and by being known as *gente decente.* But Alamán was not talking about what he considered the Creole aristocracy, of which he was a member, but rather about the parvenu titled nobility; he was reacting much like an old landed member of the *petite noblesse* witnessing the creation of so many bourgeois nobles by Louis XV. Finally, as regards merchants enjoying prestige equal to landowners, the situation in New Spain by the second half of the eighteenth century was not much different from that in most countries of western Europe, where nobles have engaged in mercantile operations for most of modern times (Brading 1971:20–25). That the landowner, the *hacendado* with a tradition going back to the *encomienda,* had more prestige and served as the model for aristocratic behavior is suggested by the fact that upon becoming aristocrats and being accepted by the traditional social and ruling class, *haut bourgeois* plutocrats invariably acquired a landed base more for expressive than for economic reasons.

In summary, I offer an outline of the stratification system of New Spain below the Creole aristocracy, that minuscule segment of the Colonial social system. At the top of this "class" system there was a small haute bourgeoisie (perhaps 30,000 or so) composed of *peninsulares* and Creoles of Spanish extraction. From this group most upwardly mobile individuals were drafted into the Creole aristocracy, for they were the richest sector of the Creole rank and file. Next was a sizable "bourgeoisie" (perhaps 300,000) composed of Creoles of Spanish extraction, *peninsulares,* and considerable numbers of mestizoized Creoles who were somatically homogeneous. This ethnically mixed sector of the stratification system were retailers, professionals, specialized craftsmen, foremen, and assorted traders. They made up a sort of middle "class," but not with quite the same socioeconomic denotation as the term carries today. The third group included almost all the non-Indian population, that is, the Mestizos, Mulattos, and *castas,* as well as some Creoles and mestizoized Creoles and a few *peninsulares.* This sector of the stratification system numbered more than two million people; it was the bulk of the colony's urban population, its working force, and the rural population not tied to Indian communities. At the bottom we find the Indian majority, the fourth group. They were not a fixed population, however, for there were always considerable numbers in the process of becoming ethnically Mestizos. The stratification system of New Spain on the eve of Independence encompassed a population of nearly six and a half million. The system was at once fluid and fixed; upward mobility was most likely to occur at the top and bottom, whereas the vast middle ground was rather static. Class consciousness, as I have indicated, is a nineteenth-century phenomenon, developing first in Europe and much later in the New World south of the Rio Grande. Indeed, the only genuine class consciousness before the demise of the ancien régime was that of the aristocracy, in both Europe and the New World. Although the class system of New Spain was not composed of well-bounded categories or classes, neither was that of most European countries at the end of the eighteenth century. But the situation was not as fuzzy as Brading maintains; it reflected rather the incipient class system of western Europe.

CHAPTER 7

The Nineteenth Century: Expressive and Structural Changes in the Transformation from an Estate to a Class System

What did the titled nobility of Mexico represent on the eve of Independence? Unquestionably, they were the social arbiters of the land and the richest men in New Spain. But they were also part of a larger group, the ruling aristocracy-plutocracy from which most of them were recruited and to which they were bound by multiple ties of kinship and ritual kinship. The titled nobility embodied the social standing to which most members of the superordinate stratum of Colonial society aspired but could not achieve. Within a decade, this estate was de jure, but not necessarily de facto, transformed into a social class when all privileges were abolished by the demise of the nobiliary system. This social class, small and tightly knit, remained largely unchanged until the Mexican Revolution of 1910, when it was reinvigorated by a third renewal. There were modifications, however, and the fortunes of the Mexican aristocracy were intimately related to the political and economic transformations of the country between Independence from Spain and the first popular revolution of the twentieth century. Moreover, the Mexican aristocracy, like all aristocracies of the Western world, underwent an increasingly significant process of embourgeoisement. What may be considered distinctive about the Mexican aristocracy—or rather distinctive about several New World aristocracies that survived the demise of the Spanish Empire—was that it retained a seigneurial component, primarily in the vast landed estates of its members, which may be attributed to the ethnic component discussed in chapter 6, but which was undoubtedly facilitated by the slow growth of class consciousness at almost all levels of Mexican society (Tannenbaum 1966:74–146).

Upon Independence from Spain, Mexico was organized into a federal republic modeled after the United States, but more so in theory than in practice. The libertarian ideas of the French Revolution and the reaction provoked by the Napoleonic Wars raised the expectations of the budding middle class. But the ideas of liberty, equality, and fraternity took nearly one hundred years to acquire true meaning and operational validity beyond the minuscule political class and the small middle class, concentrated almost exclusively in the capital and large cities of Mexico. The political vacuum left by the demise of the viceroyalty of New Spain was largely filled by the economic plutocracy—the bourgeoisie of the last fifty years of the Colonial period. From the beginning, inertia and lack of political experience militated against the Mexican aristocracy becoming the political class of the independent country. A few aristocrats did participate actively in politics and rose to prominence, but as a class, the aristocracy, partly as a result of being outmaneuvered and partly as a result of willful lack of interest, lost political and military control. Shortsightedly focusing on its landed estates and fairly secure in its alliance with the haute bourgeoisie and other powerful economic interests, the aristocracy failed to contribute to the stability of the country (Pérez de Salazar n.d.).

Independence and Its Aftermath: Economic and Social Restructuring (1810–56)

"The war of independence, which lasted from 1810 to 1821, had the effect of an earthquake. It destroyed the governing class of Mexico, drove the Spaniards from the country, and removed from office experienced administration. It left the country filled with ambitions stirred to life by the blind fury that had raged so long a time. It destroyed the capital, property, prestige, and power of the only class in the country that has exercised powers of government." Tannenbaum's (1933:74) characterization of this momentous episode accurately describes the ambiance of the upheaval and its most significant institutional consequence, namely, the political and administrative vacuum that signaled the end of Colonial rule. This inevitable consequence of colonialism affected all independent countries that were born during the collapse of the Spanish Empire in the first two decades of the nineteenth century. In Mexico, sixty years passed before the country achieved a measure of stability and relative economic well-being.

THE WAR OF INDEPENDENCE, ANTECEDENTS, AND ENSUING CONSEQUENCES

The struggle for Independence and the forces that led to it have inspired extensive scholarly treatment (see Gruening 1928; Ladd 1976; Priestley 1926; Simpson 1966; Tannenbaum 1933). Here I am strictly concerned with antecedents and consequences that impinged directly on the Mexican aristocracy during this great transformation. Lack of Creole political participation at the higher levels of government and economic favoritism for *peninsulares* are traditionally cited as the most important causes of the struggle for Independence. In the case of Mexico, these were undoubtedly the causes that, from the moment of the first *cabildo abierto* (open assembly) in 1810, brought most of the Creole rank and file and the nascent Mestizo middle class to consider opting for Independence. The titled and nontitled Creole aristocracy, however, wavered on the issue; most of its members were indecisive and probably favored a compromise settlement. Taking sides made an important difference to individuals, for as the war unfolded, an aristocrat's royalist or insurgent sympathies became a matter of life and property (Ladd 1976:105–31).

Specifically, Creole aristocrats and rank and file were equally affected by the favoritism toward *peninsulares*. Meanwhile, the economic causes and accompanying bureaucratic procedures that restricted the other various strata of Colonial society also affected *peninsulares*, and it is not surprising that many of the more than 15,000 of them in New Spain opted for Independence. Though the grievances that led to Independence affected Creoles and *peninsulares* alike, the various sectors of the dominant stratum of society usually chose sides for different reasons, motivated by different perceptions. No clear line separates those who chose one side or the other, though statistically speaking the great majority of Creoles adopted the insurgent cause, while most *peninsulares* were royalists. The majority of the Mestizo population and some of the *castas* followed the lead of Creole and *peninsular* insurgents or royalists, whereas the Indian population exhibited a marked indifference to the struggle, though they suffered, just the same, by being caught in the middle (Bulnes 1916:78–123).

Specific reasons can be pinpointed well enough but not how they affected specific individuals and groups of Creoles and *peninsulares,* beyond these two broad populations choosing in the majority the insurgent and royalist sides, respectively. First, it appears that rank-and-file Creoles strongly resented the political monopoly of *peninsulares* and chose sides primarily on political and administrative grounds. The situation, however, is more complicated. The Creole rank and file not only resented *peninsular* control of high office, but also the control exercised by the Creole aristocracy over local politics. The Creole rank and file thus lumped *peninsulares* and Creole aristocrats together (Otero 1972). Second, the Creole aristocracy and the haute bourgeoisie, meanwhile, chose sides mostly on economic grounds. They nursed grievances against the Crown for favoring administrators and *peninsulares* in high places, they opposed specific royal policies that hindered local entrepreneurs, and they resented the undue taxes levied against them. Probably the overwhelming majority of this group, which actually included significant numbers of *peninsulares* and ran the social gamut from titled nobles to Creole rank and file, was not influenced by political considerations, for they were the least influenced by the new libertarian ideas and economic liberalism. The overall situation was sufficiently blurred that the economic elite during the war was perhaps divided equally over the conflict (Mora 1972). Third, there was a social, ethnic grievance that cannot be easily pinpointed but that underlay much of the revolt against Spanish rule. Though probably not affecting the Creole aristocracy and the haute bourgeoisie, as almost all of them were *peninsulares* and Spanish Creoles, this grievance shaped proinsurgent sentiment among the mestizoized Creoles, Mestizos, and other elements that actively participated in the revolt. As in all Colonial situations, those who were not members of the superordinate stratum felt discriminated against and put down, and these feelings played a determinant role in rallying sentiment against Spanish rule, particularly among the liberal elements of mestizoized Creole extraction who constituted the leadership of the revolt (Ladd 1976:121; Urbina 1917). The following outline details the main causes and antecedents that aligned the insurgent and royalist forces and personnel in the war of Independence.

Political grievances. (*a*) Inadequate access to local politics. The Creole rank and file had a long-standing complaint against Creole aristocrats and rich plutocrats who controlled the *cabildos* of New Spain. They felt that since, together with urbanized Mestizos, they formed the great majority of the cities and towns, they should have a proportional representation in local city councils. (*b*) Near complete lack of participation in the viceregal government and colonywide administration. All Creoles, regardless of rank, felt that representatives of the Crown at all levels were corrupt or inefficient, and that good government and administration required they themselves should have access to key positions. Aristocrats and rank-and-file Creoles had been expressing this complaint since the sixteenth century, and it grew louder as the Crown lost much control of the colony during the last two decades before the war of Independence (Ladd 1976:89–104).

Economic grievances. (*a*) The Crown's intent in raising revenues provoked a series of administrative reforms that affected all sectors of the colony from titled and nontitled aristocrats to the *castas*. These reforms included new taxes and fees, engendering corruption that, during the last fifty years of Colonial rule, alienated the population from the Crown more than ever before. (*b*) Since mining began in New Spain, it had always been under rather tight Crown control, as perhaps the most important source of revenue for the central government. From 1750, mine owners had been paying exorbitant prices for primary materials such as mercury and explosives, in addition to direct taxes of exploitation and sale. (*c*) Agrarian enterprises were also subject to what *hacendados* and large-scale farmers perceived as undue economic impediments, including the *alcábala* and other direct taxes. Under this rubric must be included the prohibition against growing grapes and olives and the manufacture of wine and olive oil, all of which had to be imported from the peninsula (Young 1937:59–76). (*d*) Finally, consolidation was the most resented economic measure of the Crown. It affected not only the rich and powerful but all persons of property in the colony. This economic measure was directly tied to restricting the credit system, on which most mining, agrarian, and mercantile operations heavily depended. Every man of property was affected, particularly the great plutocratic nobles with diversified operations. It is surprising that consolidation provoked no riots and disturbances—that it did not is a tribute to able royal officials who throughout most of Colonial times were able to maintain peace in the colony. The measure placed great stress on the richest and most loyal subjects of the Crown, exacerbated shortages of basic commodities, and triggered unemployment (Ladd 1976:96–103).

Social grievances. (*a*) As the Crown began to lose control of the colony before the middle of the eighteenth century a "caste" system came into being. The mixed populations of the three basic racial stocks were pigeonholed into a large number of combinations and permutations including more than twenty-five somatic-ethnic categories. After the relatively fluid society that had prevailed until the first two decades of the century, not only the Indians but the Mestizos and *castas* felt to a considerable extent rejected by the establishment of somatic lines of demarcation and ethnic classification. Although this spurious categorization of the entire population never worked, it left a bitter residue among the mixed populations, one which was undoubtedly exploited by the Creole leadership in rallying partisans for the Independence cause (Nutini 1963). (*b*) The Creole aristocracy and the mostly *peninsular* haute bourgeoisie did not have any social grievances, but the Creole and mestizoized Creole leadership of the insurgents did. Their grievances emanated primarily from the position of social inferiority that, ideologically and behaviorally, the latter occupied with respect to the *peninsular* haute bourgeoisie. Estate and class distinctions, and even expressive distinctions, were significant inputs in structuring the leadership of the Independence movement.

From the fall of Tenochtitlán until the Mexican Revolution of 1910, revolutions, uprisings, and armed confrontations were bloody and destructive. The war of Independence was undoubtedly the bloodiest proportional to the total population involved; it was also one of the most destructive in terms of loss of property, urban destruction, disruption of the economic infrastructure, and, perhaps most devastating, discontinuing for two generations an intellectual and educational tradition. Most revolutions, of course, have these effects, but Mexico's Independence need not have been so harrowing. Humboldt (1966:78–84), for example, compares Mexico City to some of the best European cities in urbanization, the layout of street and spaces, and the excellence of its constructions. Perhaps more significant, he praises the city's educational establishments, its social and cultural institutions, and the general ambiance of the city. Nearly three generations were to pass before Mexico City regained some of its former excellence and never again did the city fully achieve its preeminent position.

The news of Ferdinand VII's abdication, which reached New Spain in July 1808, was one of the precipitators of the drive for Independence. It immediately raised the expectations of insurgent circles, which the viceroy tried to palliate by several conciliatory measures, in particular by ending the collection of consolidation. Nonetheless, independent political activities accelerated, would-be insurgents became increasingly active, and during the following two years several conspiracies were discovered and their participants tried, though, in the spirit of conciliation, they were cleared of charges. Then, in September 1810, in what is today the state of Hidalgo, Dolores erupted in opposition to the Crown, one of many such uprisings that spread like wildfire across the New World colonies within a few months. Thus began the war for Independence; during the next six years the country became polarized on the question of autonomy from Spain. Another five years of plotting, *pronunciamientos* (uprisings), irresolute action, and betrayal on both sides finally coalesced in the so-called Plan de Iguala, which halfheartedly declared autonomy from Spain (Mora 1979:87–143; Parkes 1938:133–72). No party concerned was entirely clear whether autonomy meant the radical birth of a nation, a sort of commonwealth status with Spain, or something in between. The short-lived Mexican Empire of Iturbide (1822–1823) was an ephemeral opera buffa, except perhaps that during that period Independence from Spain was completely achieved. Three years after the fall of the empire, the nascent Republic was on its way to federalism, groping for an institutional framework in the midst of political and economic instability.

One event that relates directly to the Mexican aristocracy was the expulsion of *peninsulares* from Mexico. Shortly after Mexico became independent, *peninsulares* began to leave Mexico in large numbers, taking most of their capital with them. By the time the expulsion law was passed in December 1827, probably a third of the *peninsulares* who had been resident in 1821 remained in the country. After 1821, according to most accounts, *peninsulares* became increasingly disliked, because they continued their political intrigues, because they were among the richest people in the country, and because they continued to live ostentatiously despite the general poverty brought by the war (Sims 1974:9–39). It is difficult to determine, however, exactly who hated the *peninsulares*—or *gachupines* as they were often called—enough to legislate expelling them from the country. Certainly the Indians could not have cared less; possibly the Mestizo and *casta* masses did not care that much either. The most likely candidates were the Creole and mestizoized Creole leadership of the insurgency, now the budding ruling class of the country. Starving for recognition and political power, imbued with the libertarian ideas and the promise of liberalism, the new political class vented centuries of resentment and frustration on the *peninsulares*. No doubt these leaders felt the same about the Creole aristocracy as a social and ruling class; but though they could get rid of the former, they could not even neutralize the latter.[1] The Creole aristocracy soon achieved an unspoken alliance with an essentially Mestizo political leadership; a shaky peace henceforth constituted the cornerstone of the political and economic life of the nation until the Revolution of 1910 (Nutini 1963).

ARISTOCRATIC LOSSES AND ADAPTATIONS IN THE TRANSITION TO REPUBLICAN LIFE

Like the liberal insurgents, the leadership of the movement and most politically conscious people in New Spain during the war and after Independence were indecisive and lacked a clear political course. The Creole aristocracy and haute bourgeoisie were no exception. We may assume that the Creole aristocracy wanted not independence from Spain but some sort of commonwealth association. This general stand, however, was individually modified by positions ranging from solid royalism to masonic liberalism, often conditioned by ad hoc economic constraints and considerations. Wavering thus between loyalty to the mother country and complete Independence, the aristocracy never presented a united front, as events developed from 1808 until the consummation of the revolt (Bulnes 1910:51–76). Reconstructing the situation from the battles, skirmishes, and the general conduct of the war, including the very high number of casualties on both sides, one can infer that in the country, at least, the aristocratic *hacendados* were able to muster support for the royalist cause. We know, on the other hand, that the titled aristocracy was much divided and that there were as many nobles who supported the king as who supported Independence. Certainly there were a handful of committed liberals influenced by the masonic lodges (the Yorkist and the Scottish rites), and there were a considerable number of loyalists (Ovando n.d.). Again, the nontitled aristocracy, by now composed mostly of *hacendados,* took a conservative stance.

How actively and in what capacities did Creole aristocrats participate in the armed conflict? In country and city titled nobles organized militias, sometimes on a rather large scale—occasionally as many as eight companies or roughly eight hundred men, more often two or three companies—which they completely outfitted at the expense of the individual organizer who was made regimental colonel. Urban militias were apparently not as active as rural militias. Rural militias were perhaps larger and better organized, and they often bore the brunt of military engagements. In this respect, the *haciendas* and the support system of surrounding communities played an important role in the war, and no doubt the nontitled members of the aristocracy were the most active in supporting the royalist cause (Ladd 1976:105–23). How many landed aristocrats opted for Independence is difficult to say, but I would guess only a rather small minority, judging by the nature of the armed conflict and the numbers of combatants involved. The regular royalist forces, led, to be sure, by *peninsulares,* were mainly composed of urban Mestizos and *castas.* In fact, much of the support for the royalist cause afforded by the Creole aristocracy, particularly the titled nobility, was in the form of donations or loans, to some extent extracted from them by the viceregal government (Alamán 1942, 2:79–87).

The landed aristocracy suffered greatly in the struggle. *Haciendas* were ravaged, many mansions sacked, and agricultural production much disrupted. By 1820, many *hacendados* withdrew to the cities, for rural life had become extremely unsafe. This exodus contributed to the decline of agriculture and stock raising and to the shortages of staples that characterized the war years. There was loss of income in commerce and agrarian enterprises, and mining production became almost negligible. Under such conditions, landed magnates and plutocratic merchants alike trafficked with both sides in order to make up for their great losses. But the Creole aristocracy—hereafter the Mexican aristocracy—never feared the loss of its exalted position as a social and ruling class. Most of its members correctly assessed the situation as one to which they could adapt without relinquishing their preeminent position: a change in political leadership, not a revolution (Bulnes 1910:132–47). By the time of the official decree of expulsion, the hatred and resentment toward *peninsulares,* with whom the Creole aristocracy had always been identified by reasons of social and kinship ties and racial affiliation, had been mitigated or neutralized. The unspoken alliance that was to dominate the life of the nation had been forged, and the Mexican aristocracy

as ruling class was slowly recuperating from the devastation of the war
(Nutini and Roberts n.d.). One might say that the ideas of the French
Revolution, the representative democracy of the United States, and the
seeds of economic liberalism had been effective in configuring a small,
groping middle class that was politically conscious of the course of the
nation but not strong enough to dislodge the oligarchical ruling class
(Nutini 1963).

Within the Mexican aristocracy, did the dissension between royalists and insurgents within its own ranks and the frictions and feuding
that tore families apart have any noticeable effects in the restructuring
of the class? The answer is no, and the ethnographic evidence is to be
found in the *petite histoire* of the group written during three subsequent
generations. By 1830 or so, when the fury of the struggle for Independence had abated and the new political class was groping for leadership
and making accommodations, the Mexican aristocracy was healing its
wounds, patching old grudges, and returning to its antebellum configuration as a close-knit social group (Pérez de Salazar 1928). Once
again, the expressive bond was highly instrumental for the continuity
of the group, for the old links of *hidalguía,* genuine or spurious, and its
conception as a noble estate did not disappear. Demographically, however, the configuration of the aristocracy changed in two significant
aspects: it lost a third of its traditional strength, which required two
generations to rebuild; it became more regional—stronger nuclei were
formed in several of the most important cities, and the hegemony of
the capital was diminished (Nutini and Roberts n.d.).

The transition to a representative democracy, at least in theory,
meant the demise of the estate system as it had existed throughout
Colonial times. By the time of the expulsion, the estate system no
longer existed: there were no more titles; the *mayorazgo* system had
been abolished; military orders could be boasted of only sub rosa; and
all noble privileges, of *hidalgos* and titled nobles, were gone. De jure,
then, all Mexicans became equal before the law; de facto, however, the
situation was quite different. The Indians, to be sure, ceased to pay
tribute, but their social, political, and economic status, by any measurable standard, did not improve. The Mexican aristocracy, somewhat
impoverished, without the benefit of a corporate estate, and deprived
of all its privileges, was, nonetheless, not seriously challenged, and it
remained the social and ruling class of the nation. The demise of some
of the privileges and symbols of *hidalguía* and nobility was actually

welcome, and structurally equivalent strategies were developed as a consequence of adaptive changes. Anti-Spanish and antiaristocratic actions and behaviors of the liberal leadership and general populace were short lived: a *llamarada de petate* (a flash in the pan), as cynical Mexicans would say today to describe the lack of continuity of official political and economic measures (Ovando n.d.). By the end of the 1830s, anti-Colonial feelings focused on the Mexican aristocracy had all but disappeared. But the superstructure of old symbols and privileges did not disappear from the worldview and expressive array of the Mexican aristocracy, and titles of nobility, the *mayorazgo,* and knighthood continued to play a significant role in the aristocratic way of life: as mechanisms of aristocratic affiliation, as symbols of self-identification, and as catalysts of genealogical reconstruction. The ideal of the *mayorazgo* persisted as a divisive mechanism that caused family friction until the middle of the twentieth century. Knighthood in the military orders of Santiago, Calatrava, and Alcántara remained badges of honor for the families known to have had ancestors so honored. And titles of nobility were still used in the privacy of the home and in exclusive aristocratic circles. Indeed, many titles were never discontinued, as the nobiliary connection with Spain was never severed, and several have been reactivated since Porfirian times. Titles of nobility, in this ambiance of seclusion and unofficial recognition, have become family symbols, collective representations of a family's aristocratic standing. The mere knowledge of having had a titled ancestor "ennobles" the entire family and becomes a sign of its social standing (Nutini and Roberts n.d.).

ECONOMIC DECLINE, RECONSTRUCTION, AND ESTABLISHMENT OF A NEW RULING-POLITICAL ALLIANCE

More than any other factor, economic loss affected the evolution of the Mexican aristocracy for two generations. Not only did the natural disorganization and economic losses that accompanied conflagrations such as the bloody war of Independence affect the economic dominance of the ruling class, but the transition from colony to free nation challenged its position as well. As weak as the new Republic was, it was impossible for the Mexican aristocracy to retain the institutional advantages it had enjoyed under the old regime. The continuing ruling class was nonetheless still strong enough to establish a new status quo that, despite many uprisings, coups, and aborted revolutions, was to last for some eighty years. At the end of the period the economy of the country began to improve, and shortly thereafter the landed aristocracy began its last period of florescence before the fall (Noll 1936:79–87).

Until well into the nineteenth century, mining had been the driving mechanism of the country's economy. By Independence, mining was in total disarray and ten years later was no longer one of the economic pillars of the nation. The breakdown of the credit system that for more than eighty years before Independence had worked well may be regarded as perhaps the determining factor of economic decline. Agriculture and stock raising suffered greatly; farmers near cities and small cattle and sheep ranchers were particularly hard-hit. Indeed, for more than ten years after Mexico became independent, few people, rich or poor, paid their loans, and many men of property declared bankruptcy. Not until well into the 1830s did the credit system regain a certain degree of normality. Given the lack of capital from around 1821 on, former great capitalists, almost all of them members of the aristocracy, began to sell their mining and even some of their agrarian interests to foreign companies (Bocanegra 1927:128–63).

The fifteen years following the war of Independence saw not only low capital but diminished circulating currency, which greatly hampered business and trade. The only remaining source of credit was the church, but even the church had two or three times less to give than during prewar days. Just as serious, the networks of trade and the distribution of manufactured and agricultural products were badly disrupted, and banditry and lack of safe communications made things worse (Ladd 1976:133–61). In some states and regions within states, however, the situation was not so bleak. Many of these areas became worlds unto themselves where the people could claim a measure of economic security (Pérez de Salazar 1928).

The ruling class of the country until Independence had a diversified economy including mining, agrarian enterprises, and business and trade. The richest of the rich engaged in all these enterprises, but from Independence onward, the situation changed somewhat. Whatever mining still went on fell into the hands of foreign companies, and trade and manufacturing significantly decreased. Most of the wealth of the ruling class was in the *haciendas,* where staple crops and cattle and sheep raising were the main agrarian activities. These activities now dominated regional economies, much as they had before the war, on a more modest scale, while the great agrarian wealth concentrated in the hands of a rather small group of landed aristocrats whose property was scattered throughout the country no longer existed or had been greatly curtailed. The countrywide commercial networks had also been in the hands of aristocratic magnates with diversified operations, and they did not again become an important component of Mexico's economy until after the middle of the century when the country began to recuperate definitively (Urías 1978:127—79). Agriculture and stock raising started to improve in response to the California gold rush, and this event was perhaps the beginning of the country's economic recovery (Ladd 1976:156—60). In terms of the Mexican aristocracy as a class, the stratification of core, center, and periphery also survived Independence, although the center and periphery acquired significantly more economic and social life of their own, due in part to the isolationism triggered by the birth of the nation. The core, of course, remained the model of expressive and social realization, but it no longer monopolized the wealth of the class. Indeed, until well into the Porfiriato, many of the richest families of the aristocracy and haute bourgeoisie maintained permanent residences not in Mexico City but in the traditional *hacendado* cities that had grown so important by the middle of the century. Thus, while many of the great aristocratic magnates of the core and center survived economic ruin in the aftermath of Independence, equally many did not survive, becoming downwardly mobile and eventually dropping out of the system by late Porfirian times. By contrast, peripheral *hacendados* and aristocrats with diversified operations may have survived economic disaster better, recuperated faster, and went on to amass larger fortunes than those more centrally located (Ovando n.d.).

The *hacienda* system did not change significantly in the roughly two generations following Independence. The productivity of the *hacienda* did decline, with dramatically adverse effects in some regions. But the internal organization of the *hacienda* remained constant from the late eighteenth century. Despite the legal upgrading of the Indians to the status of citizens of the Republic, their real structural position did not change. The disorganization following Independence and the deep resentment of the Indians toward the outside world made it difficult to afford them protection and fair treatment, and the problem was compounded by the fact that the Mestizo leadership, adhering to the imported European and American models of industrial liberalism, considered them an impediment to the development of the country. Debt peonage continued unabated, and it became even easier to recruit peons for the *hacienda* than it had been at the turn of the nineteenth century (Nickel 1988:93–98).

From its inception early in the seventeenth century, the *hacienda* system had been a world unto itself—not that it was completely independent of the region and the city, but that it was as self-sufficient as an agrarian operation can be, socially and economically. These isolationist aspects of the *hacienda* were exacerbated during the period in question. It became self-sufficient in most basic items of consumption and was virtually untouched by the mechanization that was beginning to affect smaller but more progressive agrarian enterprises. Most visibly, the *hacienda* more than ever before enforced its own justice and maintained a police force that, by consent or sheer necessity, extended to neighboring communities. The conditions of the time tended to perpetuate a seigneurial system, as *hacendados* retreated to their landed estates, and the countryside acquired renewed expressive significance and remained important for two generations (Ewald 1973).

I have referred to the leadership that emerged after Independence as a mixture of Creole rank and file and mestizoized Creoles. With the demise of Colonialism and the ethnic-somatic cleavages that it entailed, there came a transition toward a more fluid racial situation, in which the term *Creole* became fuzzy and ultimately lost much of its original denotation. More to the point, the new fluidity entailed a fairly high degree of upward mobility, which brought with it the mestizoization of the Creole strain. Culturally and somatically, then, the country's middle class of politicians, professionals, military officers, tradesmen, and assorted urban and rural segments was essentially a Mestizo population. Indeed, at no time in Mexico before or after the last two decades of Colonial rule have there been more inhabitants of European stock proportional to the total population of the country: in 1810, about 12 percent (of 6.5 million) were racially Spaniards; today, it is doubtful that 10 percent (of 85 million) are racially Europeans (Meyer and Sheridan 1979:207–11). It is therefore entirely proper to refer to the political class of Mexico as a Mestizo middle class.

All classes, economic groups, and ethnic sectors that participated in the Independence movement were somewhat ambivalent about choosing sides. Perhaps the most consistent of these groups were the most educated members of the Creole rank and file and the most affluent and politically conscious mestizoized Creoles. This social segment at the end of Colonial times was a small but influential and moderately educated bourgeoisie of perhaps 5 percent of the total population. Initially, the political leadership forged during the war years was a motley conglomerate of "professional" politicians, military men, and sundry "intellectuals" who had participated in the war; by the early 1830s they had coalesced as a fairly distinct segment of Mexican society and became the architects of the federal republic (Rydjord 1935:37–96). The masonic lodges played an important role in these early political developments. The Yorkist and Scottish rites were the two masonic lodges active in Mexico throughout the first half of the nineteenth century. The Scottish rite was older; its active origins can be traced to the first decade of the century. It attracted those more conservative Creole elements who opted for a degree of independence from Spain within the framework of a constitutional monarchy. The Scottish rite recruited members from the Creole rank and file and enlisted the sympathy of a few members of the more liberal elements of the Creole aristocracy. By the time of Iturbide's empire, the Scottish rite was being seriously challenged by the Yorkist rite, which soon replaced it as a main source of political ideology. From their inception during the war of Independence, the Yorkists had been more radical and indeed were perceived as revolutionaries. They established a representative federal republic, the form of government that Mexico has had ever since, though it existed in theory only; it never actually worked. The Yorkists' rather rabid nationalism promoted the expulsion of the *peninsulares* from Mexico, and their members were not above envying the wealth of the Creole aristocracy and haute bourgeoisie (Sims 1974:9–15).

It is perhaps difficult to understand why the Mexican ruling class was not able nor even seriously attempted to achieve political dominance when Colonial rule ended. The foregoing analysis implies an explanation, which may be summarized as follows. First, for three hundred years the ruling class had eschewed high political office and, under the umbrella of Colonial rule, had enjoyed with complaisance the fact of being the undisputed social and ruling class of the land. Although there are indications that nuclei of the Mexican aristocracy tried to assume direct political leadership, these attempts proved abortive. In the end, political alliance proved more expedient and less costly (Wells 1890:238). Second, demography conspired against the Mexican aristocracy becoming a powerful political presence at the national level: it was too small and scattered in the main cities of the country. Aristocrats continued to control the cities and to some extent the regions in which they were enfranchised and had their *haciendas* and other economic interests, but they were not able to control the legislative and executive government that ruled the country. Third, and perhaps most determinant, were two sociopsychological factors, one old and the other of recent origin: the sense of security engendered by having been the undisputed social and ruling class of the land for three centuries and the aristocratic dislike of the new Mestizo leadership, tinged perhaps with racial overtones, preventing political participation that required cooperation with the legislative and executive powers (Bazant 1985:75–157). The net effect of these attitudes and proclivities led to the tacit alliance that lasted until 1910 in which the Mexican aristocracy and the political class tolerated and even accommodated each other as long as the modus vivendi profited both sides.

This uneasy alliance lasted for nearly ninety years and survived all of the country's upheavals without ever resolving the fundamental goals and interests of an oligarchical aristocracy and an ever larger middle class. Laws were passed, political parties bitterly confronted each other, big and petty dictators ruled, and the masses were manipulated without benefit, but through it all the economic and social interests of the small ruling class were safeguarded and never seriously threatened, and a small Mestizo political class ruled the country unopposed, reaping economic benefits and enriching many of its members (Parkes 1938:233–311).

The conservative and liberal political parties that were formed within the decade after Independence may be regarded as the media through which the aristocratic ruling class and the Mestizo political class formally confronted each other, expressed political ideology, and legislated the destiny of the country. The liberal party sprang from Yorkist ideology and aspirations, while the conservative party adopted much of the ideology of the Scottish rite but with more rightist goals. The aims and orientations of each party were different, they were mostly in disagreement concerning the political system, and they worked to implement different economic ends. But what they had in common was the preservation of a status quo that benefited the constituencies of both parties. In their respective spheres—the conservatives dominating the city and the region, the liberals presiding over the federal system in a kind of paper-tiger fashion—they governed with various degrees of real and apparent control (Bazancourt 1931:89–142). Although the liberals ostensibly worked for the creation of a more just and equitable system, and implicitly for the growth of a larger, politically conscious middle class, they produced meager results: a Colonial mentality remained significantly in place, and the middle class remained small and powerless (Rydjord 1935:103–27).

The conservative party represented and defended the interests of the ruling class, though this by no means implies that Mexican aristocrats were directly involved in active politics at the national level, that they were representatives, senators, or ministers of state in numbers significant enough to constitute a true political body. Far from it: at no point from Independence to the Mexican Revolution of 1910 were aristocrats involved in politics except in very small numbers. For the reasons given above, aristocrats considered politics a waste of time and believed it beneath their dignity to be involved in the struggle of governing the country. Thus, the interests of the aristocratic *hacendado* class, and of the haute bourgeoisie as its complementary class, were defended by the professional politicians of the conservative party, the majority of whom were roughly of the same social extraction as the members of the liberal party. Until the first presidency of Porfirio Díaz, the liberals dominated national politics, but the legislation that emerged never seriously threatened the aristocratic ruling class and the economic interest of its close allies. Secure in their control of local (city and region) politics, the *hacendado* class was never challenged, while foreign economic interests and those of the haute bourgeoisie and political class contributed to the maintenance of the status quo. In this ambiance, these very small but all-powerful sectors of Mexican society survived and, later, prospered, as the country entered the machine age and the age of industrialization (Turner 1914: 78–107).

EXPRESSIVE RETREAT AND THE CHANGING LOCUS OF SOCIAL AND EXPRESSIVE REALIZATION

The most visible changes in the ruling class as a native aristocracy during the transition from Colonial rule to independent nation were in the expressive domain and the realization of social forms. Once again, the local aristocracy must be viewed within the context of the evolution of Western aristocracies. First, the Mexican (Creole) aristocracy reached its highest period of florescence when Western aristocracies were in decline. Consider that at no point in the history of Mexico, from the Conquest to the present, was the native aristocracy a political class. The ruling aristocracy gave nonetheless the impression of having retained many of the seigneurial attributes of the golden age of Western aristocracy, though in the limited ambiance of landed estates largely determined by the persistent Colonial mentality and ethnic-racial considerations that did not obtain in Europe. Second, the de jure transition from estate to class diminished the ceremonial, public function of the aristocracy, resulting in a process of expressive retreat that, even in the last period of florescence during the Porfiriato, the Mexican aristocracy did not entirely reverse. Third, the transition from a monarchy to a republic further eroded the expressive saliency of the aristocracy (Nutini and Roberts n.d.).

The economic factors that further diminished the expressive salience of the Mexican aristocracy for nearly two generations have already been detailed, and their effect may be gauged as follows. The virtual demise of the mining industry significantly diminished the wealth of the core aristocracy. Losses in the agrarian and trading and manufacturing sectors were also great. It was not only that wealth diminished and material and social raw resources became scarce, but that Mexico lost its ties to European expressive life, which were not reestablished until the French intervention. Moreover, contact between Mexico City and the provinces diminished, and isolation set in, leading to a measure of diversification that was not entirely reversed until the Mexican Revolution of 1910 (Pérez de Salazar 1928).

The process of withdrawal following Independence was most noticeable in the increasing importance of the *hacienda* as a more or less permanent abode. The city remained important to the Mexican aristocracy, but *hacienda* living became more central than it had been for a century and a half before Independence, and periods of rural residence were longer and more frequent. The three sectors of the aristocracy did differ, however, in their responses. The core, residing in Mexico City and two or three cities nearby, did not much alter the traditional urban-rural pattern of living, except perhaps during the years immediately following Independence. By the late 1830s, the dangers of urban living had somewhat subsided, and core aristocrats returned to city living with periodic visits to *haciendas*. This response may be explained by the fact that core aristocrats, more than all others, retained some of the economic diversification of late Colonial times, that is, they continued to engage in business as well as in the agrarian enterprises of the *hacienda*. To some extent this generalization applies also to centralized aristocrats, particularly those in the heart of Mexico, within 200 to 300 miles of the capital (Martínez del Río 1938:146–55). Peripheral aristocrats, however, rather definitively reversed the urban-rural pattern of living and became more permanently enfranchised on the *hacienda* until after the Mexican Revolution of 1910.

Some twenty years after Independence, the Marchioness Calderón de la Barca (1978) visited Mexico and wrote a clear account of life in Mexico at the time. The bulk of her account pertains to central Mexico. She visited several *haciendas* as well as the cities of Mexico City, Puebla, and Querétaro, where she stayed in mansions of some of the most distinguished members of the core aristocracy. She gave fair marks to the aristocratic urban household, praising the hospitality of her hosts and some of the expressive patterns of living. But she was not as complimentary of *hacienda* living and described country mansions as enormous establishments, most of whose rooms were empty of furniture, and a few barely furnished. Calderón de la Barca's description confirms that this segment of the aristocracy was definitely enfranchised in the city, but it also attests to the devastation that the *hacienda* suffered before and after Independence and from which it had not yet entirely recuperated in the early 1840s. In the periphery, however, most aristocratic *hacendados* had well-appointed rural residences, and many of them lived permanently on the *hacienda*. Three decades later, with the rather spectacular resurgence of landed estates, the *hacienda* system had not only regained its former splendor, but differences between core and periphery diminished, and the traditional country-city axis was reestablished (Castillo Negrete 1933:42–76).

Specifically, what were the expressive changes and social transformations that accompanied the transition from Colonial rule to Republican institutions? The retrenchment, as it were, may best be characterized as a shift from public to private domains of expression. Republican institutions, albeit weak and ineffective, nonetheless prevented the monopoly of public ceremonial and religious functions, which the aristocracy now shared with the political class and the more upwardly mobile segment of the bourgeoisie (Quintana n.d.). In direct control of the federal government and constituting the high-ranking echelons of the military, the political class insisted on a share of the public ceremonials and other expressive and symbolic validations of their new status. This state of affairs obtained primarily in Mexico City, ever the hub of a centralized political system. Provincial cities continued to be dominated by regional nuclei of *hacendados* (Nutini and Roberts n.d.).

The entire array of civil and religious public ceremonial functions shrank after Independence. Gone was the viceregal court that attracted the participation of the core aristocracy, and the new Republican government, while not devoid of pomp and circumstance, did not excel expressively. Meanwhile, competition for the public expressive domains that survived further curtailed the ruling class and enhanced the participation of the political class. From this perspective, one can speak of the "aristocratization" of the political class, which acquired a taste for expressive participation and proclivities hitherto practically impossible to attain. Conversely, the embourgeoisement of the aristocracy denoted primarily accommodation and restraint in the discharge of its expressive life. This new structural-expressive milieu was not willingly accepted by the aristocracy, but rather brought about by the active, sometimes confrontational pressure of the political class.

In the manifold domains of religious ceremonialism and sponsorships, the Mexican aristocracy fared better, retaining a greater degree of control than in civic ceremonialism. Although chantries and large-scale sponsorship of religious constructions and institutions had been greatly reduced, the aristocracy continued to express itself through the religious life, particularly in provincial cities and the *haciendas*. Overall, then, the public expressive life of the aristocracy was diminished and constrained during the decades following Independence, but not in the private domains of the household, the network of relationships binding the group, the *hacienda,* and the ambiance of provincial cities. The private expressive array remained as strong as ever, to some extent compensating for the expressive retreat in the public domains (Leicht 1934:127–69).

In conclusion, the transition from Colonial rule to Republican Mexico brought some significant changes to the expressive life and structural position of the aristocracy as a ruling class vis-à-vis the new political class. In form, the aristocracy remained basically unchanged, but the accommodations demanded by the new societal milieu entailed that it be placed in a different structural position with respect to the rising middle political class, on the one hand, and the body politic as a whole, on the other. Internally, the aristocracy changed enough so that things remained pretty much the same; externally, the process of embourgeoisement significantly shifted the position of the aristocracy, namely, it lost symbolic standing and became less visible than it had been before Independence.

The Reforma Laws and the French Intervention
(1856–76)

This period of Mexican history is marked by two important events, and both of them had determinant consequences for the development of the aristocracy in its terminal phase as a ruling class. The first, the Reforma Laws and the changes they unleashed, produced structural conditions that permitted a resurgence of the ruling class as a landed aristocracy, leading to a final period of florescence; while the second, the French intervention, provoked expressive changes that renewed the aristocracy as a social class by the diffusion of European influences affecting several domains. The social and political frameworks of the nation did change, the status quo discussed above remained the same, but despite fighting and instability, the economy began to improve, and by the end of the period, the overall conditions of the country were more propitious than they had been for more than fifty years.

TERRITORIAL GROWTH OF THE *HACIENDA* AND INCREASE OF DEBT PEONAGE

Throughout Colonial times, but especially after the expulsion of the Jesuits from the Spanish overseas possessions in 1767, the Catholic church had accumulated a great deal of arable and pasture lands. In 1856, all corporately owned lands in the country were legislated to be sold at public auction. As a result, Indian communities lost more than half of their land. In turn, church and Indian lands were acquired mostly by large *hacendados,* and their holdings reached immense proportions. In fact, such an accumulation of arable and pasture lands by the *hacendados* had never taken place on such a large scale, not even in the last part of the sixteenth century when the great landed estates were formed. Forced to leave their communities, Indian populations flocked to the *haciendas,* towns, and cities in order to survive. In this process, the *hacendados* were the great beneficiaries, and their control of a large labor force on their estates resembled the *corregimientos* of the sixteenth century (González Navarro 1957).

Shortly after Independence, there had been attempts to release the lands of the church and abolish all communal lands, which affected mostly the Indians. Nothing was done at the federal level, but some states enacted ordinances with various degrees of success. The avowed aim of abolishing all corporately owned property was to generate revenue and unfreeze the economy, for privatization fitted in well with the notions of economic liberalism. Privatization of the land was also, however, in the economic interests of the political class, and even the most revered of the liberal leaders (Juárez, Lerdo de Tejada, Comonfort) profited by the "Ley Lerdo" (*ley de desamortización;* the law passed in June 1956 requiring the sale of all communally owned property). The Ley Lerdo affected almost exclusively church and Indian communities and provoked various consequences and reactions. Those who profited most were *hacendados,* but many members of the political elite and foreign companies lost no time buying church land, *ejido,* and other kinds of corporately owned land of Indian communities (Nickel 1988:95–104). The church was allowed only to keep buildings directly related to the religious cult (churches, convents, religious retreats) and to administration (hospitals, bishops' residences), while Indian communities were allowed to keep in addition to existing privately owned property, administrative buildings, marketplaces, and *ejidos* individually exploited. Indian communities lost practically all their *tierras de repartimiento* and *propios* (two types of communal lands that had survived from Colonial times), which in many communities accounted for more than 50 percent of the total. Most of the communal lands lost to Indian communities were acquired by *haciendas,* with which the former had had turbulent relations since the early seventeenth century (Tannenbaum 1966:138–46). *Hacendados* also acquired church land, of course, but much less church land contributed to the growth of the *haciendas* during the period from the promulgation of the Ley Lerdo until 1890, when the land acquisition period ended and latifundia acquired maximal extension.

The complement to the growth of the *haciendas* was, of course, the condition of the Indians as a source of cheap labor. The Indians emerged from Colonial rule disillusioned with the world beyond their communities. The reality of citizenship did not mean much to village-enfranchised Indians, and there was apparently much resistance to the outside world during the three decades following Independence. The misguided influence of economic liberalism was largely responsible for the plight of the Indians, and some authors (see Powell 1974:84–89) even maintain that laws against vagrancy were designed to force Indians into the labor force of the *haciendas* as well as of the cities. Well-meaning measures were occasionally taken to protect and improve the lot of the Indians, but to little avail. From Porfirio Díaz's first presidency onward, all pretense of protecting the Indians was essentially abandoned until the Revolution of 1910. Possessing insufficient land, if indeed any at all, entire Indian communities sometimes became laborers attached (*acasillados*) to nearby *haciendas,* a process that had been part of the system since the seventeenth century but never on such a large scale (Nickel 1988:96–104).

The *hacienda*'s gain was the Indian's terrible loss, both in economic and cultural terms. Subjected to all kinds of influences from the Mestizo world, countless Indian villages became conglomerates of ethnic strains, and in many respects they ceased to be Indian communities. Indeed, from the middle of the nineteenth century the Indian population began to decline rapidly in proportion to the population of Mexico as a whole. By the end of the Porfiriato, the Indian population of the country was basically constituted by the Indian communities that had either been least affected by the Ley Lerdo or that by a combination of economic strategies other than agriculture had managed to preserve their cultural and ethnic identity. Debt peonage, by then a 250-year-old institution, reached unprecedented proportions, mostly associated with the *haciendas,* but also with large-scale farming. The *hacienda* had become once again a vigorous world unto itself (González Navarro 1957:107–221).

The Ley Lerdo and kindred legislation, known collectively as Leyes de Reforma, provoked not only economic but religious changes and reactions and unleashed a wave of violence and instability that lasted more than three years, until the French intervention. Almost immediately after the passage of the laws, trouble started in the provinces, and the government found itself in the midst of an insurrection that lasted for several years. The Indians ineffectually fought back, but only in exceptional cases were they able to prevent the sale of their lands (Priestley 1926:331–46). Reaction against the Reforma Laws insofar as the church was concerned was another matter altogether, aggravated by the government's high-handedness in destroying church property, symbolized by the destruction of the sixteenth-century Franciscan convent in the heart of Mexico City. Beginning in Puebla, revolts erupted throughout the country. Led mostly by the conservatives, plotted in the capital, they nonetheless inspired much public support. Although the overwhelming majority of the country undoubtedly had no sympathy for the church as a landlord, it was not about to tolerate the government's interference with the discharge of Roman Catholicism. Fundamentally, of course, the war over the reforma and the violence it generated had an economic reason, for conservatives and liberals alike were tacitly and openly in favor of ending the vast ownership of land by the church. What really provoked the reaction of conservatives and much popular support was the liberals' insistence in bringing the church under government control. The liberals did not just confine themselves to implementing a reasonable separation of church and state; they committed excesses that could have been avoided had they only controlled their ideological fervor (Parkes 1938:242–50). Predictably and regardless of personal religiosity, the Reforma Laws, insofar as they were concerned with religion, led to hardened positions, to ideological intransigence—on both sides—and, most seriously, to political rigidity and the inability to compromise, traits that continue to characterize the Mexican political system today.

The war over the reform initiated the improvement of the economy after more than four decades of instability and stagnation. During these decades few new magnates had joined the ranks of the haute bourgeoisie, as the most profitable economic enterprises were in the hands of foreign companies. From 1855 or so, a new element of the haute bourgeoisie was born: plutocrats of foreign extraction, primarily French, English, and American. This phenomenon related to the economic interests that these and other nations had in Mexico since shortly after Independence, but the families of these foreign businessmen had become Mexicans by the time the economy began to recuperate. There were not many new plutocrats, but at least a dozen became members of the haute bourgeoisie, and by the end of the Porfiriato they had been incorporated into the aristocracy (Ovando n.d.). In the traditional fashion, new domestic and foreign plutocrats became hacendados, but the main source of their wealth continued to be business and trade. From now until the end of the Porfiriato, significant members of the traditional aristocracy engaged in a diversified economy, thereby largely returning to the combined agrarian-trading-manufacturing strategy that prevailed among core and some centralized aristocrats during the last decades of Colonial rule. In the general configuration of the Mexican aristocracy, the *hacienda* loomed larger than it had for more than a century, as it constituted a significantly higher portion of the ruling class's wealth than it had, say, by the second half of the eighteenth century.

EUROPEAN INFLUENCES AND EXPRESSIVE TRANSFORMATIONS TRIGGERED BY INTERVENTION AND THE SECOND EMPIRE

If the First Empire was an opera buffa, the Second Empire was a tragicomedy. Monarchical sentiment had always been strong in Mexico, particularly among the clergy, European Creoles, the aristocracy, and even among the Mestizo middle class. Probably the great majority of Mexicans of European extraction approved of this form of government, and even though this population included many members of the ruling class and the richest people in the country, it was a minority of at best 10 percent of the total population. It was an unrealistic scheme, product of the still strong imperialistic bent of the great powers, and it succeeded for a while due largely to the involvement of the United States in its own civil war (Parkes 1938:251–56).

The foreign intervention coordinated by the French and the Second Empire resulted from a series of internal and external developments. As early as 1858, the conservative party's representatives in Europe had approached Napoleon III with the idea of finding a monarch for the Mexican throne. It should be noted at the onset that although the majority of Mexican aristocrats were monarchists, a healthy minority opposed the idea and particularly disliked the notion of an emperor not of Spanish extraction. The negotiations and search for an appropriate candidate lasted several years before Mexico acquired a new emperor (Priestley 1926:345–64). The external conditions for intervention hinged on the claims of England, France, Spain, and other nations for compensation for loss of property, investment, and lives of their nationals. For three decades the Mexican government had allowed foreign companies and private interests to operate in Mexico, conceding them land, mines, and commercial monopolies, often mortgaging some of the key resources of the country. By 1860, the nation's treasury was empty. The government was bankrupt, and the country's problems were compounded by the fact that in a still strong imperial period, the great powers could insist on their claims, real and spurious, with military force. The Mexican government could not pay its creditors, in short, and this inability led directly to the intervention of foreign troops demanding payments of more than thirty million pesos (Parkes 1938:250–56).

In October 1861, England, France, and Spain signed a treaty agreeing to send a joint expedition to Mexico. In December of that year, foreign men and material began to arrive in Veracruz, and a month later there were several thousand troops in Veracruz. The forces of Spain and England soon withdrew, for they could not agree on the claims presented to the Mexican government on the course of the intervention. The French were left alone, and in late April they moved to the interior. On May 5, 1862, they were defeated by an ill-equipped Mexican army before the gates of Puebla and forced to retreat to Orizaba. After more than seven months on the coast, the French army, by now reinforced by several thousand fresh troops, moved to the highlands and within a few months controlled most of central Mexico. By the middle of 1864, after two and a half years of campaigning, the French army controlled most of the country except the far north (Hall 1937:76–143).

In March 1864, Maximilian was informed that he had been over-whelmingly elected emperor of Mexico. He accepted in April; in May, he arrived in Veracruz; in June, he was in Mexico City and assumed the reins of government. Maximilian was a well-meaning gentle prince, with some ideas of how to reform the country. Despite his good intentions, nothing positive resulted of his three-year rule (Bauzet 1927:201–17).

Historians refer to the years following the empire as the period of reconstruction, that is, a gradual return to some orderly functioning of the government. Juárez and Lerdo de Tejada became presidents, and immediately thereafter Porfirio Díaz came to power (Priestley 1926:375–84). The country continued its economic recovery, but political events had little bearing on the reascendance of the Mexican aristocracy as a ruling class, except that the status quo continued. The French intervention and the Second Empire, however, had direct implications for the development of the superordinate class. These events provoked a wave of diffusion from Europe that redounded in an expressive renewal of the aristocracy. The renewal entailed changes in the extended domains of manners and material culture, including fashions, the household, and associated private and public sub-domains. There had been little French, English, and Italian influence in the expressive domains of the native aristocracy before the middle of the nineteenth century, but suddenly it seemed to open itself to non-Spanish European influences. The French intervention greatly enhanced their diffusion and the degree of their internalization. Again, though the configuring ideology of the aristocracy did not change appreciably, the expressive array was significantly altered and became less Spanish, changes that have marked this social class until the present.

Briefly, the expressive transformation—which required roughly thirty years, from the early 1860s to the early 1890s, to be internalized—may be detailed as follows. The French intervention firmly marked the return to the brilliant expressive life that had characterized the final decades of Colonial rule. The following fifty years had been characterized by the stagnation, if not decline, of those domains of expression centered in the household, the public image of aristocratic life, and the contributions of the ruling class to the intellectual life of the nation. Signs of recuperation appeared as early as 1855, but the establishment of the Second Empire was the impetus that expressively renewed the aristocracy and launched it into a period of high social and expressive excellence. Recuperation affected most cultural domains, and although the aristocracy never tried to challenge the political class, its control as a ruling class by the 1880s had become greater than ever.

Since its inception the aristocracy had been characterized by a concern with refinement, punctiliousness, and display. By the middle of the nineteenth century, in response to economic depression, refinement and private and public display had reached a low ebb. Significantly, however, the fact that Mexico after Independence became largely disconnected from Spain was instrumental in stirring up the waters in which the aristocracy had been stagnating. Thus, the decade of the 1860s represents a reintegration of aristocratic life with main-stream domains of European aristocratic expression, a renaissance that propelled the local ruling class from a provincial situation to a more central position in the overall expressive array of the European aristocracy (González Obregón 1911:72–109). Establishment of Maximilian's court in Mexico City became the first link to the European world of manners and material culture; it presented the aristocracy with several new expressive domains. French fashions and material innovations became predominant, increasingly augmented by similar diffusions from England and Italy. By the end of the Porfiriato, the expressive array of the aristocracy had many European flavors, some of which can be identified by nationalities but most of which were already part of the homogenized expressive life of European aristocracies. New expressive domains were created by diffusion from Europe and old domains were reinvigorated and acquired new configurations (Sodi-Pallares 1968:103–14).[2]

Behavioral inputs diffused from Europe "refined" the provincial and somewhat outmoded central expressive domains of the Mexican aristocracy. The French imperial adventure brought to Mexico many modernizing elements and social and expressive innovations; it also attracted a wide array of personnel in business and services that developed into a permanent connection with France after the demise of the Second Empire and that later extended to other European countries. As a result of this manifold process of diffusion, the following domains were most significantly affected: personal behavior and manners, dress and fashions, household decoration and display, city-country living, sports and entertainment, travel and public presentation, and intellectual and artistic participation. Reinterpreted and adapted to local conditions, diffused elements and complexes revitalized the Mexican aristocracy and brought it closer to the changing European model (José Luis Pérez de Salazar, pers. comm.).

Interpersonal behavior became more formal, less spontaneous, and regulated by rather strict rules of etiquette, a noticeable change from the traditional aristocratic norm of informality and bonhomie. The openness that had characterized the resident in city and *hacienda* living began to change toward a by-invitation-only pattern of casual and formal entertainment. The household experienced a reduction in domestic personnel and in the number of attached kinsmen. Personal behavior became affected, even prudish, and politeness in conversation replaced the frank, slightly raffish speech of Colonial society. Many usages and customs disappeared—for example, women smoking cigars in public, traditional games, and many items of the traditional cuisine—in favor of diffused ones from France and England. There was, one might say, an internalization of polite society, as a new world opened to a provincial aristocracy that had been virtually isolated from its roots for half a century. A bit insecure in this new world of manners and customs, Mexican aristocrats were fast learners and in a generation had acquired many domains of a foreign expressive array and regained their composure. The price aristocrats paid for this expressive change was an increase in social isolation and, despite their traditional penchant for ostentation, a stiltedness that did not endear them to other social classes. Until the Porfiriato, the aristocracy had been in close contact with the population at large, and ceremonial and self-serving as this rapport was, it had symbolically bridged social distance. Once this trait disappeared, the aristocracy lost an important asset.[3] One may characterize these significant changes in the expressive behavior and manners of the Mexican aristocracy as a Victorian phenomenon—a constriction of social life and repression of behavior due to a strict system of etiquette (Ovando n.d.).

Refinements in dress and fashionable apparel became more sophisticated during and after the Second Empire. Tailors, dressmakers, and dealers in men's and women's apparel from France established concerns in Mexico City and several of the most important cities. They introduced high fashion to the country, and members of the aristocracy became their most avid consumers, initiating a penchant for French attire for women and later of English attire for men. Other European fashions, particularly of Italian origin, enriched the domain of dressing before the turn of the century, and it remained unchanged until after the Second World War, when U.S. fashions began to affect the middle and upper classes of the country (Rábago n.d.).

Until the Second Empire, the urban mansions of the aristocracy, both in the capital and in provincial cities, had not undergone significant transformations since the end of Colonial rule. Some construction went on during the first two decades of the nineteenth century, but it did not appreciably alter the old patterns of Colonial architecture, particularly the building style of the second half of the eighteenth century. Aristocratic households were still almost invariably located in the center of cities, often within a few blocks of the central square. This basic pattern began to change after the Second Empire, and by the turn of the century aristocratic houses were being built away from the civic center or in suburban areas. In the case of Mexico City, for example, several exclusive neighborhoods were established on the periphery of the city, some of which until a generation ago concentrated a large number of aristocratic households. The Colonia Roma is the most noteworthy example, until it was overrun by the tremendous growth of

Mexico City. In such neighborhoods, a new, different type of architecture characterized the aristocratic household. Based on French and other architectural features, the *casa porfiriana,* as this architectural style came to be known, replaced the old Colonial residence. The *casa porfiriana* was a more functional house that accommodated the modernizing trends of the time (González Obregón 1937:76–175).

With architectural changes came a new concept of household decoration and display that was largely of modern European origin. The *casa porfiriana* demanded not only a new conception of interior decoration but an extensive array of modern furniture, ceramics, carpets, and a rather large roster of accessories such as curtains, tapestries, silver ornaments, silverware, china, and assorted bric-a-brac. The traditional decoration of the large, ample, and high-ceilinged houses, developed mostly during the last fifty years of Colonial rule, was rather simple and sparse, but characteristically dignified. The traditional aristocratic mansion created an ambiance of almost Japanese calmness and elegance, which came to contrast with the more elaborate modern aristocratic household by the end of the Porfiriato. Many of the European styles and famous manufacturers of furniture, porcelain, china, and other minor items of decoration in vogue at the time made their appearance in the Mexican aristocratic household. They blended well with some traditional patterns, particularly painting, Majolica, and silver ornaments. The modern household was significantly smaller but surrounded by gardens that the compactness of the central city had never allowed. It also had modern conveniences absent in the traditional household, including more functional kitchens and, by the turn of the century, bathrooms. By the beginning of the Mexican Revolution, the aristocratic household had been transformed, and perhaps in more than any other utilitarian or expressive domain, had internalized the modernizing trends of the time (Pérez de Salazar de Ovando n.d.). Combining European innovations with traditional patterns of decoration and display, the aristocratic household made the transition from a traditional to a modern world with dignity and elegance and without appreciable loss of time-honored values.[4]

Shortly after the Second Empire and undoubtedly spurred by the unprecedented growth of landed estates, country retreats became increasingly important. The acquisition of land proliferated into smaller *haciendas,* often relatively close to the cities, resulting in many country establishments. Another factor that contributed to the increasing importance of the *hacienda* was the conditioning of country mansions with many of the amenities of the city, not infrequently with a degree of elaboration and luxury approaching those of urban residences. By the turn of the century, *hacienda* residences were a far cry from the unfurnished drab barn reported by Calderón de la Barca (1978:205) two generations earlier (Nickel 1988:162–66). In addition, country re-reats, particularly around Mexico City, mushroomed into elaborate establishments within a few miles of civic centers, the majority of which had been engulfed by the spectacular growth of the cities by the late 1970s.

City life, too, changed noticeably in ways that may also be attributed to modernizing trends from Europe conditioned by the new emphasis on suburban living. To a great extent the traditional penchant for public display in religious and civic affairs continued unabated, but the last two decades of the century witnessed a retrenchment of the aristocracy from the social life of the cities. The seigneurial demeanor of the aristocracy began to falter, a phenomenon entailed by the increasing saliency of the political class and the slow rise of the middle class. Concomitantly, the aristocracy became more endogenous, though still retaining control of much of the religious ceremonial life of the city. Increasingly, and at the expense of public gatherings, the household became the hub of social activity, and a new kind of exclusivity now governed the life of most aristocrats, particularly in Mexico City. In provincial cities, however, the situation remained more traditional, due to the higher degree of control that aristocrats had in most realms of social and economic interaction. The glitter and pageantry of aristocratic display and public ostentation persisted, though in more exclusive and circumspect fashion: aristocrats were to be seen, their possessions were to be admired and envied, but without much of the former participation of the middle and lower classes. The political class in particular and the haute bourgeoisie in general were grudgingly accepted as partners in social interaction, as a support group if not necessarily as social equals (Ovando n.d.).

New sports, games, and other forms of entertainment arose in Mexico during and after the Second Empire. Most of them were adopted in the upper rungs of the stratification system, but they became more intimately associated with the aristocracy, and some of them became its exclusive preserve. Gambling had been a Creole passion, and it persisted after Independence, especially among the rich and the powerful (Zamora Plowes 1945, 2:299–327). By the turn of the century, public gambling had significantly decreased, probably because of the introduction of new card parlor games and the private gambling that went with it. By the middle of the nineteenth century the traditional horse games were no longer played or were rapidly disappearing. New spectator and participant sports were introduced from Europe, such as tennis and other ball games, and horse racing and equitation reinforced or redefined traditional horse sports. At the end of the period, polo was introduced, which together with equitation became the aristocratic sports par excellence. For a long time these two sports were exclusive domains of the aristocracy, which also played a leading role in the diffusion of other eventually popular games (Pedro Corsi, pers. comm.).

Until the French intervention, the Mexican aristocracy had been a rather insular society, lacking external diffusion and rarely traveling beyond the major areas of the country. Although a few aristocrats journeyed to Europe and the United States, intercity visiting and shuttling to and from faraway *haciendas* constituted the main form of traveling. During the Porfiriato, traveling became a main domain of expression for the aristocracy, and the most common destination was, of course, Europe, particularly France, Italy, and Britain (paradoxically Spain was less popular). Most aristocratic families soon became avid travelers to foreign lands. In the era of insularity, travel conferred an air of worldliness, even wisdom, and enhanced a person's public image, and these considerations undoubtedly intensified this expressive activity, which only aristocrats and plutocrats could indulge in. Traveling, however, had another expressive-utilitarian end, namely, contracting new and activating old ties to the European aristocracy—a link that had never diminished ideologically since many aristocratic families could rightly claim descent from titled nobles. Although individuals seldom bothered to activate titles, the knowledge of such connection was used expressively and pragmatically, and it was a source of social and emotional satisfaction. The Spanish source of aristocratic lineage was strengthened, but expressively Mexican aristocrats had acquired closer ties to France and Britain.

As global entities, Western aristocracies were never great bastions of intellectual realization. But for many centuries, aristocracies were virtually alone in enjoying the economic affluence and leisure time to dedicate to the pursuit of nonutilitarian activities. Thus, since early medieval times, they produced an inordinately high number of intellectuals. In fact, Western aristocracies managed to produce great scholars even during the nineteenth century. So too the scholars of the Mexican aristocracy from Gonzalo Gómez de Cervantes to Lucas Alamán extended into the economic depression and political turmoil of the first half of the nineteenth century. During the second half of the century, scholars such as Ramírez, García Icazbalceta, and Orozco y Berra contributed to the intellectual life of the nation, though perhaps not as significantly as British and French aristocrats contributed to the scientific life of their countries (Nutini, Roberts, and Cervantes 1982). The aristocracy did not produce artists, but many aristocrats were noteworthy during the Porfiriato as collectors and patrons. Last, but not least, aristocratic households had traditionally possessed the best libraries in the country, and several important collections were established during the last fifty years of Colonial rule. In the three decades before the Mexican Revolution, large and distinguished collections of Mexican and European books on literature, history, religion, and science were again amassed by aristocrats. Some of these collections rest even still in the hands of aristocratic descendants (Alfonso Cervantes Anaya, pers. comm.).

The period beginning with the Second Empire undoubtedly marked an expressive renaissance for the Mexican aristocracy, transforming many domains of the array into a coherent and modern ensemble. By the end of the Porfiriato, the aristocracy had been transformed from a rather provincial and insular class into a modern extension of the western European aristocracy. Thus the Mexican aristocracy experienced embourgeoisement, that is, the necessary aristocratic adaptations to an increasingly democratic society and plutocratic economic control.

The Porfiriato: Terminal Florescence (1876–1910)

The Díaz dictatorship was a fairly self-contained period of Mexican history.[5] It was a period of industrialization, during which railroads were built and foreign companies began the exploitation of mining and oil reserves. It was also therefore a time of rapid change and modernization; in the thirty-five years of the Díaz regime, Mexico underwent a transformation greater than any it would see the following thirty-five years. Sociopolitically, however, the Porfiriato is a continuation of the period that began shortly after Independence, when the basic accommodations of the ruling and political classes were structured. Fundamentally, no changes in this area took place during the Porfiriato; the status quo continued to work, but the industrial and modernizing transformation it provoked culminated in the Mexican Revolution. The relative prosperity of the country and the unprecedented extent of its landed estates made the aristocracy as a ruling class ever more economically powerful. But although the aristocracy continued to exercise seigneurial control of the *hacienda* and its environs, its social preeminence did not go unchallenged in the cities by the haute bourgeoisie, and it no longer received the undisputed acquiescence of the middle classes.

THE POLITICAL STATUS QUO, ECONOMIC GROWTH, AND MODERNIZATION

From the beginning of Porfirio Díaz's first presidency, it was clear that he meant to stay in power at any cost. He was able to remain in power for thirty-four years because of his ability to promote industrialization, his shrewd use of political power, and his willingness to allow the ruling class unprecedented control of economic affairs. His policy of *pan o palo* (bread or the club) worked largely because many of his measures to industrialize the country created new jobs for the urban working classes and brought prosperity to the small middle class. What he did not do was to improve the lot of the great majority of the country's population: the Indians and transitional Indian-Mestizo sectors in *haciendas,* in subsistence communities, and in various large-scale agrarian enterprises. On the whole, the Porfiriato created an ambiance of well-being and an illusion that the country was progressing inevitably toward an ultimately just society. Science and modernization would transform Mexico into a prosperous state; the sacrifices of the masses were a necessary rough patch on the road to material justice for all. The progress of the country was measured by the production of mines and factories, by the increment of means of communication, and by the general material modernization of the country. Meanwhile the majority of the country's population was tied to an agrarian society in which numbers, in land and peons, rather than efficiency generated extreme wealth for a tiny minority of the country's population (Parkes 1938:299–310). This fundamental compact structured the unspoken alliance between the aristocratic ruling class and the political class. The alliance worked for more than a generation because both allies straddled the spectrum of economic interest, namely, a new class of plutocratic merchants and manufacturers in the cities and politicians turned *hacendados* in the country. Ultimately, the alliance collapsed when sufficient pressure was brought to bear on the alliance by the ever more politically conscious and educated middle classes, a pressure that provoked in turn more oppressive measures leading to open revolt and the birth of a new political class.

Mexico's political class until the Mexican Revolution was not monolithic. The political class during the Porfiriato was a fractious entity, encompassing regional interests and divergent political orientations that required the rather outstanding political acumen of Porfirio Díaz to control. Though political dissension often arose, it was put down with minimal disruption in the system. In fact, local uprisings became rather common during the last ten years of the dictatorship, but they never spread to a state or national level, and they were easily defused. "Divide and conquer" was the basic political strategy of Porfirio Díaz, and one of his favorite ploys was to foment friction between state and federal officials, especially governors and generals, so that no official would acquire inordinate control beyond the region. It was an efficient system of maintaining law and order, but one that operated at the expense of the Indians and peasants who suffered exploitation and indignity at the hands of the federal army-police (Turner 1914:143–87).

True to their pattern since Independence, aristocrats did not participate directly in the political life of the nation in any significant number. Although they controlled local politics and thoroughly dominated the regions where their *haciendas* were located, they did so indirectly, for they rarely held political office. Their control must be understood as the weight of centuries of domination as a ruling class and their ability to maneuver as a social class, abetted by the economic aspirations of the political, upwardly mobile middle class, for which there was no other model. Concomitantly, the middle class of merchants, small manufacturers, professionals, and traders, as long as they benefited from the general prosperity of the country, were willing to accept the high-handedness and tight control of the government. Completing the picture, the plutocratic haute bourgeoisie of finance and manufacturing and the great foreign interests operating with approval of the government significantly contributed to the economic stability of the country (Thompson 1939:76–112).

How exactly did the uneasy alliance of the ruling class and political class operate, and what were its social and economic consequences? First, by the last two decades of the nineteenth century the ruling class of Mexico was constituted by the landed aristocracy and a rich plutocracy, the haute bourgeoisie, of bankers, manufacturers, and large-scale merchants, a considerable number of whom were of foreign extraction. This small but powerful sector of the ruling class held diversified economic interests throughout the country and operated in rather close social interaction with the aristocracy. As the most upwardly mobile group in the upper reaches of the stratification system and many of its members vying for aristocratic recognition, this plutocratic sector invariably supported the economic status quo of the landed aristocracy. Moreover, many plutocrats acquired land, a process that brought them closer to the aristocracy (Flandrau 1908:98–106). Regardless of social considerations, the aristocracy and plutocracy constituted the two main pillars of the ruling class and a force that the political class could not easily antagonize or confront at the national, state, and local levels.

Second, the political class during the Porfiriato was small, perhaps smaller than the combined aristocratic-plutocratic ruling class. Whereas the Porfirian bureaucracy kept expanding, given the economic growth of the country and of the federal and state administrations, the holders of effective political power certainly numbered fewer than a thousand, from Porfirio Díaz to the least important regional *jefes políticos*. At the local and state levels, politicians became landowners, some even *hacendados* on a large scale. It was to the advantage of these politicians turned landowners to support the economic interests of aristocratic *hacendados,* and even to acquiesce to their demands when they meddled in political affairs. At the national, federal level, by contrast, the situation was more fluid, but roughly the same conditions and ambiance of interaction obtained. The main distinctions were that the social distance between aristocrats and politicians was smaller than in regional environments and that the national politicians were more educated and attuned to the niceties of behavior. The political class at this level included all members of the cabinet, generals of the army, assorted high bureaucrats, and state governors, who had, since Independence, almost always been nominated or sanctioned by the president of the Republic. Particularly during the second half of the Porfiriato, many of these high-ranking politicians were businessmen and landowners. They had drawn increasingly closer to the aristocracy and its immediate circle of plutocrats, and a number of them were vying for aristocratic recognition (Parkes 1938:306–10). The ruling class of aristocrats and high-ranking plutocrats gave Porfirio Díaz his due, recognizing the necessary role he was playing in maintaining the status quo, but they never made any effort to extend social recognition to him or to his network of associates and protégés. The dictator reciprocated by regarding the ruling class with olympian condescension, by regarding their social games as below his exalted position, but he demonstrated a healthy respect for their power as a ruling class. Thus, at the highest level, both sides acknowledged that, despite social and behavioral differences, the survival of the system depended on toleration of and acquiescence to the needs and desires of all concerned (Ovando n.d.).

Third, the general prosperity of the country generated by industrialization, the expansion of trade, the construction of railroads, and the exploitation of foreign companies also benefited the small middle class and a sizable sector of the urban proletariat—roughly 20 percent of the population that, comparatively speaking, may be regarded as the privileged classes. The middle classes, though satisfied with their economic prosperity, were not happy with the political monopoly of the political class and resented the haughty social demeanor of aristocrats and plutocrats. By the last decade of the Porfiriato, the middle classes, particularly intellectuals, were restless and discontented, primarily because of their lack of political participation. Most of the actors in the uprisings of this period were peasants, but they had the unspoken support of the middle class and often received leadership from dedicated revolutionaries. In the end, the regime was brought down by a combination of peasant activism and the willingness of the middle classes to sacrifice a measure of their economic well-being for the sake of the more equitable distribution of political power that democracy would bring. This view, it should be noted, was shared by some progressive *hacendados,* who as early as 1905, three decades before the massive land reform of Lázaro Cárdenas, divested themselves of as much as half of the lands they owned (Pérez de Salazar n.d.).

Everything politically, economically, or socially noteworthy that affected the Mexican aristocracy during the Porfiriato had its roots in the previous period, except perhaps the pacification of northern Mexico, mostly in the state of Sonora and parts of the states of Sinaloa, Chihuahua, and Durango. Several Indian groups in this vast area had never been brought under control, and communities of Yaquis, Mayos,

Coras, and other Indian groups suffered the painful, sometimes cruel, process of incorporation. Most significantly, much fertile land became available to local *hacendados* and Mestizo farmers, as the 1856 laws pertaining to communally owned property were reactivated. The northern *hacienda* experienced unprecedented affluence, for the lands expropriated from the Indians, particularly in Sonora, were very fertile and appropriate for intensive cultivation. By the late 1880s, similar measures had been taken in the southern states of the country, particularly Yucatán, and in extension and the quality of arable lands, the *hacienda* had reached its zenith (Parkes 1938:295–303).

It is difficult to assess the accomplishments and historical implications of the Díaz dictatorship. That it was a rather benevolent dictatorship most historians agree. They might also agree that he was not directly responsible for much of the oppression and injustice that occurred in the name of law and order. In terms of the national interest, the biggest mistake Díaz made was to allow foreigners to dominate several aspects of the economy. From the humane standpoint, meanwhile, he could have curtailed the abuses and exploitation at all levels of society. These failings notwithstanding, Díaz's regime did introduce the country to the machine age and create the infrastructure for a modern state. This transformation could no doubt have been achieved by less repressive measures, but the Porfiriato was less violent and destructive than most other dictatorships in Latin America, many of which produced no positive results. The Mexican Revolution was the first popular revolution of the twentieth century, which explains the ambivalent judgment that history has passed on the Díaz dictatorship.

THE *HACIENDA* AS THE LAST BASTION OF ARISTOCRATIC SEIGNEURIALISM

As a consequence of the Reform Laws of 1856, the subsequent twenty years witnessed unprecedented growth of the *hacienda* system, but it was not until the onset of the Díaz regime that the *hacienda* as a seigneurial estate reached its zenith. By the turn of the century, enormous landed estates dotted the countryside, particularly in the north, where a single *hacienda* might encompass millions of hectares. Under the protective mantle of the Porfiriato, *hacendados* had undisputed control of the regions where their landed estates were located, including the available labor force, water, and other agrarian resources. Un-

questionably, then, the aristocratic landowners were the greatest beneficiaries of the *pax porfiriana*, which allowed them to run their *haciendas*,
dominate the economic and social ambiance of the towns and cities of
the region, and exploit the resources of the land with the connivance of
state and local authorities. In some regions, the *hacendados* directly
participated in state and municipal politics, either by holding office or
by supporting candidates unconditionally indebted to them. In the
confines of the *haciendas*, landed aristocrats exercised virtual seigneurial
authority, including judicial, administrative, and social control, over
the labor force of Indians and Mestizos.

The *haciendas* varied greatly according to size, the quality of the
land, access to water, and the type of agrarian enterprises. The largest
haciendas were in northern Mexico and in the lowlands of the Gulf of
Mexico, where most of the great plantations were to be found. In
central Mexico (from Oaxaca to Zacatecas), the *haciendas* were smaller,
generally more fragmented, but more valuable, given the better quality of the soil, accessibility to market towns, and irrigation. An extension of 100,000 hectares within 150 miles from Mexico City or
Guadalajara was generally more valuable than 1,000,000 hectares in
Chihuahua or Coahuila. Indeed, there were moderately small *haciendas*,
10,000 to 20,000 hectares, in the states of Mexico, Puebla, and
Morelos that were among the most valuable in the land because of
irrigation, the intensity of cultivation, and the ample labor force. The
labor force was a critical factor accounting for much of the value of
haciendas, particularly in areas where the population was sparse. The
population of the country grew from roughly seven million in 1850 to
fourteen million in 1910, contributing greatly to the growth of the
hacienda. Still, *hacendados* had to compete for the labor force with each
other and not infrequently with the more efficiently cultivated *ranchos*
of Mestizo farmers (Nickel 1988:104–23).

Granted significant variations, the *hacienda* was generally an inefficient, land- and labor-intensive system of production. Undoubtedly,
the most efficient *haciendas* were those dedicated to the cultivation of
sugarcane, coffee, ixtle, and other specialized crops, while the most
inefficient were those dedicated exclusively to cultivating grain and
raising livestock. The former employed modern machinery and had
achieved some mechanization, while the latter still used the traditional
technology of the early nineteenth century. There were, of course,
progressive *hacendados* who strived for efficiency by the introduction of

modern machinery and means of production, but most of them relied mostly on traditional methods, a large labor force, and extensive but wasteful exploitation. The richest *hacendado* combined extensive land and labor with the best of modern technology, while the average great landowner derived sufficient income to satisfy his aristocratic way of life simply through the labor-intensive exploitation of tens of thousands of hectares (Pérez de Salazar n.d.).

The general industrialization of Mexico and the rather extensive network of railroads that had been established by the turn of the century affected the modernization of the *hacienda* and the distribution of its products. The railroad system, however, was a blessing that facilitated the transportation and distribution of agricultural products and overall enhanced the productivity of the *hacienda*. Grain and livestock *haciendas* were the most conservative, as we have seen, and relatively few technological innovations were introduced during the Porfiriato, while those engaged in the production of nonstaples—including *pulque,* coffee, cotton, tobacco, and so on—did modernize considerably, in order to compete successfully in the domestic and foreign markets. This dichotomy cannot be explained in terms of conservative and progressive *hacendados,* but rather in the very nature of the specialized crops: Some were sufficiently productive to satisfy the *hacendado*'s lifestyle without the introduction of new technology, while others required the introduction of modern machinery in order to stay productive. *Haciendas* that produced nonstaple, more commercial crops may be characterized as plantations, and their workers and peons were better off economically than laborers on traditional *haciendas* (Couturier 1968).

During the Porfiriato, *hacendados* continued to recruit labor as they had for more than two hundred years: primarily through debt peonage, sharecropping, contract labor, and the employment of technical and administrative personnel. Sharecropping and contract labor were fairly widespread practices, particularly in areas of low population density, such as in the north and coastal areas. The bulk of the *hacienda*'s labor force was recruited through several forms of debt peonage, which varied from region to region. Whatever the initial and continuing amounts of the debt and the reasons for the indenture, the intent of the *hacendados* was to maintain a labor force permanently tied to the land. The peons attracted and retained in this fashion were mostly Indians, and the system worked because of their dire economic necessity and lack of effective labor protection (Nickel 1988:153–58). This process reached a peak at the end of the Porfiriato, with rather drastic consequences for Indian ethnicity and the growth of a modern Mestizo nationality: uprooted from their ancestral communities, Indians accelerated the process of mestizoization that had been gathering momentum since Independence.

The technical and administrative personnel of the *hacienda* were different matters altogether. Technical personnel, almost exclusively on the plantation-type *haciendas* engaged in the production of nonstaple crops, were recruited in a modern fashion, and on the whole they were not subjected to the abuses inflicted on the peons. These workers were Mestizos who were part of the specialized labor force that had developed as the result of Mexico's industrialization and the building of the first railroads in the late 1860s. Administrative personnel included a variety of nonhomogeneous positions ranging from the administrator of the *hacienda* and foremen to gang leaders (*caporales, cuadrilleros*) and clerical people. With the exception of the administrator, most of these positions were again filled by Mestizos of different extractions, constituting a body of personnel closely associated with the *hacendado* (*personal de confianza*) and recruited by him and the administrator on the basis of *compadrazgo* and long-standing acquaintance. The administrator occupied a crucial position in the organization of the *hacienda,* quite often he was foreign, most likely a Spaniard, and not infrequently a friend or a poor relative of the *hacendado*. As the executive officer in charge of the labor force, planning and organizing production and distribution, and administering the *hacienda* as a socioeconomic entity, the administrator was a powerful figure with ample opportunity to enrich himself by abusing his powers (Ovando n.d.). The possibilities for perfidy multiplied when, as occasionally happened, an administrator became a partner in the *hacienda* operations. Perhaps on most *haciendas* throughout the country the authoritarian, somewhat despotic image of the administrator contrasted rather sharply with that of the benevolent, paternalistic *hacendado,* who, as the good lord, was concerned for the welfare of his workers and honored his ritual kinship obligations. Whether this vision of the patron-peon relationship was to any significant extent realized throughout the country is difficult to ascertain.

The stereotypical image of the *hacendado* dating to the seventeenth century is that of the absentee landlord. From the beginning of the system until its demise after the Mexican Revolution, *hacendados* never lived most of the time on the *hacienda,* but they kept in close touch with this expressive and economic cornerstone of aristocratic life. The physical presence in the *hacienda* of the owner, his family, and his large retinues of kinsmen and friends varied throughout the several Colonial and Republican periods in response to economic conditions. At no time, however, was the *hacienda* so disregarded and physically abandoned by aristocrats as the twentieth-century literature on the subject would lead us to believe. The portrayal of the *hacendado* and his family living in Paris, London, or New York, or permanently enfranchised in Mexico City or any of the large provincial cities, utterly oblivious to the affairs of the *hacienda,* is simply false. That most *hacendados* spent a majority of their time in Mexico City or provincial cities is true, but it is doubtful that more than a third of them had been to Europe, let alone lived in any of the favored European capitals for extended periods of time. Reliable ethnographic information suggests that most *hacendados,* perhaps the great majority, kept in close touch with the land, visited the *hacienda* two or three times a year, and spent an average of two and a half months of the year in the country. Moreover, at least 15 percent of the *hacendados* and their families spent more time in the country than in their urban residences, particularly when landed estates were within a hundred miles of the city (Ovando n.d.). Indeed, at no period in the *hacienda*'s existence was the city-country axis more balanced than during the Porfiriato, which reflected both the changing socioeconomic conditions of the time and the improvements in transportation and communication. On the eve of the Mexican Revolution, the landed aristocracy was still based primarily in the city, but country living was looming significantly more important.

An integrated socioeconomic, religious, and even political system, almost a state within a state, the *hacienda* was the last surviving manifestation of an agrarian social system that extended from Feudalism to seigneurialism. Having replaced the *encomienda* as the main socioeconomic institution of the aristocratic ruling class, the *hacienda* was, practically if not officially, a seigneurial system made possible by ethnic differences and the peripheral evolutionary development of a Colonial society. The *hacendado* was the lord of the land, his wishes were undisputed, and through a stern administrative apparatus his will was enforced: the *hacienda* had its own system of justice, its own police force, and through these mechanisms it enforced its own standards (Kaerger 1901). The control of the *hacendado* over the land's resources and the labor force was always high, but, ironically, it reached a peak after Independence. The Spanish Crown's policy of controlling the ruling class as tightly as possible had furnished Indian communities with a modicum of protection against excessive exploitation by the *hacendados*. This protection disappeared when Mexico became a federal republic. After nearly a century of Republican life, the landed aristocracy, despite democratization in other areas of the body politic, enjoyed more seigneurial control over its estates than it had during Colonial times. This effect evidently would not have occurred without the connivance of the political class, which during Colonial rule had remained separate from the ruling class and somewhat antagonistic to its economic interests.

The social structure of the *hacienda* encompassed all personnel associated with the estate, from *acasillados* and contract laborers to the administrator and owner, all bound by clearly defined rights and obligations. The *hacendado,* the administrator, and some of his key personnel had many rights and few obligations; the peons, of course, had no power to redress the balance. The peons, particularly the *acasillados,* were obliged to pay police duties, serve periodically in the *hacendado*'s country and city residences, meet the requirements of the social and religious organization of the estate, and so on. Onerous duties notwithstanding, the *hacienda* represented a measure of security and stability for the *acasillados,* and to some extent for contract laborers, that, given the conditions of the countryside at the time, they could not find in their native communities. Many of the *acasillados* had been residents of the *hacienda* for generations and knew no other home. On the positive side, the peons, especially those of Indian extraction, brought to the *hacienda* much of their village culture, including traditional religious practices, kinship and ritual kinship practices, and their ritual and ceremonial life became centered in the *capilla*—chapel, a prominent structure of the landed establishment—much as it had been in the village church. The paternalistic concerns of the *hacendado* and his family and the asymmetrical ritual kinship ties that bound them to some of the peons functioned as symbolic links to temper some of the more blatant inequalities of the system. The *hacendado* demanded unquestioning loyalty from his peons and administrative personnel, and thanks to the traditional hierarchical fashion of Indian society, he apparently received it from the former (Zamora Plowes 1945, 1:217–41).

The dominion of the *hacendado* was not confined to the landed estate he controlled but extended to the region in which the estate was located, including towns and villages. This ripple effect was particularly strong when several estates owned by a single *hacendado* or his family dominated the region, as was often the case in north and some areas of central Mexico. The autarchic dominion of the *hacendado* over his estates was, of course, not exercised in the region dominated by the *hacienda*, but one can speak of an extended seigneurial domain by virtue of the power and influence of the *hacendado* in areas of public justice, political office, and economic activities. The more traditional *haciendas*, dominating the production of staple crops for the regional market, exercised more control over the region than the modernizing *haciendas*, which were geared mostly to the national and international markets. There are significant seigneurial considerations associated with the *hacendado*'s hegemony over the region, extending with diminishing intensity to the city where he was enfranchised. He was undoubtedly the most prominent personage in the region, and he enhanced his prominence by contracting multiple ties of patronage and ritual kinship and by sponsoring religious and civil festivities in the agricultural and commercial centers (Pérez de Salazar n.d.). Homage alone accrued to the *hacendado* by virtue of these multiple involvements, and homage was in fact very important in upholding his image as an aristocratic leader and justifying the expenses of his involvements. In short, the autarchy that he exercised in his landed domains and the homage he received from the peoples of the region made the Porfirian *hacendado* the center of one of the last seigneurial systems in the long history of Western stratification.

The *hacienda* also reached a zenith of expressive activity during the last decade of the Porfiriato, fueled by the economic well-being and the control over the agrarian labor force that had prevailed during the last three decades of the nineteenth century. The *hacienda* mansion was conditioned as it had probably never been before, preparing it for permanent living and entertaining on a large and lavish scale. The country mansion was outfitted with elegant furniture, imported carpets and tapestries, artwork, fine china and silverware, and all the paraphernalia of the aristocratic household. The large *haciendas* became enormous establishments with many dozens of rooms, including large halls and living rooms, elaborate dining rooms, billiard and play rooms, many well-appointed guest bedrooms, and other amenities. The *hacienda* mansion became an elegant and elaborate residence, a worthy rival, in a less formal and rigid fashion, to the city mansion, reflecting a noticeable shift from the traditional urban orientation of the landed aristocracy. There was, of course, significant regional variation, depending on the size and economic productivity of the *hacienda,* but the foregoing remarks depict an often realized model to which aristocrats of smaller landed estates aspired (Nickel 1988:163–66).

THE THIRD RENEWAL (1850–1900) AND CLASS STRATIFICATION

Some thirty years after Mexican Independence was a time of trial, instability, and economic decline. These conditions affected the entire spectrum of the stratification system, but none more so than the tiny minority at the top and the vast majority at the bottom: the aristocracy's economic power was diminished, and its control of the country as a ruling class was challenged by a nascent political class of Mestizo-Creole origin; meanwhile, the Indian population became more vulnerable to exploitation in their new egalitarian status in the new republic. Independence also slowed the development of class stratification and class consciousness, and it is not until the twentieth century that the phenomenon achieves maturity. Moreover, the aristocracy, though deprived of its minimal privileges as members of the superordinate estate and no longer enjoying the protection of the Spanish Crown, successfully accommodated to the exigencies of the new order. After the middle of the century, the overall situation changed, and conditions improved steadily until the Mexican Revolution and the demise of the aristocracy as a ruling class. As in the case of the second renewal, the fundamental socioexpressive orientations of the aristocracy did not change, though they had to be adapted to new constraints. Neither was the basic principle of upward mobility appreciably modified.

By 1850, the aristocracy was smaller than it had been since the sixteenth century, probably no more than nine hundred families. Downward mobility was significant, particularly among peripheral aristocrats in the far north and the far south, a trend that did not reverse until the onset of the Porfiriato and the incorporation of plutocratic magnates who had risen between Independence and the French intervention. The core and center of the aristocracy were enfranchised in Mexico City and in the most important cities from Guadalajara to Oaxaca. The aristocracy experienced fission to the extent that several important cities traditionally associated with large-scale landed enterprises became replicas of Mexico City as centers of aristocratic activity. The appeal of the capital nonetheless persisted as a centralizing feature of the Colonial past that never waned (Nutini, Roberts, and Cervantes 1982).

In terms of upward mobility, the period between Independence and the middle of the century was virtually static, as no new great fortunes of plutocratic extraction were made and the haute bourgeoisie became much smaller and much less wealthy and influential than it had been in the first decade of the nineteenth century. From midcentury onward, the haute bourgeoisie once more became prominent and vied for aristocratic recognition. A few plutocratic magnates were accepted into the ranks of the aristocracy before the French intervention, in greater numbers thereafter, and by the turn of the century many were solidly placed. Extrapolation from oral histories and extensive genealogical information indicates that roughly two hundred families successfully made the transition. Thus, by the end of the Porfiriato the strength of the Mexican aristocracy was about eleven hundred families. The second half of the nineteenth century witnessed almost no aristocratic downward mobility, due to the period's economic affluence and increasing social retrenchment, but the aperture to plutocratic newcomers may be explained on expressive grounds; the new wealth of the haute bourgeoisie made the most outstanding members of this class desirable allies (Ovando n.d.).

The ethnic composition and social extraction of the plutocratic magnates that became aristocrats throughout the third renewal were at once more varied and more restricted than in the two previous renewals. In Colonial times, throughout the first and second renewals, the Creole aristocracy was not exclusively composed of individuals of pure Spanish ancestry. Since the sixteenth century the aristocracy had included Mestizo elements, which became more noticeable in the eighteenth century. With Independence, however, this Mestizo element nearly disappeared. Whatever Mestizo somatic elements had been present were Europeanized throughout the nineteenth century, and plutocratic recruits throughout this period were almost invariably of European extraction. The transition to Republican life, then, did not put an end to ethnic discrimination and racial exclusivity in the uppermost sectors of the stratification system, but indeed exacerbated them. More than ever the Mexican aristocracy became an endogenous class. Threatened by or in contention with the Mestizo political class, and symbolically and to some extent physically distanced from Spain, aristocrats insisted on endogamous marriages and reinforced European alliances.

The upwardly mobile personnel of the third renewal included three groups. The first group was composed of Spaniards who had escaped the expulsion from Mexico, their sons, and others who migrated from Spain or its former colonies after the initial xenophobia had died down. Between the 1840s and 1860s, fortunes were made by members of this group, and they became prime candidates for aristocratic incorporation. Most of these fortunes were made in trade, some in manufacturing, but almost all led to the acquisition of landed estates. The second group boasted foreigners, primarily English and French, who had become enfranchised in many Mexican cities in the pursuit of trading, manufacturing, and banking activities during the four decades after Independence. This group included several highly placed personnel who came to Mexico with Maximilian and during the French intervention. Many second-generation families of this group became rich and influential by the onset of the Porfiriato, and a significant number, some in the capital but mostly in provincial cities, acquired aristocratic status. The third group included exclusively members of traditional, mostly provincial families of Spanish-Creole extraction who had accumulated land and urban property after two generations of independent life (Whetten 1972).

In principle, the ideology and worldview of the Mexican aristocracy have not changed since the Spanish Conquest. But they have adapted to the changing socioeconomic and political conditions of the country. Republican life imposed new constraints that essentially deprived the aristocracy of certain privileges entailed by the estate system that came to an end in 1821. The process of embourgeoisement became perhaps the most significant factor in the adaptation of the aristocracy to an increasingly more democratic society. Not even the great economic affluence that the aristocracy enjoyed during the Porfiriato compensated for the loss of ceremonial standing and intrinsic homage and respect that had accrued to them under the estate system. Only in the protective environment of their landed estates could the ambiance of bygone times be maintained—hence the increased expressive importance of the *hacienda*. In testimony to this adaptive strategy, only a handful of aristocrats after 1830 bothered to reactivate the titles of nobility to which many families in Mexico were entitled, for most aristocrats knew—and wished to avoid—the criticism and adverse consequences that such an action would elicit from the political class and educated segment of the middle class. The mere knowledge that a title belonged in the family satisfied pride in lineage and established aristocratic standing in the group. Even terms of address, such as count or knight of one of the military orders, had disappeared in most endogenous contexts of the aristocracy (Rábago n.d.).

Throughout the second renewal, the plutocrats who became aristocrats significantly augmented the economic horizons of the ruling class by demonstrating that a combined agrarian-business strategy generated greater wealth than the traditional landed strategy of the aristocracy. No such input took place throughout the third renewal, for to a considerable extent the aristocracy had been pursuing this strategy since the last decades of the eighteenth century. The third renewal entailed a smaller acculturative component than the second renewal, and I suggest the following explanation. By the end of the nineteenth century, the European haute bourgeoisie, already the richest class in society, was asserting itself independently from the aristocracy and was creating its own expressive standards that significantly influenced the aristocracy. The case differed in Mexico, whose peripheral position had been more constrained by isolation from Europe. The Mexican aristocracy, therefore, vis-à-vis the haute bourgeoisie, was significantly more dominant than in Europe (Weckmann 1983, 2:419–32). Aristocrats still thoroughly dominated expression, lacked social rivals, and experienced no challenge to their behavioral standards. The aristocracy was still wealthy and powerful and could accept or reject upwardly mobile candidates without adverse consequences.

To conclude with a general outline of the stratification system of Mexico at the end of the Porfiriato: The main aspects of the evolution of class stratification throughout the nineteenth century were the elimination of the last vestiges of estate privilege, the abolition of Indian tribute, and the institution of equality before the law for all Mexicans. In the new republic, all citizens, from Indian to aristocrat, possessed equal rights. From the beginning, Mexico adopted the most advanced and liberal models of Republican government, and, de jure, the country was at the forefront of progress. De facto, much of Mexico remained seigneurial, and the development of class consciousness proceeded slowly and painfully. But the seeds of class stratification had been planted in the late Colonial period, and continuity governed the transition to Republican life, which was marked by the significant diminution of ethnic components in the classes that came into being. In sociological terms, this means that the denotation and connotation of terms such as *Creole* and *Mestizo* changed significantly, while terms such as *peninsular* and the various *castas* ceased to exist as meaningful categories.

The following description roughly outlines class stratification in Mexico ninety years after Independence. At the top was a minuscule aristocracy of perhaps 1,100 families, less than 10,000 people, in firm control of the agrarian sector of the country. Just below, and in close alliance with the *hacendados,* was a haute bourgeoisie of traders, merchants, manufacturers, and bankers controlling much of the non-agrarian wealth of the nation. This group numbered perhaps 20,000 people, enfranchised in the main cities of the country. The political class is difficult to conceptualize; it constituted a sort of very small "upper-middle class," a subsection of the haute bourgeoisie of businessmen and landowners, and, from the beginning of Republican times, it included a huge number of lawyers. The bourgeoisie, or the middle classes, if you will, had increased several times after Independence and constituted perhaps 12 percent of the total population, or close to two million people. The bourgeoisie was an urban middle class of professionals, retailers, traders, and some specialized craftsmen that constituted the core and economic life of cities and towns throughout the country. Below these categories, one can speak only of incipient classes, in which ethnicity continued to play a determinant role and class consciousness was minimal or nonexistent. But one can speak of an urban proletariat (a mixture of lower-middle and upper-lower classes in modern sociological parlance), Mestizo peasants, Mestizo *acasillados,* Indian *acasillados,* transitional Indian communities, and traditional Indian communities. By the end of the Porfiriato, the urban proletariat was groping for class consciousness, though nothing of the sort can be detected in the social groups below it. Indeed, in the various Mestizo and Indian populations in rural Mexico the situation was not perceptibly more fluid than it had been at the end of Colonial rule. On the *haciendas,* as I have indicated, the situation was actually less fluid, and the same can be said for Indian communities. It is more difficult to reconstruct the stratification of the country in 1910 than in the years leading to Independence, largely because the middle sectors had become more fluid while the lower sectors had hardened. However, in assessing the global stratification system on the eve of the Mexican Revolution, one must consider that ethnic considerations had ebbed, old categories had become obsolete, and clear-cut sectors no longer existed.

From its inception, as embodied in the conquistadors, to its maturity, as embodied in the *hacendado* class during the Porfiriato, the Mexican aristocracy was never challenged as a social class. But its luster and ceremonial functions diminished throughout the nineteenth century as a result of the democratization of society. As a ruling class, the aristocracy was as powerful as it had ever been, given the growth of the population from 6.5 million in 1810 to more than 14 million in 1910. Even though the aristocracy never became a political class and few of its members directly participated in politics, the aristocracy at the end of the Porfiriato had reached a new peak of power and control. Having reached such heights, the decline of the aristocracy after the Mexican Revolution was more dramatic than the slower, less drastic decline of most Western aristocracies after the demise of the ancien régime.

CHAPTER 8

The Twentieth Century: Political Obliteration, Economic Decline, and Expressive Survival

The Mexican Revolution of 1910 was disastrous for the aristocracy, and it has never recuperated. In less than three generations, from an undisputed position as the ruling class of the country, the aristocracy was reduced to a marginal social class. Its overthrow as a ruling class was swift; by the end of the armed phase of the revolution, the aristocracy no longer existed at the national level, though it retained a modicum of influence at the state and local levels until the mid-1930s. The decisive economic blow was the massive land reform of 1934, which reduced most of the aristocracy to an upper-middle-class standard of living. Socially, however, aristocrats were prominent until the 1970s, and they provided the expressive model for the new plutocracy that came into being. Within the wider context of the haute bourgeoisie, including the plutocracy and political sector, having largely lost its social and expressive raison d'être, the aristocracy survived until today in a sort of underground fashion.

Armed Phase of the Mexican Revolution and Its Aftermath (1910–34)

The Mexican Revolution of 1910 was the first massive popular revolt of the twentieth century. It was a violent and bloody confrontation— more than a million people lost their lives—and only after ten years did the country begin slowly to return to normalcy. The revolution utterly transformed the political and economic landscapes of the country within two generations, ushering Mexico to the brink of modern industrialization. The economic catalyst of the revolution was land reform, and the ideological catalyst was Indianism, or the search for roots in the Indian past. There were actually two movements in this transformation: the purely political action of middle-class Mexicans pressing for political liberalization and the peasant revolt, first in the states of Sonora and Morelos, then spreading through much of the country (Parkes 1938:126–42). It took more than twenty years for a political class to emerge, and not until the presidency of Lázaro Cárdenas was the agrarian reform thoroughly implemented.

MILITARY STRUGGLE AND THE TRANSFORMATION OF THE COUNTRY

The history of the Mexican Revolution has been written many times, and I need not repeat even the most salient events. What follows is a bare outline of occurrences within which to place the fall of the aristocracy as a ruling class. The 1910 Revolution has been incorrectly characterized as a transformation in which the country's Mestizo political class abandoned its long-standing alliance with the traditional ruling class, the *hacendados,* and allied itself with the lower elements of the old order, the peons on the *haciendas* and the Indians in Indian communities. This misinterpretation stems from the inexact use of the term "political class" (Tannenbaum 1966:116–74). In fact, a new political class came into being that gropingly constituted the leadership of the revolution and ultimately asserted itself as the ruling class of the country after some twenty-five years of contradictory ideological struggle and scattered power plays. For the last fifteen years of the Porfiriato there had been much vocal and active discontent throughout the country, mainly concerning lack of political participation and what the middle class perceived as the dictatorship's blatant favoritism of foreign interests. Out of this milieu the new political class of Mexico emerged between the onset of the armed revolt and the establishment of the official part of the revolution, later on the Partido Revolucionario Institucional (PRI), shortly before 1930. The old Porfirian political class, also of basically Mestizo extraction, was so closely allied to the aristocratic ruling class of *hacendados* and assorted plutocratic magnates that it was rejected by the new political class. One element that survived was the centralization of power. The actual fighting was done by Mestizo and Indian masses, led by peasant leaders and by many local, provincial leaders who did not reap the benefits of victory after the fighting was over. The leadership, the vision and aims of a "revolutionary" society, was provided by an urban middle class out of which the new political class emerged (Thomson 1937). By the time Lázaro Cárdenas became president, the new political class had fashioned a new presidency, and for the next fifty-five years it ran the affairs of the nation with a mixture of authoritarianism and populism.

In September 1910, Porfirio Díaz was fraudulently elected president of Mexico for the sixth time by defeating Francisco E. Madero. Madero did not accept the results of the election and declared himself provisional president. Thus began the revolution in Sonora and Chihuahua, and it spread quickly to other states of the union. On May 21, Porfirio Díaz resigned. Five days later he was off to exile in Europe. Meanwhile Mexico smothered in a devastating civil war involving the forces of Carranza, Villa, and Zapata (Parkes 1938:311–25).

From the start, revolutionaries targeted state authorities and *jefes políticos* as the most visible subjects of Porfirian despotism. But the equally visible *hacendados* did not suffer as much as the political representatives of the regime, nor did the plutocratic magnates, who benefited from their greater anonymity to the revolutionary masses. Destruction and loss of property on a large scale occurred everywhere, and many of the *haciendas* were destroyed and did not recuperate in the lull of nearly fifteen years of relative peace in the countryside that preceded the massive land reform (Priestley 1926:411–32). Most *hacendados* weathered the years of fighting in the cities that they had controlled or in Mexico City, but those who stayed on the *haciendas* with their families were often protected by their peons and neighboring communities when guerillas and revolutionary armies fought battles or devastated the countryside.

The revolution that Madero led was a movement against the Díaz regime, concerned exclusively with political liberalization; he did not have an economic program, and he certainly did not envision the massive land reform proposed by the budding political class, expressing the aspirations of the Indian and Mestizo masses. The leaders of the revolution, of both middle-class and peasant extraction, sought nothing less than the obliteration of the system, overthrowing what they regarded as remnants of the Colonial past as well as the new capitalist oppressors from abroad (Parkes 1938:382–84). Hence, their emphasis in searching for the origins of the nation in its Indian past. *Indigenismo,* then, became a byword that shaped many of the vague programs of the new leadership in the years to come.

Almost as soon as Madero became president, several rebellions erupted. By the beginning of 1913, the situation was extremely volatile, provoked mainly by the conflicting interests of peasant leaders. The fatal blow was delivered by Victoriano Huerta, who had Madero assassinated and assumed the presidency. Huerta quickly became a dictator and established a regime more despotic than the Porfiriato had ever been. Reaction was swift. A coalition of northern and southern revolutionary armies under Carranza, Villa, Obregón, and Zapata forced Huerta to resign less than eighteen months after the onset of his bloody regime. During this most ferocious period of the entire revolution, more than one-half of all *hacienda* mansions were destroyed or badly damaged.

After Huerta's demise, Carranza was installed as president, but the uprisings continued, and revolutionary leaders could not agree upon a course of action. Obregón tried to mediate between Carranza and Villa, ultimately to no avail, and fighting now resumed among the partisans of Carranza, Villa, and Zapata. Villa and Zapata were neutralized, and in April 1916, Carranza was recognized as provisional president by most of the country. The federal bureaucracy was incompetent and dishonest, and corruption and abuses of power continued as they had in the past. Yet the six years of struggle had made a difference, and many changes were now a distinct possibility. In December 1916, Carranza called a national convention that ultimately resulted in the constitution of 1917. The views of the more radical conventioneers prevailed, and the constitution became an enlightened document. Still, the fundamentally sound articles of the 1917 constitution took more than two generations to mature. During this period, Villa ceased to be a political presence and Zapata was assassinated, putting an end to the main factional disputes and the country on the way to recuperation. Carranza wanted to stay in power for one more term, but he was abandoned by most of his supporters. He fled to the Gulf coast and was assassinated in a Veracruz village. Obregón, the favored candidate to replace Carranza, was inaugurated president in November 1920 (Gibbon 1934:84–96).

Obregón's presidency ushered in a period of reconstruction: the fighting stopped and bloodshed became minimal, but democracy had not come to Mexico. The ills that had plagued the Díaz dictatorship remained: graft, abuse of power, and generals and bureaucrats who behaved like the old *jefes políticos*. But the promise of a just and democratic society persisted as well. Obregón was an able statesman, and he did much to improve the conditions of the country: neutralizing the army, establishing the primary and secondary education system, and normalizing the country's bureaucracy. Most significant for the central problem of this book, he initiated the land reform on behalf of Indian and Mestizo communities, forcing neighboring *haciendas* to allot land to individual families and compensating *hacendados* with government bonds. Obregón was opposed to a thorough land reform, however, for he thought the *hacienda* system essential to the economic well-being of the nation (Parkes 1938:372–80). This respite allowed *hacendados* to retain possession of most of the arable land of the country until fourteen years later.

After a short uprising at the end of Obregón's administration, Calles was elected president and he took office peacefully in July 1924. The Calles administration, though markedly progressive, was marred by an authoritarianism that became a dictatorship. Power concentrated rapidly in the hands of the emerging ruling class, and from this time onward one can speak of a new political class, which crystallized a few years later in the PRI. Almost equally important, one can pinpoint the Calles administration as the source of the phenomenon of supposedly socialistic politicians becoming capitalists, before and after their terms in office expired. Land reform proceeded more rapidly than during the Obregón administration, and perhaps as many as five million acres were distributed among landed peasants (Beteta 1935:132–57). During the second year of the Calles administration conflict between the Catholic Church and the government began, and by summer 1926, open hostility between church and state led to the so-called rebellion of the *Cristeros*, one of the most shameful episodes of the post–armed revolutionary period, during which government troops devastated entire regions of the states of Jalisco, Colima, and Michoacán (Meyer 1976).

By the middle of 1927, Calles decided to nominate Obregón as the new president, and at this time the constitution was amended by extending the presidency from four to six years. Unfortunately,

Obregón was assassinated, but Calles defused the dangerous situation with consummate statesmanship, and Portes Gil was elected president of Mexico (Parkes 1938:390–400). During Portes Gil's administration, significant institutional developments took place, primarily the foundation of the National Revolutionary Party (PNR), later renamed Partido Revolucionario Institucional, the most important event in the life of the nation since the armed phase of the revolution. From the beginning, the revolution had pursued contradictory aims, spanning the socialist-capitalist spectrum and ranging from dictatorial powers to representative democracy. During the period between the nomination of Portes Gil and the election of Cárdenas, some of these contradictions were eliminated, an accommodation of free enterprise and socialist measures was achieved, and the government moved from executive authoritarianism toward consensus vested in the party. By 1933, the budding political system was veering sharply to the left, tempered by the conservative tendencies of Calles and his followers. At this juncture Cárdenas was the candidate of compromise, and in December 1934, he was installed as president (Thomson 1937).

Cárdenas was the last innovator of the Mexican Revolution. He invented the cosmetic, ideological apparatus of the official party, which was designed to mask the authoritarian, nearly dictatorial character of the Mexican presidential system with a mantle of democracy, and a populism that catered to the masses but was liberal enough to accommodate a rather strong capitalist component. Thenceforward, the incoming president was nominated (the *tapado*) by the outgoing president with the advice of the party's inner circle, the core of the political class. The PRI always allowed a modicum of opposition, but presidential elections became gigantic shows, the congress little more than a rubber stamp, and the president reigned supreme for six years. With slight modifications, the political system of Mexico has persisted in this vein for nearly sixty years. The two most important economic achievements of the Cárdenas administration were the land reform and massive institution of the *ejido* system and the nationalization of the oil industry. Both were carried out successfully but with mixed economic results. Nothing as institutionally significant and economically and politically eventful as these events took place in Mexico in the subsequent fifty years, as the country slowly moved toward economic improvement and democratic reform.

THE NEW POLITICAL CLASS AND SOCIAL AND ECONOMIC CONSEQUENCES

The armed struggle of the Mexican Revolution and the twenty years of unrest and reorganization that followed did not radically transform the political and socioeconomic structure of the nation, for the movement was not a Russian-style revolution, and the socialist elements that it introduced were tempered with capitalist ideas; free enterprise was never explicitly an object of suppression. The fighting was seldom dictated by ideological considerations; rather it was the expression of basic, historically rooted inequalities that major segments of the body politic wanted to redress quickly. Pragmatic economic and political considerations rather than ideological convictions initiated and sustained the Mexican Revolution, and although the latter were present, they were never strong enough to have radically transformed the country politically, economically, and stratificationally.

By the time Carranza became president, the Porfirian political class had ceased to exist, and the country was being chaotically governed by revolutionaries of varied extractions. In fact, it is difficult to identify any clear segment that may properly be termed a political class from the fall of Díaz to the assassination of Carranza. Throughout this period, the main revolutionary leaders, from *jefes máximos* to local guerilla chieftains, came from almost the entire spectrum of the stratification system, including a few *hacendados*. Most leaders, however, came from local middle-class or peasant stock. They were generally motivated by a genuine desire for political and economic reform, but, also quite generally, by the hope for personal gain as well. One ideological trait shared by virtually all revolutionary leaders was *indigenismo*, which, of course, took different forms but focused essentially on creating a new Mexico for Mexicans, emphasizing native over foreign.[1]

Out of this motley configuration of personages, a political class began to emerge during the Obregón regime that came to fruition with the institution of an official party during the Calles dictatorship. But not until the fateful years of the Cárdenas administration did a political class coalesce that centered on the official party. From then on, the new rulers of Mexico kept a tight rein on the political affairs of the nation. With the exception of the higher position of revolutionaries in the hierarchy—the president, state governors, and a few other offices—the new ruling class was not staffed exclusively by members of revolutionary extraction, and indeed after the Second World War it was composed mostly of militant party officials with no revolutionary antecedents at all (García Purón 1964). Until the end of the Cárdenas administration, the background of the budding ruling class was uniformly middle class, with a sprinkling of politicians from peasant stock who had risen to important positions. There were, of course, no formal prohibitions against individuals and groups that had been associated with the ruling and political classes of the Porfiriato, but most circles of the new political class rather jealously guarded entrance to political participation (Nutini, Roberts, and Cervantes 1982). In other words, from the start of the revolution, politics became a rather restricted arena available mostly to individuals of kindred orientation and class position.

The revolution did not destroy the old industrial, manufacturing, and banking establishments of Mexico, but it certainly modified them, reconfiguring labor practices, management, and ownership. Much foreign capital remained in place, some plutocratic magnates retained control of their enterprises, but access to capitalist ventures became more fluid. Under revolutionary conditions and the dictatorial ambiance of governments until the Cárdenas administration, one could not speak of a ruling class vested in great plutocratic magnates, owners of the most important means of production. The budding political class was in a sense also the ruling class, for the remaining plutocratic magnates did not influence the functioning of the government. By 1940, the population of Mexico was nearly double that of 1910, industry had proliferated, and large manufacturing and business concerns had become common throughout the country. Foreign capital was increasing, but foreign investors from Europe and the United States also made their home in Mexico, and this segment significantly affected the powerful economic interests of a new plutocracy. Old plutocrats, with interests mainly in banking and manufacturing, made a comeback; more significantly, new entrepreneurs were making increasingly large fortunes, benefiting from the massive land reform that was not having a significant effect on the overall economy of the country. The last, by no means least, important input in the formation of this new plutocracy was from the political class. During the first twenty years after the fall of Porfirio Díaz, the political and ruling classes were basically indistinguishable, but with the growth of the private economic sector, they began to differentiate. In the 1930s, the Mexican political system became fairly well structured along the lines of a career pattern that culminated with just one opportunity at high political office, although exceptional individuals could occupy several high positions in succession. In short, from the Calles administration to the end of the Cárdenas administration, a ruling class was configured, constituted primarily by politicians turned businessmen after a term at high office and the growth of a private plutocracy (García Purón 1964).

The aristocracy's influence in conducting governmental actions disappeared quickly after the onset of the revolution. Once uprisings in the countryside became common and largely uncontrolled, aristocrats and their plutocratic allies suffered not only loss of property but physical violence and loss of control as well. Most *hacendados* enfranchised in the country left their landed estates and took refuge in the capital or large provincial cities, while a few temporarily left the country. Many country mansions were sacked and destroyed, and not infrequently peasants occupied land of the *haciendas*. Most *hacendados* nonetheless retained legal possession of the land, as revolutionary leaders, from Carranza to Calles, engaged largely in token land reform. From 1911 to 1920, a certain amount of land was either allotted to landless peasants by the federal and state governments or illegally occupied by Indian and Mestizo villages. The real problem, however, was that most *haciendas* throughout the country were abandoned by their owners, or else that productivity fell dramatically due to revolutionary activity and turmoil caused by intermittent fighting. With some notable exceptions in areas not directly trampled by revolutionary activity, the *hacienda* did not survive well the disastrous years of the armed conflict (Nutini, Roberts, and Cervantes 1984).

The loss of agrarian income dealt a deathblow to the aristocracy as a ruling class during the first phase of the revolution. Meanwhile, deep-seated antagonism, both of an economic and political nature, prevented aristocratic participation at all levels of government and administration. Only at the local level, once revolutionary activity ebbed, did *hacendados* retain a modicum of control. In the cities, aristocrats succeeded in protecting their mansions, but they lost the determinant influence and control that they had enjoyed during the Porfiriato. Significant numbers of aristocrats, both in the country and the city, suffered a modicum of violence and outrage, and perhaps a few were killed, but these acts generally resulted from immediate individual or group resentment and not from a concerted effort on the part of responsible revolutionaries and guerrilla leaders.

The reluctance of Obregón and Calles to dismantle the great landed estates and the return to a modicum of peaceful prosperity led *hacendados* to hope that further redistribution and illegal appropriation of land by the government would stop and that the *hacienda* system, though modified, would survive. The years from 1920 to 1934 were a period of relative recuperation for the aristocracy, whose expectation of retaining their landed estates fueled a relative improvement as a social class. Upwardly mobile elements of the political and economic sectors sought rapport with the aristocracy as a legitimating mechanism, which many aristocrats welcomed as a survival strategy. Despite Calles's anticlericalism and his openly antagonistic policy toward the church, the aristocracy did not unduly suffer throughout these troubled times, and to a certain extent it even reasserted its former place as a social class. Although a few aristocrats were able to retain a foothold in the new plutocracy by virtue of converting agrarian and urban property into banking and manufacturing operations, the overwhelming majority of aristocrats languished in the expectation that ultimately the land problem would be resolved in their favor.

The *hacienda* system survived in its overall configuration until 1934, and though crippled by violence, it continued to produce a modicum of income. As an instrument of expression and as a focal point of the aristocratic *imago mundi,* however, it had been mortally wounded by 1920. The destruction and pillage of most *cascos* were too great to allow the *hacienda* to recuperate its former expressive preeminence. Those *haciendas* that survived the fury of the revolution or that could be repaired and refurbished continued to play a role in the expressive life of aristocratic families even after the massive land reform, but by then most families did not have enough money to undertake the massive job of reconstruction. In fact, as early as 1930, many aristocratic families began to acquire country residences, if they did not already have them, within relatively short distances of Mexico City and a few other urban centers. After 1940, most *hacienda cascos* lay in ruins or had been badly damaged, many had been bought by members of the new political and ruling classes and ostentatiously refurbished, and only a few were still occupied by aristocrats.

As a social class, the aristocracy survived, both as a clearly discernible group and as the collective carrier of superordinate expressive behavior. Simply put, as the model of upwardly mobile aspirations, aristocrats provided a unique commodity and this expressive component alone made the aristocracy a viable social group until the late 1970s. Until the beginning of the Cárdenas administration, most of the great aristocratic mansions in Mexico City and important provincial cities were still inhabited by their original owners. Not until after the massive land reform were almost all of these mansions either expropriated or sold by their owners for economic reasons. In the old Colonial mansions and in the new, nearly suburban residential areas established during the Porfiriato, many aristocratic families played leading roles in homogenizing the disparate elements of the evolving political and ruling classes. Some aristocrats played a substantial role in business and industry, and their visibility enhanced the desirability of aristocratic expression for those vying for a place in the superordinate stratification of the country. For the upwardly mobile people of the time, the ineffable aristocratic aura was still strong, and this was perhaps the main expressive attribute that sustained the aristocracy for another fifty years or so.

The Massive Land Reform and Aristocratic Concentration in Mexico City (1934–50)

These sixteen years were the most critical period for the Mexican aristocracy since the onset of the Revolution of 1910. Stripped of their land and rapidly losing social and economic control of the provincial cities traditionally associated with the *hacienda,* a massive migration to Mexico City took place. The ambiance of the capital had always promised security in violent and uncertain times, and there in the security of numbers the aristocracy experienced one last moment of social saliency and visibility. Though revolution did not directly cause the obliteration of the aristocracy, the massive land reform most certainly launched this social class into a final process of disintegration.

DEMISE OF THE HACIENDA SYSTEM AND ECONOMIC DISINTEGRATION

The massive land reform initiated by Cárdenas was a shock of cataclysmic proportions for the Mexican aristocracy. In the short period of six years, the *hacienda* system had come to an end. Whatever hopes the *hacendado* aristocracy cherished of retaining its landed estates dissolved and its residual inputs as a ruling class vanished overnight. Expressive constraints conspired against aristocrats becoming successful pluto-crats, and most aristocratic families were reduced to relative poverty. A small number, however, made the transition successfully, and between the end of the Cárdenas administration and the late 1960s, they could be counted among the rich and powerful. These exceptions may be explained in two ways. First, throughout the nineteenth century there had always been aristocrats who successfully combined agrarian opera-tions with banking and industry, and when these families lost their landed estates, they were not totally ruined. Second, another small group of aristocratic *hacendados* were realistic enough to realize that the *hacienda* would not survive, given the reluctance of Obregón and Calles to break up the great landed estates. Thus, between 1920 and 1933, this group sold most of their land to small farmers, individual peas-ants, and even to Indian communities, investing the profit in urban property and the manufacturing industry. By the 1960s, perhaps 10 percent of aristocratic families had survived economically and had estab-lished a plutocratic basis in the new haute bourgeoisie. But the great majority of aristocrats were devastated by the Cárdenas land reform and forced into the liberal professions.

During the Cárdenas administration, the great landed estates of Mexico were abolished and the *ejido* system came into being. The *ejido* was land expropriated from private individuals—including the great *haciendas* as well as large farming enterprises and agrarian enterprises owned by foreign companies—by the government and given to groups of landless peasants, not as personal property but with rights of cultiva-tion and transmission to their children (Mendieta y Nuñez 1966). Except in broad outline and intention (the termination of the landed estates), the agrarian reform was not uniform throughout the country. Taking into account density of population and the availability of land—that is, the incidence and size of *haciendas*—the land allotted to individuals directly or as part of collective *ejidos* varied greatly from adequate, plot sizes ranging from ten to twenty hectares, to miserably inadequate, plots ranging from one-half to one hectare. In most parts of the country, particularly in the more densely populated areas, the land reform was a failure, for it did not significantly improve the living standards of peasants. Only in the north and along the gulf coast was reform successful in ameliorating the overall economic situation, and this success may be attributed to lower population density resulting in larger plots of land allotted to individual and collective cultivation, particularly of commercial crops such as sugarcane (Nickel 1988:171–81). By the late 1950s, the agrarian reform had become a political weapon to defuse potentially violent situations, and thus led to the further breakup of medium-size, efficiently cultivated farms.

The agrarian reform not only distributed land among landless peasants, but also legislated the amount of land that could be owned by individuals. The legislation varied from state to state with respect to the quality of the land and the use to which it could be put, limits which remain in effect. For example, an individual can own no more than 100 hectares of irrigated land, and no more than 200 to 300 hectares of nonirrigated land, though these limits may be stretched depending on the region or state and the cultivation of specialized crops. Animal husbandry, mostly in the north, south, and coastal areas, requires larger plots regulated by the quality of land and livestock (Mendieta y Nuñez 1966). *Hacendados* could own land as allowed by law in addition to the *casco*. Many *cascos* had been damaged beyond repair during the armed phase of the revolution, while perhaps many more were in various stages of disrepair in 1934, and, given the economic decline of their owners, were allowed to deteriorate further.

About half of aristocratic *hacendados* sold the land that the law allowed them to retain by 1955. They either sold the land to peasants of nearby communities or to prosperous farmers, who frequently accumulated land in excess of what the law allowed. In these cases, former *hacendados* became almost entirely disconnected from the land, and as they gravitated toward Mexico City their ties with the ancestral *hacienda* loosened, particularly when the *hacienda* was located in such faraway places as the far north and Yucatán. In areas closer to the capital, the *hacienda* connection persisted longer, but by the late 1960s, less than a fourth of former aristocratic *hacendados* derived income from the exploitation of their ancestral estates. In a few cases, aristocrats bought land elsewhere and have continued to farm, sometimes on a scale larger than the law allows.

The land reform had another aspect that, though illegal, may have been a plus for the agrarian productivity of Mexico. Before the Cárdenas land reform, many revolutionary leaders acquired land, and some of them may even be called *hacendados,* given the large tracts that they had managed to accumulate. After 1934, land holdings beyond what the law allowed continued under veiled government protection and by the use of *presta nombres* (name lenders). Since the onset of massive agrarian reform, it has been a standard practice to register land under the names of several individuals (usually kinsmen or close friends) in order to circumvent the law and consolidate larger parcels of land. The most powerful members of the political class probably do not even bother with this subterfuge, but most politicians and average large-farm operators do, including aristocratic farmers. On the lands of their former *haciendas* or of nearby communities, an appreciable number of aristocrats continue to farm on a moderate scale and derive good incomes from these agrarian operations (Carlos de Ovando, pers. comm.).

The Cárdenas land reform terminated nearly four centuries of aristocratic agrarian dominance and eliminated perhaps the most salient feature of the expressive configuration of the Mexican aristocracy. During the past fifty years the land has had little or no economic value for the aristocracy as a class, but it still looms large in the consciousness of most aristocrats and continues to play an important role in the expressive retreat that has been going on for more than two generations. The city-country axis of expressive realization was not entirely destroyed, as considerable numbers of *hacienda* mansions are still in the hands of aristocrats, and they continue to provide solace and psychic support to their owners. Economically, the agrarian reform transformed the aristocracy into urbanite professionals and small-to-medium businessmen with a foothold in the world of powerful plutocrats. The aristocracy is no longer rich, and it has lost all its once great power and influence.

EXODUS TO MEXICO CITY AND PROFESSIONAL (EMBOURGEOISEMENT) GROWTH

Since its formation in the sixteenth century, the Mexican aristocracy had always gravitated toward Mexico City. By the turn of the twentieth century, a degree of decentralization had taken place and more than ever before aristocratic families were enfranchised in important provincial cities; still, perhaps as many as 50 percent kept residences in Mexico City. This traditional pattern began to change with the fall of Porfirio Díaz, and by 1950 more than 80 percent of all aristocratic families resided permanently in the capital. In 1910, and to some extent until 1934, the most important nuclei of aristocratic families were located in the following cities: Puebla, Guadalajara, Querétaro, Oaxaca, Mérida, Morelia, Chihuahua, Xalapa, Durango, San Luis Potosí, Zacatecas, Tampico, and three or four smaller centers. The violence and disruption of the early revolutionary years meant the abandonment of *haciendas*. With Obregón, relative peace and order came to the countryside and *hacendados* and their families cautiously resumed the routine of the city-country axis. The *acasillados* and contract labor continued to work the land, producing an income for *hacendados* and reestablishing a semblance of normality. Despite the low profile they were forced to adopt as a consequence of their loss of power and control, the aristocracy continued to dominate the social life of the city.

Massive migration to Mexico City began in 1936, triggered not only by the total loss of *haciendas* and a serious decrease in income but by a new awareness of middle-class action and revolutionary assertion that made provincial life uncomfortable for aristocrats accustomed to undisputed control. The upwardly mobile element in provincial cities was asserting itself as never before and was no longer willing to accept passively the haughtiness and paternalism of aristocrats. With their *haciendas* gone and their local business interests in shambles, most aristocratic families opted for migration to Mexico City, a process completed by the early 1950s. Within the next two generations, those aristocratic families that remained in provincial cities became downwardly mobile, and most of them lost aristocratic affiliation; they became part of local elites of politicians, new businessmen, and small-scale industrialists that in time developed into local plutocracies. These former aristocratic families are known today as *familias venidas a menos* (dropouts, downwardly mobile families). Bona fide aristocrats regard them as no longer part of the group but still accord them minimum recognition. Only in Guadalajara, Querétaro, and perhaps one or two more cities do there remain small nuclei of aristocratic families that are recognized as an integral part of the Mexican aristocracy.

In Mexico City the provincial arrivals found a much larger, more congenial environment than in the rapidly changing cities that they had once so thoroughly controlled. In the capital, aristocrats found a measure of security in numbers; they presented a fairly united front against the hostile world developing around them. For *hacendado* aristocrats who did not have any other source of income, migration to

Mexico City was simply a matter of economic survival. For a considerable number of aristocrats, however, the demise of the *hacienda* system was not a crashing blow, for they possessed a diversified economy in banking, industry, and urban property. Thus, during the two decades following the massive land reform, the Mexican aristocracy concentrated in the capital included rich aristocrats, well-off ones, and those who had to start pretty much at the bottom.

The main economic survival strategy of the majority of aristocrats was to join the liberal professions. Becoming a doctor, a lawyer, or an engineer was nothing new to aristocrats. But, whereas a career was undertaken in the nineteenth century as a hobby or in pursuit of strictly scientific or intellectual interests, it was now done in order to survive. Aristocrats became architects, chemists, business administrators; some became archaeologists, anthropologists, and historians, choosing fields in which members of the aristocracy had excelled in the nineteenth century. The great majority of male aristocrats born between 1920 and 1940 entered the university, and already by the late 1950s, most of them had received degrees in the liberal professions. Female aristocrats, however, did not receive a similar education until later, as female university graduates in the liberal professions, most commonly art history and psychology, became common only in the 1960s. In a short generation, the aristocracy had made the transition from a rich landed base to a fairly comfortable economic position by engaging in the professions and a rather wide array of business and industrial enterprises.

Ideologically and expressively, the Mexican aristocracy remained unified and unchanged, supportive of its members, and quite close as a social group until the late 1940s. Even before 1940, however, diversification and the growing formation of smaller networks were apparent. In pursuing new means of economic survival, once cohesive aristocratic networks grew apart, both in the process of building new nonaristocratic connections and establishing different patterns of social and economic activities that were not entirely compatible. From 1950 onward, two types of aristocratic families emerged, types that have remained distinct throughout the past forty years. On the one hand, there are those families that, most constrained by the aristocratic *imago mundi,* have totally refrained from social interaction with the haute bourgeoisie, have centered their lives in the household, interacting exclusively with small selected networks of kinsmen and friends of their own class. This conservative sector adheres to a traditional view of aristocratic behavior and to a static conception of aristocratic roles. It refuses to make any concessions to the rich and powerful and has therefore not participated in the expressive process of aristocratic-plutocratic acculturation since its inception in the early 1940s. True to their exclusive, endogenous principles, this segment has gone underground, living mostly in the past. On the other hand, there are those families least constrained by the aristocratic *imago mundi,* more forward looking, and with the most entrepreneurial skills. This group constitutes the majority of aristocratic families, among them are the most affluent, with a firm foothold in plutocratic circles, and with whom the haute bourgeoisie has interacted rather closely, beginning right after the end of the Second World War. Since the late 1930s, this sector has provided the model for expressive aristocratic-plutocratic acculturation of the emerging haute bourgeoisie. Intermarriage between aristocrats and plutocrats began in the late 1940s and became fairly common in the next generation, when the expressive arrays of these social classes began to coalesce and a new acculturative entity was born.

Even during the most difficult and insecure times of the 1920s and 1930s, the Mexican aristocracy was the undisputed social leader in the capital, while in provincial cities this position of superordination was lost. Aristocratic life experienced a renaissance in Mexico City. Their ranks increased by migration, the aristocracy dominated social and religious events. Despite their loss of wealth, a rather large number of aristocratic families were sufficiently affluent to be in the limelight, constantly reported in the press, and still universally recognized by the middle and even lower classes of a city of nearly three million people. This state of affairs continued until the late 1940s. Another generation had to pass for the aristocracy to lose this position, and for the population at large to lose the ability to discriminate between traditional aristocrats and new plutocrats. The phenomenal demographic growth of the city, the growth and assertion of the middle classes, and the final formation of a very rich and powerful plutocracy caused this terminal transformation. While the renaissance lasted, the aristocracy remained a closed social class, its social life admired, and its expressive culture envied. What made this last outburst of aristocratic control possible was, above all, the sheer weight of four hundred years of domination and the symbols that went with it.

Ascendance of a New Plutocracy and Its Interaction with the Aristocracy (1950–70)

By the late 1950s, only a few isolated pockets of aristocrats were still enfranchised in provincial cities, and from this time onward the Mexican aristocracy must be regarded as a social class enfranchised in Mexico City. In contrast with the plutocracy, this period marks the economic decline of the aristocracy, marked by a significant lowering of living standards and a discontinuity in many domains of expression that had always been central to this social class. Thenceforward, 10 percent of aristocrats at most were plutocrats as well, that is, had fortunes of several million dollars. The traditional recognition of aristocratic membership began to blur, the lower and middle classes were increasingly unable to discriminate between social standing and power and wealth, and only at the highest rungs of the stratification system were aristocrats recognized as a distinct class or group.

Three rather distinct classes had come into existence: a political class embodied in the ruling party; a ruling class of plutocrats; and a social class still constituted by the aristocracy. This superordinate segment of the Mexican stratification system I have elsewhere called the haute bourgeoisie (Nutini, Roberts, and Cervantes 1984). The aristocracy remained for generations the preeminent social class by virtue of expressive and behavioral attributes that were desirable to political and plutocratic elites in their quest to validate social standing. Slightly different forms and mixtures of the political-ruling-social triad have been the basic model of superordinate stratification and upward mobility in Western stratification throughout modern times. As the aristocracy declined, the model paradoxically acquired renewed importance in shaping new political and ruling classes in superordinate positions. The model, with the aristocracy as an essential element, ultimately falters when ruling and political classes begin to create new expressive arrays independent of the acculturative aristocratic model.

SOCIOECONOMIC ACCOMMODATION AND ARISTOCRATIC-PLUTOCRATIC PREPONDERANCE

As I have indicated, there is little if any continuity between the membership of the political and ruling classes from the Porfiriato to the second half of the twentieth century. The aristocracy remained the preeminent social class of the capital, in a kind of precarious balancing act with the plutocracy. An already powerful plutocracy constituted the majority of the country's ruling class in close social and economic interaction with the political class. The political class, as defined above, provided the undisputed political leaders of the country and constituted also a strong minority of the ruling class. Thus the political class developed a close relationship with the ruling class, both because of the overlapping membership and the economic interests they had in common. The aristocracy had but a minor foothold in the ruling class, as aristocratic plutocrats were not among the magnates of the ruling class. Roughly four decades ago, then, the Mexican haute bourgeoisie achieved a constitution that has remained rather constant: its composing sectors were distinct classes that significantly overlapped each other, particularly along economic boundaries. The political class as such had no significant interaction with the aristocracy, and only as plutocrats, mostly after discharging high political office, did members of the former have an input in the development of the latter.

The presidency of Miguel Alemán (1946–52) was a period of industrial growth and economic advances. In the fifteen years after World War Two, many new fortunes were made and older ones increased. Industry, manufacturing, banking, and service concerns experienced unprecedented growth, and the new plutocracy came to maturity. Disregarding the important minority of former politicians, the composition of the plutocracy was as follows: The majority were self-made men of middle-class origins, a considerable number of whom had a university education. A considerable number were foreigners of U.S., European, and Near Eastern extraction, most of whom had been residents of Mexico for more than a generation. Finally, a sprinkling were aristocrats and old plutocrats of Porfirian extraction who had managed to retain a modicum of wealth and now came into their own.

While this plutocracy spread throughout the country, the richest and most powerful plutocrats, in the traditional centralist fashion of Mexico, were enfranchised in Mexico City. Demonstrating another aspect of centralization, many plutocrats who made fortunes in the provinces or initiated business concerns in provincial cities eventually moved to Mexico City.[2] By the late 1950s, the great majority of plutocratic magnates resided very visibly in Mexico City. Together with some members of the political class, plutocratic magnates began to dominate the social life of the city, and certainly they occupied the limelight. Plutocrats' mansions proliferated in the most fashionable quarters of the city, their doings and activities were prominently reported by the press, and their economic success made them as talked about as prominent politicians. Mexico City already had more than six million people, and in this environment the aristocracy had little or no visibility, except in the upper range of the stratification system, whereas the plutocracy commanded attention second only to that of highly placed political leaders. It is difficult to pinpoint the wealth of plutocratic magnates, for it ranged considerably, but the average fortune was on the order of fifty to sixty million dollars. More difficult still is to calculate the strength of this group, but an educated guess is that it surpassed one thousand families.

Throughout these twenty years, social interaction between aristocrats and plutocrats was generalized, no longer consisting of aristocratic condescension toward upstart plutocrats. Since Colonial times the aristocracy had always had a rather close circle of social "retainers." These were well-to-do, "upper-middle-class" families, or *gentes propias* (proper people) as they were called, with whom the aristocracy interacted on a basis of near equality. By standing tradition, these "proper" people and the aristocracy had enough in common expressively to ensure smooth and fluid social interaction and occasional intermarriage. By plutocrats, by contrast, I mean middle-class individuals who had risen to power and wealth during the previous generation and were socially upwardly mobile, but did not enjoy a standing relationship with the aristocracy. This statement, however, should be qualified. Some, perhaps 15 percent, of the plutocratic families could claim proper genteel extraction, and in the process of upward mobility, these families interacted most successfully with the aristocratic group. The average plutocratic family, meanwhile, though it did not traditionally share with the aristocracy a complex of social and expressive forms, was composed of fast, willing learners.

In the 1940s, plutocratic families established a modicum of social interaction with aristocratic families and learned some of their expressive domains. During the following two decades, the plutocracy came into its own. As its power and wealth vastly surpassed that of the dwindling aristocracy, the plutocracy no longer accepted a passive role in its upwardly mobile aspirations. Aristocrats and plutocrats came into rather continuous and occasionally close contact in a wide array of social, economic, and "cultural" contexts and situations that tended to homogenize the two classes. It cannot be said, however, that the entire aristocracy and plutocracy participated in this process of rapprochement; rather the process was dominated by the interaction of the most forward-looking, liberal segment of the aristocracy and the most upwardly mobile and powerful segment of the plutocracy. As these segments constituted the majority of the two classes, the overall social and expressive rapprochement of a single superordinate group was strengthened. The conservative aristocratic minority retreated and dropped out of the system, and the less rich and powerful plutocratic minority—the segment of the plutocracy of more humble origins—uninterested in upward social mobility also remained outside the system. Economically, aristocrats emulated plutocrats and not infrequently occupied important positions in plutocratic enterprises. Socially, aristocrats and plutocrats interacted in several contexts and occasions: in the household, albeit with a certain degree of reticence on the part of aristocrats; in the more public ambiance of weddings, balls, and kindred events outside the household; in clubs, theaters, and musical affairs; and so on.

What dynamic propelled this increasing interaction? The answer is twofold. First, in the time-honored fashion thrice described and analyzed, aristocratic-plutocratic interaction was configured in terms of needs: the desire of plutocrats to validate social standing in the game of upward mobility after reaching a high level of power and wealth and the necessity of aristocrats to gain or consolidate economic assets or to make new economic allies to preserve their social predominance. The difference between the present situation (the last renewal of elites) and the three situations described previously is social and economic dominance. In the three earlier transformations the aristocracy had total predominance, it was secure in its social and economic position of superordination, and the process of plutocratic acceptance and internalization was imbalanced. Now the situation was reversed: the aristocracy was little more than a social class, no longer in control and insecure of its social predominance, whereas the plutocracy was richer and more powerful and able to assert itself in several domains.

Second, though need configured aristocratic-plutocratic rapprochement in a fairly balanced manner, compromise established the guidelines of the process, and the give and take of aristocrats and plutocrats culminated in a reversal of fortune. For the first time aristocrats were incorporated into a budding social class of plutocrats, while the majority of aristocrats retreated, socially and expressively unable to surrender their traditionally undisputed role. But as long as the acculturative role of aristocrats survived, they remained an active social class, still visible, and grudgingly accepted as a superordinate segment.

EXPRESSIVE TRANSMISSION AND BEHAVIORAL ACCULTURATION

In the short-range historical perspective, the aristocracy, as the traditional social class of Mexican society, is still largely endogamous, and no less endogenous in behavior and expression. A large complex of manners and behavior obtains that constitutes the endogenous parameters of the group. Those who do not behave according to the rules are not regarded as aristocrats, and this reality is subtly manifested in social and economic situations. It was under these conditions that plutocrats until 1950 had always acquired aristocratic recognition and were eventually fully incorporated into the group. Throughout the 1950s and 1960s, plutocrats in one fashion or another sought aristocratic recognition, but incorporation did not necessarily follow, primarily because the plutocracy innovated socially and expressively on its own and pursued an independent course and secondarily because the aristocracy no longer exercised political and ruling functions.

Aristocrats regard themselves as the arbiters of social life, specialists in the niceties of ritual and ceremonial behavior, practitioners of complex codes of etiquette and traditional standing, and upholders of good manners and family traditions. Members of the plutocracy most likely internalized the social ambiance to which they had been exposed outside Mexico City, rather than copying directly from the aristocracy. Still, the aristocracy in situ was the validating group of good manners and genteel behavior. The catalysts in the aristocracy-plutocracy interaction are economic necessity and social ambition: the desire of the former to expand its economic horizons and acquire a measure of ruling control, and the ambition of the latter to be regarded not only as economically and politically powerful but as socially acceptable as well. These factors, however, cannot entirely explain the persistence of the aristocracy as a largely endogamous, viable, quite self-contained class. What has ensured this survival are the aristocracy's expressive components, which buttress the group's identity and strengthen the structure of the group.

What are the main components of this large complex of expressive behavior? They belong mainly to the domains of the household and kinship behavior, the life cycle and socialization of children, etiquette and personal behavior, patterns of entertainment and celebrations, the fine arts, interpersonal relations, and patterns of dress and demeanor. In all instances of social mobility, what attracts or compels the aspiring individual or group to acquire and master the behavior of a superordinate stratum is not the notion that such mastery will bring acceptance and make him or the group more similar to the aspired object, but the belief that it will confer the security, sense of superiority, and natural demeanor that distinguishes those superordinately placed. Why else would plutocrats care about the social standing of aristocrats, when they have most of the economic and political power and prestige and could create their own standards?

For aristocrats, the common body of expressive behavior unites them as a self-directed group and at the same time affords them significant security. They regard the various domains of expressive behavior as a legacy of the past, a validation of the exalted place that they once occupied. The refinement of behavior, the protocol of certain ritual and ceremonial occasions, and the circumspection and savoir faire that social interaction requires are always very much in the individual and group consciousness and are regarded as epitomizing civilized living. This kind of behavior and social interaction impose restrictions upon the average aristocrat, who is generally quite willing to restrict his or her social life to the familiarity of an increasingly poorer social milieu.

When plutocrats reach a certain plateau of wealth and economic power, they seem to develop a rather strong desire for social recognition and interaction with the aristocracy. Certainly this desire has characterized the Mexican plutocracy since the early 1940s. The Mexican plutocracy is composed of two generations: those who initiated the enterprises that brought them wealth and their married or unmarried children. The older generation had its beginnings when the aristocracy was significantly more visible than it is today, that is, before World War Two. Curiously, would-be plutocrats either developed a strong desire for social acceptance and actively sought to interact with the aristocracy, or they had been somehow scarred and developed a strong aversion to imitating the ways of their social superiors. The younger generation, however, has assiduously sought acceptance and increasing social interaction with the different segments of the aristocracy, and they have not overlooked any opportunities in this quest. The natural resistance of aristocrats to social rapport with the plutocracy has slowly broken down. By the early 1970s, the average plutocrat had acquired such outward trappings of aristocratic behavior as dress, certain patterns of language and demeanor, expressive travel, forms of entertainment, and so on. But plutocrats know that they cannot manufacture pedigrees or an illustrious past. They realize that these values come only with time, and as time passes and they achieve more wealth, they worry less.

Aristocrats are well aware that by acquiring their expressive behavior, plutocrats are vying for social recognition. Aristocrats regard this recognition as an important commodity, a source of satisfaction and self-validation to be used wisely. They know too that they cannot press their expressive claims too strongly, for wealth and power will eventually bring plutocrats the social recognition they desire anyway. At this juncture, the relationship between aristocrats and plutocrats is a delicate one. The former expect to maximize expressive claims by engaging in social interaction without totally giving in, while the latter try to encourage social interaction without appearing overly obsequious. Both sides of this acculturative equation exhibit a rather wide range of behavior: from aristocrats who adamantly refuse to accept plutocrats as their social equals and have nothing but contempt for them to those who maintain that as a matter of survival it is necessary to achieve an intimate rapport between social status and power and wealth; from plutocrats who regard aristocrats as anachronistic, unproductive drones with whom they would have nothing to do to those who feel drawn strongly to aristocrats and wish to cement strong social and matrimonial alliances. By the mid-1970s, the equation was skewed significantly toward the liberal side of the spectrum, including primarily the richest and the younger on both sides.

The principal context of interaction has always been economic: the world of business, banking, and manufacturing. Rich aristocrats are of course part of that world, and they therefore interact intimately with plutocrats in business clubs and associations and at the attendant social occasions. Most aristocrats, however, interact with plutocrats from a position of economic subordination: as high- or middle-level executives in banks and business enterprises, or as borrowers of money or buyers of products. In all cases, social occasions arise when plutocrats and aristocrats interact: club reunions, dinner parties, cocktail parties, and so on. Quite often executive and middle-level male and female person-nel with aristocratic background are drawn into the ranks of banking and business enterprises. Given the international character of many such enterprises, this personnel is regarded as a considerable asset, capable of the social nuances and interpersonal savoir faire that such business transactions involve.

The other significant contexts of aristocratic-plutocratic interac-tion are the world of music and fine arts and the domain of sports (polo, equitation, sailing). Aristocrats and plutocrats join forces in sponsoring artistic and musical events. For public relations purposes, the main banking institutions often sponsor exhibitions of the best collections of Colonial pottery, family portraits, porcelain, furniture, and so on. These various events are always social occasions, but they invariably occur in the fairly impersonal ambiance of banks and other public buildings. Social gatherings of aristocrats and plutocrats in the context of sports are probably the most intimate and include the homes of the two groups. Thus, the greatest rapport between aristocrats and plutocrats has occurred among this small group, where the highest degree of social homogeneity and recognition can be observed.

The confrontation between these two sectors of the haute bourgeoi-sie has not been uniform; many subtleties and shades of this process of acculturation cannot be detailed here. Suffice it to say that the richer and more powerful plutocrats are, the more they are drawn into the process, and the more plutocratic- or business-oriented aristocrats are, the more rapidly and thoroughly does acculturation proceed. In the sometimes reluctant, tentative, still somewhat asymmetrical rapproche-ment between the aristocracy and the plutocracy, there remains one domain that the aristocracy regards as the last bastion of its social life, namely, the ambiance of the household. When the endogenous exclusiv-ity of the household as a place of social gatherings and as a symbol of the group's self-identity comes to an end, the aristocracy will have consciously relinquished all claim to social superordination. This sur-render was beginning to happen in the mid-1970s and by 1990 it was nearly accomplished. From the early 1940s there has been a slow but steady progression of social recognition of the plutocracy by the aristoc-racy (Nutini, Roberts, and Cervantes 1982).

One may summarize the interaction of the aristocracy and plutoc-racy from the early 1950s to the 1970s as displaying a significant degree of asymmetrical expressive transmission complemented by symmetrical behavioral acculturation. Many domains of the aristocratic expressive array were internalized by plutocrats, both as the price of social recognition and as the realization that such an expressive acquisition was intrinsically valuable as an economic tool. Aristocrats and plutocrats reciprocally influenced each other, and their respective worldviews were substantially modified to accommodate disparate behaviors.

The Terminal Stage: Plutocratic Predominance and Aristocratic Withdrawal (1970–90)

This period witnesses the divergent paths of the aristocracy and plutocracy and the near demise of the former as a distinct social class in the Mexican stratification system. The aristocracy by now is little more than a self-defined and self-recognized group, although it continues to be somewhat vaguely recognized by the political and ruling sectors of the haute bourgeoisie and the upper-middle class. The plutocracy, meanwhile, asserts itself overwhelmingly, pursues its own social and expressive course, and insofar as the aristocracy retreats, becomes *the* social class. The situation is more complex than this characterization, for some aristocrats are rather completely plutocratized, while some plutocrats are significantly aristocratized. The essential consideration of this terminal period, however, is that the aristocracy loses its last asset, the expressive component, and no longer plays a determinant role in the emerging superordinate system.

A New Superordinate System Comes into Being

By the mid-1970s, the Mexican plutocracy residing in the capital and two or three provincial cities had reached a plateau of power and wealth unparalleled since the mining boom of the second half of the eighteenth century. More than one thousand millionaire families constituted the ruling class of the country, with an important political class component, and it was on the verge of becoming the social class. The plutocracy had come of age and, during the following decade and a half, dominated most aspects of public life, achieved a high level of recognition, and acquired a wide network of international connections. The plutocracy had been growing in wealth and self-awareness since the late 1940s, and by the late 1970s it had transformed into a self-directed group with a clear vision of its position within the body politic. With close ties to the political class, the plutocracy was second only to the highest holders of political office in directly and indirectly formulating policy, managing its consequences, and supporting the status quo engendered by the ruling party.[3] In this respect, the economic interests of the plutocracy are tied to the political aims of the ruling party, even though at times they diverge on important issues.

The social composition of the plutocracy has not changed since the late 1940s, except perhaps that during the present period more plutocrats of foreign extraction, mostly of European and Near Eastern extraction, have joined its ranks. Plutocrats of European extraction were usually moderately rich capitalists when they settled in Mexico, and only a handful made their original fortunes in the country. Equally significant, European plutocrats had better class positions than domestic ones; they were mostly of upper-middle-class and upper-class origin. Thus European plutocrats became the most fully integrated into aristocratic circles by virtue of shared expressive domains. In terms of overall social and economic configuration, the plutocracy does not change in the roughly twenty years of this period, but for the first time, it displaces the aristocracy as the goal of upward mobility from the upper rungs of the middle classes, and the masses look to the rich and powerful as the ideal of attainment. Translated into the language of social stratification, from now on the so-called objective (structural) criteria are more visible than the subjective (expressive) criteria of class membership (Baltzell 1966).

The devaluation of the peso in 1976 was a blow to the Mexican economy, and it affected the wealth of the plutocracy. At that point, the absolute wealth of the plutocracy peaked, but comparatively speaking successive devaluations did not diminish the power of the ruling class. Though the average plutocratic fortune decreased in absolute value, and many of the several hundred million, perhaps billion, dollar fortunes were significantly scaled down, this effect was to some extent compensated by the increasing number of foreign capitalists who acquired plutocratic status and reinforced the power of the plutocracy as a class. By now the plutocracy had acquired extensive international networks, and its economy extended beyond the domestic operations of a generation before. This multinational tie not only enriched the Mexican plutocracy economically but socially and expressively as well, giving it a new maturity and confidence. During the last two decades the plutocracy became the overwhelmingly predominant class of the superordinate system. The majority of plutocrats no longer feel the attraction that in the early years of upward mobility had so impelled them to seek alliances with the aristocracy. The plutocracy has become an independent social class, no longer in awe of aristocratic lineage and expression, and to some extent it creates its own expressive domains. For at least the last twelve years, the plutocracy has been interacting with the aristocracy on a basis of social equality and, indeed, the last ten years of aristocratic-plutocratic interaction may even be characterized as a growing apart, a situation of studied indifference.

Throughout the centuries, the Mexican aristocracy, more than any of the Western aristocracies, has been a very small endogamous and endogenous group.[4] Although dispersed throughout the country, the overwhelming majority of aristocratic families knew the boundaries of the group, its membership, and its composite segments in terms of prominence and antiquity of lineage. Nothing of the sort characterizes the plutocracy, which by definition is an open, mobile group with shallow lineage and tradition. The plutocracy is a fairly open and loosely bounded superordinate segment, essentially no different from other classes in the overall stratification system. Membership in the plutocracy is achieved and recognized solely as a result of economic and political achievements. Regardless of social extraction, any individual, and by extension his family, who reaches a plateau of power and wealth is recognized by other plutocrats as a member of the plutocracy, provided that he displays his power and wealth visibly enough. Despite its openness and lack of precise boundaries, the plutocracy does exhibit considerable consciousness of kind and awareness of its social and economic roles. But the plutocracy is not homogeneous. It exhibits a degree of differentiation that has direct implications for assessing its interaction with the aristocracy in the terminal phase.

Three fairly distinct groups compose the Mexican plutocracy. First, there are plutocratic families expressively impervious or new to the game of upward mobility. This group includes both plutocrats of old standing—that is, who have been rich and powerful since the 1940s—and plutocrats of more recent standing. The former are plutocratic families who never manifested any inclination to upgrade their social status, despite the fact that many of them counted among the richest and most powerful. They were quite content to retain their middle-class origins and showed little or no interest in wealthy display. The latter, on the other hand, are plutocrats too recent to assess the advantages and disadvantages of upward mobility. They do not yet have the required connections and are among the least affluent. Altogether this group is a minority that accounts for no more than 20 percent of plutocratic families.

The second group is comprised of plutocratic families of old standing and most of the families of foreign plutocrats of more recent standing. This group constitutes the majority of plutocrats, roughly 65 percent, and includes the richest and most powerful. Well-connected to the aristocracy, some of them for two generations, this majority pursues an independent social life, does not allow itself to be patronized by aristocrats, and is undoubtedly creating its own expressive domains. This is the most visible segment of the plutocracy; their members are constantly in the limelight, and as far as the middle classes are concerned, they are *the* social class, as the term is employed throughout this monograph. Expressively and behaviorally, they have internalized many aristocratic patterns and domains, but they have also been influenced by the foreign elements in their ranks. This plutocratic majority is becoming the model of upward mobility and may in the future develop into a new "aristocracy" if the superordinate system retains sufficient traditional elements.

Third, about 15 percent of plutocratic families who achieved that standing forty-five to fifty years ago have successfully integrated into aristocratic circles, and to all intents and purposes they have been accepted as members of the group by all liberal aristocrats. This group of plutocrats ranges from a few among the richest to a majority with medium-size fortunes, mostly in manufacturing and agrarian enterprises. Most intermarriages of aristocrats are contracted with members of this group. In the traditional fashion, this group of plutocrats has followed the path of acculturative integration and is the most likely to become a main pillar of the Mexican superordinate stratification system in the decades to come.

Aristocrats themselves present a varied interaction with the plutocracy that may be outlined as follows. First, the conservative sector of the aristocracy, a distinct minority, has, so to speak, gone underground: totally centered in the household, entirely endogamous, and under no circumstances willing to interact with anyone but its own. All grown-up members of this group fit this characterization, but their children are another matter. Some of them adhere to the views of their elders, but many are in open revolt and in search of wider social horizons, namely, interaction with the rich and powerful, among whom their names still count in the marriage game. Second, the majority of aristocrats are still open and maintain social relations with the various sectors of the plutocracy in several contexts. While the household is still the endogenous center of social activity, it is now more open to social interaction with plutocrats, and the overall configuration of relationships has become fairly symmetrical. Intermarriage with plutocrats has increased since the late 1970s, and it is now accepted as a matter of course and necessity. Third, 10 percent of aristocrats, as I have stated, straddle the aristocratic-plutocratic spectrum, they are the most acculturated to plutocratic ways, and their intermarriage with plutocrats is common.

TERMINAL VALUE OF THE ARISTOCRATIC EXPRESSIVE COMMODITY

The process of acculturation that has affected the aristocracy and plutocracy of Mexico since 1940 may be summarized in three developmental stages. (1) During the early 1940s, the new plutocracy made its appearance as a group to be reckoned with economically. Its social recognition by the aristocracy came fairly slowly, and it was not until the mid-1950s that its presence was generally established. This period was characterized by tentative, groping advances on the part of the plutocracy and cautious appraisal and grudging acceptance on the part of the aristocracy. Within fifteen years, the majority of the plutocracy shed its outward middle-class trappings and acquired those of the aristocracy. The social interaction of the two sectors occurred mainly in the public context of business and banking, and on the whole it remained quite formal. (2) From the mid-1950s until about the mid-1970s, the plutocracy became well versed in the details of upper-class genteel behavior. It took a more forceful social position, making its wealth and economic power an explicit instrument of assertive mobility. The aristocracy became increasingly willing to extend social recognition, some aristocrats opened themselves completely, as the manners and mores of the plutocracy came to resemble their own. Social interaction was extended to the home, though still somewhat asymmetrically, in that plutocrats extended themselves willingly and lavishly, whereas aristocrats largely retained the home as a last bastion of endogenous expression. (3) Since the mid-1970s the acculturative cycle of expressive transference from the aristocracy to the plutocracy has ended, and a significant homogenization of expressive and behavioral patterns has been achieved, including the transference of plutocratic attitudes to the aristocracy. Most plutocrats have been sufficiently transformed to pass for upper-upper class, while aristocrats have toned down their ancient claims so as to interact as equals with those who have most of the wealth and economic power. The center of social interaction has now significantly shifted to the almost sacred preserve of the aristocratic household, and only the most conservative and recalcitrant aristocrats do not extend full social recognition to the average plutocrat.

Intermarriage between aristocrats and plutocrats has taken place in all three acculturative stages, but only recently has it become common. There is no doubt that intermarriage will soon become generalized. When it does, and the cherished endogamy of the aristocracy comes to an end, it will certainly accelerate the conclusion of the final stage: the last gasp of the aristocracy as a self-defined, highly conscious, and delineated group.

Throughout this chapter, I have used the term *aristocracy* with some hesitation to characterize the descendants of the old ruling class of Mexico. My justification for using the term is essentially taxonomic, in that it discriminates properly the three main sectors of the haute bourgeoisie since the Mexican Revolution. Despite their self-awareness as a class and pride in their illustrious past, most aristocrats acknowledge their anomalous position: they are the holders of social prestige but cannot buttress it with the kind of wealth that had traditionally accompanied it. When asked to define their social class, most aristocrats today respond "éramos aristócratas pero ahora somos de clase alta" (we were aristocrats but now we belong to the upper class). Even the few who quixotically maintain that they are still aristocrats by virtue of lineage and tradition qualify their answer by saying "aunque ahora lo único que vale es el dinero y pronto vamos a pasar a la historia" (though today money is the only thing that counts and we shall soon pass into oblivion). Eighty years of hardship and dwindling wealth have made aristocrats realize that social status and prestige without adequate wealth can carry them only so far and that they are reaching a stage when they will no longer be able to maintain collective consciousness and self-identity.

The younger married generation expresses this final transformation well when they say that their children will grow up in a different world: they will no longer be able to guide their interaction with youngsters of the plutocracy and upper-middle class, and as a consequence, many of the customs and manners that were exclusively theirs will disappear. Indeed, most sensible parents are in subtle ways preparing their children for the change. Young married couples view the transformation not altogether negatively, as a kind of release from the past, representing a more realistic attitude consonant with their present economic position. The older generations, however, are experiencing a sad blow, and for them, the future promises only the painful experience of witnessing the demise of centuries of development.

It is more difficult to gauge the ideology and general attitudes of the plutocracy toward the aristocracy. It is clear, however, that they have not gloated over their overwhelming economic dominance. The average plutocrat has learned from aristocrats not to flaunt wealth and to discourage ostentatious displays. Their wealth and economic power are enough to sustain them as the dominant sector of the haute bourgeoisie and to dismiss the slights of the most snobbish aristocrats. Plutocrats know that the future is theirs and that in the end, social status, prestige, and the material symbols that accompany them cannot contend against wealth and economic power. Even more than aristocrats, plutocrats know their history well: lineage, social manners, and expressive comportment are essential, but they persist only when buttressed with appropriate power and wealth.

The aristocratic-plutocratic synthesis or amalgamation that was taking place and heading for a resolution until the early 1970s was not realized, and from the early 1980s onward, the aristocracy and plutocracy began in fact to diverge. On the one hand, most aristocrats are either withdrawing or no longer seeking social interaction with plutocrats. The main reason for this attitude is the perception that, if their survival as a class is nearing an end, they should perish true to their aristocratic ideology. Here again, the cleavage between the younger and older generations has the aristocracy in a state of disarray that accelerates the pace to disappearance. On the other hand, the majority of plutocrats no longer exhibit a conscious rapport with aristocrats—they have learned all they desired from aristocrats and are no longer drawn to the aristocratic worldview. In the emerging *imago mundi* of plutocrats, achievement, power, and wealth supplant lineage and tradition, and this independent realization sustains recent plutocratic assurance. But plutocrats know that if they are going to survive and prosper as a social and ruling class they must create their own "lineage" and tradition. The younger generation of aristocrats will be the purveyors of these commodities that plutocrats are still eager to acquire, as the rapidly increasing marriages of aristocrats and plutocrats indicate, and from this standpoint, a sort of acculturative synthesis will perhaps emerge in the near future.

The Fourth, Terminal Renewal (1940–90) and Economic Stratification

We come to the end of a long journey, and the unbroken continuity of a social class is nearly over. Three renewals (1550–1630, 1730–1810, and 1850–1900) marked the evolution of the aristocracy, and during these periods, the superordinate class was restructured and renovated socially and expressively. The three renewals differed from one another with respect to the circumstances that provoked them and the economic and political circumstances that configured them, but in three respects they were the same: the numerical strength of the aristocracy remained rather constant, due primarily to a balanced rate of upward and downward mobility; the upwardly mobile sector was invariably constituted by nouveaux riches plutocrats and men of affairs who had amassed large fortunes, not infrequently in rather short periods of time; and the process of social and expressive acculturation was always asymmetrical, that is, upwardly mobile plutocrats had to acquire and internalize the *imago mundi* of aristocrats to earn incorporation.

The fundamental common denominator of renewals and periods of slackening upward mobility until the Mexican Revolution of 1910 was that the aristocracy uninterruptedly remained the preeminent social and ruling class. It was never threatened by the plutocracy, and the aristocracy recognized and accepted upwardly mobile plutocrats on its own terms. Nonetheless, the plutocracy did contribute to the acculturative social and expressive process, and from this standpoint the aristocracy was truly renewed not only by new blood joining its ranks, but perhaps more significantly by learning new economic lessons from the plutocracy.

In terms of lineage and tradition, who are aristocrats today? (1) Descendants of conquistadors, *encomenderos,* and settlers (quite often founders of cities and towns), the original nucleus of the aristocracy that by 1560 was the budding social and ruling class of New Spain.

This group of aristocratic families is very small, numbering less than 10 percent. (2) Descendants of plutocrats of various extractions who achieved aristocratic rank by the end of the first renewal, most of whom had become or would soon become great *hacendados* engaged in mining and commercial operations. Perhaps 25 percent of all aristocratic families can substantiate this claim, and they are among the most prominent families today. (3) Descendants of plutocrats who achieved aristocratic status during the second renewal, that is, the great *hacendado*, mining, and trading plutocracy that dominated New Spain from the middle of the eighteenth century until the end of Colonial times. Slightly over 50 percent of aristocratic families fall into this category. (4) Descendants of plutocrats who achieved aristocratic status during the third renewal, mainly bankers, manufacturers, and assorted businessmen of domestic and foreign extraction who amassed great fortunes during the second half of the nineteenth century. Perhaps 15 percent of families fall into this category. These are recognized segments of the aristocracy today. But within the wider context of the haute bourgeoisie, the aristocracy is perceived as a fairly homogeneous group, as social and expressive relations with the plutocracy have unfolded during the terminal renewal.

The last transformation to affect the Mexican aristocracy departs radically from all previous transformations. Strictly speaking, it is not a *renewal* as the term has been used in this monograph. *Terminal renewal,* as the term indicates, entails the beginning of the end of the aristocracy as a distinct sector of superordinate stratification. The final renewal may be encapsulated as entailing the following consequences. The aristocracy lost all political influence with the revolution, which was a blow severe enough to affect its social and ruling predominance. But the aristocracy survived economically until the 1934 land reform, when almost overnight it ceased to be a factor in the economic life of the nation. Even this second blow was insufficient to dislodge it from its position as the social class of the nation concentrated in Mexico City. From 1940 to 1970, the aristocracy was still the recognized social class of the country. In the early part of this period it underwent a sort of renaissance, and throughout most of these years, it played its traditional role as the expressive model for upwardly mobile plutocrats. Up to this point, then, the aristocracy still may be considered as undergoing a renewal of sorts. From 1970 onward, however, the aristocracy has withdrawn while the plutocracy has asserted itself socially.

The Mexican Revolution is the sufficient but not necessary cause of the aristocracy's political, economic, and social decline over the past eighty years. It would have taken longer, and the aristocracy would have survived with a greater social role, had the revolution not taken place. In short, the aristocracy would not have been able to compete economically with the rising plutocracy: agrarian-generated wealth since the early nineteenth century has never been able to compete with industrial wealth; and, as Pareto (1980:31–93) brilliantly describes, elites come to an end and are superseded by newer elites because they cannot adapt themselves to new constraints and are not able to innovate sufficiently to prevail. The Mexican aristocracy was not able to adapt to an economic world in which land was no longer the main wealth-producing mechanism. Though a few aristocrats became successful businessmen, the great majority were constrained by an *imago mundi* that even dire economic necessity could not totally overcome.

The Mexican aristocracy survived because of the unusual ethnic and colonial conditions that existed in Mexico until the turn of the century. With these conditions gone or greatly altered since 1910, the aristocracy eighty years later is reduced to an almost subterranean social class. Still, even with its expressive commodity largely unmarketable, the aristocracy survives as a marriage market, as an almost stavistic symbol of the past. By contrast, western European aristocracies have survived somewhat better, perhaps because, for the past 130 years at least, revolutions have not accelerated their demise and their symbolic and physical presence—as embodied in titles of nobility, the ritual roles that aristocrats still occasionally play, and the palaces still in their hands—is more historically imprinted in the societal consciousness. In Mexico, lack of awareness of the aristocracy has been a negative factor for its survival as a distinct social class, as its palaces and titles are beyond the perception of the overwhelming majority of the population.

The plutocracy, on the other hand, still ascends socially and as a ruling class, and barring a major upheaval it will have reached maturity within a generation. The continuing democratization of society will undoubtedly preclude the configuration of a social class approaching the position of the aristocracy eighty years ago, for it was the de facto estatelike configuration of Mexican society until the 1910 Revolution that allowed the aristocracy to constitute an endogenous, largely endogamous, and quite closed social class. It is in this sense that aristocracies have come to an end in the twentieth century, as the last one hundred years have witnessed a thorough transition to a class system. The last vestiges of estate privilege, and the implicit and explicit constraints that it imposes on the development of society, have been largely eliminated. The Mexican plutocracy today is a fluid social class with none of the characteristics of a possible "aristocracy" of the future. This is not to suggest that the plutocracy is so fluid and unstructured that it would entail renewal every generation or so. Indeed, as the superordinate class in the stratification system, the Mexican plutocracy has developed along quite similar lines as those of the established plutocracies (ruling classes) of the United States and Western Europe.

Finally, to round out the analysis, a few remarks on the Mexican stratification system as a whole: The main factors that structured the changes in class stratification since the 1910 Revolution were the disappearance of the traditions and constraints of the estate system, the significant elimination of ethnic considerations in class formation, and the growing awareness of citizenship among the population at large. In postrevolutionary society, the nineteenth century idea that all Mexicans have equal rights before the law slowly came to fruition, and in this respect the leadership of the Mexican Revolution played a crucial role. By the mid-twentieth century, Mexican society was basically democratic, though still saddled with political and economic systems that did not reflect the global evolution of society. Since then, and particularly during the past few years, Mexico has been evolving into a full-fledged democracy, as clearly expressed in the diversification and fluidity of the entire stratification system. In the twentieth century, ethnic terms such as *Creole* and *Mestizo* have lost almost all categorizing value, at least as far as stratification is concerned. They do, of course, survive, but mostly as entities with little or no descriptive value or in the context of interaction with Indian society, a segment of the country's population that remains largely outside the national culture. In a nutshell, the Mexican stratification system in 1990 presents an array of classes fundamentally no different from the U.S. stratification system. Mobility has increased greatly since the Second World War, particularly from the middle to the top rungs of the stratification system, and although the middle classes are still much smaller than in industrial countries, their ranks have been growing rapidly during the past two decades. The categorization of class in Mexico today is essentially the same as that of most modern industrial countries, and it is based on the following criteria: wealth, occupation, residence, education, antiquity in place of origin, and prestige (see Ossowski 1963; Mills 1966). In Mexico these criteria receive differential weight, to be sure, and they reflect a stratification system that, on its way to maturity, still exhibits some of the constraints of the past: ethnicity, cultural somaticism, and a certain lack of citizenship. Moreover, with respect to the expressive and behavioral components of class, a leveling process has occurred across the entire spectrum of the stratification system, and only the upper and lower rungs have retained largely distinct expressive arrays.

I would venture the following outline of class stratification in Mexico today. At the top, we find a very small haute bourgeoisie enfranchised in Mexico City and a few provincial cities composed of a minuscule, dying aristocracy, a larger plutocracy, and a small tottering political class. Below these three clearly discernible rungs the distinctions become somewhat murky, caused mainly by the sudden mobility that set in after World War Two. Nonetheless, one can speak of a lower-upper class of medium-size manufacturers, large-scale merchants, and assorted businessmen. This group is still relatively small and is found in all large and medium-size cities of the country. Just below is an upper-middle class of professionals enfranchised in the cities and affluent farmers enfranchised in the country and small cities and towns. This class is the most difficult to configure for in the capital as well as in many provincial cities it includes many *familias venidas a menos* and even more families who had attained solid middle-class position at the turn of the century. This array of the rich and powerful and of the country's economically privileged constitutes no more than 8 percent of the population. Below this group the situation is even more confused, primarily because mobility has been most evident into the middle-middle and lower-middle classes. The former includes some professionals, retailers, and small businessmen, and the latter is composed essentially of the urban factory workers and small farmers. The middle-middle and lower-middle classes constitute probably 35 percent of the total population and are mostly urban dwellers. Below this point, it is impossible to discriminate in terms of upper, middle, and lower; under the rubric of lower class is included an immense and varied conglomerate of manual workers, small artisans, peasants, and so on—not including the Indians. The lower classes constitute about 60 percent of the population, and they are, of course, found in all the types of cities, towns, and villages of the country.

Regional variations are important. As one moves from the city to the country and through the many distinct regions of the nation, the equivalence of classes changes greatly. For example, shortly after the migration of aristocrats to Mexico City in the late 1930s and early 1940s, their positions as provincial social and ruling classes were occupied by locally bred plutocracies that a generation or so later became the new social and ruling classes of large and medium-size cities throughout the country. These new provincial plutocrats were of foreign (Spain and the Near East) and local extraction that in a relatively short time had come to dominate the business and manufacturing of the cities. They became the local "upper" classes, but most of them could not be so classified in terms of a national standard. Today, they are undoubtedly the ruling classes of many cities, but they are not part of the national plutocracy, and socially they are equivalent to the upper-middle class of Mexico City. This is the case, for example, in my preliminary study of the stratification of the cities of Puebla (1,750,000), Córdoba (250,000), Orizaba (200,000), Tehuacan (80,000), and Texmelucan (60,000) in the states of Puebla and Veracruz. Another noticeable phenomenon is that the stratification of provincial cities and regions is less elaborate than that of Mexico City, Guadalajara, and Monterrey, where the full array of classes and its subdivisions resemble most the U.S. system described by sociologists (Bendix and Lipset 1966; Coleman and Rainwater 1978; Ossowski 1963).

Conclusions

The recurrent themes of the monograph may be summarized as follows: there is an unbroken continuity in the ideology and *imago mundi* of the Western aristocracy from classical times to the present; the Mexican aristocracy is a variant of the Western aristocracy; the differences between the Spanish and Mexican aristocracies are underlined by ethnic and demographic conditions that prevailed in the New World; regardless of the drastic changes that twice marked the 450-year evolution of the Mexican aristocracy, and despite upward and downward mobility, there is unbroken structural and ideological continuity; superordinate stratification constitutes the fundamental milieu in which the aristocracy, haute bourgeoisie, and political class exercise exclusive and complementary functions as the dominant sectors of the nation; and every significant period from the Spanish Conquest to the present is characterized by an expressive array that, albeit reflective of a largely unchanging worldview, is modified by changing economic and political conditions.

I conclude this monograph by addressing three major topics: (1) The analytical significance of the fourfold approach (see Introduction) for the historical and evolutionary study of superordinate stratification in particular and stratification in general. I seek thus to establish the relationship between expressive and structural components in a single conceptual framework. (2) A synoptic assessment of what has been accomplished in the study of the aristocracy as an estate and class within the Mexican context in particular and the Western context in general. (3) The effects of the aristocracy on the configuration of class stratification and on the democratization of society in modern times.

Analytical Significance and Results of the Study

STRUCTURAL AND IDEOLOGICAL IMPLICATIONS IN THE TRANSITION FROM ESTATE TO CLASS

Estate and class as defined by modern social science are two categorically different sociological entities. Logically and epistemologically, of course, class has historically been a sociologically meaningful category of estate, the most common examples, as discussed in chapters 1, 2, and 3, being the upper and lower nobility composing the superordinate estate and the various categories composing the commoner estate in traditional western European society. The characteristic defining property of class is equality before the law for the entire body politic, though customary inequalities are bound to arise in the most egalitarian system. Classes thus are the product of the past two centuries, whereas in the Western tradition the preceding two millennia are characterized by the invariable presence of an estate organization. Thus, "Athenian democracy" is a misnomer, since there were probably as many slaves as there were citizens, and the latter were divided into a mild estate system. Keeping estate and class as separate and distinct conceptual categories is not a mere terminological matter, but a matter of capital importance for the historical analysis of stratification everywhere.

Although Toennies (1931) made the distinction between estate and class more than seventy years ago, historians and historical sociologists still confuse these stratification categories. Often, too, they employ the term *estate* to refer to divisions in Western society without drawing appropriate stratificational implications, as for example in the division of late medieval and early modern Western society into the noble, ecclesiastic, and commoner estates. In this case the ecclesiastic is an estate—as the priestly hierarchies had privileges that, at least vis-à-vis the commoner estate, placed the latter in a position of inequality before the law—but not a stratificational category. A conceptual distinction between estate and class is necessary to understand and explain the evolution and structural configuration of stratification, certainly in the Western cultural tradition and perhaps in all other civilized traditions. From the dawn of Western society until the late eighteenth century the estate system was the fundamental form of stratification. One can speculate, however, that under the influence of

Greek and Roman naturalism during the first two centuries of our era, classes in the modern sense could have developed by the abolition of slavery. The spread of Christianity, however, fostered a slightly new form of the estate system and supported the divine right of kings to rule, orientalizing society. One could encapsulate the role of Christianity by saying that it sacralized Western society and forged the feudal and seigneurial systems that operated for a thousand years as the cornerstone of the Western stratification system. The Dark Ages that followed after the middle of the fifth century constituted the formative period of Feudalism; the classical estate system was redefined, becoming unwieldy and more endogenous than ever before. From 800 to 1200, Feudalism reigned supreme, the noble and commoner estates sharply bifurcated Western society, and only in a few Italian and northern European cities did the fluidity of stratification survive. From 1200 onward, Feudalism rapidly declined and seigneurialism took its place, and this change ushered in a return to the fluidity of the first centuries of the Christian era. In this new milieu, roughly until the beginning of the sixteenth century, the bourgeoisie, as a distinct social class of the commoner estate, had its inception and began to thrive. With the rise of absolutism, from as early as the last quarter of the fifteenth century, the noble estate began to decline: by 1650, it had ceased to be a political class; by 1800, its role as a ruling class was being seriously challenged; and by 1900, it had been reduced to a mere social class.

Class stratification began during the second half of the eighteenth century, but its period of gestation began with absolutism, perhaps even earlier. The first class that came into existence, as a reasonably well bounded entity with a fairly high consciousness of itself, was the haute bourgeoisie. This class constituted the top rung of the mercantile, and later the manufacturing and industrial, bourgeois segment of Western society; it was already a presence in the first half of the fifteenth century, matured in the sixteenth and seventeenth centuries, and began to assert itself powerfully from the middle of the eighteenth century. From roughly 1600 to 1750, the haute bourgeoisie may be regarded as a class in the modern sense. Class stratification did not, of course, come into existence overnight. Not only the haute bourgeoisie but kindred segments of commoner society as well had a long period of gestation that began in late medieval times. What I am emphasizing is simply that after the two great revolutions of modern times—when most of the privileges of the noble estate had been abolished and national states instituted equality before the law—classes based on property, occupation, education, and other classical determinants came into existence as the main if not sole configuration of society. Thus, as long as the noble estate retained a significant modicum of privileges, classes remained at the formative period.

The nearly eight hundred years from the fall of the Roman Empire to the transition from Feudalism to seigneuralism constituted the most stringently stratified period of Western society. The estate system approached the configuration of a caste system. The transition from Feudalism to seigneuralism is the starting point of the liberation of the masses, and every juridical and customary gain from Magna Carta to the American and French Revolutions brought Western society closer to class stratification. Some of the changes during the late Middle Ages can be explained as aspects of the overall evolution of Western society. More difficult to explain are the evolutionary changes in the period between 1500 and 1750 that led to the egalitarian society triggered by the American and French Revolutions. While undoubtedly these changes owe to specific material causes—the invention of the printing press, the intensification of technology and production, and the great discoveries of the time—they are ultimately the result of the naturalization and secularization of society that, rejecting deus ex machina as the only approach to understanding and explaining the external world, break the control of the church and give birth to modern sciences. In this ambiance of intellectual liberation and increasingly naturalistic approaches to all domains of existence, the French philosophers of the Enlightenment and kindred scholars everywhere rejected the divine right of kings to rule, asserted the basic rights of man, and challenged the privileges of the aristocracy.

The composition and overall configuration of the aristocracy as the superordinate estate have varied significantly in the long history of Western society. Disregarding the ancient, classical period, how can the situation be characterized since the onset of Feudalism in about 800? First, during this thousand-year period there was a significant degree of national and even regional variation, both with respect to the composition of the aristocracy and its social, economic, and political power. A brief example may clarify this complex problem. In Britain, the feudal system was always milder and less controlling than on the continent, and even the Norman Conquest did not significantly equalize the situation. On the continent itself there was much variation, resulting in a wide range of confrontation but seldom in compromise and accommodation. Moreover, overall variation also obtained longitudinally, with the most exploitation of the commoner estate occurring in the twelfth century.

Second, the divisions into which the superordinate and subordinate estates were configured characterized this long period universally. These divisions were classes in the modern, sociological definition of the term: they were configured along occupational, ruling, manufacturing, and producing lines; they exhibited a modicum of endogeny and a tendency toward connubial endogamy; and their membership had distinct juridical status. The superordinate estate was composed of two basic classes, namely, the greater and the lesser nobility, which is to say the great feudal lords (tenants-in-chief, king's barons, and vavasors) and the lords of the manor and knights. When titles of nobility came into existence by the middle of the thirteenth century, the former became the titled or higher nobility and the latter the lower nobility. As classes, the titled nobility and the gentry significantly overlapped, for they shared the same *imago mundi* and had similar expressive arrays and connubial rights. The subordinate, commoner estate, by contrast, was more diversified. Moreover, composition of the commonality changed throughout the feudal and seigneurial periods. During most of Feudalism there were basically four commoner classes: the burghers ("bourgeoisie," traders, and merchants); the free farmers and peasants (sometimes known collectively as the yeomanry in England, as *behetrías* in Spain, and by other names elsewhere in western Europe); the villenage (semifree peasants tied to feudal demesnes); and the serfdom (totally bound to feudal lords). By the end of the Middle Ages, serfdom had largely disappeared. The burgher class of merchants and traders had diversified, and an elite of their members, the haute bourgeoisie, had come into existence.

Third, concentrating exclusively on the superordinate estate, the position of the aristocracy changed as western European society evolved from Feudalism to seigneurialism to a less stringent form of seigneurialism from the sixteenth to the eighteenth century. Throughout Feudalism, the social, economic, and political control of the aristocracy over the commonality was nearly absolute, for centralized authority vested in the king was very weak. From 1200, as the military components of Feudalism waned and the king acquired more control, the seigneurial nobility lost some political power but continued to dominate its vast domains socially and economically. From the last decades of the fifteenth century, the aristocracy, particularly the titled nobility, increasingly lost political control as the king became an absolute monarch. And by the end of the eighteenth century, the aristocracy had no political functions, except perhaps at the local level, but it was still a powerful economic factor.

The onset of the class system as the sole configurational mechanism of society engaged political and economic forces that, first slowly but with increasing rapidity during the second half of the nineteenth century, radically changed the power, control, and configuration of the aristocracy. At this stage of development, the aristocracy was no longer an estate but an anomalous class. Most of its privileges were gone, but the force of tradition and a few surviving privileges allowed it to continue to play an important role in the superordinate stratification system. From the demise of the ancien régime until the present, the economic power of the aristocracy has declined continuously, and by the turn of the twentieth century few European aristocrats could be counted among the rich and powerful.

How does the haute bourgeoisie fit the foregoing context? Equivalents of the haute bourgeoisie, as a kind of intermediary class between the noble and commoner estates and as a breeding ground of upward mobility into the superordinate estate, are rather common in Western society. The best known of these historical "haute bourgeoisies" is the knightly class that took root as the Romans expanded throughout the Mediterranean world. By the onset of the principate, the *equites* as a class had risen out of their role as *publicani* and came to occupy a special position between the patrician and plebeian estates. The haute bourgeoisie in modern times has different origins, but it is nonetheless striking how by the end of the seventeenth century it had come to occupy a position similar to that of the *equites,* namely, as a class straddling the noble and commoner estates. By the last decades of the eighteenth century, the haute bourgeoisie was already a powerful economic force, and in the following decades its members counted among the most prominent architects of the Industrial Revolution. Throughout the nineteenth century they became the driving economic force of European nations, and in the twentieth century they rivaled the declining aristocracy socially.

CONTINUITY, CHANGE, AND TRANSFORMATION IN THE EVOLUTION OF SUPERORDINATE STRATIFICATION

Superordinate stratification in Western society has been constant from classical times to the present, reflecting the changing continuity of the estate system from the mature stage of Feudalism in the tenth century. The best way to describe this millennium is as the continuity of an aristocratic ideology and *imago mundi* that configured a way of life circumscribed by the noble estate, but periodically undergoing changes and transformations in the structure of personnel and its articulation to the global society. The evolution of the aristocracy, nobility, and superordinate stratification is best explained by the combined models of Aron's tripartite configuration of superordinate stratification and Pareto's renewal of elites.

The Roman aristocracy throughout the entire Republican period (510–44 B.C.) constituted the absolute social, ruling, and political class, although the patricians were seriously challenged politically by the plebeians beginning in the middle of the second century. Throughout the principate (27 B.C.–A.D. 280), the aristocracy remained the social class, faced constant challenge from upwardly mobile elements as a ruling class, and ceased to be a political class, as all political power emanated from the emperor (*princeps*). During the empire (280–476), a motley aristocracy continued to be the preeminent social class, sharing its position as a ruling class with diverse upwardly mobile elements, while the political class was the imperial bureaucracy and the army as emperor-makers. The Germanic conquest was the most drastic change undergone by Western society in its entire existence. This period, extending roughly until the death of Charlemagne in 814, may be regarded as the gestation of Feudalism, during which Roman and Germanic institutions underwent a period of amalgamation characterized by acculturation. The new estate system that came into existence included Roman and Germanic elements but reflected an ideology that was more Germanic than Roman and that has pervaded the configuration of the aristocracy until the present. The two most important inputs to the acculturation equation of this period were the Germanic notion of kingship as derived or sanctioned by the gods and the division of the noble estate into a two-tier system of kingly families and a large retinue of knightly warriors.

The feudal period lasted roughly four hundred years. Early in this period, the feudal aristocracy acquired its classic two-tier configuration, and so did the commoner estate. Throughout this entire period, the noble estate constituted the overwhelmingly dominant social, ruling, and political class of western Europe. In the transition to seigneurialism, the aristocracy continued its social, economic, and political domination, though it was somewhat curtailed by the increasing power of the king, the economic growth of the bourgeoisie, and the de facto abolition of serfdom. This state of affairs lasted until the close of the Middle Ages, when, with the rise of modern absolutism, the nobility ceased to be a political class. The sixteenth century was a period of transition, as the aristocratic class acquired a slightly different social and ruling configuration: absolutism forced perhaps the majority of the titled nobility to become courtiers and to disregard their landed estates; the haute bourgeoisie as a class began to make itself felt economically and politically; and the lesser nobility, as the result of centralization, began to lose local political power. From 1600 until the French Revolution, the aristocracy as social class still reigned supreme but was steadily challenged by the haute bourgeoisie as a ruling class. The last two centuries in the development of Western aristocracy fall into two periods. During the nineteenth century the aristocracy remained unchallenged as a social class, but by the middle of the century it had been surpassed as a ruling class by the haute bourgeoisie. During the twentieth century, the last vestiges of ruling power vanished, and the aristocracy precariously maintained social class superordination until the Second World War. Thenceforward the aristocracy steadily lost ground to the haute bourgeoisie and is now a vanishing social class.

A number of problems remain to be addressed concerning the configuration of superordinate stratification if the model is to be applied comparatively and synchronically. First, we must circumscribe and delimit the membership of social, ruling, and political classes and assess their functions synchronically and diachronically. I have demonstrated how the Mexican aristocracy discharged superordinate social and ruling functions, while political class functions rested in the hands of *peninsulares,* direct representatives of the Spanish Crown. The superordinate social and ruling segment of the aristocracy, as an essentially Creole group, coexisted with the *peninsular* political class without undue friction and antagonistic interests, demonstrating that social, ruling, and political functions in superordinate stratification can be, and in modern times almost invariably have been, vested in separate classes.

Second, the interrelation of social, ruling, and political classes requires more analysis. As structurally circumscribed as social, ruling, and political classes may be, they are to a large extent open social groups, and their functions cut across class boundaries. This cross-cutting occurs particularly during periods of revolutionary transition or rapid change, as for example during the Roman principate on a gigantic scale, or after the Mexican Revolution of 1910 on a minor scale. More specifically, during Colonial times in Mexico, the division between the social and ruling functions vested in the Creole aristocracy and the political functions vested in the Crown were clear-cut. Yet some Creole aristocrats held political office, while significant numbers of Crown officials became great landowners and married into the local aristocracy.

A third issue, the relationship of upward and downward superordinate mobility and the division of social, ruling, and political functions was addressed implicitly in the chapters dealing with the Mexican aristocracy. It is evident, for example, that the more completely social, ruling, and political functions are vested in a single stratificational unit, the less the degree of upward or downward mobility. The more diversified social, ruling, and political functions are within the superordinate system, however, the higher the degree of upward and downward mobility. The problem is complicated by conquest and revolutionary upheavals as demonstrated by the Spanish Conquest and the Mexican Revolution of 1910. Moreover, when superordinate social, ruling, and political functions are primarily discharged by distinctly separate classes, it is important to establish the mechanisms that condition, foster, or impede membership in these classes, particularly social upward mobility.

Whereas the tripartite conception of superordinate stratification has enabled me to articulate the synchronic and diachronic configuration of the aristocracy into a coherent system by itself and vis-à-vis the global society, Vilfredo Pareto's concept of the renewal of elites has been instrumental in explaining the continuity and adaptation of the aristocracy as a social, ruling, and/or political class. Most significantly, my study indicates that the continuity of aristocracy is greatest in the ideational order, while in the structure of personnel the class is most vulnerable to transformations produced by wider societal changes and adaptations to new environmental, demographic, and political-economic conditions. Indeed, the *imago mundi* of the aristocracy has remained one of the most constant elements in the culture and society of Western Civilization. Several points must be emphasized in order to clarify the renewal of aristocratic personnel.

First, from the macroevolutionary perspective, conquest and revolution have caused the most extreme transformations of the aristocracy's personnel. These events, in fact, are so drastic for the reorganization of superordinate stratification that they can hardly be accounted for by Pareto's renewal of elites: They should be regarded, evolutionarily speaking, as the starting points of new cycles. Thus, the transformation from the republic to the principate ushered in by Augustus radically altered the patrician estate and led to the inclusion of the *equites* in the superordinate estate. Similarly, the establishment of Germanic-Roman societies in western Europe led to the consolidation of Feudalism, which represents a new cycle that came to an end during the second half of the eighteenth century. Within this one thousand-year period one can properly speak of the renewal of elites, for while the feudal ideology and *imago mundi* of the aristocracy hardly changed, the personnel of the aristocracy and its configuration evolved as a series of renewals. On a smaller, more peripheral scale, the case of the Mexican aristocracy is even more illustrative. The Spanish Conquest of Mexico established a Creole aristocracy that, from the middle of the sixteenth century to the middle of the twentieth century, underwent four clear-cut renewals. Each example shows that, although the aristocracy was periodically renewed by the influx of upwardly mobile elements from the top of the subordinate estate, a continuity of personnel often extended for many hundreds of years. In the case of the Mexican aristocracy, about 10 percent of families today can trace descent from conquistadors and *encomenderos* of the sixteenth century, and increasing numbers of families trace direct descent from the ensuing renewals during the first half of the seventeenth century (25 percent), the last fifty years of colonial times (50 percent), and the dictatorship of Porfirio Díaz (15 percent). I intuit that for this time span, and perhaps for two hundred to three hundred years longer, percentages of aristocratic continuity are not much different from most aristocracies of western Europe.

Second, when I assert continuity of content and form I refer primarily to the ideational order, for broader structural features of the aristocracy such as its economic base and variants of political control are much more likely to change in response to global societal transformations. Undoubtedly, the ideational order of Western aristocracy was given definitive form during the first two centuries of Feudalism and has remained basically the same until today. What has changed is the position of the aristocracy vis-à-vis the rest of society: changes brought about by demographic, technological, and revolutionary transformation as Western society moved from Feudalism to seigneurialism to attenuated seigneurialism and finally to a class system. The question is, to what extent have these structural changes affected the ideational order of the aristocracy? Although the aristocracy's political role and its economic base have changed, sometimes greatly, during the past millennium, as a social entity it has remained largely the same; socially, its predominance has not been disputed until very recently; and its self-image is not attuned to the great changes that have affected Western society over the past two hundred years.

Third, the renewal of elites as a concept underlying the evolution of the aristocracy in particular, and superordinate stratification in general, has been discussed in this monograph. Two further points come to mind. The main structural reason for the high degree of continuity of the aristocracy over such a long period of time may very well be that it has always allowed for upward mobility, even at its most endogenous. The renewal of elites thus means a periodic burst of upward mobility from the ranks immediately below, namely, the acquisition of privileges enjoyed exclusively by the superordinate estate and, more specifically, aristocratic recognition after the demise of the ancien régime.[1] The evolution of the Mexican aristocracy indicates that this periodization has been tied intimately to wider economic and political developments and that the bursts of upward mobility lasted for decades followed by periods of stability in which aristocratic recognition took place only occasionally. Furthermore, the peaks and valleys in the renewal of elites must be refined and expanded to other variants of the Western aristocracy. That the peaks and valleys of upward mobility are quantitatively very different among different aristocracies is evident, but a formal implementation of the model requires a precise quantification beyond the scope of this monograph.

To summarize the evolutionary account of the aristocracy, then, I offer the following outline of the relationship of the tripartite configuration of superordinate stratification and the renewal of elites. There is a fairly high degree of concomitance between these synchronic and diachronic models. Specified renewals bring new realignments of the social, ruling, and political functions of the aristocracy enriched by upwardly mobile elements. Of particular importance is the realignment of class functions that obtains at the beginning of a cycle. Thus, the Spanish Conquest established the Creole aristocracy as the social and ruling class of New Spain, with a minimum of political functions, a situation that continued unchanged throughout Republican times until the Revolution of 1910. These initial conditions predicated future renewals of the Mexican aristocracy: a new version of the aristocratic *imago mundi* came into being that to a large extent determined the mechanisms of upward mobility and of each consecutive renewal. But the initial conditions also impeded the discharge of political function, when, after Independence, the aristocracy could have also become the political class.

THE CONFIGURATION OF EXPRESSIVE AND STRUCTURAL INTERPLAY

My basic assumption here is that stratification is one of the most natural domains of realized expression. Classes and estates exhibit expressive arrays that have more in common cross-culturally—that is, in several related but not necessarily adjacent societies—than intraculturally—that is, among the several ranks of a single society. This problem has been discussed elsewhere (Nutini 1988:387–91) and outlined in the Introduction. It pertains only to the exclusive domain that defines and characterizes all social classes today and estates in the past. Two subsidiary assumptions come into play: the most visible component of all stratification units is the expressive array; moreover, this visibility is most striking in superordinate stratification. Though economic and material conditions unquestionably structure the units of stratification, their expressive arrays are the sufficient manifestation of the domains they can configure with the means at their disposal. Thus, the higher the class, the more elaborate the expressive array, particularly in its exclusive domains. This fact explains the vicarious interest that the middle and lower rungs of society have always had with the aristocracy and more recently with the expressive life of the rich and powerful. It should be noted, however, that the expressive array of the aristocracy everywhere since the onset of the twentieth century is no longer a manifestation of their wealth and power, for in these roles they have been superseded by the haute bourgeoisie. Rather, what has maintained the aristocracy as a social class until recently is the atavistic concern with lineage and antiquity and the association to places and events that they evoke.

Chapters 4 and 5 demonstrate how the expressive array of the Mexican aristocracy derived from the ideology and *imago mundi* brought by conquistadors to the New World and modified by the Conquest and the ethnic and demographic situation of the new land. These conditions enabled conquistadors and their descendants to configure an expressive array determined both by the Spanish aristocratic ideology and by the vast land and peoples they conquered, that is, by the vision created by the Conquest itself. Generatively more significant is the fact that the expressive array of the Creole aristocracy was also determined by the social and ruling functions that the aristocracy discharged in the Colonial order. Here again the expressive life of the aristocracy reflects its position in the wider organization of society. The seigneurial components of the Spanish expressive array were continued and to some extent reinforced by the position of the Creole aristocracy as the social and ruling class of New Spain.

Structure and expression are always concomitant—not that this entails a causal relationship; only that structure sets the parameters for the realization of expression, and expression may in turn influence the development of structure. In concrete terms, the expressive array of the Mexican aristocracy was molded by the social, economic, and political control that it had over the Indian population and its influence over the wider Colonial and, later, Republican society. Conversely, the expressive array was instrumental in fostering or impeding the renewals themselves, to the extent that aristocrats were constrained by their expressive array in adapting to changing economic, political, and even demographic conditions, while upwardly mobile plutocrats by contrast profited by such constraints. Thus, the *imago mundi* of any class, particularly a superordinate class, discharged in the exclusive domains of the expressive array may either be a positive or negative force for adaptation and survival.

Two examples may illustrate the inhibiting and enhancing effects of the *imago mundi*–expressive array. For roughly seven hundred years the feudal and seigneurial aristocracies of western Europe did not have to adapt fundamentally to new societal conditions. From 1500 onward, however, western European aristocracies experienced increasing difficulty in adapting to the changing political, economic, and more naturalistic tenor of modern times. First, as a political class, Western aristocracies were never able to reconcile the new requirements of absolutism with the total control exercised under Feudalism and seigneurialism. Second, landownership had been the economic mainstay of the aristocracy since before feudal times and its importance continued uninterrupted until after the demise of the ancien régime. As an ideological consequence, the aristocracy mythologized the land as an end in itself, the only expressively proper way of generating wealth for a warrior caste that by the second century of modern times was a caste in name only. After 1500, many aristocrats indeed engaged in business and mercantile activities, but they did so almost surreptitiously, through intermediaries, for these occupations were still regarded as undignified activities beneath their dignity. Consequently, the aristocracy as a whole never developed the inclination and skills for business, banking, and manufacturing that from the seventeenth century onward became such important wealth-generating activities and that by the beginning of the Industrial Revolution surpassed agrarian enterprises as the economic mainstay of western Europe. By the end of the nineteenth century, therefore, the aristocracy had been replaced as the ruling class by the haute bourgeoisie. Third, the ideology of the Western aristocracy forged during feudal times created an expressive array that made it very difficult for aristocrats to adapt to the naturalization of society, political democratization, and an egalitarian conception of human interaction. Under such conditions, Western aristocracies have been in retreat for more than a century and a half, and they have survived mainly as a function of natural stavism and by implicitly marketing an expressive array that upwardly mobile plutocrats desired. Primarily, then, it was expressive considerations that impeded aristocracies from adapting to the changing conditions of western Europe, and by default they relinquished ruling and political roles.

The evolution of the Mexican aristocracy detailed in this monograph parallels the formation, development, and, particularly, the decline of European aristocracies. After its formation and for two centuries of social and economic domination, the Mexican aristocracy was equally inhibited: after Independence it missed the opportunity to become the political class of the country; throughout the nineteenth century it remained the ruling class but did not follow in the footsteps of the plutocracy, failing to monopolize banking, trading, and manufacturing; and once again after the 1910 Revolution, it did not take advantage of its structural position to share emerging ruling functions with the new plutocracy. What, then, are the enhancing effects of the aristocratic *imago mundi*–expressive array? In periods of strong domination and control, it endows the aristocracy with a unitary ideological configuration that heightens a monolithic self-image and in feedback fashion reinforces domination and control. In periods of decline, however, its effects are entirely negative and accelerate decline. The strongest beneficiaries of the enhancing effects of the aristocratic *imago mundi*–expressive array, in periods of dominance and decline alike, are the upwardly mobile elements vying for aristocratic recognition—that is, in modern times, the haute bourgeoisie.

Mobility in Western stratification from the commoner to the noble estate always proceeded according to fairly well established patterns and circumscribed contexts. Thus, in medieval times, knighthood as a reward for excellence in battle was the main avenue of ennoblement. Beginning in the late fifteenth century, with the feudal aristocracy as a warrior class gone, the context of upward mobility shifted to the economic and political domains, associated respectively with the rise of the bourgeoisie and absolutism. In modern times, the haute bourgeoisie was the most important group vying for aristocratic recognition, and it pursued two avenues of upward mobility: becoming rich and powerful by generating wealth in the increasingly diversified forms available from the sixteenth century onward; and becoming powerful and influential as part of the political class created by the requirements of absolutism. The structural configuration of upward mobility is then established by powerful members of the haute bourgeoisie on the way to staffing new ruling and political classes. The aristocracy nevertheless remained the undisputed social class, and vying for aristocratic recognition became a necessity for most members of the haute bourgeoisie as the final step of upward mobility. Aristocratic recognition and acceptance mean fundamentally expressive recognition and acceptance, that is, that those vying for membership must acquire the manners and behavior of the aristocracy. Such has been the case for more than three hundred years, from the formation of the *noblesse de robe* in seventeenth-century France, to ennoblement of the captains of the Industrial Revolution in nineteenth-century England, to aristocratic acceptance of plutocrats during the regime of Porfirio Díaz in Mexico.

The expressive component entailing positive and negative effects has been crucial in configuring the evolution of the aristocracy as the foremost superordinate entity: it has triggered the renewal of elites by facilitating upward mobility, and it has determined the composition of the aristocracy in terms of social, ruling, and political functions by inhibiting adaptation to changing conditions. At least in modern times, the dynamics of stratification and mobility at the upper rungs have been determined by the traditional conservatism of aristocrats and their virtual inability to change and adapt and by the adaptive capabilities and innovative spirit of upwardly mobile haut bourgeois. Already in the formative years of the Industrial Revolution it had become known that agrarian wealth would have difficulty in competing with business and manufacturing wealth, a fact that had become confirmed by the middle of the nineteenth century. Yet the *imago mundi* and expressive array of aristocrats consistently conspired against a diversification that in the end would have saved most of the land of the great landowners and secured for them a prominent place in the ruling class. Plutocrats and assorted haut bourgeois, on the other hand, innovators, as most upwardly mobile individuals are, took full advantage of their economic power and wealth and successfully adapted to the social requirements of the aristocratic milieu.

The Western and Mexican Aristocracies in Perspective

COMPARATIVE DIMENSIONS IN STRUCTURE AND EXPRESSION

The main substantive theme of this monograph is that the Mexican aristocracy is a marginal version of western European aristocracy, in principle the same, but modified by local ethnic and demographic constraints. Another variable that caused divergent development was the continuation in the New World of an aristocratic pattern that in western Europe was declining, namely, seigneurial control. Furthermore, the Mexican aristocracy did not achieve the physical-expressive realization of the Spanish aristocracy. This disparity can be explained by distance from Europe and the fact that, outside of the aristocracy's landed domains, the Colonial social and political milieux were more egalitarian than those of the mother country.

There is a dichotomous aspect of the Mexican aristocracy that slightly deviates from that of Spain and other European countries. On the one hand, the aristocracy was ideologically enfranchised in its estates, first as *encomenderos* and then as *hacendados*. In this role, the Mexican aristocracy continued the seigneurial system that was declining in Europe even as it had its inception in the New World. Through at least two and a half centuries of Colonial rule, the Creole aristocracy was a throwback to the fifteenth century, and one can make the case that the Mexican aristocracy was one of the last extant manifestations of the seigneurial system in the Western mold. The necessary conditions for this aristocratic variance are the ethnic and demographic considerations that structured the relationship between *encomendero/hacendado* and Indian/surrounding population in a fashion similar to that of the relationship between seigneur and villein, which by the end of the seventeenth century had been outgrown in western Europe. On the other hand, in the urban, wider Colonial and Republican world, though the aristocracy was the undisputed social class and the preeminent ruling class, its control and dominance were significantly tempered by a more "democratic" milieu, which in Colonial times included Creoles and *peninsulares* and after Independence an increasingly powerful plutocracy and Mestizo political class.

Conquistadors and their ideological descendants the *encomenderos* and *hacendados* founded and configured the Creole aristocracy as a seigneurial system and as a model for the Creole and *peninsular* rank and file to emulate, and this social class was indeed perceived in the colony as the epitome of social and ruling excellence. The aristocracy of the mother country, conversely, considered Creole aristocrats parvenue poor cousins that had become uppity and self-important. Thus the aristocracy locally embodied the legendary deed of the Conquest and the myth of the last conquerors that was shared by Creoles and *peninsulares,* while all these perceptions and behaviors were regarded as Colonial conceits by peoples in Spain. The situation reversed after Independence, and the Mexican aristocracy came to be regarded in a different light. As the rising Mestizo middle class of the country came to dominate politics and the professions, to become more educated, and to assert itself as it never had in Colonial times, it lost much of the traditional respect and subservience toward the aristocracy. The new enlightenment of the middle classes created class resentment toward the aristocracy among the majority. Meanwhile, as Colonial times receded, the upper classes of Spain underwent a significant transformation toward their former colonies, and the Conquest acquired an almost mythological aspect. The deeds of the conquistadors acquired heroic proportions, and a new respect for their descendants was generated. Many titles vacated after Independence were reactivated by Spaniards, who forged new links with Mexican aristocrats. By the second half of the nineteenth century, many Mexican aristocrats had developed extensive ties to Spanish aristocrats and renewed old family bonds. By the mid-twentieth century, this marginal aristocracy was more strongly connected to western Europe than it had ever been before.

There are five variants of Western aristocracy: Italian, French, Spanish, English, and German. Each variant has its own slightly different configuration in the domains of ranking organization of dignities, mobility, traditional privileges, power and prestige, and overall position within the global stratification system. The case of the Mexican aristocracy, and perhaps another four or five similarly marginal ones in Latin America, must be regarded as essentially faithful manifestations of the Spanish aristocracy, exhibiting variations even less pronounced than those found among European aristocracies. The unitary meaning of all European and New World variants is to be found in their common ideational order. The ideology, *imago mundi,* and core of expressive domains of Western aristocracies exhibit few perceptible deviations today. With some significant exceptions, the continuity of aristocratic ideational configuration may be traced to classical times. The explanation for this continuity lies in the invariant existence of an estate system that remained fairly constant until the end of the eighteenth century and in the ownership and exploitation of the land as the most important source of generating wealth. Few features of Western culture and society have had such a high degree of continuity for such a long time, and they testify to the ideological persistence and efficacy of an ideology that was the creation of specific structural conditions more than 2,500 years ago.

The Mexican aristocracy was always much smaller than the aristocracies of western Europe. The French aristocracy was the largest, nearly 10 percent of the total population of France by the middle of the eighteenth century, England's aristocracy was less than 5 percent of the population, and Spain's was somewhere in the middle, with some 7 percent.[2] At no time was the total membership of the Mexican aristocracy more than 3 percent of the total population, and at the end of the nineteenth century it was less than 1 percent. These demographic factors indicate that, comparatively speaking, the power and control of the Mexican aristocracy were greater than those of any western European country after the sixteenth century, given that by the end of the nineteenth century, roughly twelve hundred families owned perhaps 50 percent of the arable land of the country.

With the exception of the Germanic conquest of the Roman Empire, when two sociocultural traditions at quite different levels of evolution and complexity met head-on, western European aristocracies have functioned and developed in rather homogeneous ethnic milieux—unlike the marginal aristocracies in the New World. In the Mexican case, the aristocracy as a superordinate estate and class was an imposition on a vast mass of Indian and Mestizo populations that gave a quite different twist to the overall stratification system. The division of the population into two distinct ethnic groups resulted in a stratification system that occasionally surpassed some of the worst aspects of seigneurialism of the fourteenth century, with a degree of control of the dominated population that contrasted sharply with the democratizing changes Europe had been experiencing since the late sixteenth century. In addition, demographic differences between the superordinate and subordinate estates and classes contributed significantly to the inequalities of stratification in the Spanish New World that persist today. This deep inequality led to a slow and quite late development of the middle classes that only recently have most Spanish-speaking countries been able to begin to redress. From a strictly expressive viewpoint, the ethnic component also contributed significant inputs. Though most of the exclusive expressive domains of the Mexican aristocracy were shared with those of western European aristocracies, its inclusive domains were influenced by the expressive culture of the Indian and Mestizo populations. Indeed, since the beginning of the expansion of western European peoples throughout the world five hundred years ago, the aristocratic model has had determinant effects without which many aspects of Colonialism cannot be properly understood.

Even a cursory look at the aristocracies of ancient civilizations and of the modern world reveals how strikingly much they have in common, despite the widely diverse structural contexts in which they flourished. Every civilization since the city-state came into being more than five thousand years ago has had an aristocracy in which most superordinate social, ruling, and political functions have been vested. Not surprisingly, it is in their ideational order that aristocracies worldwide resemble each other most, particularly in the realization of their *imago mundi* in terms of kinship, lineage, and heredity, and in claims of racial superiority and/or supernatural sanction for their exalted position. Even expressive proclivities such as social exclusivity, exalted endogeny, claims to excellence, and a priori belief in inherent superordinate position manifested in every domain of social and cultural life are shared by the most structurally varied aristocracies throughout the world, across time and culture alike.

The Significance of Superordinate Stratification for Stratificational Studies in General

This study demonstrates that Western stratification in general and Mexican stratification in particular must be conceived with reference to the aristocracy for maximum effect. Diachronically, the aristocracy has been the motivating force that has configured other entities of the global stratification system, and it has provided the dynamics for social mobility in the middle and upper rungs of the system. Synchronically, the aristocracy has been the model for the new superordinate class that has been in the process of formation since the demise of the ancien régime. This view of stratification assumes that the effects of stratification are most effectively conceptualized with reference to the superordinate class or estate. Thus, as conquests and revolutions structure new social, ruling, and political classes, as Pareto (1935:176–83) rightly emphasizes, the cycle is renewed and a new superordinate entity comes into being. The transformation from estate to class was heralded by most scholars of the late nineteenth and early twentieth centuries as democratic and promising a nonstratified society. Indeed, Western society and its extensions have become more democratic, but the classless society has not materialized. This new form of stratification, particularly at the top, can best be understood with reference to the dying aristocracies.

Several reasons can be given for adopting this strategy. First, though the transition from estate to class has entailed important, perhaps radical, changes, the latter has retained some characteristics of the former. This continuity is most notable in the upper rungs of the system, where superordinate classes have retained many characteristics of traditional aristocracy. Structurally, social endogamy, exclusivity, and a strong tendency to endogeny have been internalized by the haute bourgeoisie as it creates a new social class after its ruling and political predominance. Expressively, the transference has been even greater, as the century-long process of acculturation has entailed the survival of countless characteristically aristocratic expressive domains. Indeed, there is no sharp break between the aristocracy and haute bourgeoisie; a new expressive array entails most domains of the former, somewhat reinterpreted by the new power and wealth of the latter.

Second, a question I do not explore in this monograph is the extent to which the haute bourgeoisie has been able to transcend the underpinnings of the aristocracy. If we assume that a new superordinate class emerges from the slow decline of an old one, can the initiation of a new ideology and *imago mundi* be established so as to signal the birth of a new superordinate system? I cannot answer this question in terms of the Mexican case. Western European haute bourgeoisies, on the other hand, are at a more advanced stage, and there are indications that they have begun to fashion a number of expressive domains that unmistakably demonstrate a change in the traditional aristocratic *imago mundi*. Thus we see a shift from religion, certain aspects of kinship and descent, and ritual and symbolic functions toward economic activity as an end in itself, the secularization of social relations, and a much more pragmatic and utilitarian view of the world.

Third, one of the premises of this monograph is that every social class has its own expressive array quite distinct from those of other classes in the stratification system. In this regard, the case of the Mexican aristocracy may serve as a model to investigate the structure and expressive composition of the middle and lower classes of any stratification system. Of particular significance within a single stratification system is determining the enhancing and inhibiting effects of the *imago mundi* and expressive array, the exclusive and inclusive domains of the array, and the feedback effect of expressive components in every class. Cross-culturally, however, the study of stratification demands the comparison of classes occupying similar positions in diverse systems. This comparative expressive approach undertaken with reference to superordinate stratification may also elucidate mechanisms that have fashioned similar expressive responses.

Fourth, not much is known about the structural configuration of the new superordinate class that has been emerging for generations, much less about its patterns of interaction with other classes of the global stratification system. The haute bourgeoisie, or plutocratic and political elites, has not expressively matured as an independent social class, but for all intents and purposes it has functioned as the ruling and political class of national states for more than fifty years. Nonetheless, a few generalizations are in order. The Mexican haute bourgeoisie has not yet developed a class consciousness that gives it a unitary view of its position in the global society. Its slowness is understandable, since the model that it internalized from the aristocracy is essentially expressive and not that of a ruling class. At the moment, the ruling and political classes of Mexico appear to be a disjointed conglomerate of sectors looking for a position of leadership that reflects specific interests that have not yet coalesced. Structurally, the ruling and political classes of Mexico still exhibit significant divergent interests and have not yet developed a firm united front. There are some indications, however, that this situation is already changing, and one can expect a more integrated ruling-political class configured along more defined ideological and pragmatic lines and with a higher consciousness of itself. Finally, as a social class, this ruling-political elite has almost arrived, for the aristocracy has practically ceased to be the arbiter of mores, manners, and expressive behavior.

Finally, a word about the class system of the United States. Due to the unusual Colonial situation, centered mostly on lack of a large native Indian population, the composition of the immigrant settlement, and the relationship to England, the thirteen colonies never had an estate system comparable to that of New Spain. That an estate system existed in these colonies until Independence there is no doubt, as they were an extension of England, but it was mild and did not leave a marked impression after Independence. Unconstrained by significant survivals of the estate system and molded by the liberalizing and egalitarian tenets of the Declaration of Independence, the United States initiated the first Western class system. As a consequence of these early egalitarian conditions, the configuration of the superordinate class was never as monolithic as in Mexico or western Europe and the social, ruling, and political classes have always been more diversified. Which discrete groups constitute the ruling and political classes of the United States in the twentieth century has been a matter of considerable debate. No doubt exists concerning the preeminent social class of the country, or more precisely, the regional social classes known by such popular terms as Boston Brahmins, Philadelphia Mainliners, and Virginia Gentry. These social elites are unquestionably the closest the United States has to an aristocracy, as defined in this monograph, and they embody some surviving elements of the *imago mundi* and expressive array of the Colonial estate system.

Concluding Remarks

Midway (1984) in the synchronic, data-gathering investigation of the Mexican aristocracy, I searched for sociological and anthropological studies of the Western aristocracy and associated aspects of nobility in their manifold manifestations that in some systematic fashion addressed these concepts in historical, evolutionary, or sociological perspective. I found none, but I did find a great deal of modern historical accounts of specific periods and problems that contained miscellaneous information on the aristocracy, and a few works dealing directly with the aristocracy. I also found a vast literature written by genealogists, aristocrats, and panegyrists of the aristocracy containing valuable information on many aspects of this social class. Astonishingly, not a single book written by professional historians deals with the aristocracy as a class or estate per se. These glaring omissions led me to expand Part 1 of this monograph from the mere outline I had originally intended.

Reading this literature made me realize that in approaching the study of Western stratification in evolutionary perspective, the aristocracy is the pivotal entity, at least until the formation of modern classes. One cannot understand the historical development of Mexican stratification without a thorough grounding in the aristocracy and *hacienda* system. By the same token, the political and ruling transformation of the Western aristocracy under absolutism is a necessary requirement for understanding the rise of the haute bourgeoisie. This basic premise has guided every phase of the present study. Beyond a purely descriptive contribution, however, this monograph contributes analytically and theoretically to the study of stratification.

(1) Concentrating on superordinate stratification requires a dynamic conceptualization of estate and class and offers a clearer understanding of social mobility. In this framework, expression constitutes the sufficient conditions of upward mobility that, centered on the upper rungs of the system, may apply to all stratification levels. Downward mobility, on the other hand, is conceived as failure to comply with expressive requirements and constraints, which, configured by economic and other nonexpressive variables, allows one to determine the profile of downwardly mobile individuals and groups. This monograph

demonstrates how structural and expressive variables are inextricably interrelated, constituting, respectively, the determinant necessary and sufficient conditions of a wide array of stratification phenomena.

(2) Another analytical contribution is the notion that the transition from estate to class was not violent and that it was conditioned by a long period of development. The variables that determined the transition are reasonably well established, particularly with reference to the last three hundred years of Western stratification. This book demonstrates how the ideational order of the old estate system conditioned the structural development of class and provided the model that resulted in a new realignment of personnel in fashioning the modern superordinate class. Concomitantly, the acculturative, at times syncretic, nature of the emerging superordinate class is thoroughly explored.

(3) A third analytical point of theoretical significance is the distinction between class as the basic, primary unit of stratification and class as a unit of estate. Without this distinction one can understand neither the complexities of the estate system nor its evolution since the beginnings of Western Civilization. In the context of the past two centuries, the distinction helps us to understand the transition from estate to class and how several aspects of the former have influenced the configuration of the latter, particularly in the upper rungs of the system.

(4) The general form of explanation in this study is nomonological, in that at every turn I establish covariations and consistently try to replicate the superordinate model under different conditions. In other words, specific explanations go beyond the simple linear entailment of history without adducing independent concomitant variables. Specific explanations are formulated at various levels of complexity, which at times pertain exclusively to the superordinate class and at times to the entire stratification system. Functionally, the Mexican aristocracy in particular and Western aristocracies in general are explained within the context of global societies, and the estates and classes of the stratification system are socially, economically, and politically configured with respect to the aristocracy. Evolutionarily, the ideological continuity and structural adaptation of the aristocracy are explained in the context of the periodic transformations entailed by the social, economic, political, and demographic conditions of crucial periods of transition.

(5) A theory of sufficiently ample comparative applications is not yet feasible, but several analyses of this monograph bring its realization

much closer: the realization that in all forms of stratification the structural and expressive components are inextricably interrelated; the feedback effect between the expressive and structural components of stratification and the effect of this factor in the dynamics of upward and downward mobility; and the differentiation of class and estate in evolutionary and synchronic perspective.

Notes

Introduction

1. Several students of culture and society during the past two hundred years have been aware of the role of expression in the conceptualization of human behavior. Notable among them have been Montesquieu, Millar, and Ferguson. Even Marx's notion of class consciousness entails an expressive component, but whether he himself was aware of it, I am not certain. At any rate, the organized conceptualization of expression is a recent phenomenon, and Warner must be credited with having been perhaps the first to apply the concept more or less systematically to the study of social stratification in the United States.

Chapter 1

1. There is every indication from Aristotle's compilation of the 158 constitutions of the ancient world that he was a good data gatherer in the modern, conventional sense. Aristotle favored democracy, but we cannot say that his reasons were entirely projective and ideological; he must be credited with some empirical reasons for favoring this form of government and organization of society.

2. The long struggle of the plebeians for political recognition represents the earliest concerted effort on record of any subordinate estate or class toward political and economic equality. The plebeian-republican struggle must be regarded as the earliest massive manifestation of class consciousness in civilized society and as the first incipient manifestation of representative democracy, unparalleled until the framing of the United States constitution. The much vaunted system that slowly emerged in England out of Magna Carta covenant may be regarded in form as the mother of parliaments, but not in

content and conception, for it was a struggle of the feudal estate against centralization and power of the monarchy. Undoubtedly the English parliamentary system affected the rise of modern democracy, but it did not emanate from the subordinate estate.

3. By Christianity being an oriental religion I mean that, in contrast to Greco-Roman polytheism, it contained many affective elements, "mysteries," and ritual elements that contrasted with the generally more rationalistic *imago mundi* of the Greeks and Romans. In several respects, Christianity (entailing such elements as virgin birth, a revealed human god, otherworldliness, and so on) must be categorized with Orphism, the mystery religions, and other religious elements that begin to appear in the West in the sixth century B.C. Being a monotheistic religion, Christianity was a total transaction that admitted no compartmentalization, and its belief system and *imago mundi* affected every domain of social life.

4. I am not concerned with the eastern Roman Empire. The Byzantine Empire, as it came to be known, had its inception with the division of the Roman Empire into an eastern and a western part under Constantine. After Emperor Justinian's abortive attempt in the mid-sixth century to reconquer the territories of the west that had fallen into the hands of Germanic kingdoms, the Byzantine Empire took a different course and was effectively cut off from the west (Boak 1943:483–89).

Chapter 3

1. Under this category fell that infamous privilege or right of noble landed magnates variously known as *jus primae noctis, droit de seigneur,* or *droit de pernage,* that is, the customary or legal right of a feudal lord to deflower or have sexual intercourse with a commoner vassal's bride on the night of the wedding. The actual incidence of this practice is unknown, and the best guess is that it took place very rarely, as few lords would dare disturb the peace of their realm. What apparently happened was that a due was paid by the groom to rescind the right of the lord.

Chapter 4

1. As I have indicated, Feudalism is a much misused concept. Its original meaning was precise, and the system that developed out of it and persisted until the demise of the ancien régime is seigneuralism, that is, a kind of Feudalism deprived of certain social, military, and political aspects. Historians and social scientists use Feudalism almost as a pejorative, generic term, particularly in discussing the late Middle Ages, when the correct term to use is seigneurialism. By the time of the Spanish Conquest of Mexico

seigneurialism was a going concern on the peninsula, and what the conquistadors sowed in the new land was seigneurialism, not Feudalism.

Chapter 5

1. By today's standards, the Mexican aristocracy has been extremely concerned with upholding its racial and cultural integrity. When an individual deviates from the standards of the group, it elicits immediate disapproval and occasionally indirect social sanctions, including gossip that becomes prevalent when a member looks somatically different from the norm, that is, looks "Mestizo" or exhibits other racial admixtures. If this state of affairs holds sway today, one can imagine the equivalent situation of Mexico at the end of Colonial times, when the Creole aristocracy dominated the social and economic life of the nation.

2. While throughout the entire Colonial period *peninsulares* monopolized the political life of the colony beyond local government, which created friction with and resentment on the part of the Creoles, in most other domains of Colonial life this situation did not obtain. Historians have consistently overemphasized Creole-peninsular political antagonism and by extrapolating to other domains have distorted several aspects of the social and cultural life of New Spain.

Chapter 6

1. My own estimate is that the population of the Tlaxcalan Confederacy at the time of the Conquest was roughly 250,000. When the Velasco Census was taken in 1556, the population had been reduced to roughly 80,000, and by the turn of the seventeenth century it had been further reduced to about 50,000. These estimates are based on my study of Tlaxcalan settlement patterns, twenty-three partial and complete community censuses from 1642 and 1684, and a partial analysis of many documents in the parochial archives on the western slopes of La Malintzi volcano on subjects as varied as tribute, church organization and administration, community descriptions, parochial-diocesan correspondence, and some demographic information. Extrapolating from Tlaxcala, and assuming that this region was typical of Mesoamerica, the total population of the latter at the time of the Conquest was between 12 and 13 million. It declined to about 2 million by the first decade of the seventeenth century, and from then on it slowly began to increase. By the middle of the seventeenth century, the Indian population of New Spain was certainly more than 2 million.

2. In a study conducted in 1985 with a sample of 120 aristocratic men and women residing in Mexico City, family portraits and furniture

ranked first and second in expressive importance in a list of ten different types of heirlooms. Silver objects, including trays, tea sets, and flat silverware, ranked eighth in the same list. This ranking is independently confirmed by the fact that so little has survived from the eighteenth century made of silver and gold, as most of the silver that the average aristocratic household has today is of recent acquisition. By the same token, the survival of portraits and furniture still in the hands of aristocratic families is also explained.

3. For example, at the end of the sixteenth century, the descendants of Leonel Gómez de Cervantes were some of the richest and most distinguished families in New Spain. Two centuries later, the Cervantes family was still rich and probably the most distinguished family in the land: its members held four of the seven original titles granted in New Spain (Santiago de Calimaya, Salinas del Río Pisuerga, Valle de Orizaba, and Mariscal de Castilla). Despite the fact that the Cervantes family was no longer rich by the last two decades of the nineteenth century, it has retained its preeminent social standing until the present. The same aristocratic continuity characterizes the Pérez de Salazar, Rincón Gallardo, Sánchez Navarro, and at least another dozen families that acquired aristocratic standing from the second half of the sixteenth century to the second half of the seventeenth century.

4. From the American and French Revolutions onward, it is the rare modern historian that has been able to give an unbiased sociological analysis of the concepts of nobility, aristocracy, and the estate system and to rise above preconceived ideas engendered by the belief that class is the only tolerable form of stratification. Thus, even the descriptions of estate organization and nobiliary systems have suffered distortion. No doubt there is merit in the criticisms by Otero (1972) and Lizardi (1966) of the seventeenth-century nobility as irrelevant, lacking in political power, and concerned with nothing but self-gratification. But there is more to this segment of the ruling class of New Spain that is lost in ad hominem characterizations. More seriously, these characterizations are regarded a priori as the exclusive traits of aristocracies, and not, as it has been demonstrated by Pareto (1935:265–341), as a universal component of whatever ruling class (elite) is in a superordinate position at a given time.

5. The nuances of stratification, particularly of superordinate groups, simply do not yield easily to historical investigation, and sociological extrapolation from situations that have been studied with the benefit of in-depth fieldwork, or equivalently hard ethnohistorical data, may be a necessary requirement in studies of class and estate. In the present case, reliable information on the Mexican aristocracy exists from the middle of the nineteenth century onward, and this corpus of data has been indispensable for understanding many historical aspects of this social group.

Chapter 7

1. Most Spanish-speaking countries in Latin America have had an understandable love-hate relationship with the mother country. But Mexico is perhaps unique in harboring a strange symbolic resentment. This emotion again is understandable, but not the conscious, almost concerted use of latent proclivities as a political tool. It began with the somewhat unjustified expulsion of the *peninsulares* from Mexico in 1826, continued latently throughout the nineteenth century, and became an important aspect of *indigenismo,* the search for Mexico's Indian past, to denigrate things Spanish. In the mythologies of most Spanish-speaking countries, for example, at least some recognition is given to Spain and the Hispanic cultural tradition. The Chilean mythology, as a case in point, is centered on the premise that the country is the issue of "el altivo español y el indómito araucano" (the haughty [proud] Spaniard and the indomitable Araucanian [Indian]), and the statue of Pedro de Valdivia, the conqueror of the country, is prominently displayed in the capital. So is the statue of Francisco Pizarro in Lima, Peru—an honor that he does not deserve—and the statues of eminent conquistadors are similarly displayed in the capitals of several Latin American countries. In Mexico, however, not even the humblest street in the smallest town of the country is named after Hernán Cortés. And in a country that today is much more Spanish than Indian in culture, society, and institutional framework, one cannot but conclude that something is out of joint. One hears schoolteachers and sometimes supposedly serious intellectuals, for example, making wildly unrealistic or at best distorted claims about the Indian contribution to Mexican culture, in the process glaringly misinterpreting the true glory and greatness of pre-Hispanic Indian culture. What happened in New Spain's colonialism, and what events took place during the war of Independence, that are different from what transpired in other Spanish-speaking countries to have made Mexico so significantly different, is a mystery to me. But I have the feeling that one day a statue of Cortés will be placed, not perhaps in the capital's main square, but at least in front of the hospital that he founded after the fall of Tenochtitlán. More perhaps than other Latin American countries, Mexico is a nation of great contrasts and contradictions, as was most tellingly manifested when the Mexican government, nobly and generously and without hesitation, opened the doors of the country to tens of thousands of refugees fleeing the dictatorship of Franco's Spain.

2. The expressive array of the Mexican aristocracy will be analyzed in depth in the third volume of the series. Suffice it to say here that the exclusive domains of the array have remained constant since 1910, when the last changes can be documented. During the past eighty years, there have been many changes in the inclusive array, mostly the result of adaptation to the changing political conditions of Mexico and the obliteration of the aristocracy as a ruling class.

3. This is not particularly a Mexican phenomenon. Rather, it appears to be universal among all Western aristocracies in their period of decline after the demise of the ancien régime. This is shared with all haute bourgeoisies that have become the new ruling classes in Western countries during the past hundred years. Ironically, in several respects the social distance that separates classes in the stratification system that came to replace the ancien régime is greater than what it was in the traditional estates of European society.

4. This important point has several implications for understanding the terminal transformation of the Mexican aristocracy—to be analyzed in the second volume of the series. It should be noted, however, that substantively the expressive domain of the household and associated domains of behavior have changed little since the turn of the century, and they can be reconstructed from informants in the context of the short-range historical perspective of this social class.

5. What I call the short-range historical perspective (Nutini and Bell 1980:232–35) begins with the dictatorship of Porfirio Díaz. From roughly the middle of the 1870s, the social and expressive life of the Mexican aristocracy can be reconstructed from oral history. Nine informants aged eighty or more in 1978–81 spoke authoritatively and reliably about the aristocratic life of the last two decades of the nineteenth century based on accounts of their fathers and grandfathers and on what they themselves experienced as children before the Mexican Revolution. In addition, family archives are rich in many kinds of information pertaining to most of the social, religious, and economic milieux of aristocratic life. Given the fact that independent information on these domains is difficult to find or nonexistent, oral history becomes the primary source of information. Thus, beginning more than a century ago, strictly speaking, we leave the domain of history and enter that of ethnology.

Chapter 8

1. *Indigenismo* was a kind of nativistic movement, with which one cannot but sympathize, but it was doomed to failure because of the overwhelming predominance of Western-Spanish cultural components in the institutional and overall configuration of the nation. Nonetheless, *indigenismo* was a salutary reaction to centuries of oppression of the masses of peasants and the disposed; it fostered a new pride in being Mexican, and I think it was instrumental in creating a Mexican national mentality.

2. My observations of superordinate stratification of several elites in central Mexico—primarily Puebla, Jalapa, Orizaba, and Córdoba—indicate the formation of plutocratic nuclei at the top of the system beginning in the late 1930s. This formation coincides with the massive migration of local aristocrats to Mexico City, and the vacuum they left in the cities they formerly

controlled was undoubtedly related to the form that local superordinate stratification took throughout the country. Without the benefit of an aristocratic input, provincial plutocracies, as local ruling and social classes, acquired different configurations. Expressively, for example, plutocratic magnates in Córdoba and Veracruz would rank nationally as upper-middle class.

3. Throughout Colonial times, the ruling class and the political class were distinctly separated and occasionally antagonistic to each other. Since Independence, however, the demarcation between the political class and the ruling class was never clear, and throughout the nineteenth century an uneasy alliance brought them together. During the Porfiriato, their common interests coincided to a high degree, even though the ruling class and the political class embodied different social strata. The 1910 Revolution destroyed this state of affairs, but the new ruling and political classes that replaced the traditional ones retained the unspoken principle that had held together the "ancien régime."

4. This peculiar situation may be explained by the Colonial environment that, even after Independence, harbored the Mexican aristocracy, and by the ethnic milieu that tended to configure the aristocracy as a highly exclusive group even within the Creole sector of the population. Always in complete control of a large agrarian population regarded as ethnically inferior and with a high sense of exclusivity with respect to the population of urban environments, the aristocracy maintained until the end an aloofness, an awareness of who they were, and a sense of relatedness akin to a centrifugal community or an extended kinship system.

Conclusions

1. I have deliberately avoided the superordinate stratification of the United States because since its independence from England it has not had an aristocracy in the traditional western European pattern. Throughout Colonial times, the thirteen colonies were, of course, an extension of England, but with the Declaration of Independence, the United States became the most democratic and egalitarian country in the world, at least as far as stratification is concerned.

2. It seems that the extremely large upper and lower nobility of France as a privileged state unduly taxed the resources of the country, which may have been one of the variables that precipitated the French Revolution. This opinion gains some validity considering that in the overwhelming majority of estate stratified societies of the past the superordinate estate was never more than 7 percent of the total population. On the other hand, the rather low percentage of the noble estate in England may have been instrumental in the more democratic, less violent modern transformation of the country compared to continental nations.

Glossary

Spanish, French, Latin, and Hispanicized Nahuatl terms used in the text are explained when they first occur, but for the convenience of the reader, those that are used twice or more have been compiled here. Proper nouns are capitalized.

acasillado   resident laborer on a landed estate; during the Porfiriato, debt peon

alcalde   mayor of Spanish towns and cities; the highest executive officer in town and city government

alcalde mayor   governor; regional and provincial Indian administrator

alguacil   police officer of Spanish towns and cities

alguacil mayor   constable, peace officer; regional and provincial Indian police officer

ancien régime   old political and ruling system; in France, and in all Western countries, the old estate system

arrivista   upwardly mobile individual; socially uppity person

Audiencia   Royal Justice Court; Spanish institution entailing judicial, administrative, and executive powers in the absence of a viceroy or captain general

ayuntamiento (cabildo)   municipal government; town and city government; city hall; municipal council

behetría   free, independent settlement in late medieval Spain largely independent of seigneurial control

beneficium   benefice; conditional type of land tenure in early medieval times; one of the three main institutional Roman antecedents of Feudalism *caballero*   knight; gentleman; the lowest dignity in the Spanish nobiliary system; ambivalent term in all Western aristocracies due to usurpation after 1500

cabildo   see *ayuntamiento*

capellanía   chaplaincy; a salient domain of religious expression among aristocrats throughout Colonial times

capitulacion   agreement, stipulation; agreement signed by all members of a group of conquistadors prior to a conquest or colonization

casa porfiriana   architectural style, based on some French features, developed during the last two decades of the Porfirio Díaz regime

casa solariega   ancestral house in medieval Spain and Mexico until the end of Colonial times

casco   mansion or manor of a landed estate; after the Mexican Revolution of 1910, mostly the gutted framework of a mansion or manor

castas   racial mixtures of Indians, Whites, and Blacks; an elaborate system of racial classification in eighteenth-century Mexico

cofradía   sodality; a significant form of religious expression among aristocrats until the Mexican Revolution of 1910

colonia   until the 1940s, exclusive neighborhoods of Mexico City; since then, any new subdivision of the city

comes (comites)   count (counts); originally a follower of the Roman emperor; during the last century of the empire a frontier administrator; since then, through a series of transformations, it evolved into the late medieval dignity

comitatus   until the end of the Roman Empire, another name for the emperor's following; after Frankish times, a countship

comitia   name for the several assemblies of the Roman people until well after the onset of the principate

comitiva   after the onset of the first century A.D., following of a Roman emperor; council of state

congregación (reducción)   congregation; Indian reserve in Colonial times

corregidor   Crown official in charge of the political and economic administration of Indian congregations

corregimiento   the basic administrative Indian unit in Colonial times; circumscribed region including several congregations

Criollo   Creole; Spaniard born in Mexico; originally in the sixteenth century a strictly racial, somatic category; subsequently it acquires cultural definitional characteristics

dux (duces) duke (dukes); originally at the end of the fourth century, a military commander; after the establishment of Germanic monarchies it became the most important administrative official of the realm, and subsequently developed into the late medieval dignity

ejido after the Mexican Revolution of 1910, land given in tenure by the state to individuals or groups of individuals

embourgeoisement literally, becoming bourgeoislike; after the onset of the nineteenth century, the changes undergone by Western aristocracies due to their loss of political power and wealth

encomendero Spanish or Creole grantee of Indian labor; until roughly the middle of the seventeenth century, latifundia owner

encomienda Indians granted as tributaries to individual Spaniards or Creoles during the sixteenth and seventeenth centuries

eques (equites) knight (knights); in early Roman times, those who fought on horseback; from the first Punic War onward, capitalists, businessmen, and tax collectors by the late Republic organized as an intermediate social order between patricians and plebeians

estado llano commoner estate; one of the two main divisions of Spanish society until the nineteenth century

estancia latifundia dedicated primarily to stock raising

familias venidas a menos downwardly mobile families; dropout aristocratic families

federales during the Porfiriato, federal army-police

fideicomiso feoffment in trust; the Roman antecedent of entailed property in Spain

fuero during Colonial times, juridical privileges apart from the common system of justice

gachupines disparaging term of reference for Spaniards born in Spain, particularly at the end of Colonial times

gañan Indian laborer attached to a landed estate by placing him in debt, primarily in the seventeenth century

gente decente decent or proper people; a rather ambivalent term used from the middle of the seventeenth century onward, referring primarily to affluent Creole and Spanish populations standing below the aristocracy

gente propias proper people; primarily in the twentieth century, upper-middle class families with whom the aristocracy interacted on a slightly superordinate foot of equality

godo   Goth; self-address term used by conquistadors as a badge of honor and pride

habitante (morador)   inhabitant of sixteenth-century towns and cities; later arrival that did not enjoy the rights and privileges of original settlers

hacendado   latifundia owner from the middle of the seventeenth century until the Mexican Revolution of 1910

hacienda   latifundia; the form of land tenure that predominated in Mexico from the middle of the seventeenth century until the Mexican Revolution of 1910

haute bourgeoisie   high bourgeoisie; rich and powerful plutocracy; social class in all Western societies that had its inception in the fifteenth and sixteenth centuries, competed with the aristocracy in the seventeenth and eighteenth centuries, and asserted itself in the nineteenth and twentieth centuries

haute noblesse   higher nobility; titled nobility in France and most Western countries

hermandad   brotherhood; a significant form of religious expression among aristocrats until the Mexican Revolution of 1910

hidalgo   member of the lower nobility or gentry; individual entitled to a coat of arms with access to other nobiliary privileges

hidalgo a fuero de España   member of the lower nobility according to Spanish nobiliary law

hidalgo de gotera   lesser known member of the gentry, known mostly locally, and who perhaps could not prove his lesser nobility

hidalgo de rebozo   local member of the gentry at the end of Colonial times; term referring to provincial Creoles who pretentiously regarded themselves as lesser nobles

hidalgo segundones   second-born sons of members of the gentry according to Spanish nobiliary law

hidalguía   lower, lesser, or nontitled nobility; gentry; the second rank of the Spanish aristocracy, with counterparts in all Western aristocracies

imperator   emperor; in traditional Roman society, an individual empowered to rule and command, usually a consul or a praetor

imperium   the power to command and make military, political, and administrative decisions by the will of the senate and the Roman people

indiano   in Spain, term of reference for a person who had come to the New World

indigenista   cultural revolutionist; after the onset of the Mexican Revolution, an individual engaged in searching for the nation's Indian past

indigenismo   the ideological stance, adopted by many intellectuals and most revolutionary leaders after the onset of the Mexican Revolution, essentially focused on creating a new Mexico for Mexicans, emphasizing what was native at the expense of the foreign

jefe máximo   the highest, generally acknowledged revolutionary leader; a common term of reference for the president of Mexico until the 1940s

jefe político   during the Porfiriato, regional political boss directly responsible and subservient to the president of the republic

juegos de cañas   a kind of jousting practiced exclusively by members of the gentry until nearly the end of Colonial times

juegos de sortijas   lancing rings at the gallop; popular equestrian sport that became common to all classes by the onset of the seventeenth century

lanzas   a tax paid by titled nobles as an exemption from military service, echoing the feudal obligation of a vassal

limpieza de sangre   purity of blood; status of a Christian of long standing

mayorazgo   entailed property; primogenit; until well into the nineteenth century, perhaps the main institution perpetuating titles of nobility and aristocratic status in Spain and Mexico

merced   in New Spain, a grant of land, Indians, or any other property awarded by the Crown or any Crown-empowered official for services rendered or other reasons

Mestizo   half-breed; an individual of mixed Indian and Spanish ancestry; originally in the sixteenth century a strictly racial, somatic category; it evolved, and by the nineteenth century it had become essentially a cultural category

morador   see *habitante*

nobleza titulada   titled nobility; upper nobility

noble a fuero de España   member of the upper and lower nobility according to Spanish nobiliary law

noblesse d'épée   nobility of the sword; roughly the traditional seigneurial aristocracy of France from the time of Louis XIV until the French Revolution

noblesse de robe   nobility of the robe; the new civil-service aristocracy created by Louis XIV and continued until the French Revolution

obras pías   endowed charities; a form of social expression practiced by aristocrats from the eighteenth century to the Mexican Revolution of 1910

oidor   royal justice; member of a royal court of justice

patrocinium   patron-client relationship; the old Roman institution of placing oneself under the protection of a powerful magnate

pechero   member of the commoner estate; villein; in Spain, tribute-paying member of the two lowest classes of the commoner estate

peninsular   Spaniard born in Spain; a Spaniard who, during Colonial times, resided in Mexico in an official or private capacity

pequeña propriedad   small landholding; small-scale farming after the Cárdenas land reform

perulero   rich Spaniard returning to Spain from the New World; Spaniard who made a fortune in Peru

petite histoire   minor history; personal history; family, genealogical, topical, and regional history written by aristocrats

petite noblesse   lower or lesser nobility; gentry in all continental countries

pobladores   settlers after the Spanish Conquest; later Spanish arrivals who founded new towns and cities and were granted Indians and land

precarium   a late Roman form of land tenure; conditional form of land tenure granted to an individual in friendship or to secure a debt

presta nombres   name lenders; after the Cárdenas land reform, the practice of registering land under the names of several individuals in order to circumvent the law

princeps   prince; originally, the elite, veteran soldier of the Roman legion; the title taken by Augustus as the first citizen of the state

probanzas   proof submitted to a court in order to claim nobility according to Spanish nobiliary law

pronunciamiento   uprising; plot against the central government, particularly between Independence and the Díaz dictatorship

pulque   alcoholic beverage made of fermented agave juice

pureza de sangre   purity of blood; being of pure Spanish stock; being of noble, gentry origin

reducción   see *congregación*

regidor   councilman; alderman; member of the town or city council

repartimiento   periodic allotment of Indians to individual Spaniards and Creoles during the sixteenth and seventeenth centuries

República de Indios   Republic of Indians; Indian congregation; Indian reserve in Colonial times

ricos hommes   rich, powerful men; plutocrats; nouveaux riches; a rather deprecatory term for Spaniards born in the New World

santa hermandad   holy brotherhood; centralized police force established by the Catholic kings and directly responsible to them

tequio   corvée; Hispanized Nahuatl term for communal labor

tienda de raya   company store; the landed estate's store that served to keep peons tied to the land until the Mexican Revolution of 1910

vecinos   citizen-neighbors of newly founded municipalities in New Spain; conquistadors and founders of towns and cities having first rights to exploitation of the land, Indians, and natural resources

villano   see *pechero*

Bibliography

Adams, Brooks
1896   *The Law of Civilization and Decay.* New York: Macmillan.
Aguirre Beltrán, Gonzalo
1946   *La Población Negra de México.* Publicaciones Fuente Cultural: México, D.F.
1967   *Regiones de Refugio. El Desarrollo de la Comunidad y el Proceso Dominical en Mestizoamérica.* México, D.F.: Instituto Indigenista Interamericano.
Alamán, Lucas
1942   *Disertaciones Sobre la Historia de la República Mexicana.* 3 vols. México, D.F., Editorial Jus.
1952   *Historia de Méjico Desde los Primeros Novimientos que Prepararon su Independencia en el Año de 1808 Hasta la Época Presente.* 5 vols. México, D.F.: J. M. Lara.
Alberro, Solange
1990   "La Sociabilidad Criolla como Processo Aculturativo." In *Messico Terra d'Incontro: La Cultura Mestiza,* ed. Italo Signorini. *L'Uomo* 1 and 2 (2).
Alessio Robles, Vito
1938   *Bosquejos Históricos.* México, D.F.: Editorial Polis.
Allen, Frederick L.
1935   *The Lords of Creation.* New York: E. P. Dutton.
Altamira, Rafael
1967   "Spain Under the Visigoths." In *The Cambridge Medieval History,* vol. 2, ed. H. M. Gwatkins and J. P. Whitney. Cambridge: Cambridge University Press.

1969 "Spain 1252–1410." In *The Cambridge Medieval History,* vol. 7, ed. J. R. Tanner, C. W. Pruité-Orton, and Z. N. Brooks. Cambridge: Cambridge University Press.

Amory, Cleveland
1947 *The Proper Bostonians.* New York: E. P. Dutton.
1952 *The Last Resorts.* New York: E. P. Dutton.

Anderson, Paul
1974 *Lineage of the Absolutist State.* London: Nilsoon and Sons.

Andrews, Anthony
1982 "The Growth of the Athenian State." In *The Cambridge Ancient History,* vol. 3, pt. 3, ed. J. Boardman and N. Hammond. Cambridge: Cambridge University Press.

Aristotle
1923 *Politics.* Translated by Benjamin Jowett. Oxford: The Clarendon Press.

Aron, Raymond
1966 "Social Class, Political Class, Ruling Class." In *Class, Status, and Power: Social Stratification in Comparative Perspective,* ed. Reinhardt Bendix and Seymour Martin Lipset. New York: The Free Press.

Arróniz, Marcos
1952 *Manual de Biografía Mejicana o Galería de Hombres Célebres de Méjico.* Paris: Rose Buret.

Ashburn, Frank D.
1944 *Peabody of Groton.* New York: Coward McCahn.

Baldwin, John F.
1897 *Scutage and Knight-Service in England.* Chicago: University of Chicago Press.

Baltzell, Digby E.
1966 " 'Who's Who in America' and 'The Social Register': Elite Upper Class Indexes in Metropolitan America." In *Class, Status, and Power: Social Stratification in Comparative Perspective,* ed. Reinhardt Bendix and Seymour Martin Lipset. New York: The Free Press.

Bancroft, Hubert Howe
1972 *History of Mexico.* San Francisco: A. L. Bancroft.

Baudot, George
1977 *Utopie et Histoire au Mexique.* Paris: Privat.

Bauzet, Charles
1927 *La Intervención Francesa en México.* Barcelona: Isola Pujol.

Bayle, Constantino
1952 *Los Cabildos Seculares en la América Española.* Madrid: Sapientia, S.C.

Bazancourt, Claude L. de
1931 *Le Mexique Contemporain.* Paris: La Rochelle.

Bazant, Jan
1975 *Cinco Haciendas Mexicanas. Tres Siglos de Vida Rural en San Luis Potosí (1600–1910).* México, D.F.: El Colegio de México.
1985 *Antonio Haro y Tamariz y sus Aventuras Políticas (1811–1869).* México, D.F.: El Colegio de México.
Beals, Carleton
1954 *Porfirio Díaz.* México, D.F.: Editorial Sánchez.
Bendix, Reinhardt, and Seymour Martin Lipset, eds.
1966 *Class, Status, and Power: Social Stratification in Comparative Perspective.* New York: The Free Press.
Benítez, Fernando
1953 *La Vida Criolla en al Siglo XVI.* México, D.F.: El Colegio de México.
Beteta, Ramón
1935 *Economic and Social Program of Mexico.* San Francisco: Johnson and Sons.
Bloch, Marc
1940 *La Société Feodale.* 2 vols. Paris: Editions Albin Michel.
Boak, Arthur E. R.
1943 *A History of Rome to 565 A.D.* New York: Macmillan.
Bocanegra, José María
1927 *Memorias para la Historia de México Independiente, 1822–1846.* México, D.F.: Imprenta del Gobierno.
Bottomore, Tom B.
1969 *Classes in Modern Sociology.* New York: Pantheon.
Boyd-Bowman, Peter
1964 *El Habla de Guanajuato.* México, D.F.: Imprenta de la Universidad.
Brading, David A.
1971 *Miners and Merchants in Bourbon Mexico, 1780–1810.* London: Cambridge University Press.
1972 "Government and Elite in Late Colonial Mexico." *Hispanic American Historical Review* 53 (3): 389–414.
1974 "The Capital Structure of Mexican Haciendas: León 1700–1850." *Ibero-Amerikanisches Archiv,* NF, Nos. 1 and 2: 197–237.
Bulnes, Francisco
1916 *The Whole Truth about Mexico.* Detroit: Blaine Ethridge Books.
Bush, Michael L.
1983 *Noble Privilege.* London: Holmes and Meier.
1984 *The English Aristocracy: A Comparative Synthesis.* Manchester: Manchester University Press.
Calderón de la Barca, Frances
1978 *Life in Mexico.* New York: Doubleday.
Calmette, Jacques
1938 *La Société Feodale.* Paris: A. Gallimard.

Carrasco, Pedro
1976 "La Sociedad Mexicana Antes de la Conquista." In *Historia General de México,* ed. Daniel Cosío Villegas. México, D.F.: El Colegio de México.

Carreño, Alberto María
1961 *La Real y Pontificia Universidad de México, 1536–1865.* México, D.F.: Imprenta Universitaria.

Carrión, Antonio
1897 *Historia de la Ciudad de Puebla de los Angeles.* Puebla: Escuela Salesiana de Artes y Oficios.

Cary, M., and H. H. Scullard
1975 *A History of Rome Down to the Reign of Constantine.* New York: Saint Martin's.

Casariego, Juan E.
1946 *El Municipio y las Cortes en el Imperio Español de Indias.* Madrid: Talleres Gráficos Marsiega.

Castañeda, Carlos E.
1929 "The Corregidor in Spanish Colonial Administration." *Hispanic American Historical Review* 9:446–67.

Castillo Ledón, Luis
1932 *La Conquista y Colonización Española de México.* México: Imprenta del Gobierno.

Castillo Ledón, Amalia
1940 *Apuntes para la Historia de Tamaulipas.* Guadalajara: Editorial Cruz.

Castillo Negrete, Emilio
1933 *Cedulario Heráldico de Conquistadores de Nueva España.* México, D.F.: Museo Nacional de Arqueología, Historia, y Ethnografía.

Castro, Américo
1948 *España en su Historia: Cristianos, Moros y Judios.* Buenos Aires: Editorial Losada.
1954 *Dos Ensayos.* México: Editorial Porrúa.

Céspedes, Guillermo
1976 "Las Indias Durante los siglos XVI y XVII." In *Historial de España y América Social y Económia,* vol. 3, ed. J. Vicens Vives. Barcelona: Vicens.

Chadwick, H. Munroe
1963 *Studies in Anglo-Saxon Institutions.* New York: Russell and Russell.

Chaunnu, Pierre
1951 "Le Galeon de Manille. Grandeur et Decadence d'une Route de la Soie." *Annales* (Paris) 6 (4): 67–94.

Chaussinard-Nogaret, Georges
1975 *Histoire des Elites: 1700–1848.* Paris: A. Gallimard.

Chevalier, Francois
1948 "La Signification Sociale de la Fondation de Puebla de Los Angeles." *Revista de Historia de América* 32:112.
1952 *La Formation des Grands Domaines au Mexique: Terre et Société aux XVI–XVII Siècles.* Institut d'Ethnologie, Université de Paris à la Sorbonne, Travaux et Mémoires.
1963 *Land and Society in Colonial Mexico: The Great Hacienda.* Berkeley: University of California Press.
1970 "The Ejido and Political Stability in Mexico." In *The Politics of Conformity in Latin America,* ed. C. Véliz. London: Oxford University Press.

Cicero, Marcus Tullius
1928 *De Republica de Legibus* (Anotada por Grabiel Fernández Santander). Madrid: Imprenta del Nuevo Mundo.

Clavero, Bartolomé
1974 *Mayorazgo: Propiedad Feudal en Castilla 1369–1836.* México, D.F.: Siglo Veintiuno Editores.

Cobban, Arthur
1969 "The Decline of Divine-Right Monarchy in France." In *The Cambridge Modern History,* vol. 7, ed. J. O. Lindsay. Cambridge: Cambridge University Press.

Coleman, R. P., and L. Rainwater
1978 *Social Standing in America.* New York: Basic.

Comhaire, J., and W. J. Cahman
1959 *How Cities Grew: The Historical Sociology of Cities.* Madison, N.J.: Florham Park Press.

Conde Díaz Rubín, José Ignacio
n.d. *Historia Genealógica de la Familia Cervantes.*

Cook, Sherburn, and Woodrow Borah
1960 "The Indian Population of Central Mexico, 1531–1610." *Ibero-Americana* 44.

Corbett, William J.
1967 "The Foundation of the Kingdom of England." In *The Cambridge Medieval History,* vol. 2, ed. H. M. Gwatkins and J. P. Whitney. Cambridge: Cambridge University Press.

Cortés, Hernán
1963 *Cartas de Relación.* México, D.F.: Editorial Porrúa, S.A.

Cosío Villegas, Daniel
1975 *La Sucesión Presidencial.* México, D.F.: Editorial J. Mortiz.

Couturier, Edith B.
1968 "Modernización y Tradición en una Hacienda (San Juan Hueyapan, 1902–1911)." in *Historia Mexicana.* México: Editorial del Gobierno.

Covarrubias, Diego de
 1953 *Opera.* Madrid: Imprenta de la Luz.
Cué Canovas, Agustín
 1946 *Historical Social y Económica de México: 1521–1810.* México, D.F.:
  Editorial América.
Davis, Kingsley
 1942 *Human Society.* New York: Macmillan.
Davis, Kingsley, and Wilbert E. Moore
 1945 "Some Principles of Stratification." *American Sociological Review* 10
  (2): 242–49.
Díaz del Castillo, Bernal
 1967 *Historia Verdadera de la Conquista de la Nueva España.* México, D.F.:
  Editorial Porrúa, S.A.
Domínguez Ortiz, A.
 1955 *La Sociedad Española en el Siglo XVIII.* Madrid: Imprenta Nuevo
  Mundo.
 1970 *La Sociedad Española en el Siglo XVII.* Madrid: Imprenta de San
  Miguel.
 1974 *El Régimen Señorial y el Reformismo Borbónico.* Madrid: Imprenta de
  San Miguel.
Dorantes de Carranza, Baltasar
 1970 *Sumaria Relación de las Cosas de la Nueva España.* México, D.F.: Jesús
  Medina, Editor.
Doucet, Armand
 1948 *Les Institutions de la France au XVIe Siècle.* Paris: F. Artois.
Douglas, Donald C.
 1939 "The Norman Conquest and English Feudalism." *Economic Historic
  Review* 9:128–43.
Duby, Georges
 1968 "The Nobility in Eleventh- and Twelfth-Century Maconnais. In
  Lordship and Community in Medieval Europe, ed. F. L. Cheyette. New
  York: Macmillan
Durand, José
 1953 *La Transformación Social del Conquistador.* 2 vols. México, D.F.:
  Porrúa y Obregón, S.A.
Enríquez, Manuel
 1938 *Conquistadores de la Nueva España.* Buenos Aires: Imprenta del
  Campo.
Ewald, Ursula
 1973 "Organización y Explotación de la Gram Propiedad Agrícola en la
  Época Colonial." *Comunicaciones* 7:43–76.

Fernández Echeverría, Mariano
    1931   *Historia de la Puebla de los Angeles en la Nueva España. Su Descripción y Presente Estado.* Puebla: Edición Fidel Solis.

Fernández de Recas, Guillermo
    1965   *Mayorazgos de la Nueva España.* México, D.F.: Biblioteca Nacional.

Ferrero, Guglielmo
    1958   *A Short History of Rome.* New York: Putnam.

Fisher, Lillian E.
    1951   *Viceregal Administration in the Spanish American Colonies.* New York: Russell and Russell.

Flandrau, Claude M.
    1908   *Viva México.* México: Imprenta Flores.

Foster, George M.
    1960   *Culture and Conquest: America's Spanish Heritage.* Viking Fund Publications in Anthropology, No. 27. New York: The Fund.

Fox-Davis, A. C.
    1895   *Armorial Families.* Edinburgh, Scotland: Sutherland Publications.

Frank, Tenney
    1927   *A History of Rome.* New York: Harcourt Brace and Company.

Frazer, John
    1982   *America and the Patterns of Chivalry.* Cambridge: Cambridge University Press.

Fustel de Coulanges, Numa Denis
    1899   *Histoire des Institutions Politiques de l'Ancienne France.* Vol. 4. Paris: A. Gallinard.
    1963   *The Ancient City.* New York: Doubleday Anchor.

Gage, Thomas
    1978   *Travels in the New World.* Norman: University of Oklahoma Press.

Galván Mariano
    1984   *Ordenanzas de Tierras y Aguas.* México, D.F.: Imprenta del Gobierno.

Ganshof, François L.
    1952   *Feudalism.* London: Longmans Green.

García Carraffa, Alberto, and Arturo Carraffa
    1919   *Enciclopedia Heráldica y Genealógica Hispanoamericana.* Madrid: A. Marzo.

García Martínez, Bernardo
    1969   *El Marquesado del Valle. Tres Siglos de Régimen Señorial en Nueva España.* México, D.F.: El Colegio de México.

García Pelayo, Manuel
    1946   "El Estamento de la Nobleza en el Despotismo Ilustrado Español." *Moneda y Crédito* 6:73–92.

García Purón, Manuel
  1964 *México y sus Gobernantes: Biografías.* México, D.F.: M. Porrúa.
García Soriano, Manuel
  1954 *El Conquistador Español del Siglo XVI.* Tucumán, Argentina: Universidad Nacional.
Garretón, Antonio
  1933 *La Municipalidad Colonial. Buenos Aires Desde su Fundación Hasta el Gobierno de Laris.* Buenos Aires: J. Menéndez.
Genestal, Robert
  1911 *La Parage Normand.* Caen, France: P. Lalande.
Gibbon, Edward
  1913 *The Decline and Fall of the Roman Empire.* London: Bohn's British Classics.
Gibbon, Thomas E.
  1934 *Mexico Under Carranza.* London: L. Green.
Gibson, Charles
  1964 *The Aztecs Under Spanish Rule: A History of the Indians of the Valley of Mexico: 1519–1810.* Stanford: Stanford University Press.
Gil Munilla, Ladislao
  1955 "La Ciudad de Hispanoamérica." *Estudios Americanos* 10.
Gómara, Francisco López de
  1971 *Historia de la Conquista de México.* México, D.F.: Editorial Pedro Robledo.
Gómez de Cervantes, Gonzalo
  1944 *La Vida Económica y Social de la Nueva España al Finalizar el Siglo XVI.* México, D.F.: José Porrúa e Hijos.
González Navarro, Moisés
  1957 "El Porfiriato. La Vida Social." In *Historia Moderna de México,* ed. D. Cosío Viellegas. Buenos Aires: Ed. Hermes.
González Obregón, Luis
  1900 *México Viejo.* México: Vda. de C. Bouret.
  1911 *La Vida en México en 1810.* México: Vda. de C. Bouret.
  1937 *Ensayos Histórico y Biográficos.* México, D.F.: Editorial Botas.
González Serrano, Manuel
  1876 *Historia de Tamaulipas.* México, D.F.: Imprenta Nacional.
Goodwin, William K.
  1953 *Decline and Survival of the Aristocracy.* Liverpool: Landon Brothers.
Gordon, Milton M.
  1949 "Social Class in American Sociology." *American Journal of Sociology* 55 (3): 262–68.
  1958 *Social Class in American Society.* Chapel Hill: University of North Carolina Press.

Goubert, Paul
  1973 *The Ancien Régime.* London: Routledge and Kegan Paul.
Greenidge, Arthur J.
  1973 *Roman Public Life.* London: Macmillan.
Gruening, Ernest
  1928 *Mexico and Its Heritage.* New York: The Century Company.
Hall, Frederic
  1937 *The Laws of Mexico.* San Francisco: A. L. Bancroft
Hammond, Nicholas G. L.
  1958 *The Classical Age of Greece.* London: Weidenfeld and Nicholson.
Hanke, Lewis
  1965 *The Spanish Struggle for Justice in the Conquest of America.* Boston: Little Brown.
Haring, Clarence Henry
  1939 *Comercio y Navegación Entre España y las Indias en la Época de los Habsburgos.* México, D.F.: El Colegio de México.
  1953 *Las Institutciones Coloniales de Hispanoamérica.* San Juan: Instituto de Cultura Portorriqueña.
Hartman, Lewis H.
  1967 "Italy under the Lombards." In *The Cambridge Medieval History,* vol. 2, ed. H. M. Gwatkins and J. P. Whitney. Cambridge: Cambridge University Press.
Heitland, William E.
  1923 *The Roman Republic.* Cambridge: Cambridge University Press.
Higley, John, and Lowell Field
  1972 *Elites in Developed Societies: Theoretical Reflections in an Initial Stage.* Beverly Hills, Calif.: Sage Publications.
Homans, George C., and Charles P. Curtis, Jr.
  1934 *An Introduction to Pareto: His Sociology.* New York: Alfred A. Knopf.
Honigmann, John J.
  1976 *The Development of Anthropological Ideas.* Homewood, Ill.: Dorsey Press.
Humboldt, Alexander von
  1966 *Ensayo Político Sobre el Reino de la Nueva España.* México, D.F.: Editorial Porrúa, S.A.
Icaza, Francisco A.
  1969 *Diccionario Autobiográfico de Conquistadores y Pobladores de Nueva España.* Guadalajara, México: Edmundo Aviha Levy.
Ihne, Wilhelm
  1937 *The History of Rome.* London: Longmans, Green, and Sons.
Isidore of Seville, Saint
  1954 *History of the Kings of the Goths, Vandals and Suevi.* Leiden: E. J. Brill.

Israel, Jonathan I.
  1974 "Mexico and the General Crisis of the XVII Century." *Past and Present* 63 (3): 158–89
  1975 *Race, Class and Politics in Colonial Mexico: 1610–1670*. Oxford: Oxford University Press.
Iszaevich, Abraham
  1979 "Social Organization and Social Mobility in a Catalan Village." Ph.D. Dissertation, University of Michigan.
Kaeger, Karl
  1901 *Landwirtschaft und Kolonization im Spanischen Amerika*. Leipzig: Die Südamerikanischen Weststaaten und Mexiko.
Kamen, Howard
  1971 *The Iron Century*. London: Longmans.
Kasdan, Leonard
  1965 "Family Structure, Migration, and the Entrepreneur." *Comparative Studies of Society and History* 27 (3): 87–103.
Kemble, John M.
  1876 *The Saxons in England*. London: Max Press.
Konetzke, Richard
  1951 "La Formación de la Nobleza en Indias." *Estudios Americanos* 3(10): 136–54.
Konetzke, Richard, ed.
  1953 *Colección de Documentos para la Historia de la Formación Social de Hispanoamérica, 1493–1810*. 3 vols. Madrid: Consejo Superior de Investigaciones Científicas.
Kornhauser, Arthur
  1966 " 'Power Elite' or 'Veto Groups'." In *Class, Status, and Power: Social Stratification in Comparative Perspective*, ed. Reinhardt Bendix and Seymour Martin Lipset. New York: The Free Press.
Kubler, George A.
  1942 "Mexican Urbanism in the XVI Century." *Art Bulletin* 9 (3): 37–52.
Labatut, Pierre
  1972 *Les Ducs et Pairs de France au XVIIe Siècle: Étude Social*. Paris: Flon.
Ladd, Doris M.
  1976 *The Mexican Nobility at Independence, 1780–1826*. Austin: University of Texas Press.
Last, Hugh
  1969 "The Kings of Rome." In *The Cambridge Ancient History*, vol. 7, ed. S. A. Cook, F. E. Addock, and M. P. Charles Worth. Cambridge: Cambridge University Press.
Laurand, Louis
  1925 *Manuels des Etudes Grecques et Latines*. Paris: A. Picard.

Lefevre, Georges
 1970 *The Great Fear of 1798.* London: Longmans.
Leicht, Hugo
 1934 *Las Calles de Puebla.* Puebla: Imprenta del Estado.
Lewis, Arthur R.
 1974 *Knights and Samurai: Feudalism in Northern France and Japan.* London: Oxford University Press.
Lira Montt, Luis
 1976 "Bases Para un Estudio del Fuero Nobiliario de Indias." *Hidalguía* (Madrid), 138:881–917.
Liss, Peggy K.
 1975 *Mexico Under Spain: 1521–1556. Society and the Origins of Nationality.* Chicago: University of Chicago Press.
Lizardi, José Joaquín Fernández de
 1966 *El Periquillo Sarmiento.* México, D.F.: Editorial Porrúa.
Lockhart, James
 1972 "The Social History of Colonial Latin America." *Latin American Research Review* 7 (1): 61–87.
Lohmann Villena, Guillermo
 1947 *Los Americanos en las Ordenes Nobiliarias, 1529–1900.* 2 vols. Madrid: Consejo Superior de Investigaciones Científicas.
Lopreato, J., and J. Hazelrigg
 1972 *Class, Conflict, and Mobility.* San Francisco: Chandler.
Lot, Ferdinand
 1948 *Naissance de la France.* Paris: Presses Universitaires de France.
Lucas, Charles R.
 1973 "Nobles, Bourgeois, and the Origins of the French Revolution." *Past and Present* 60:84–96.
Luchaire, Achilles
 1938 *Manuel des Institutions Francaises.* Paris: A. Picard.
Lynd, Robert S., and Helen M. Lynd
 1937 *Middletown in Transition.* New York: Harcourt Brace.
McAlister, L. N.
 1963 "Social Structure and Social Change in New Spain." *Hispanic American Historical Review* 43 (3): 132–48.
Mackrell, J. Q. C.
 1973 *The Attack on "Feudalism" in Eighteenth-Century France.* London: Routledge and Kegan Paul.
Madariaga, Salvador de
 1963 *The Fall of the Spanish American Empire.* New York: Collier.
Martin, Frederick T.
 1911 *The Passing of the Idle Rich.* New York: Doubleday.

Martínez de Cosío, Leopoldo
1946 *Los Caballeros de las Ordenes Militares en México.* México, D.F.: Editorial Santiago.
Martínez del Río, Pablo
1938 *El Suplicio del Hacendado y Otros Temas Agrarios.* México: Ediciones Polis.
Medieta y Nuñez, Lucio
1966 *El Problema Agrario de México.* México, D.F.: Porrúa Hermanos.
Mendizábal, M. O. de
1972 "El Origen Histórico de Nuestras Clases Medias." In *Las Clases Sociales de México,* ed. M. O. de Mendizábal. México, D.F.: Editorial Nuestro Tiempo.
Meyer, Jean A.
1976 *The Cristero Rebellion: The Mexican People between Church and State, 1926–1929.* New York: Cambridge University Press.
Meyer, Michael C., and William L. Sheridan
1979 *The Course of Mexican History.* New York: Oxford University Press.
Mills, C. Wright
1966 "The Middle Classes in Middle-Sized Cities." In *Class, Status, and Power: Social Stratification in Comparative Perspective,* ed. Reinhardt Bendix and Seymour Martin Lipset. New York: The Free Press.
Mingay, George E.
1976 *The Gentry.* London: Longmans.
Miranda, José
1947 *La Formación Económica del Encomendero en los Orígenes del Régimen Colonial.* México, D.F.: Stylo.
1952 *El Tributo Indígena en la Nueva España Durante el Siglo XVI.* México, D.F.: El Colegio de México.
Momigliano, Arnaldo
1955 *Contributo alla Storia degli Studi Classici.* Rome: Università di Roma.
Mommsen, Theodor
1898 *Roman Chronology to the Time of Caesar.* New York: Doubleday.
Moncrieffe, Sir Iain
1970 Foreword to *More Equal than Others: The Changing Fortunes of the British and European Aristocracies* (Lord Montagu of Beaulieu). London: Michael Joseph.
Montagu of Beaulieu, Lord
1970 *More Equal than Others: The Changing Fortunes of the British and European Aristocracies.* London: Michael Joseph.
Moore, John P.
1954 *The Cabildo in Peru Under the Hapsburgs.* Durham, N.C.: Duke University Press.

Mora, José María Luis
1972 "Las Clases Privilegiadas." In *Las Clases Sociales de México*, ed. M. O. de Mendizábal. México, D.F.: Editorial Nuestro Tiempo.
1979 *México y Sus Revoluciones*. México, D.F.: Editorial Porrúa.
Moses, Bernard
1898 *The Establishment of Spanish Rule in America*. London: G. P. Putnam.
Motolinía (Fray Toribio de Benavente)
1903 *Memoriales*. México: Casa del Editor.
Muñoz Camargo, Diego
1948 *Historia de Tlaxcala*. México, D.F.: Edición Rosell.
Muñoz, Juan Bautista
1793 *Historia del Nuevo Mundo*. Madrid: Edición Nueva.
Murray, Gilbert
1951 *The Five Stages of Greek Religion*. Boston: Beacon Press.
Myers, Arnold R.
1975 *Parliaments and Estates in Europe to 1789*. London: Oxford University Press.
Navarro, J. C.
1930 *El Municipio en América Durante la Asistencia de España*. Madrid: Compañía General de Artes Gráficas.
Nickel, Herbert J.
1988 *Morfología Social de la Hacienda Mexicana*. México, D.F.: Fondo de Cultura Económica.
Noll, Arthur Howard
1936 *From Empire to Republic*. Chicago: Grant Press.
Nutini, Hugo G.
1961 "Roman Social Organization." *Comentari*, (Rome), January, 17–61.
1963 "A Comparative Study of Mesoamerican and Andean Indian Cultures." *Revista Austral*, September, 120–53.
1971 "The Latin American City: A Cultural Historical Approach." In *The Anthropology of Urban Environments*, ed. Thomas Weaver and Douglas R. White. The Society for Applied Anthropology Monograph Series, No. 11.
1972 "Anthropology and Comparative Epistemology." *Bijdragen Tot de Taa-Land en Volkenkunde* 128 (2): 19–37.
1984 *Ritual Kinship: Ideological and Structural Integration of the Compadrazgo System in Rural Tlaxcala*. Princeton: Princeton University Press.
1986 "La Ciudad de Puebla y el Medio Poblano-Tlaxcalteca: Significado Pre-Hispánico e Importancia Colonial y Contemporánea." *Casas y Gentes* (Mexico City), February, 13–27.

1988 *Todos Santos in Rural Tlaxcala: A Syncretic, Expressive, and Symbolic Analysis of the Cult of the Dead.* Princeton: Princeton University Press.

1990 *Componentes Sincreticos y Aculturativos del Culto a los Santos en el Medio Poblano-Tlaxcalteca.* Tlaxcala, Mexico: Imprenta del Estado.

Nutini, Hugo G., and Betty Bell

1980 *Ritual Kinship: The Structure and Historical Development of the Compadrazgo System in Rural Tlaxcala.* Princeton: Princeton University Press.

Nutini, Hugo G., and John M. Roberts

1991 "Mexican Titles of Nobility: An Expressive Code with Focussed Concordance." *L'Uomo* 15:32–67.

n.d. "The Secular Cult of the Ancestors as Manifested in Mexican Interior Decoration." N.p.

n.d. "The Aristocratic Image of Mexico City and the Rise of the *Haute Bourgeoisie.*" N.p.

Nutini, Hugo G., John M. Roberts, and María Teresa Cervantes

1982 "The Historical Development of the Mexican Aristocracy: 1519–1940." *L'Uomo* 6:3–37.

1984 "The Mexican *Haute Bourgeoisie:* An Outline of Its Ideology, Structure, and Expressive Culture." *L'Uomo* 8:3–28.

Nuttal, Zelia

1922 "Royal Ordinances Concerning the Laying Out of Towns." *Hispanic American Historical Review* 5:148–79.

O'Gorman, Edmundo

1942 "La Nobleza Colonial, Último Tercio del Siglo XVIII." *Archivo General de la Nación,* Boletín 13, No. 4; México, D.F.

Ortega y Pérez Gallardo, Ricardo

1908 *Historia Genealógica de las Familias más Antiguas de México.* México: A. Carranza Editores.

Ossowski, Stanislaw

1963 *Class Structure in the Social Consciousness.* London: Routledge and Kegan Paul.

Otero, Mariano

1967 *Obras.* 2 vols. México, D.F.: Editorial Porrúa.

1972 "El Régimen de Propiedad y las Clases Sociales en el México Independiente." In *Las Clases Sociales de México,* ed. M. O. de Mendizábal. México, D.F.: Editorial Nuestro Tiempo.

Ots Capdequí, José María

1934 *Instituciones Sociales de la América Española en el Período Colonial.* La Plata, Argentina: Imprenta Gómez.

Ovando, Carlos de
  n.d.   "Documentos Miscelaneos del Archivo Pérez de Salazar de Ovando.
         N.p.

Ovando, Carlos de, and Carmen Pérez de Salazar de Ovando
  1986   "Talavera Poblana: Apogeo, Decadencia y Resurgimiento de una
         Artesanía Singular que Embellece Cúpulas de Templos y Mesas
         Cotidianas." *Casa y Gentes* (Mexico City) April, 38–47.

Palgrave, Sir Francis
  1921   *Rise and Progress of the English Commonwealth.* Cambridge: Cam-
         bridge University Press.

Pareto, Vilfredo
  1935   *The Mind and Society.* New York: Harcourt Brace.
  1980   *Trattato di Sociologia Generale.* Milano: Edizioni di Comunitá.

Parkes, Henry B.
  1938   *A History of Mexico.* Boston: Houghton Mifflin.

Parra, Porfirio
  1906   *La Reforma.* México: Imprenta de San Miguel.

Parsons, Talcott
  1965   "Vilfredo Pareto: Contributions to Sociology." In *International Ency-
         clopedia of the Social Sciences,* ed. D. L. Sills. New York: Macmillan.

Peña, José F. de la
  1983   *Oligarquía y Propiedad en Nueva España (1550–1624).* México, D.F.:
         Fondo de Cultura Económica.

Pérez de Salazar, Francisco
  1923   "El Primer Marqués de Sierra Nevada." In *Memorias de la Sociedad
         Alzate,* No. 41, 415–22.
  1928   *La Fundación de Puebla.* México: Sociedad Mexicana de Geografía y
         Estadística.
  n.d.   "Documentos Varios del Archivo de Don Francisco Pérez de Sala-
         zar." N.p.

Pérez Pujol, Emilio
  1947   *Historia de las Instituciones de la España Goda.* 2 vols. Madrid:
         Imprenta López de Arce.

Perret, Jacques
  1962   *Tacite la Germanie: Text Etablie et Traduit.* Paris: Société d'Edition
         "Les Belles Lettres."

Perrot, Roy
  1968   *The Aristocrats: A Portrait of Britain's Nobility and Their Way of Life
         Today.* New York: Macmillan.

Pfister, Christian
  1967   "Gaul Under the Merovingian Franks. Institutions." In *The Cam-*

bridge Medieval History, vol. 1, ed. H. M. Gwatkins and J. P. Whitney. Cambridge: Cambridge University Press.

Pike, Ruth
1972 *Aristocrats and Traders: Sevillian Society in the Sixteenth Century.* Ithaca, N.Y.: Cornell University Press.

Pirenne, Henri
1966 "Stages in the Social History of Capitalism." In *Class, Status, and Power: Social Stratification in Comparative Perspective,* ed. Reinhardt Bendix and Seymour Martin Lipset. New York: The Free Press.

Powell, Philip W.
1952 *Soldiers, Indians and Silver. The Northward Advance of New Spain, 1550–1600.* Berkeley: University of California Press.

Powell, T. G.
1974 *El Liberalismo y el Campesinado en el Centro de México.* México, D.F.: Sepsetentas.

Powis, Jonathan K.
1984 *Aristocracy.* New York: Basil Blackwell

Prescott, William H.
1973 *History of the Conquest of Mexico.* 3 vols. Philadelphia: J. B. Lippincott.

Priestley, Herbert I.
1926 *The Mexican Nation, a History.* New York: Macmillan.

Pruite-Orton, C. W.
1968 "The Italian Cities till c 1200." In *The Cambridge Medieval History,* vol. 5, ed. J. R. Turner, C. W. Pruite-Orton, and Z. N. Brock. Cambridge: Cambridge University Press.

Quintana, Manuel
n.d. *Colección de Documentos Genealógicos.*

Rábago, Daniel
n.d. *Documentos Inéditos Sobre la Familia Rabago.*

Rascher, John M.
1904 *Colonial Society in Mexico.* London: Faber.

Ridgeway, Cecilia L., and John M. Roberts
1976 "Urban Popular Music and Interaction: A Semantic Relation." *Ethnomusicology* 20 (2): 233–51.

Riesman, David
1959 *The Lonely Crowd.* New York: Doubleday.

Roberts, John M.
1976 "Belief in the Evil Eye in World Perspective." In *The Evil Eye,* ed. Clarence Maloney. New York: Columbia University Press.

Roberts, John M., Chen Chiao, and Triloki N. Pandey
1975 "Meaningful God Sets from a Chinese Personal Pantheon and a Hindu Personal Pantheon." *Ethnology* 14 (2): 121–48.

Roberts, John M., and Gary E. Chick
1979 "Butler County Eight Ball: A Behavioral Space Analysis." In *Sports, Games and Play: Social and Psychological Viewpoints*, ed. Jeffrey H. Goldstein. Hillsdale, Ill.: Lawrence Erlbaum.

Roberts, John M., and Thomas V. Golder
1970 "Navy and Polity: A 1963 Baseline." *Naval War College Review* 23 (3): 3041.

Roberts, John M., Frederick Koening, and Richard B. Stark
1969 "Judged Display: A Consideration of a Craft Show." *Journal of Leisure Research* 1 (2): 163–79.

Roberts, John M., Quentin S. Meeker, and James C. Aller
1972 "Action Styles and Management Game Performance: An Exploratory Consideration." *Naval War College Review* 24 (10): 65–81.

Roberts, John M., and Susan M. Nattrass
1980 "Women and Trapshooting: Competence and Expression in a Game of Physical Skill with Chance." In *Play and Culture*, ed. Helen B. Schwartzman. West Point: Leisure Press.

Roberts, John M., and Brian Sutton-Smith
1962 "Child Training and Game Involvement." *Ethnology* 1 (2): 166–85.

Roberts, John M., Melvin D. Williams, and George C. Poole
1982 "Used Car Domain: An Ethnographic Application of Clustering and Multi-dimensional Scaling." In *Classifying Social Data*, ed. Herschel Hudson and Associates. San Francisco: Jossey-Bass.

Rodríguez Arzúa, Juan
1947 "Las Regiones Españolas y la Población de América (1509–1538)." *Revista Indiana* 30:695–748.

Romano, Giovani
1910 *Le Dominazioni Barbariche in Italia*. Milano: Editoriale Manfredi.

Romero de Terreros, Manuel
1944 *Bocetos de la Vida Social de la Nueva España*. México, D.F.: Editorial Porrúa.
1956 *Antiguas Haciendas de México*. México, D.F.: Editorial Patria.

Rostovtsev, Mikhail
1926 *The Social and Economic History of the Roman Empire*. Oxford: The Clarendon Press.

Rozas de Oquendo, Manuel
1964 *Elegías del Perú*. Buenos Aires: Imprenta La Plata.

Rydjord, John
1935 *Foreign Interests in the Independence of New Spain*. London: Charles Cullen.

Sahagún, Fray Bernardino de
1956 *Historia General de las Cosas de la Nueva España*. 4 vols. México, D.F.: Editorial Porrúa.

Saravia, Anastasio G.
    1941   *Apuntes para la Historia de la Nueva Vizcaya.* 2 vols. México, D.F.:
           Reveles.
Schama, Simon
    1989   *Citizens: A Chronicle of the French Revolution.* New York: Alfred A.
           Knopf.
Schumpeter, Joseph
    1951   *Imperialism and Social Classes.* Chicago: Augustus M. Kelly.
Selden, John
    1937   *Titles of Honor.* London: Joseph Paul.
Serrano y Sanz, Manuel
    1918   *Orígenes de la Dominación Española en América.* Madrid: Bailly Bailliere.
Simpson, Leslie B.
    1934   *Studies in the Administration of the Indians in New Spain.* Berkeley:
           University of California Press.
    1966   *The Encomienda in New Spain.* Berkeley: University of California
           Press.
    1967   *Many Mexicos.* Berkeley: University of California Press.
Sims, Harold D.
    1974   *La Expulsión de los Españoles de México (1821–1828).* México, D.F.:
           Fondo de Cultura Económica.
Sinclair, Andrew
    1969   *The Last of the Best: The Struggles of Europe in the Twentieth Century.*
           New York: Macmillan.
Slicher van Bath, B. H.
    1963   *The Agrarian History of Western Europe, A.D. 500–1850.* London:
           Routledge and Kegan Paul.
Sodi Pallares, Ernesto
    1968   *Casonas Antíguas de la Ciudad de México.* México, D.F.: La Prensa.
Solís (y Rivadeneira), Antonio de
    1968   *Historia de la Conquista de México, Población y Progresos de la América
           Septentrional, Conocida por el Nombre de Nueva España.* México, D.F.:
           Editorial Porrúa, S.A.
Solórzano Pereyra, Juan
    1930   *Política Indiana.* 5 vols. Buenos Aires: Ibero-Americana de Pu-
           blicaciones.
Spring, Donald, ed.
    1977   *European Landed Elites in the Nineteenth Century.* Baltimore: Johns
           Hopkins University Press.
Starr, Chester G.
    1977   *The Economic and Social Growth of Early Greece, 800–500 B.C.* New
           York: Oxford University Press.

Stenton, Frank M.
  1961   *The First Century of English Feudalism*. Ithaca, N.Y.: Cornell University Press.
Stephenson, Carl
  1942   *Medieval Feudalism*. Ithaca, N.Y.: Cornell University Press.
Strayer, Joseph R.
  1965   "Feudalism in Western Europe." In *Feudalism in History*, ed. Rushton Coulborn. Princeton: Princeton University Press.
Stuart Jones, Howard
  1916   *The Roman Empire: 29 B.C. to 476 A.D.* Oxford: The Clarendon Press.
  1969   "The Primitive Institutions of Rome." In *The Cambridge Ancient History*, vol. 7, ed. S. A. Cook, F. E. Addock, and M. P. Charles Worth. Cambridge: Cambridge University Press.
Tacitus, Cornelius
  1961   *Complete Works*. New York: Random House.
Tamayo, Fausto
  1960   *La División Racial en la Puebla de los Angeles Bajo el Régimen Colonial.* Puebla: Instituto Poblano de Antropología e Historia, Publicación No. 14.
Tannenbaum, Frank
  1933   *Peace by Revolution. Mexico After 1910.* New York: Cambridge University Press.
  1966   *Mexico: The Struggle for Peace and Bread.* New York: Alfred A. Knopf.
Thompson, F. M. L.
  1977   "Britain." In *European Landed Elites in the Nineteenth Century*, ed. D. Spring. Baltimore: Johns Hopkins University Press.
Thompson, William
  1939   *The People of Mexico*. London: Charles Cullen.
Thomson, Charles A.
  1937   *Mexico's Social Revolution.* Foreign Policy Reports, vol. 13, no. 10. Washington, D.C.
Toennies, Ferdinand
  1931   "Stände und Klassen." In *Handwörterbuch der Soziologie*, ed. Alfred Verkandt. Cologne, Germany.
  1966   "Estates and Classes." In *Class, Status, and Power: Social Stratification in Comparative Perspective*, ed. Reinhardt Bendix and Seymour Martin Lipset. New York: The Free Press.
Torquemada, Fray Juan de
  1969   *Monarquía Indiana.* 3 vols. México, D.F.: Editorial Porrúa.
Tovar de Teresa, Guillermo
  1986   "La Arquitectura Colonial de Puebla." *Casas y Gentes* (Mexico City), April, 20–32.

Tumin, Melvin M.
 1966 "Some Principles of Stratification: A Critical Analysis." In *Class, Status, and Power: Social Stratification in Comparative Perspective,* ed. Reinhardt Bendix and Seymour Martin Lipset. New York: The Free Press.
Turner, John K.
 1914 *Barbarous Mexico.* Austin: University of Texas Press.
Urbina, Luis
 1917 *La Literatura Mexicana Durante la Guerra de Independencia.* México: Imprenta el Sol.
Urías, Margarita
 1978 *Formación y Desarrollo de la Burguesía en México. Siglo XIX.* México, D.F.: Siglo Veintiuno.
Veblen, Thorsten
 1931 *The Theory of the Leisure Class.* New York: Modern Library.
Velasco Ceballos, Rómulo
 1937 *La Administración de Don Antonio María de Bucareli y Urzúa, Cuadrigésimo Sexto Virrey de México.* México: Talleres Gráficos de la Nación.
Verlinden, Charles
 1954 *Précédents Médiévaux de la Colonie en Amérique.* México: I.P.G.H.
Vico, Gianbattista
 1965 *The New Science.* Ithaca, N.Y.: Cornell University Press.
Villanueva, Carlos
 1912 *La Monarquía en América.* 4 vols. Paris: P. Ollendorff.
Villar Villamil, Ignacio de
 1910 *Las Casas de Villar y de Omana en Asturias y el Mayorazgo de Villar Villamil.* San Sebastián, Spain: Vangirard.
Vinogradoff, Paul
 1948 *English Society in the Eleventh Century: Essays in English Medieval History.* Oxford: The Clarendon Press.
 1968 "Feudalism." In *The Cambridge Medieval History,* vol. 3, ed. H. M. Gwatkins and J. P. Whitney. Cambridge: Cambridge University Press.
Viollet, Paul
 1948 *Historire des Institutions Politiques et Administratives de la France.* Vol. 4. Paris: A. Gallimard.
Warner, Arthur R.
 1960 *English Genealogy.* Oxford: Oxford University Press.
Warner, W. Lloyd
 1942 *The Saga of American Society.* London: Routledge and Kegan Paul.
 1957 *American Life: Dream and Reality.* Chicago: University of Chicago Press.

1959   *The Living and the Dead: A Study of the Symbolic Life of Americans.*
        New Haven: Yale University Press.
1961   *Social Class in America: A Manual of Procedure for the Measurement of
        Social Status.* New York: Harcourt Brace.
1963   *Yankee City.* New Haven: Yale University Press.
Warner, W. Lloyd, and Paul S. Hunt
1941   *The Social Life of a Modern Community.* New Haven: Yale University
        Press.
Weber, Max
1946   *Essays in Sociology.* London: Oxford University Press.
Weckmann, Luis
1984   *La Herencia Medieval de México.* 2 vols. México, D.F.: El Colegio de
        México.
Wecter, Dixon
1937   *The Saga of American Society.* New York: Scribner's.
Wells, David A.
1890   *A Study of Mexico.* New York: Appleton Century.
Whetten, Nathan L.
1972   "Factores Históricos de la Clase Media en México." In *Las Clases
        Sociales en México,* ed. M. O. de Mendizábal. México, D.F.: Edito-
        rial Nuestro Tiempo.
Wiener, Martin J.
1981   *English Culture and the Decline of the Industrial Spirit, 1850–1980.*
        Cambridge: Cambridge University Press.
Wright, Marie Robinson
1965   *Picturesque Mexico.* Philadelphia: Alsop Press.
Young, Wilfred
1937   *Mexican Martyrdom.* Chicago: Thompson and Jones.
Zamora Plowes, Leopoldo
1945   *Quince Uñas y Casanova Aventureros: Novela Histórica Picaresca.* Mé-
        xico, D.F.: Talleres Cráficos de la Nación.
Zavala, Silvio A.
1943   *Ensayos Sobre la Colonización Española en América.* Buenos Aires:
        Emecé Ediciones, S.A.
1948   *Estudios Indianos.* México, D.F.: El Colegio de México.
1973   *La Encomienda Indiana.* México, D.F.: Editorial Porrúa, S.A.

Index

IAKZ8572 8-15-96 Hill